Human Rights and
Transnational Democracy
in South Korea

PENNSYLVANIA STUDIES IN
HUMAN RIGHTS

Bert B. Lockwood, Series Editor

A complete list of books in the series is available from
the publisher.

HUMAN RIGHTS AND TRANSNATIONAL DEMOCRACY IN SOUTH KOREA

Ingu Hwang

PENN

UNIVERSITY OF PENNSYLVANIA PRESS

PHILADELPHIA

Publication of *Human Rights and Transnational Democracy in South Korea* was supported by the 2020 Korean Studies Grant Program of the Academy of Korean Studies (AKS–2020–P04).

Published by
University of Pennsylvania Press
Philadelphia, Pennsylvania 19104-4112
www.upenn.edu/pennpress

Printed in the United States of America on acid-free paper
10 9 8 7 6 5 4 3 2 1

Library of Congress Cataloging-in-Publication Data
Names: Hwang, Ingu, author.
Title: Human rights and transnational democracy in South Korea / Ingu Hwang.
Other titles: Pennsylvania studies in human rights.
Description: 1st edition. | Philadelphia : University of Pennsylvania Press, [2022] | Series: Pennsylvania studies in human rights | Includes bibliographical references and index.
Identifiers: LCCN 2021030588 | ISBN 9780812253597 (hardcover), ISBN 9780812298215 (eBook)
Subjects: LCSH: Democratization—Korea (South) | Human rights movements—Korea (South) | Human rights advocacy—International cooperation. | Human rights—Political aspects—History—20th century. | International law and human rights—History—20th century. | Korea (South)—History—1960-1988. | Korea (South)—Politics and government—1960-1988. | Korea (South)—Foreign relations—United States. | United States—Foreign relations—Korea (South)
Classification: LCC JC599.K6 H93 2022 | DDC 320.95195—dc23
LC record available at https://lccn.loc.gov/2021030588

Dedicated to my father, Hwang Ho-sŏng (황호성, 1935–2002), a brave father, farmer, worker, and educator who taught me how to participate in the world

and to my mother, Kim Ok-ja (김 옥자, 1939–), a wise and insightful mother, who guided me in how to contribute to the world as a global citizen

그립습니다, 감사합니다, 사랑합니다.

CONTENTS

ABBREVIATIONS

AAFLI	Asian American Free Labor Institute
ACF	Armacost Chron File
ACHR	American Committee for Human Rights
ACLU	American Civil Liberties Union
ACTS	Ad Hoc Committee Against Torture and the Fabrication of Spies
AFL-CIO	American Federation of Labor and Congress of Industrial Organizations
AHRC	Asian Human Rights Commission
AI	Amnesty International
AIIS	Amnesty International's International Secretariat
AIUSA	Amnesty International USA
APF	Association of Prisoners' Families
CBCK	Catholic Bishops' Conference of Korea
CCIA	Commission of the Churches on International Affairs (WCC)
CCJP	Catholic Commission for Justice and Peace
CFC	Combined Forces Command
CINCUNC	Commander in Chief of the United Nations Command
CPAJ	Catholic Priests Association for Justice
COI	Commission of Inquiry (UN)
CSCE	Conference on Security and Cooperation in Europe
CWU	Church Women United
DA	Diplomatic Archives, Ministry of Foreign Affairs, Republic of Korea
DDRS	Declassified Documents Reference System
DMZ	demilitarized zone
ECOSOC	Economic and Social Council (UN)
EJB	Edward J. Baker Collection
FKTU	National Federation of Korean Trade Unions

FMS	foreign military sale
GFPL	Gerald Ford Presidential Library
GSF	Gaston Sigur Files
ICC	International Criminal Court (UN)
ICCPR	International Covenant on Civil and Political Rights
ICESCR	International Covenant on Economic, Social, and Cultural Rights
ICJ	International Commission of Jurists
ICUIS	Institute of the Church in an Urban Industrial Society
IEC	International Executive Committee (AI)
IISH	International Institute of Social History (AI)
JECCKP	Japan Emergency Christian Conference on Korean Problems
JCPL	Jimmy Carter Presidential Library
KAUIMG	Korean Association of Urban Industrial Mission Groups
KCAO	Korean Christian Action Organization
KCIA	Korean Central Intelligence Agency
KDF	Korea Democracy Foundation
KDYL	Korean Democratic Youth League
KIHR	Korea Institute for Human Rights
KSCF	Korea Student Christian Federation
LAT	*Los Angeles Times*
MF	microfilm
NACHRK	North American Coalition for Human Rights in Korea
NARA	National Archives and Record Administration (US)
NCCCUSA	National Council of Churches of Christ in the United States
NCCK	National Council of Churches in Korea
NCDC	National Coalition for Democratic Constitution
NCRD	National Council for the Restoration of Democracy
NDP	New Democratic Party
NDYSF	National Democratic Youth and Student Federation
NHRCK	National Human Rights Commission of Korea
NIKH	National Institute of Korean History
NKDP	New Korea Democratic Party
NSA	National Security Agency (US)
NSC	National Security Council (US)
NSP	National Security Planning
NYAD	National Youth Alliance for Democracy
NYT	*New York Times*

OAT	Organizing Activities Troupe
PCFEAP	Presidential Country Files for East Asia and the Pacific
PL	public law
POC	prisoner of conscience
PRC	People's Republic of China
PRM	presidential review memorandum
PRP	People's Revolutionary Party
RDP	Party of Reunification and Democracy
ROK	Republic of Korea
ROKG	Republic of Korea Government
RRPL	Ronald Reagan Presidential Library
SMFE	Staff Material Far East
SOFA	Status of Forces Agreement
SRS	Senior Research Staff (CIA)
TRCK	Truth and Reconciliation Commission of the Republic of Korea
UDHR	Universal Declaration of Human Rights
UIM	Urban Industrial Mission
UN	United Nations
UNC	United Nations Command
UNCHR	United Nations Commission on Human Rights
UNHRC	United Nations Human Rights Council
WCC	World Council of Churches
WP	*Washington Post*

TIMELINE OF MAJOR EVENTS

1910   Japan formally colonizes Korea.

1919   March First Movement, a series of demonstrations for Korean national independence from Japan, erupts.

1945   Korea is liberated from Japanese colonial rule but is divided at the 38th parallel into Soviet and US zones of occupation.

1948   South and North Korean governments form their respective polities.

1950   June 25: The Korean War begins.

1953   Korean War ends in a ceasefire with the signing of the Korean Armistice Agreement.

1960   A student uprising catalyzes the April Uprising (or Revolution), which in turn leads to Syngman Rhee's resignation as president. Syngman Rhee is replaced by a democratically elected government led by Prime Minister Chang Myŏn and President Yun Po-sŏn.

1961   May 16: Military forces, led by Park Chung-hee, overthrow the first democratically elected government in South Korea.

          July: Amnesty International (AI) is launched in London and initiates its first campaign for prisoners of conscience (POCs), including Song Chi-yŏng and others.

1962   The Second Vatican Council is held and continues until 1965. Its ecumenical and sociopolitical tone deeply influences Christian human rights and social justice activism in the late 1960s.

1968   AI launches its global expansion campaign.

          The World Council of Churches (WCC) initiates its global human rights advocacy program.

1969   September: Park Chung-hee's ruling party passes constitutional amendment that allows Park to be elected for his third term.

December: Ivan Morris visits Seoul on behalf of AI.

1970   November: Chŏn T'ae-il sets himself on fire to protest inhumane working conditions at P'yŏnghwa Market.

1972   March 28: The Amnesty Korean Committee is established as the first human rights organization in South Korea.

October: President Park Chung-hee suspends the constitution and dissolves the legislature. A new constitution, the Yushin Constitution, is announced that allows for Park's lifelong rule.

1973   August: Kim Dae-jung, a vocal opponent of the Park regime, is kidnapped by the Korean Central Intelligence Agency (KCIA) while in Japan.

November: The National Council of Churches in Korea (NCCK) holds its first consultation on human rights as part of the WCC's global advocacy initiative. The result is the first indigenous "Declaration of Human Rights."

1974   January: Park Chung-hee enacts the first of a series of emergency decrees that place strict limitations on political dissent.

May: The NCCK establishes the Human Rights Committee.

June–July: US lawyer William J. Butler visits South Korea to conduct a fact-finding mission on the latest crackdowns in Seoul on behalf of AI.

July: US congressman Donald Fraser organizes the first US congressional hearing on human rights in South Korea; Butler is invited to testify.

November: US president Gerald Ford visits South Korea, sparking a transnational contestation on US foreign policy in relation to human rights in South Korea.

December: Rev. George Ogle is expelled from South Korea after speaking out on behalf of eight prisoners accused of leading a Communist conspiracy (the People's Revolutionary Party [PRP] case). Shortly thereafter, Ogle testifies before Congressman Fraser's human rights hearing.

1975   February: Pro-democracy activist Na Pyŏng-sik and other
released prisoners begin articulating their experiences of torture in
government custody and call on international organizations to
investigate.

April: In response to dissident calls for investigation, AI launches
a fact-finding mission that coincides with Congressman Fraser's
visit to Seoul. These two visits pave the way for the second US
congressional hearing on human rights in Korea.

April 9: The Park regime executes the eight PRP prisoners.

May 13: Park Chung-hee enacts Emergency Decree No. 9, which
bans all criticism of the regime. Political dissident Kim Chi-ha is
imprisoned for his role in publicizing the torture of the PRP
prisoners. While in prison, Kim Chi-ha writes "Declaration of
Conscience," which his supporters circulate globally with the help
of Catholic and other transnational networks.

November: The North American Coalition for Human Rights in
Korea (NACHRK), a transnational human rights network, is
established to develop and promote the politics of human rights in
Washington, DC.

1976   March 1: At a mass commemorating the 1919 independence
movement, a group of *chaeya* (a broad nonpartisan, antiregime,
and prodemocracy political coalition) and ecumenical leaders
issue a joint statement that challenges the Park regime's rule by
emergency decree and offers a vision for democracy, human rights,
and unification in Korea.

October: US news media exposes Koreagate—the illegal lobbying
of ninety US officials and congressmen by the South Korean
government.

1977   January: Jimmy Carter, who ran on a campaign promise of
promoting human rights abroad, is sworn in as president of the
United States.

March 10: Ecumenical pro-democracy and labor activists release
one of the earliest labor-specific human rights statements, "The
1977 Declaration of Laborers' Human Rights."

November 1: The newly established Human Rights Council for the
P'yŏnghwa Market Workers publishes "Korean Laborers' Charter

for Human Rights," which calls for a minimum wage, an eight-hour workday, safe working conditions, free and autonomous trade unions, and an equitable distribution of income.

December 29: Twenty human rights and people's rights groups establish the Coalition for Human Rights Movements in Korea to investigate human rights violations and offer legal aid to victims. For the first time, one group represents the interests of multiple fields.

1978   February: Dong-il Textile Company attempts to thwart union elections. Female union workers, who protest the company's actions, are fired and placed on a blacklist preventing their employment elsewhere. NACHRK intervenes, transforming this local labor conflict into a transnational human rights dispute.

June: Female factory workers at Taehyup, a toy manufacturing company in Seoul, demand fair wages. Church Women United (CWU) plays a leading role in publicizing internationally the plight of these workers. Three thousand workers at Signetics Korea launch a hunger strike during wage negotiations. As at Dong-il and Taehyup, the workers articulate their suffering utilizing the language of human rights.

1979   January: Three prominent *chaeya* leaders send a letter to President Carter asking that he make the upcoming summit contingent upon the Park regime introducing significant political reform.

June 29: President Carter arrives in Seoul for the scheduled summit with Park. Journalists from two South Korean newspapers stage a sit-in protest against Carter's visit at AI Korea headquarters.

August 9: A female worker is killed by police during a peaceful demonstration against YH Company. This incident escalates into a national and international contestation on human rights.

October 16: An anti-regime protest at Pusan University in Pusan, South Korea, spreads beyond campus, marking the beginning of the Pusan-Masan Uprising.

October 19: The Carter administration announces that it will not intervene in South Korean domestic affairs.

October 26: Against the backdrop of widespread civil unrest, Park Chung-hee is assassinated by the KCIA chief.

December: Military coup, led by Chun Doo-hwan and Roh Tae-woo, seizes power. Ch'oi Kyu-ha is named president of South Korea, but the real power rests with Chun.

1980   March: President Ch'oi announces the restoration of the rights of 687 political dissidents, marking the beginning of the so-called Seoul Spring.

April 14: Chun moves to consolidate his power, taking on the role of acting director of the KCIA. Combined with his existing position as chief of the Army Security Command, he now controls both the civil and military security domain.

May: Chun declares martial law, prompting nationwide protests by students, labor activists, and other pro-democracy groups.

May 17: Kim Dae-jung is arrested on charges of treason.

May 18: Hundreds of students gather at Chŏnnam National University in Kwangju to protest the university's closure and the institution of martial law. The protest spreads beyond campus, marking the beginning of the Kwangju Uprising (later called the Kwangju Democratization Movement).

May 21: Protesters in Kwangju force the retreat of Republic of Korea (ROK) troops and gain control of the city. The Church Committee on Human Rights in Asia, based in Chicago, sends a letter to the *Chicago Tribune* claiming that US authorities "trained and equipped" the South Korean troops being used to suppress the Kwangju demonstrators.

May 26: Student protesters appeal to the US State Department to act as an intermediary to arrange a truce.

May 27: The US State Department rejects the request; one hour later, the Chun regime violently suppresses the demonstration.

1981   January: US president Ronald Reagan invites Chun to Washington for the first state visit of his presidency. Chun's invitation resulted from behind-the-scenes negotiations to save Kim Dae-jung, who had been sentenced to death in the wake of the Kwangju Uprising.

1982   March: A group of college activists set fire to the American
Cultural Center in Pusan to protest the US government's role in
suppressing anti-regime demonstrations in Kwangju.

May: Female union leaders at Wŏnp'ung Textile Company
demand workers' right to subsistence (*saengjonkwŏn*) and challenge the existing political order after being blocked by company
officials from accessing union offices and being sexually assaulted
by male workers hired by the company to disrupt union activity.

June: South Korean police storm a meeting between Control Data
Corporation representatives and union leaders on the pretext of
rescuing the representatives from a hostage situation. Forty union
leaders and members are arrested.

July: The human rights violations vocalized by workers during the
above grassroots disputes are codified at the NCCK's annual
consultations on human rights.

August: US Congress holds hearings on reconciling US strategic
interests and human rights in Asia.

October: To celebrate 1983 International Human Rights Day, the
Catholic Bishops' Conference of Korea organizes "Human Rights
Sunday."

December: The Reagan administration negotiates Kim Dae-jung's
release from prison and exile to the United States. The administration depicts it as a victory for quiet diplomacy.

1983   January: Kim Dae-jung, in a televised interview on CNN, accuses
US administrations, including the Reagan administration, of
supporting dictatorial regimes in the name of anti-Communism,
security, and US economic interests.

February: The Chun regime introduces a series of liberalization
measures (*yuhwa choch'i*) that set 350 student prisoners free, allow
1,300 expelled students to return to school, and remove 200
dissidents from the political blacklist.

April: The newly formed National Youth Alliance for Democracy
(NYAD) releases "An Open Complaint to the Minister of Domestic Affairs on the Violation of Human Rights Throughout the
Nation," articulating the dire socioeconomic hardships workers
experienced due to low wages and long working hours.

November: President Reagan's arrival in Seoul for a summit with Chun Doo-hwan repeats the established pattern of exacerbating debates on US responsibility for human rights violations in South Korea.

1984   Spring: Former leaders of the P'yŏnghwa Market (Ch'ŏnggye) Clothing and Textile Trade Union, dissolved by the government in 1981, campaign to restore the union.

September: Taking advantage of Chun's liberalization measures, students reopen the Democratic Student Association, which the government had shut down in 1980.

November: Kim Dae-jung announces his plans to return to South Korea to participate directly in pro-democracy movements.

1985   January: The New Korea Democratic Party (NKDP) is established as an opposition political party.

February 8: Kim Dae-jung returns to Seoul. His return contributes to the NKDP's success in securing 67 out of 276 seats in the National Assembly.

September 4: The torture of Kim Kŭn-t'ae, NYAD's founder, while in police custody, sparks national and transnational anti-torture campaigns.

October: A host of pro-democracy and human rights advocacy groups launch the Ad Hoc Committee Against Torture and the Fabrication of Spies (ACTS, Komun Kongdaewi).

November: 120 pro-democracy leaders, including Kim Dae-jung and Kim Young-sam, take part in a three-day protest against the government's use of torture that culminates with the call for Home Minister Chŏng Sŏk-mo's resignation.

1986   February: The NKDP initiates a nationwide signature campaign in support of amending the constitution to allow for direct presidential election in 1988.

October: Students from twenty-seven universities occupy Konkook University in Seoul to protest Chun's dictatorial rule and the presence of US troops and nuclear bases in South Korea.

1987   January: Pak Chong-ch'ŏl, a twenty-one-year-old student, dies while in police custody; the autopsy concludes that the likely cause of death was torture. The government initiates a cover-up, blaming low-ranking officials for Pak's death.

March 3: Tens of thousands of protesters, including students, religious leaders, and opposition party members, gather for the "Grand March Against Torture and for Democratization."

April 13: Chun cancels ongoing talks on constitutional revision and announces that the 1988 presidential election will occur under the existing system.

May 30: Acting prime minister Yi Han-gi apologizes for Pak's death and for the cover-up.

June 10: Hundreds of thousands of protesters take to the street to protest Chun's cancellation of constitutional talks.

June 18: Representatives Thomas Foglietta of Pennsylvania and Fortney H. Stark of California draft a bill denying favored nation trading status to South Korea until that nation demonstrates "respect for internationally recognized human and labor rights" and introduces fair elections and freedom of the press.

June 29: Roh Tae-woo, the ruling party's 1988 presidential candidate, issues an eight-point proposal for democratization that largely acquiesces to the opposition's demands.

1997   December: Kim Dae-jung is elected as president, marking the first peaceful regime change.

NOTE ON ROMANIZATION AND TRANSLATION

In romanizing Korean words, I have used the McCune-Reischauer system and have generally followed the stylistic guidelines established by the Library of Congress. In romanizing the names of Koreans, I have placed a hyphen between the two personal names, the second of which is not capitalized (e.g., Park Chung-hee). In ordering the elements of a person's name, I have used the traditional Korean ordering, whereby the surname appears first followed by the first name. One notable exception is Syngman Rhee, whose name is commonly given in Western sequence. All translations of interviews and documents in Korean are my own, unless otherwise noted.

The Human Rights Turn

A Transnational Perspective on Democratization Movements in South Korea

Overview

In the early 1970s, as President Park Chung-hee gradually moved the Korean government in an authoritarian direction, pro-democracy activists were eager to link their domestic struggles with global human rights advocacy campaigns. On March 28, 1972, seven months prior to Park establishing his lifelong regime, a group of twenty-four democratic leaders held the first official meeting of the Amnesty Korean Committee (Aemnest'i Han'guk Wiwŏnhoe), also known as the Korean Section of Amnesty International (AI), or AI Korea. In his inaugural speech, AI Korea chair Rev. Kim Chae-jun, a prominent ecumenical leader, expressed a deep commitment to building the first human rights organization dedicated to advancing democratization movements: "It is a natural endeavor . . . to build a global connection through which global voices of conscience can together deliver our outcries . . . if our individual freedom of conscience, expression, and religion as well as our basic liberties stipulated in our Constitution are infringed."[1] Kim imagined AI Korea as a platform for translating democratic struggles into global human rights issues. But his understanding of the new section's role did not correspond with that of AI. Attending the inaugural meeting, AI International Executive Committee (IEC) member Thomas Hammarberg spoke out that it should be "a nonpolitical organization" in keeping with AI's founding principles.[2]

But Kim, like many initiators of the Korean Section, had contacts with and belonged to another global human rights network, whose orientation in sharp contrast to AI was political and ecumenical. By November 1973, the National Council of Churches in Korea (NCCK) in concert with the World Council of Churches (WCC) had produced the first indigenous human rights declaration in South Korea; this declaration embraced social, economic, and political justice as human rights and did not shy away from engagement in domestic democratic struggles. As participants in the NCCK/WCC network as well as the newly formed AI Korea, local activists combined the two approaches to human rights to create a language of protest, which they mobilized for their local democratic struggles. In the following decades of democratic transition in South Korea, this process of appropriation, vernacularization, and adaptation of human rights critically served for the translation and transformation of domestic pro-democracy disputes into transnational contestations on human rights issues in South Korea.[3]

Frustrated by the repeated failure of world powers to recognize their concerns about national self-determination, economic unfairness, and human rights, citizens in Third World nations formed populist movements that sought to determine the economic and political direction of their respective nations. In nations such as South Korea, Taiwan, the Philippines, and Chile, where right-wing regimes ruled with the support of the United States, local protesters mobilized human rights politics to link their local campaigns with emerging social movements for human rights that transcended territorial, socioeconomic, and ideological borders. In the case of South Korea, the nascent pro-democracy and human rights movements of the 1970s set the stage for South Korea ultimately to join the democracy club as part of what political scientist Samuel P. Huntington classified as "the third wave of democratization."[4]

This book investigates the internationalization of South Korea's democratization movements during the 1970s as one of the most understudied cases for the global expansion of human rights. It argues that South Korea's disputes over democracy became part and parcel of global human rights activism and politics. In concert with global advocates, pro-democracy activists transformed local struggles into transnational human rights contestations against the backdrop of authoritarian industrialization in South Korea. In so doing, they built a transnational coalition for social, political, and economic justice that challenged US Cold War policy addressing South Korea. When this coalitional activism materialized, both the South Korean regime and US administrations devised counteractive human rights policies. The South Korean regime mobilized anti-Communist mechanisms to suppress democratic dissidents and utilized American concerns about political prisoners as a bargaining chip to leverage the US government for economic and security aid. US administrations, in turn, attempted to advocate for incarcerated dissidents without jeopardizing regime stability or US Cold War security interests in the region. But rather than pacifying moralist criticism at home, as US administrations had hoped, this policy intensified such criticisms and fueled the development of transpacific human rights politics, which regime opponents in South Korea appropriated to transform local pro-democratic struggles into transnational contestations on democratization.

Through a bottom-up approach that emphasizes the constitutive role of local non-state actors, this book contributes to a growing body of literature that challenges diffusionist narratives of human rights in which civil and political rights radiate outward from the Global North (or center) to the Global South (or periphery). In this paradigmatic narrative, the global advocacy group AI, which rose to prominence in the 1970s, is frequently the lens through which the spread of global human rights is evaluated. AI prioritized the promotion of civil and political rights over social and economic rights; but many indigenous groups did not accept this prioritization in their campaigns for human rights. Thus, rather than simply translating universal human rights into vernacular form, indigenous perspectives incorporated local concerns, such as the pursuit of industrialization at the expense of worker welfare. Understanding these indigenous perspectives and how they influenced the trajectory of global human rights history requires a thick approach—one that utilizes indigenous sources to reveal local perspectives on human rights, while at the same time seeking points of contact with transnational social and political forces.

The South Korean case offers a unique and underexplored vantage point from which to examine such interactions between center and periphery, because there, local activists developed contacts with two transnational organizations with very different approaches to human rights: the secular AI and the ecumenical WCC. Unlike AI, the WCC was an umbrella organization that encouraged member groups to develop a Christian understanding of human rights that took into account the civil, political, social, and economic concerns of indigenous populations. Consequently, the WCC adopted a maximalist understanding of human rights that made no attempt to be apolitical. In fact, its concept of human rights was contingent upon the way in which geopolitics contributed to human rights abuses in South Korea and in other Third World nations.

In presenting the bottom-up (re)shaping of global human rights activism and politics, this book also departs from one of the dominant narratives in the historiography on modern South Korea. Utilizing a national lens, most scholars have depicted pro-democracy struggles in South Korea as the *minjung* (people's) resistance against the regime. This narrow national focus means that little attention has been paid to the transnational/international dimensions of this conflict or to the evolution of the language of human rights during the democratization process. Yet, both pro-democracy activists and the Korean regime utilized the frame of human rights to create momentum in international politics. In this transnational politicization of human rights, social and economic rights became closely tied with civil and political rights. In addition, Washington, rather than the United Nations, became the epicenter for the transnational politicization of human rights. Thus, this book also calls into question the conventional approach to US-Korean diplomatic relations that to date has largely focused on bureaucratic politics in a binary frame of realism versus idealism.

Human Rights and Democratization: Beyond National, *Minjung*, and Diplomatic Perspectives

The global history of human rights is a relatively new field of scholarly inquiry. As the twentieth century entered its final decade, a number of narratives appeared that sought to pinpoint when the idea of universal human rights first emerged. These early narratives tended to have a celebratory tone, date human rights to ancient Greek or Roman times, and use history to confirm the inevitable rise of human rights, rather than to highlight the contingencies that informed it.[5] But these teleological narratives were soon replaced by a growing body of literature that highlighted the 1970s as a breakthrough moment in human rights history. In his seminal work *The Last Utopia*, Samuel Moyn claims that the 1970s marked the moment at which liberal human rights became a delocalized and grassroots cause, owing in part to the efforts of nongovernmental organizations (NGOs), especially AI. AI's minimalist and apolitical orientation, Moyn contends, allowed AI to emerge triumphant over other competing international ideologies as the "last utopia."[6] Kenneth Cmiel also highlights the role of NGOs in the 1970s, detailing how they pioneered "a new style of reform politics that succeeded by combining thick rivers of fact to influence elites, direct mail and foundation money to keep going, and media savvy to appeal broadly." The cumulative result of these tactics, Cmiel concludes, was that "the very phrase 'human rights' developed an aura around it," even though no one could agree on exactly what the term meant. In fact, Cmiel contends, its "vagueness" was its strength: "To the extent that the ideal of human rights captures wide public support, it does so because it allows people to attach their own meaning to the term."[7] Yet, like the earlier triumphalist accounts, these new histories remained West-centric, describing the spread of human rights as a unilateral process from the Global North to the Global South. They also tended to ignore the role of religious organizations in the spread of human rights and assigned little importance to indigenous perspectives.

Slowly, however, studies emerged that incorporated these alternative perspectives. For example, in his book *The World Reimagined*, Mark Philip Bradley challenges West-centric narratives, by arguing that the United States was a "latecomer to human rights" and by stressing that human rights history is best understood as having evolved through interdependent dynamics in a transnational domain.[8] The polycentric origins of human rights are also a major theme of the political scientist Kathryn Sikkink's monograph *Evidence for Hope*. For example, she argues that the inclusion of social and economic rights in the Universal Declaration of Human Rights (UDHR) was primarily the result of Latin American interventions in contrast to most mainstream narratives underlining Soviet interventions. Similarly, she points out that it was the Brazilian delegate Bertha Lutz and the Dominican delegate Minerva Bernardino who pushed for the inclusion of women rights despite opposition from the American and Canadian delegates, as well as from the women advisers to the British delegates.[9] Rather than highlighting non-European contributions to a universal language of human rights, Patrick William Kelly's *Sovereign Emergencies* utilizes case studies of Brazil, Chile, and Argentina to underscore the multiple meanings that human rights ideals had at the local, national, international, and transnational levels. In tracing the intersection of these different meanings, Kelly offers one of the few accounts that addresses the religious dimensions of human rights politics. For example, he notes that the WCC, based in Geneva, was "the nexus for exchanges among civil society actors" like AI, the UN human rights office, and exiles from South America and accentuates the "profoundly Christian" nature of the notions of testimony and confession adopted by activists in the 1970s.[10] Yet, neither historians nor political scientists have written much on the role of religious actors in human rights development, and some of what has been written portrays religious organizations in a negative light.[11]

Just as global studies of human rights in the 1970s largely ignore the contribution of indigenous populations and religious actors, studies of South Korea's democratization movements in the 1970s rarely touch upon the geopolitical or human rights dimension of pro-democracy struggles. For example, in the edited volume *Yushin kwa panyushin* (The Yushin system versus the anti–Yushin opponents), pro-democracy movements are depicted as "anti–Yushin system" protests.[12] Similarly, historian Namhee Lee analyzes the role of intellectuals and college students in the democratization movement, also known as the *minjung* (people's) movement. Against the backdrop of post-colonialism, anti-Communism, and crony capitalism, she examines how these *minjung* practitioners "articulated, contested, and practiced the notion of *minjung*" so as to make it "the driving force for the country's transition from an authoritarian military regime to a parliamentary democracy."[13] Both studies focus primarily on domestic developments and tensions, and human rights activism and rhetoric do not figure prominently in either narrative.

In contrast, political scientist Hak-kyu Sohn's study of "extra-parliamentary," or *chaeya*, opposition movements between 1972 and 1979 does address human rights and social justice issues, including concerns about unfair economic distribution, but it does so only in relation to the late 1970s. Moreover, he limits his analysis to domestic politics and bilateral US-Korean relations.[14] In his monograph, sociologist Paul Chang also offers a sustained discussion of human rights by focusing on lawyers, journalists, and Christian leaders' protests over civil and political rights. In tracing a dialectical process between the Park regime and protesters, Chang highlights the evolution of the tactical repertoire of protesters, including the adoption of human rights rhetoric. Chang's study offers a notable quantitative and qualitative analysis of the role of intellectuals, but the international and diplomatic dimensions of the conflict are beyond the scope of his narrative. He does not broach how and why workers' rights and economic rights emerged amid the conflict.[15] Theologian Son Sŭng-ho's work details the historical evolution of the NCCK's Human Rights Committee as a human rights advocate in the 1970s South Korea. But like the other studies, his analysis is limited to national and theological aspects without offering a contextualization of transnational and international factors.[16]

Yet even these limited discussions advance a bold direction, given that the Korea Democracy Foundation's *The History of Korean Democratization*

Movements states that "human rights" entered the public discourse only after the opening of procedural democracy in 1987. According to the account, prior to this democratic opening, only some religious (Christian) communities explicitly challenged the regime's violence and suppression through "human rights" activism, but they failed to develop their activism into major political struggles.[17] Thus, in the current literature on South Korea's democratization, the global/transnational perspectives on human rights remains marginalized.

There are, in fact, a few works that utilize human rights to advance a transnational perspective on democratization movements in South Korea. Sang-young Rhyu's edited volume *Democratic Movements and Korean Society* points to "overseas democratization" (*haeoe minjuhwa*) in spotlighting international/transnational campaigns and networks of democratic figures.[18] However, this discussion remains in embryonic form. Political scientist Hyug Baeg Im and communication scholar Misook Lee highlight the cross-boundary network of Christians, particularly ecumenical activists, and historian Patrick Chung illustrates international journalists' engagement with human rights campaigns in South Korea.[19] Still, there is no comprehensive study that analyzes the impact of global secular and religious advocacy groups on pro-democracy movements in South Korea as well as addresses how US Cold War policy influenced confrontations on democracy in South Korea.

In studies of US-Korean relations, there are a substantial number of works that address how various US administrations balanced human rights violations and security issues in dealing with South Korea. For example, Jerome Cohen and Edward Baker, legal scholars and human rights activists, provide a thorough survey of human rights issues in South Korea in relation to US foreign policy during the democratic transition. But without archival examinations, their study only hints at tensions within US administrations over policy direction.[20] Diplomatic scholars, including Yong-Jick Kim and Yi Samsŏng, focus primarily on President Carter's human rights policy and its relation to US military forces in South Korea and to the Kwangju crisis. In so doing, they filter human rights issues through the lens of state-level bureaucratic politics and rely on a binary framework of realism versus idealism.[21] Thus, they largely overlook the rise of transnational contestations that involved human rights and US Cold War policy on South Korea that developed in Washington, DC, in the first half of the 1970s. A very recent work by diplomatic historian Sarah Snyder is a notable exception, utilizing a transnational approach to US-ROK relations to examine the issue of President Park Chung-hee's human rights abuses. She highlights the role of American missionaries in South Korea, human rights advocates in the United States, and US mid- or lower-level diplomats' moralist orientations in facilitating debates in the US Congress that contributed to a boomerang effect on the Park regime.[22] Still, due to her focus on American diplomacy toward South Korea, she pays little attention to local pro-democracy actors' (re)actions to transnational human rights talk and activism and to international politics or to the Park regime's active intervention in human rights politics. As a consequence, her study does not fully engage the complex dynamics that shaped Washington politics on human rights in South Korea.

Toward a Transnational Perspective: Methodology and Sources

This book is centrally concerned with how the language, ideas, and norms of global human rights gained meaning in the context of pro-democracy movements in South Korea. It pays special attention to the transnational process in which local and global state and non-state actors coalesced and contested social, economic, and political issues.[23] It examines how these actors contentiously articulated, appropriated, and adapted the language of human rights in relation to other significant subjects such as national security, political development, and economic development.

This book advances three analytical points to shed new light on the current literature. First, it situates South Korea's pro-democracy movements within the global history of human rights. It posits that human rights served to create critical connections, coalitions, and/or conflicts that transcended the traditional sovereign-territorial boundaries. It analyzes multifold and multilayered interactions between global and local state and non-state actors. In short, utilizing the lens of human rights, it builds upon a growing literature that highlights the inadequacy of the national framework to capture the history of an increasingly interconnected world. For example, historian Akira Iriye asserts that the dichotomy of realism versus idealism that international relations scholars utilize to explain phenomena that do not easily fit the realist paradigm cannot capture the dynamic challenge that NGOs posed to traditional geopolitics beginning in the 1970s. These NGOs operated outside the national framework and challenged "the 'real' world" of bipolarized Cold War politics by creating an alternative "'imagined' world in which human rights figured prominently.[24] Similarly, the historians Charles Bright and Michael Geyer also question the tendency of scholars to see the nation as "a presumptive and preexisting unit of containment" for analyzing all historical processes. The globalization of human rights language, norms, activism, and networks during the global détente era, they explain, engendered contentious or coalitional points of connection across sovereign territorial boundaries that cannot be addressed adequately using the nation "container."[25] As historians Mark Philip Bradley and Patrice Petro stress, the "new politics of human rights" arose in the context of globalization and fundamentally reshaped "the boundaries among the rights of individuals, states, and the international community."[26] This "new politics of human rights," I argue, did not stop at the borders of South Korea; its appropriation and adaptation by local pro-democracy advocates allowed them to translate local struggles into transnational human rights campaigns that captured the attention of a global audience.

This book's second analytical point is that local non-state actors played constitutive roles in (re)shaping transnational contestations on human rights; thus, it situates the South Korean democratic struggle within a growing body of global human rights scholarship that decenters the United States and Western Europe, in order to elucidate the contribution made to human rights history by grassroots actors and organizations on the periphery. For example, Brad Simpson, an expert in US foreign relations and Southeast Asian history, analyzes human rights discourse and activism in Indonesia to demonstrate why recovering the diversity of Indonesian perspectives on human rights is critical for understanding "why international activists selectively engaged with certain Indonesian human rights discourses and not others, and how this selective engagement inflected domestic politics and Indonesia's human rights diplomacy." As Simpson notes, human rights talk inside of Indonesia in the 1970s extended beyond the political and civil rights championed by international NGOs, such as AI, to include economic and social rights as well as Indonesia's place in the world economy. The Indonesian government's constant invocation of the tropes of economic development and modernization to legitimize President Suharto's New Order "created political space for local human rights activists to challenge the regime on the same ground." Understanding these local dynamics, Simpson explains, requires an examination of the international politics of human rights with which these local dynamics were deeply entangled. This more comprehensive narrative of the 1970s' human rights trajectory requires an analysis that works from both "the inside out and the outside in," that is, one that takes into account local sources and conceptions of human rights and traces their points of intersection with transnational perspectives.[27]

In keeping with this focus on global processes and multiple human rights vernaculars, this book highlights two critical interventions made by local non-state actors in the sphere of human rights. First, it offers a history of South Korean democratization movements in the 1970s that focuses on how these movements mobilized, adapted, and indigenized the language of human rights in response to national and international socioeconomic and geopolitical conditions. In particular, it analyzes pro-democracy actors' pragmatic interactions with two global advocacy groups: AI and the WCC. In promoting human rights throughout the world, these two global advocacy organizations, as noted earlier, adopted contrasting approaches to human rights. As a secular organization, AI pursued a top-down, minimalist, and apolitical orientation to advance campaigns that promoted civil and political rights. As a religious organization, the WCC took an indigenous, maximalist, and political course that embraced local communities' socioeconomic rights in addition to civil and political rights. Second, through an analysis of the frictions between the local (periphery) and the global (center) that produced the Korean human rights vernaculars and elevated local actors' interactions onto the global stage, this book seeks to provide a case history that calls attention to the constitutive role played by non-state actors at the periphery in transforming the global human rights landscape. Because this aspect of global human rights history remains underexplored, it is important to take a comparative approach, so as to show how incorporating an analysis of the Korean understanding of human rights (as one of many that differed from the dominant American and European narratives) enriches the understanding of the globalization of human rights.

The third analytical point is the emergence of Washington, DC, as the epicenter of transnational contestations on human rights and US Cold War policy. To make this point, on the one hand, the book spotlights local non-state actors' (re)actions to US administrations' foreign policy toward South Korea. It traces how these local actors engaged with US–South Korean diplomatic relations through transnational contestations that principally took place in institutions of the US Congress. In duly weighing geopolitical and economic factors under US Cold War hegemony, it discusses the ways in which the existing bipartisan realpolitik orientation of US foreign policy that had dominated US foreign policy since the emergence of the US security state in 1947 was confronted by a revitalized liberal internationalism in the US Congress in the early 1970s.[28] It pays attention to how in the wake of the global détente, the Watergate scandal, and the collapse of Vietnam, some US politicians, including Minnesota congressman Donald Fraser, initiated a campaign to provide a framework for reimagining the end goal of US interventions abroad based on US moral leadership on the global stage. In so doing, they posited a role for international institutions and nongovernmental organizations in the formulation of US foreign policy aims and in the promotion of democracy abroad. Specifically, in fall 1973, they sought to make the receipt of US security and military assistance contingent upon an allied state's adherence to international human rights standards.[29]

On the other hand, in tracking transnational human rights campaigns, this book highlights the parallel development of counteractive human rights policies by South Korean governments and by US administrations. The liberal international campaigns advanced in the US Congress resulted in US foreign policy dynamics that produced a corresponding change in the Korean regime's strategy vis-à-vis the United States. The Korean regime began using domestic political suppression as a diplomatic bargaining chip to put pressure on the US administration. Under the presidencies of Nixon, Ford, Carter, and Reagan, White House and State Department officials actively devised strategies aimed at minimizing moral criticism of US foreign policy as well as safeguarding US Cold War containment policy. Thus, this book closely examines how Henry Kissinger and other US security officials pursued human rights policy through "quiet diplomacy" in order to maintain the status quo with its undemocratic ally regime. As a descriptive term and a classic diplomatic method, "quiet diplomacy" refers to diplomacy based on confidential, private discussions behind closed doors to achieve desired ends as opposed to pursuing public talks to achieve those same ends.[30]

Periodically, the Korean regime released political prisoners to create the facade of supporting human rights in order to ensure continued US aid that was contingent upon US congressional support. This strategic action by the regime allowed US presidential administrations to claim "quiet diplomacy" was working, thus lessening public moral criticism at home and safeguarding the US Cold War security system. At the same time, it ensured that the Korean regime would not have to make any fundamental changes to its political system. It could continue to issue emergency decrees that suppressed democracy.

This book illustrates how security-concerned officials in Washington strategically adopted quiet diplomacy to counter the interventions of local and transnational advocacy groups in international politics and to ensure US Cold War hegemony. Moreover, it shows that multinational corporations and American labor organizations participated in this counteraction coalition that sought to maintain US security interests on the Korean peninsula. Thus, this book shows how bilateral diplomatic relations between the United States and South Korea became entangled in transnational contestations on labor, democracy, and human rights.[31]

In narrating South Korea's democratization process within a global context, this book operates on two levels. At one level, it traces the process through which pro-democracy actors in South Korea translated their local socioeconomic and political causes and struggles into transnational human rights campaigns, thereby elevating domestic disputes into international politics. In so doing, it assesses the impact of human rights issues for domestic and international relations. At the other level, it analyzes how human rights actions and counteractions emerged on the international stage and assumed geopolitical significance, especially in the sphere of US Cold War hegemony. Hence, it argues that pro-democracy protesters in South Korea built transnational campaigns demanding socioeconomic and political justice that challenged the authoritarian regime and US Cold War policy toward South Korea.

I believe we can learn much by incorporating the role of South Korean actors into studies of transnational human rights campaigns. It was complicated, however, since it was often unclear where relevant sources might be, and the reasoning behind the location was often unclear as well. For example, some former dissidents, such as Kang Ki-jong, and missionaries, such as David Satterwhite, claimed they sent packages of documents to Amnesty International's International Secretariat (AIIS). I hoped, thus, to find such documents within the AIIS collection in Amsterdam. Surprisingly, the number of documents I actually found was exceedingly small. I was similarly disappointed with my visit to Columbia University in New York to examine the Amnesty International USA (AIUSA) collection. I decided to travel to Columbia inspired by a brief notation in an essay by human rights scholar Kenneth Cmiel mentioning stored Korea-related documents. Yet, in that collection, there were few documents pertaining to well-known Korean political dissidents.

This dearth of materials contrasted sharply with my experience with other archival collections, such as UCLA Library, Emory Library, the Korean Democracy Foundation (KDF), and the Kim Dae-jung Presidential Library, that housed materials on human rights activism by missionaries and other religious groups in South Korea. Wanting to understand the reason for this disparity, I continued to read the AIUSA materials that were available, such as the papers of Ivan Morris, chairman of AIUSA from 1966 until his death in 1976. As I read his papers, it became clear that the distinction that AI drew between prisoners of conscience (POCs) and political prisoners meant that many Korean dissidents, accused of treason and/or Communist ties by the South Korean government, did not qualify for AI assistance. Such dissidents had two options: reaching out to religious organizations that did not draw this distinction and/or convincing AI that the Korean government's label was wrong.

In examining the desperate appeals of Korean activists to religious organizations and to AI, I tried not to assume the preexistence of human rights issues or language in South Korea. Instead, I tried to analyze the dynamic and frictional processes of localization, vernacularization, and translation that highlight the role of local actors in (re)shaping transnational human rights discourses and international norms.

In addition to interactions between international advocacy organizations and local pro-democracy actors, I was interested in interactions between state actors, nongovernmental organizations, and local actors. I thus consulted US government documents on policies toward South Korea and East Asia at the Nixon, Ford, Carter, and Reagan libraries. I hoped these documents would help me understand the decision-making process of various US administrations on human rights and democracy in the region. In examining inter- and intragovernmental correspondence, I paid particular attention to how US administrations and Congress responded to local protest actions, such as letter-writing campaigns to the White House and demonstrations at the US Embassy in Seoul. Similarly, in conducting research at the Korean Diplomatic Archives, I focused on how South Korea's diplomatic and intelligence officers in the United States and in South Korea tried to anticipate US reaction to local protests and counteract potential fallout.

To augment the information gained from these sources, I also consulted the oral histories of pro-democracy actors collected by the Korea Democracy Foundation, governmental reports (Korean and American), and articles from newspapers and periodicals published in Korean and English. In addition, I conducted extensive interviews as part of my research. Among those interviewed were pro-democracy and human rights movement organizers, such as Han Sŭng-hŏn, Yun Hyŏn, O Chae-sik, and Kim Sŏng-jae. I also interviewed international human rights activists, including Pharis Harvey, as well as former Korean intelligence officer Yi Chong-ch'an, US security officer and diplomat Michael Armacost, and US intelligence officer Donald Gregg.

Cold War, Human Rights, and Democratization in South Korea

South Korea's liberal capitalist course began under the guidance of the US Army Military Government (1945–48) after the defeat of Japanese imperialism in August 1945. When the US forces landed in Korea on September 8, 1945, they did not recognize the Korean Provisional Government, an exile organization in Shanghai since 1919. They also moved to outlaw the Korean People's Republic, the self-governing body established and upheld by the leaders of grassroots bodies or people's committees two days earlier. This suppression meant the premature demise of many socioeconomic and political justice agendas, such as land reform, freedom of the press, and economic reforms, an eight-hour workday, and abolition of child labor.[32] Under the US Army Military Government, Korea's colonial legacy was strengthened through the absorption of Japanese colonial bureaucrats, the police, the military, and the legal institutions. The result was that the South Korean state apparatus became overdeveloped vis-à-vis civil society. On August 15, 1948, Syngman Rhee became president of the newly established Republic of Korea (ROK) and held that office until 1960. This imbalance between a strong state and weak civil society was further aggravated by the Korean War (1950–53). To combat North Korean forces, Syngman Rhee further strengthened the state apparatus, while civil society remained in disarray. Political scientist Jang-Jip Choi notes that while the country's early architects ultimately intended to establish a liberal democracy, the means of reaching such a political order was through Cold War anti-Communism. Because they believed that democracy was not possible without first realizing national security and internal political stability, the South Korean government was never fully vested in establishing democratic institutions or upholding principles of democracy.[33] The increasing authoritarian direction of the Rhee government, as well as widespread allegations of election fraud in 1960, led university students to launch massive demonstrations against the regime, which ultimately led to Rhee's resignation as president.

At the time of Rhee's resignation, South Korea's per capita gross national product (GNP) was significantly lower than that of North Korea.[34] The short-lived democratic government that replaced Rhee's authoritarian regime developed an agenda of socioeconomic and political reforms. However, in May 1961, a military junta led by General Park Chung-hee seized power in a coup. A three-decade-long struggle for democracy ensued; pro-democracy advocates confronted first the Park regime (1961–79) and then the regimes of his disciples, Chun Doo-hwan (1980–87) and Roh Tae-woo (1988–92).

Around 1960–61, Washington launched its "modernization" policy to compete with the Soviet model that prioritized heavy industry, defense, and collectivization.[35] In theory, the US model linked economic development to democratic development; nations proceeded through a series of developmental steps that ultimately led to the realization of a Western liberal democratic form of government. In practice, however, officials in Washington rarely incorporated democratic values into the developmental and political policies implemented in developing allied nations. As Victor Korchmann shows in his study of Japan and Asia, US officials conceptually identified "modernization" with "industrialization" or economic development.[36] Under the guidance of the John F. Kennedy administration, the Park regime initiated its planned economy in 1962. In 1965, Walt W. Rostow, a leading modernization theorist, declared during a visit to Seoul that South Korea had reached the "take-off" stage after which point an economy can expand rapidly. This program of economic development was accompanied by a program to reshape the attitudes of South Korean youth. Concerned by Korean youths' tendency to wreak political havoc, the United States Information Service (USIS) was charged with creating cultural programs for college and student youth leaders that encouraged them to take a new view of their role in national and global affairs.[37]

The Park regime also benefited from the normalization of South Korea–Japan diplomatic relations and from the nation's participation in the Vietnam War, which allowed it to develop its export industries. Economist Alice Amsden describes the years 1966 to 1977 as the "Golden Age of Korea's industrial expansion."[38] Yet, in the late 1960s, rather than continuing the import substitution industrialization (ISI) policy, the Park regime initiated a heavy-chemical industry policy called the "Big Push." In conjunction with this industrial transition and the introduction of global détente, South Korea went from being a relatively liberal state to an authoritarian one. This transition culminated with the adoption of the Yushin (Revitalization) Constitution in 1972, which recognized Park Chung-hee as ruler for life. This political and economic transition, in turn, became the backdrop for South Korea's democratization in the 1970s, as did the global rise of human rights.

Yet, the 1970s were not the first time in the twentieth century that the concept of human rights achieved international prominence. In 1945, the UN Charter included a reference to "human rights," and in 1948 the United Nations adopted the UDHR. However, human rights soon became entangled in the Cold War confrontation between the two superpowers, with each side championing particular rights based on its ideological orientation.[39] As legal scholar Eric Posner highlights, owing to the confrontation between the United States and the Soviet Union, it took an additional twenty years to transform the "declaration" into international human rights treaties—the International Covenant on Civil and Political Right (ICCPR) and the International Covenant on Economic, Social, and Cultural Rights (ICESCR).[40] In fact, most likely these treaties would never have come to pass if not for a fundamental change in the leadership of the UN Third Committee, which dealt with human rights. By the 1950s, the Western powers had ceded leadership on human rights matters at the UN to Third World nations in exchange for solidarity on Cold War security matters. Moreover, because human rights were one of the few topics on which Third World nations and nonaligned states could voice an independent opinion without fearing pressure from Western powers or the Soviet Union, Arab Asian and Latin American groups utilized the topic of universal human rights to write into resolutions their grievances about self-determination, state sovereignty, and economic independence. The change in leadership also hinted at the emergence of new era—one in which UN debates would no longer be divided along East-West lines, but rather along the so-called North-South axis; at the Bandung Conference in 1955, many participants propagated the idea of a distinct Third World identity.[41] By the early 1960s, the rapid influx of decolonized nations ensured that the North-South antagonism permeated every area of UN activity, but especially human rights and developmental policy, owing to decolonized nations' desire for full economic independence.[42] The complexion of the United Nations changed yet again in the late 1960s and early 1970s; this time, rather than an influx of newly decolonized nations, this transformation was in the nature of the regimes represented. Across Asia, Africa, and Latin America, military coups had placed authoritarian regimes in power. The end result was that Third World and nonaligned nations that had once championed the universalism of human rights, now did an about-face and supported cultural relativism. It was against this backdrop that the "human rights revolution," or "breakthrough," led by NGOs, occurred in the 1970s.[43]

In South Korea, human rights talk and politics also developed in the late 1940s against the backdrop of growing Cold War hostility. In 1947, at the request of General Douglas MacArthur of the Far East Command, Roger Baldwin, cofounder of the American Civil Liberties Union (ACLU), traveled to Korea to introduce American-style civil liberties. Baldwin met with Yŏ Unhyŏng, the vice-premier of the Korean People's Republic, and observed the repressive policies of the US military government. Baldwin criticized MacArthur's hypocritical "crusade of democracy." Still, his visit ushered in Korea's first "human rights" organization, Chosŏn Inkwŏn Ongho Yŏnmaeng. But this group did not significantly impact the direction of Korean politics.[44] As in the United Nations, human rights in Korea fell victim to Cold War politics. The Korean peninsula was divided into two states; the new South Korean state fell within the sphere of US influence and North Korea within the Soviet sphere. Anti-Communism significantly shaped the South Korean constitution, and the Syngman Rhee regime pursued a violent state-building course, as epitomized by the brutal suppression of the Cheju Uprising (April 1948–May 1949). During the Korean War, the regime began holding "human rights" events—including the celebration of the anniversary of the UDHR in 1950. But the primary aim of these events was to portray the US and South Korean forces as waging a battle for human rights.[45] In 1953, lawyer Yi Hwal organized the first postwar "human rights" group, Taehan Inkwŏn Ongho Yŏnmaeng. In 1955, this human rights organizations changed its name to Kukche Inkwŏnongho Han'guk Yŏnmaeng and became affiliated with Baldwin's International League for the Rights of Man. This organization survived into the 1970s and onward. However, over the years, it had become closely tied to the South Korean government and so never spoke out against the government's antidemocratic actions.[46] In the 1960s, President Park actively utilized *inkwŏn* (human rights) language to legitimize his new military regime and to leverage the United States (see Chapter 1).[47] Moreover, many political critics or dissidents preferred to speak of *minkwŏn*, which can be translated into English as "civil rights" or "people's rights." Yet, by the early 1970s, local pro-democracy protesters had opted for *inkwŏn* as a means of capitalizing on the global rise of human rights to bring global attention to their struggle for democracy.

Organization

This book consists of seven chapters, followed by an epilogue. Proceeding chronologically, each chapter highlights a specific theme and analytical question, thereby illustrating the global process of South Korea's democratization in the frame of global human rights activism and politics. Chapter 1 addresses the emergence of "human rights" as a protest language for pro-democracy movements in the early 1970s. It focuses on local pro-democracy actors' interactions with two international organizations that had fundamentally different understandings of human rights, AI and the WCC. In tracing the points of contact between AI, the WCC, and local activists, it highlights how local actors attempted to indigenize global human rights initiatives. It argues that the globalization of human rights developed through the convoluted and constructive effects of interactions at the periphery.

Chapters 2 and 3 illuminate the emergence of global human rights politics in South Korea under Park Chung-hee's emergency rule beginning in January 1974. These chapters analyze how local activists in South Korea and Japan created momentum and internationalized the regime's crackdown by framing governmental repression as violations of international human rights norms. Chapter 2 focuses on AI's fact-finding mission and the resulting first human rights hearing in the US Congress. It argues that local protesters' geopolitical considerations transformed Washington into the epicenter of global human rights politics, while the role of the United Nations dwindled. In parallel with the development of transnational human rights campaigns, this chapter shows another engine of global human rights politics: the formation of the Nixon/Ford administrations' countermobilization policy, namely, "quiet diplomacy," to safeguard the Cold War security consensus. Chapter 3 analyzes the role of the normative terms "conscience" (*yangsim*) and "torture" (*komun*) to show the evolution of pro-democracy protest repertoires and techniques that made possible the linking of local disputes with international campaigns and politics on human rights. It then details the complex and convoluted actions and counteractions of the Ford administration, the US Congress, the Park regime, and local and transnational actors in an effort to advance their respective political, economic, and security agendas. It argues that East Asia, and more specifically South Korea, largely did not experience the so-called "Helsinki effect." The new "modern methods," touted by Kissinger at the 1975 US-Japan summit as the only means of containing the Soviet Union in the era of global détente, did not materialize in East Asia, where US foreign policy aimed at advancing US security interests frequently impeded the progress of pro-democracy actors and human rights activists.

Chapter 4 analyzes the transnational developments associated with the historic, but little historicized, pro-democracy protest known as the 1976 March 1 Incident. The chapter focuses on the development of the South Korean version of the Charter 77 campaign, which posed a diplomatic quandary for the Ford and Carter administrations. It comparatively investigates how this incident became a transnational human rights issue and a US-Korean foreign policy dilemma in the years from 1976 to 1978. In doing so, it details the deterioration of human rights conditions in South Korea at the very point in time that the Carter administration intensified moralist interventions in South Korea. It shows how the Park regime utilized repressive measures against dissidents, especially Kim Dae-jung, to secure security aid and other concessions from US negotiators. Rather than attributing these developments to internal inconsistencies in Carter's moralist foreign policy, the chapter points to the ascendancy of a group of top advisers and officials for whom security was paramount. Rather than a moralist approach, these officials advanced a realpolitik approach, that is, quiet diplomacy, to safeguard US security interests in East Asia.

Chapter 5 examines the politicization and mobilization of human rights in people's protests (*minjung*) for democracy between 1977 and 1979. It argues that people's protests for democracy and human rights were embedded in international political and economic systems that were underpinned by US Cold War hegemonic policy. In making this argument, this chapter first examines how low-income workers, farmers, and their supporters appropriated the term "right to subsistence" (*saengjonkwŏn*) to consolidate their democratic struggles. Next, it shows how these labor disputes that mobilized the language of human rights became contestations on US Cold War policy. The expansion of these disputes, in turn, led ordinary Koreans to realize the negative impact of US containment policy on their daily lives.

Chapter 6 examines the escalation of violent confrontations between pro-democracy forces in South Korea and the new military regime of Chun Doo-hwan. It discusses three critical events that took place between late 1979 and early 1980—the so-called Seoul Spring, the Kwangju Incident, and the Kim Dae-jung case—to highlight the cumulative effects of local and transnational non-state actors' human rights activism during the 1970s and their growing cognizance of the anti–human rights orientation that underpinned US implementation of "quiet diplomacy." It argues that democratic actors and transnational supporters became openly critical of US policy in May 1980, after the new military regime massacred protesters at Kwangju.

Chapter 7 illustrates the continued centrality of human rights for local and transnational contestations for democracy in the 1980s. It shows that, as in the 1970s, human rights language and politics remained a crucial framework for articulating local grievances and for building transnational coalitions on socioeconomic and political suffering in South Korea. In detailing the long hours, poor working conditions, and sexual attacks against female workers who tried to organize, activists spoke of *saengjonkwŏn* (the right to subsistence) and of sexual torture. In protesting the regime's brutal interrogation techniques (e.g., waterboarding, sexual abuse, and beatings), they made clear that these government-sponsored practices constituted a violation of international human rights norms. Moreover, the repressive measures instituted by the regime to suppress protests and the Reagan administration's failure to actively support pro-democratic actors contributed to the growing size and cohesion of pro-democracy movements in the 1980s.

The Epilogue extends the discussion of human rights in South Korea to the post-democratization and global justice era. Focusing on three human rights issues in contemporary South Korea—"comfort women," forced labor, and human rights in North Korea—it challenges a growing body of scholarly literature that takes a dim view of the future of human rights. Through these contemporary struggles, it illustrates how local actors in South Korea continue to redefine the boundaries of human rights based on local needs, build new local and transnational networks, and create unique strategies predicated on changing local and international circumstances. Thus, rather than the demise of human rights, it points to an ongoing process of adaptation, vernacularization, and indigenization that continues to expand the horizon of transnational human rights contestations.

CHAPTER 1

Protest Language

Appropriating, Translating, and Transforming the Language of Human Rights

In January 1973, Ko Sŏng-sin and Yim Kyŏng-ja, along with four hundred female textile workers (most from rural areas and in their early twenties) demanded that the Taehan Mobang Company, where they were employed, redress abusive working conditions. Their demand was made against the backdrop of the 1972 Yushin Constitution, which had transformed South Korea into a full-scale authoritarian state, and Park Chung-hee's heavy industrialization drive, which was contingent upon the maintenance of low wages and the ruthless suppression of any attempts by labor organizations to negotiate better hours or wages. Yet, despite this anti-labor atmosphere, the women insisted that the company no longer require an eighteen-hour shift on the weekends and voiced their objections to the company's mandatory prayer requirement. The women asserted that these requirements breached the Labor Standards Law. They also claimed that as a global "common holiday," the weekend break should be "inviolable" and that "forced prayer" constituted "forced labor."[1] In February 1973, the company responded to their demands by firing four workers, including Ko and Yim.

While sociologist Hagen Koo has argued that female textile workers in the early 1970s appealed to "humanitarian" arguments to advance their struggles for social justice and democracy,[2] as shown in this chapter, the women fired by Taehan Mobang Company ultimately translated their suffering into human rights issues, making it one of the earliest labor struggles in 1970s South Korea to appropriate the language of human rights. This translation stemmed from the contacts that these women developed with South Korean ecumenical activists, who had close ties to AI and to the WCC—two global organizations, as noted in the Introduction, with fundamentally different approaches to human rights.

This chapter examines how and why local pro-democracy and ecumenical activists in the early 1970s turned to human rights as a means of promoting their struggles for democracy and social justice in South Korea. It pays particular attention to the emergence of AI Korea and how confrontations between AI's International Secretariat (AIIS) and local actors over AI's neutrality policy led to the appropriation, adaptation, and vernacularization of the language of human rights. This transformation of the language of human rights, the chapter also shows, resulted from the contacts that local actors developed with the WCC through the NCCK. The NCCK would produce the first indigenous South Korean declaration of human rights in which the distinct approaches of the two international organizations converged—a pattern that continued as local actors continued to build transnational human rights networks through which they gained global attention for their pro-democracy struggles.

Human Rights Discourse in South Korea Before 1970

Even before democratization movements adopted the language of human rights in the 1970s, the South Korean government in the 1960s had eagerly promoted human rights programs. In May 1961, Park Chung-hee ousted South Korea's first democratic government in a military coup. After seizing power, Park initiated a series of policies to promote "human rights." In December 1961, at a celebration in honor of International Human Rights Day, Park explained that his "military revolution" ultimately aimed at realizing "human rights" and declared that "freedom from want" was at the core of his regime's plan for economic rehabilitation. In making this assertion, he noted that his policy echoed the values of the international regime of human rights.[3] In 1962, he established the first government office for human rights under the umbrella of the Prosecutors' Office; this office would be responsible for creating human rights legislation as well as organizing human rights campaigns. That same year, his government began publishing an annual report on human rights, which continued until 1972.[4] His government also established human rights consulting centers for ordinary citizens that achieved huge popularity in the 1960s for the handling of *minwŏn* (civil petitions for government arbitrations on civilian disputes).[5]

In addition to operating human rights offices and programs, Park's regime endorsed two civil "human rights" organizations, including lawyer Yi Hwal's Kukche Inkwŏnongho Han'guk Yŏnmaeng, which in 1955 became affiliated with Roger Baldwin's International League for the Rights of Man. These two organizations pursued human rights campaigns that became entangled with US-Korean diplomatic relations. In 1962, they publicized crimes committed by US soldiers; utilizing a human rights frame, they linked this issue to the regime's prolonged efforts to conclude the Status of Forces Agreement (SOFA) in the post–Korean War era.[6] Notably, the two organizations requested Baldwin's assistance in mobilizing a letter-writing campaign that demanded that the Kennedy administration sign the treaty immediately. They also publicized Baldwin's correspondence with the White House on this topic. In short, they launched an effective international human rights campaign centered on a sensitive diplomatic issue.[7] Between 1963 (the year that Park became South Korea's civilian president) and 1966 (the year that the United States and South Korea concluded the treaty), campaigns publicizing crimes of American soldiers continued.

Pointing to the Park government's promotion of human rights discourse and programs in the 1960s and to the emergence of human rights organizations in South Korea since the late 1940s, sociologist Yi Chŏng-ŭn posits a straight developmental line from these earlier engagements with human rights to that which took place in Korea in the 1970s.[8] But this continuity thesis leaves unaddressed the Cold War ideological baggage associated with human rights in the late 1940s and 1950s and the increasingly disingenuous character of Park's human rights regime in the 1960s. Just as Pakistan's autocratic ruler had instituted "basic democracy" and Indonesia's Achmad Sukarno had established "guided democracy," Park in 1961 had justified his coup with the slogan "Korean–style democracy."[9] Although Park abandoned this slogan once he became president in 1963, ten years later he revived it as he moved to institutionalize his authoritarian rule. Like other Third World authoritarian regimes of this era, he also quickly abandoned the human rights programs that he had initially championed.[10] By the 1970s, the South Korean government had become the nation's principal violator of human rights, and the two government-sponsored human rights organizations never investigated these violations. As conditions deteriorated in South Korea and government-sponsored human rights groups failed to respond, pro-democracy activists broke with the human rights programs and offices of the Park regime. Recognizing the disingenuous character of the Park program, they did not look to the past as the model for their struggle; instead, they looked to the transnational human rights networks, especially AI and the WCC, that were emerging in the 1970s.

Establishing the Amnesty Korean Committee

In protesting President Park Chung-hee's increasing authoritarian turn in the late 1960s, a group of pro-democracy activists turned their attention to AI and the possibility of establishing a national section. Their pursuit of this goal was indicative of the global rise of human rights in the 1970s; however, the establishment of AI Korea was anything but smooth; instead, it followed a convoluted course. For two years, AIIS and local promoters debated how AI's policy of political neutrality would be safeguarded in South Korea. Yet, few historians have devoted significant space to internal conflicts in AI during the 1970s. Jan Eckel briefly comments on the incongruence between AI's "bureaucratized" institutions and AIUSA's "active grassroots membership."[11] Kenneth Cmiel also notes in passing disputes between AIIS and AI Adoption Groups over the distribution and flow of information.[12] Yet, as the two-year process of launching AI Korea shows, the globalization of human rights was a contentious, interactive, and constructive process.

AI's Global Expansion to Korea

Prior to 1970, almost no one in South Korea had heard of AI, but AI's presence in South Korea dates back to the organization's inception in 1961. In summer 1961, Amnesty, AI's forerunner, initiated a one-year worldwide campaign for freedom of expression and faith, "Appeal for Amnesty, 1961."[13] On October 30, British lawyer and AI founder Peter Benenson telephoned the South Korean embassy in London to appeal for clemency for Cho Yong-su, Song Chi-yŏng, and An Sin-kyu, three journalists who had been arrested shortly after Park Chung-hee's coup.[14] Two days after Benenson's call, an appeals court sentenced the three men to death. In December 1961, Cho was executed; but the other two journalists were not. On Park's order, their sentences were commuted to life imprisonment.[15] AI counted the commutation of their sentences among its first successful campaigns.[16] In the wake of this success, AI continued to monitor the South Korean situation; for example, AI followed the 1962 case against law professor Hwang San-dŏk, and its members sent letters to Song Chi-yŏng until his release in 1969.[17] Nevertheless, in the 1960s AI's actions attracted neither the media's attention nor that of the South Korean public.

So, what changed in the 1970s that allowed AI to develop a presence in South Korea that garnered the attention of pro-democracy communities and prompted them to consider establishing a local chapter? Of the plausible factors, I pinpoint AI's decision at this time to develop a widespread global presence. Prior to 1968, despite occasional campaigns that extended to South Korea, I argue, AI's geographic orientation remained European. However, once Martin Ennals became secretary-general in 1968, AI launched an initiative aimed at moving beyond its previous Eurocentric (and soon North American) orientation.[18] During Ennals's first year in office, AI dropped the European Convention as foundation for its statutes and adopted the UDHR, in particular Article 5 on torture, Article 9 on arbitrary arrest, Article 18 on religious freedom, and Article 19 on freedom of expression. By shifting its orientation to the UDHR, AI expanded the geographic breadth of its human rights claims, while enhancing the international credibility of its statutes. In addition, Ennals pointed to AI's "wider membership" and "greater financial resources" to convince the leadership that AI should expand its global reach over the next decade to include member nations from Africa, Asia, and the Americas. By 1972, AI had initiated the "Long-Range Planning Report," an action policy aimed at systematically promoting the establishment of national sections in non–European countries.[19]

In pursuing global expansion, AI reaffirmed and implemented its two pivotal principles. The first was its minimalist policy that prioritized an individual's civil and political rights over social and economic rights. In 1970, Ennals confirmed this policy as AI's core objective, although he acknowledged that some members preferred a maximalist orientation that encompassed social and economic rights. He also noted practical constraints on campaigns due to the Cold War setting, for example, the difficulties of conducting fact-finding missions in Communist countries, including North Korea.[20] The second principle was political neutrality or impartiality. In 1980, reflecting on AI's remarkable development during the 1970s, Ennals cited AI's across-the-board application of this principle to its entire agenda from membership to research and action as a key factor in AI's success.[21] Thus, AI's global expansion to non-European areas was seen as requiring the precise application and execution of these two core principles.

In 1969, AIIS began crystallizing its global expansion policy in East Asia. In addition to hiring its first full-time research staff member for this area, it charged Ivan Morris, a Columbia University professor and founding member of AI and of AIUSA, with launching its mission to Japan, South Korea, and Taiwan. Unlike the other two countries, Morris could not enter Taiwan, because the government refused entry. However, by 1971, AI declared Taiwan as its "greatest single expansion" and released a list of thousands of prisoners under Chiang Kai-shek's rule.[22] In Japan, Morris, a scholar of Japanese literature, actively encouraged Japanese promoters to establish AI Japan. He considered Japan an "ideal country" for AI campaigns and commented to Ennals: "We should do everything we can to encourage its development here."[23] By January 1970, AI Japan had become AI's first national section in East Asia.

However, upon completing his mission to Seoul in December 1969, Morris did not recommend creating a national section, because he did not feel that South Korean promoters would uphold AI policies. In his "confidential" report to AIIS, he characterized South Korea as "a country in which Amnesty can accomplish a good deal, provided that we proceed with the necessary tact and caution." As for the political conditions, he identified the South Korean government as a "democratic" system in theory but a "thoroughgoing dictatorship" in practice that operated repressive apparatuses such as the National Security Law and the Korean Central Intelligence Agency (KCIA). Against this backdrop, he discussed appropriate AI policy toward South Korean political prisoners, particularly college students arrested for protesting President Park's revision of the constitution to allow him to serve a third term, and those arrested in connection with two other political cases, the 1967 German espionage case and the 1969 European spy case. Morris argued that among these prisoners, there were "very few" prisoners of conscience (POCs) who deserved AI's official support. In reaching this conclusion, he drew on AI's policy of denying POC status to political prisoners charged with committing violent acts or advocating violence, as well as those accused of espionage. He mentioned student prisoners arrested for alleged violent actions as well as two cases in which espionage was at issue.[24]

In the report, Morris expanded on what AIIS's future policy should be toward those not granted POC status. For example, with reference to

University of Cambridge professor Park Tong Su (Pak No-su), who had been sentenced to death in connection with the 1969 spy case, he maintained that AI should "avoid direct interference in the cases of Park . . . and others who are not POCs." He further proposed that any future appeals on behalf of Park or other non-POC prisoners should be made "entirely on humanitarian grounds."[25] Morris formulated this guideline without undertaking any serious investigation into the veracity of the allegations made against prisoners denied POC status. Throughout the 1970s, AI continued to apply this guideline; yet many AI Korea leaders did not have a clear understanding of these terms and conditions. As we shall see in Chapter 2, in 1974 family members of those accused of espionage challenged AI's assumption that the charges of espionage were true. In 2009, the Korean Truth and Reconciliation Commission of the Republic of Korea (TRCK) ruled that Professor Park, whom AI had denied POC status, was innocent of all charges. Professor Park had been executed in 1972. The commission reached the same conclusion in numerous other political prisoner cases.[26]

Morris also made a series of recommendations concerning AI's engagement strategies in South Korea. In reaffirming that AI should maintain its impartial and apolitical image in dealing with the Korean government, he elaborated: "In approaching the authorities of countries like South Korea (the same would apply to e.g., Formosa, South Vietnam, East Germany) it is very useful to establish Amnesty's total impartiality by showing a genuine interest in the situation of political prisoners in the other country (e.g. North Korea, Communist China, etc.)." He urged AI chair Sean MacBride to assist the South Korean Red Cross in initiating international campaigns for the repatriation of displaced Koreans who had been trapped in North Korea during the Korean War or in Sakhalin during Japanese colonial rule. In addition, Morris requested that Ennals express his gratitude to the South Korean Ministry of Justice for its cooperation.[27] In outlining AI's current and future engagement in South Korea, Morris emphasized the importance of the Korean government's cooperation, if AI campaigns were to be effective.

Based on these engagement strategies, Morris did not recommend establishing a national section in South Korea. Instead, he recommended creating an information network. Rev. Kang Wŏn-yong and Professor Ham Pyŏng-ch'un, Morris advised, could collect and deliver factual information on cases of political repression in South Korea. Morris also found a visiting scholar, the German theologian Gerhard Breidenstein, who agreed to act as a volunteer secret courier for messages from Kang and Ham to AIIS. Morris asked Ennals to give AI international membership to Breidenstein.[28]

As a result of his Seoul mission, Morris emerged as one of the most influential figures in determining AI's expansion policy in East Asia. His 1969 mission report served as a critical guideline for years to come. In early January 1970, Morris recapitulated the policy line from his mission report to Hillis Hinze, AIIS's first research expert on East Asia: "Amnesty should involve itself only with genuine POCs, not with political prisoners in general; otherwise, we shall quickly destroy our credit with the South Korean Government and become completely inoperative in that country." He also reaffirmed his previous recommendation that AI should focus its efforts on supporting the campaign of the South Korean Red Cross for the repatriation of Koreans in North Korea and Sakhalin.[29]

In short, AI took steps to seamlessly launch its global expansion based on its founding principles. In his mission statement, Morris reaffirmed AI's distinction between political prisoners and legitimate POCs. He advocated for a cooperative relationship with the South Korean government and insisted on the preservation of AI's policy of political neutrality. Based on AI principles, he advised against establishing a South Korean section of AI. Instead, AI should support the South Korean Red Cross's campaign for displaced persons. But in advancing this approach, Morris and AIIS overlooked a crucial factor—that is, the reaction of local pro-democracy activists to the idea of an international human rights organization.

Koreans: Building an International Connection Through AI

Morris's mission made clear that AIIS had no interest in establishing a national section, if local leaders' aspirations for the section did not align with AI policy. In fact, by the early 1970s, only a few national sections had been established in Third World countries, and none of these were in East Asia. Nevertheless, pro-democracy activists in South Korea actively pursued establishing an AI national section, because they envisioned AI as a tangible means for advancing democracy in South Korea. Their imaginings catalyzed a two-year debate on AI's neutrality policy, thereby transforming AI's global expansion into a contentious and interactional process.

In early spring 1970, three months after Morris's visit to Seoul, local pro-democracy activists began giving serious consideration to establishing an AI national section. It was Breidenstein who submitted to AIIS the first proposal.

In addition to serving as a secret courier for AI, Breidenstein, since his 1968 arrival in South Korea, had also been working with ecumenical communities on social justice campaigns. On March 7, 1970, Breidenstein updated AI's East Asian specialist on the political situation in South Korea and asked, "Why is it not advisable to found a group?" He added that he would be willing to work with Song Chi-yŏng to launch the section. Song had been designated a POC by AI in 1961 and released from prison in July 1969. Breidenstein admitted that establishing a national section in South Korea came with risks. If, for example, AI Korea adopted POCs from Asian Communist countries, it could provoke unwanted international media attention, given the authoritarian anti-Communist regime in place in South Korea. In acknowledging these potential difficulties, Breidenstein asked Hinze if there were other sections in similar situations that had devised alternative formats acceptable to AI.[30]

On receiving Breidenstein's letter, AIIS placed his proposal under official advisement, and the IEC rejected it that same month. In their decision, the IEC expressed doubts that a national section in South Korea could fulfill two critical criteria: the operation of the section free from government interference and the guarantee of safety for members participating in AI campaigns. However, in evaluating AI Korea's ability to meet these conditions, the IEC never contemplated the possibility that members' safety might be jeopardized due to political engagement in domestic politics.[31] By June 1970, AIIS had removed from the official agenda the possibility of an AI Korea.[32] For the next three months, Ennals received no further inquiries from Seoul and assumed that the matter was closed. But local activists, intent on creating an international platform for promoting democracy in South Korea, refused to abandon the idea of a national section.

At the PEN Club International Assembly in late June, Breidenstein found a new promoter for the proposed national section, Yun Hyŏn. As acting chair of the Korean Civil Rights Committee (Han'guk Minkwŏn T'ujaeng Wiwŏnhoe), Yun was campaigning for the release of poet Kim Chi-ha, who had recently been arrested for his poem "Ojŏk" (Five bandits), in which he satirized five archetypal figures of corrupted modernization in South Korea.[33] Through his encounter with Breidenstein at the assembly, Yun learned of AI for the first time. A few days later, Breidenstein sent Yun a booklet on AI.[34] Years later, Yun recalled this encounter and described how he immediately imagined applying AI's human rights concepts to the political situation in South Korea, noting that AI's "opposition to the death penalty, the termination of torture, and so on were so compatible to my everyday thought and what should be done in our country."[35] Yun acknowledged that Breidenstein had made clear at that time that the establishment of a national section would have no direct bearing on the domestic campaign to free the arrested poet. Still Yun proposed, "Why don't we establish a national section of this international organization [for international campaigns on Kim's arrest]?"[36] At roughly this same time, Song Chi-yŏng informed Yun: "My life was saved thanks to Amnesty's campaign."[37] Thus, despite Breidenstein's qualification, local activists, such as Yun, imagined the new national section advancing the domestic struggle.

Shortly after his meeting with Breidenstein, Yun sent his first letter to Ennals, in which he informed him about the case against the poet Kim as well as expressed "the desire of his organization to become a member" of AI. Over the next two months, Yun's group met with Breidenstein to discuss submitting another proposal for a national section. During these meetings, Breidenstein carefully explained the reasons that Ennals had rejected the previous proposal. On October 6, the decision was reached to have Breidenstein submit a new proposal on behalf of Yun's group.[38]

In writing this second proposal, Breidenstein faced a unique challenge. He knew that Yun's group wanted to continue its local advocacy, and he understood and supported this goal. However, he also understood and respected AI's neutrality policy. To reconcile the two perspectives, Breidenstein advanced the notion of a "double purpose" in the new proposal: "Our Korean friends were thinking of doing both, working for other countries' prisoners and for people in South Korea." To justify this "double purpose," Breidenstein pointed out that it was "quite natural" that Yun's group would want to continue its domestic advocacy, given that until now this had been its "exclusive concern." Additionally, the current dire political realities in South Korea made it understandable that the group would not want to abandon local advocacy. Breidenstein explained that the local promoters were willing to take steps to safeguard neutrality, such as choosing a "representative body of concerned citizens" as founding members and even inviting government officials to join this body. Additionally, he noted that "former Amnesty prisoners," such as Song Chi-yŏng, would not assume leading roles in AI Korea nor would foreigners.[39]

Breidenstein also advanced a series of proposals aimed at overcoming various organizational and financial obstacles. For example, according to AI statutes, a national section must have three adoption groups, with each group responsible for supporting three POCs. Lacking the resources to operate three adoption groups, Korean promoters suggested an alternative format, namely, a "committee" (*wiwŏnhoe*) that would serve in the place of three adoption groups.[40] Another obstacle involved money; AI required national sections to pay dues; this money was used to fund campaigns. But for personal and political reasons, the required dues presented a major challenge. As Yun Hyŏn recalled, there were few Koreans, who "were willing to pay membership fees to assist foreign POCs whom they had never seen before." In addition, Yun noted, the government did not permit the remission of foreign currency.[41]

In January 1971, Ennals acknowledged the determined efforts of the promoters in Seoul, but he remained unconvinced that Yun's group was committed to upholding AI's impartiality policy. A correspondence ensued between Ennals and Yun, in which Ennals tried to instill in Yun the importance of this policy, and Yun tried to show appropriate respect for the policy. Still, Ennals remained anxious about the Korean promoters' motives; he felt that the Korean promoters wanted to mobilize the proposed national section to influence the upcoming presidential and National Assembly elections. Thus, Ennals decided to postpone any further discussion of establishing a national section until after the elections.[42]

Meanwhile, Yun's group began drafting statutes for AI Korea, in which they carefully articulated their understanding and respect for AI's impartiality policy. On July 6, 1971, Yun sent Ennals a copy of the draft statutes in English. In this draft, the promoters clarified that the committee "shall not concern itself directly" with human rights issues in South Korea.[43] One week later, in his final letter to AIIS before returning to Germany, Breidenstein revealed that at Yun's request, he authored the draft and adopted "all the points I felt necessary to be included in the interest of Amnesty." Breidenstein added that Yun and other initiators readily accepted the draft and made only minor revisions, such as to the organizational structure. Breidenstein concluded the letter by noting that the future AI Korea would be distinct from Yun's Korean Civil Rights Committee, although there would be some overlap in membership.[44]

Impressed by the draft statutes, Ennals sent a letter on July 26, 1971, to both Yun and Breidenstein, in which he approved the establishment of AI Korea for January 1972. He asked Yun to recruit ten members who were committed to upholding the statutes. He also encouraged local promoters to continue their efforts at improving AI's apolitical image in South Korea.

Specifically, he requested that they campaign for POCs in countries outside Asia. In fact, he described the draft as "excellent" and kept it as a "model for other [prospective national] sections." In September, he invited Breidenstein, now residing in Germany, to the International Council meeting, as a quasi-representative of the future AI Korea.[45] On October 15, he again praised the draft as "a model for other sections in the course of establishment." In this letter, however, he reiterated to Yun the IEC's demand that steps be taken to ensure impartiality. The IEC requested that AI Korea conduct campaigns for "prisoners selected on a balanced political basis," meaning in non-Asian countries.[46]

When Yun finally received Ennals's letter from July, which had been lost in transit and did not arrive until December, he communicated local promoters' acceptance of all additional demands. At the same time, he expressed his anxieties about the increasingly authoritarian direction taken by the Park regime in tandem with the rapprochement of US-Sino relations.[47] A few days later, on December 6, 1971, President Park declared a state of emergency.

Against the backdrop of the changing political climate in South Korea, the local promoters entered the final stages of preparation. Yun began publishing a local bulletin in Korean, *Aemnest'i T'ongsin* (*Amnesty Newsletter Korea*), that provided information on AI's recent reports and decisions as well as information on promoters' activities. Through these bulletins, Yun found twelve new promoters, including Rev. Kim Chae-jun, lawyers Yi Pyŏng-rin and Han Sŭng-hŏn, and journalist Ch'ŏn Kwan-u. Shortly thereafter, at the request of AIIS, Yun and the new promoters launched a campaign for Brazilian politician Rubens Paiva, who disappeared following a raid on his house in January 1971.[48]

By all indications, Yun's Korean opposition group had become an international human rights group. In February 1972, Ennals notified Yun that the IEC had endorsed the Korean promoters' statute draft and that IEC member Thomas Hammarberg would visit Seoul the next month. In a subsequent letter dated March 2, Ennals asked Yun to assist Hammarberg in explaining AI's political neutrality policy to Korean officials: "A national section does not adopt prisoners in its own country."[49]

Although by now Yun understood and respected AI's neutrality policy, many of the recently recruited promoters did not; they envisioned AI Korea playing a direct role in local pro-democratic protests. In fact, many of these new promoters were founding members of the *chaeya* movement, a broad nonpartisan, anti-regime, and pro-democracy political coalition.[50] At the

Figure 1. AI Korea's inaugural
meeting in March 1972.
From left, Thomas Hammarberg,
Kim Chae-jun, and Han Sŭng-hŏn.
Courtesy of Han Sŭng-hŏn.

inaugural meeting on March 28 (Figure 1), Rev. Kim Chae-jun called for the
internationalization of South Korea's democratic struggle through engagement with AI. His speech coincided with the release of AI Korea's founding
statement in which the new national section expressed its support for the UDHR
and for AI's "nonpolitical" (*pijŏngch'ijŏk*) policy.[51] In short, the new promoters
had revived the concept of "double purpose," previously rejected by AI.

The WCC and the First Indigenous Declaration of Human Rights in Korea

In parallel with AI's global expansion policy that led to the founding of AI
Korea, the WCC's global human rights advocacy network reached out to ecumenical communities in South Korea. In fact, the WCC's formation and its
human rights advocacy more than likely can be traced to the 1937 Oxford
Conference. As historian Samuel Moyn explains in *Christian Human Rights*,
the conference crystallized transatlantic Protestant ecumenism, thereby laying the foundation for the WCC in 1948. Moreover, Moyn asserts, "it was
thanks to this event that the rhetoric of 'the human person' as a moral alternative to power politics—and likewise defined against the totalitarian
specter—entered Protestant thinking."[52] Concomitantly, a similar development was taking place within Catholicism. Thus, human rights ideology at
this time was decidedly Christian and conservative, and it was in this form
that it was incorporated into the UN Charter.[53]

Yet, the role of Christian ecumenical groups, such as the WCC, in global
human rights advocacy in the late 1960s and 1970s has received little attention.

Although Moyn identifies human rights ideology in the immediate postwar era as Christian, he largely describes 1970s human rights discourse as secular, arguing that the secular left in Europe had "achieved predominant ownership over human rights" by that time.[54] In focusing predominantly on Europe and the United States as the locus of human rights discourse, Moyn and other historians have largely left unexplored the role of religious groups in human rights advocacy in Third World countries in the 1970s.

In the case of South Korea, the WCC in concert with the NCCK developed coalitional networks for advancing human rights campaigns. As this section will show, ecumenical groups in Korea were involved in drafting the first indigenous declaration of human rights. In contrast to AI's minimalist and paternalist approach, this indigenous declaration advanced an expansive definition of human rights that took into account the harsh social and economic realities faced by Koreans in the wake of rapid industrialization and urbanization. These ecumenical activists, I show, mobilized theological concepts in the service of local pro-democracy campaigns and as part of the WCC's global initiative on human rights. In short, the WCC played a critical role in globalizing South Korean democratic struggles and the local understanding of human rights based on concrete needs.

The WCC's Global Initiative on Human Rights

According to Philip Potter, who became general secretary of the WCC in the early 1970s, the WCC initiated a new orientation in human rights advocacy at roughly the same time that AI introduced its global expansion policy. Unlike AI's focus on freedom of expression and faith, the WCC paid attention to the social milieu, specifically the economic and social hardships it engendered. At the Fourth Assembly of the WCC held in 1968 in Uppsala, Sweden, the WCC called special attention to two questions: "What is happening to man?" and "How should Christians faithfully understand and respond to these happenings?" Within this framework, the WCC singled out human rights as one of its new long-term initiatives. In July 1971, David Jenkins, director of the WCC's Humanum Studies, addressed the two questions raised at the 1968 meeting in his paper "Human Rights from a Theological Perspective."[55] Over the next few years, this document served as the foundation for developing concrete human rights policies. To assess the significance of the WCC's initiative in South Korea, I compare and contrast the WCC global initiative with AI's global advocacy. I argue that the WCC pursued a comprehensive and self-deterministic course that offered local activists in South Korea an alternative model for globalizing human rights.

Following the 1968 assembly, the WCC continued to clarify what human rights encompassed and how each church could promote these rights in practice. In January 1971, at the WCC's Central Committee meeting in Addis Ababa, Ethiopia, the WCC clearly moved in the direction of a maximalist and pragmatist orientation to human rights. In discussing "What is man?" member churches expressed their concerns on "injustice in the world from the point of view of the 'poor,' the 'underprivileged,' and the 'oppressed,' paying special attention to economic factors." They asserted: "As never before, human survival depends upon the realization of human rights." They also proclaimed that "the Bible . . . demands concrete action to safeguard human life and dignity." Based on this pragmatic and realistic view of the world situation, committee members developed immediate action strategies. For example, rather than looking to the United Nations to promote human rights, each member church should push its government to take action. The United Nations, the committee explained, lacked the judicial mechanism to implement the "utopian" laws of human rights.[56] In focusing on the relationship between poverty and human rights as well as on political solutions to the problem, the WCC diverged from AI, which in 1980 declared that it would not "seek to explain the root causes of political repression," nor would it "attempt to advance political solutions for their eradication."[57]

The WCC also initiated a global discussion of human rights through consultations. On the initiative of the Commission of the Churches on International Affairs (CCIA), the 1971 Central Committee meeting at Addis Ababa announced consultations to "focus member churches' concern on human rights, to stimulate greater awareness of, and interest in, the problems involved vis-à-vis human rights." The meeting also clarified that after each consultation report, the WCC would revise and create new "guidelines for future appropriate action."[58] In the wake of the 1971 Addis Ababa meeting, the 1972 Central Committee meeting in Utrecht, in the Netherlands, adopted a document developed by the CCIA, "Report and Further Recommendations on Human Rights." In the report, the CCIA stated, "The implementation of existing international standards of human rights is a matter of the highest priority" and that ongoing study was needed "to relate the provisions of existing international instruments for the protection of human rights to the struggle for social and economic justice and other fundamental rights." In so doing, the Utrecht Central Committee issued a resolution outlining specific instructions for the human rights consultation, which the 1971 Addis Ababa meeting had first proposed: "[The consultation] should include men and women from the various parts of the world with knowledge and practical experience of the application of Human Rights and the results of their violation; (and) that the main theme of this consultation be how to relate standards of human rights to cultural, socio-economic and political settings of different parts of the world, attention being given to religious liberty as a basic right; and emphasis being laid on finding more effective means of international cooperation for the implementation of Human Rights."[59] Both the 1971 and 1972 meetings of the Central Committee had taken steps to advance the bottom-up formation of human rights consciousness and consensus.

In guiding the content of consultations, the WCC required "critical reflection on human rights" in the four following areas. First, it pointed out that "international contradictions have emerged which make implementation of fundamental human rights difficult," such as those between "the rights of individuals and those of groups" and "between the rights of those in the position of power and those of ordinary citizens." Second, it described "the traditional approach to human rights" taken by ecumenical movements and church members, that is, an exclusive focus on religious freedom, as not sufficiently "adjusted to the new world reality or to new, more profound insights into international behavior." It also stated the inadequacy of "judicial machinery" to guarantee the application of international instruments; they were not equipped with a consistent set of international standards capable of meeting "the deep need of the underdeveloped world." Finally, it highlighted that "human rights are a political matter." In making this assertion, it noted that "some groups have been inclined to consider them as purely 'humanitarian' and 'apolitical'" and that "this lack of consciousness of the proper political dimensions of human rights has allowed them to be misused in ideological struggles and political conflicts."[60] This criticism seemed to target AI's global policy, although it never mentioned AI by name. Throughout the text, the WCC consistently emphasized that consultations should concentrate on the needs of local communities where human rights violations occurred. In short, the WCC had moved away from its longtime concentration on "religious freedom" and now paid attention to the comprehensive implementation of human rights based on the needs of local communities.

Thus, the WCC presented the consultation as a platform for building an indigenous and maximalist orientation to human rights on a global scale. In reconfirming the consultation project during the Central Committee meeting in Geneva, Switzerland, in August 1973, the WCC expected to explore "how to relate standards of human rights to the cultural, socio-economic and political settings of different parts of the world." In so doing, it wanted Christians to "become directly involved in processes of change of all social structures in which human rights are not fully implemented." It proposed one strategic option: to capitalize on the events associated with International Human Rights Day.[61] Based on national consultations, the 1974 general consultation "Human Rights and Christian Responsibility" would "develop further a new approach to human rights concretely linked to human reality."[62]

The WCC global human rights initiative developed in parallel with AI's global expansion policy. In contrast to AI's minimalist, apolitical, and top-down approach for global engagements, the WCC advanced a maximalist, political, and indigenous perspective. Upon returning from the meeting in Geneva, NCCK general secretary Rev. Kim Kwan-sŏk noted to the South Korean church community: "The future theme of world churches will be 'human rights.'" Two months later, the NCCK began organizing a national consultation for South Korea on the global formation of human rights and its meaning for pro-democracy movements.[63] The next month, the NCCK consultation produced the first indigenous declaration of human rights in South Korea.

Ecumenical "Mission" and "Fields" (Hyŏnjang) and Human Rights

Against the backdrop of accelerating industrialization and urbanization in late-1960s South Korea, ecumenical communities began implementing the bottom-up and maximalist orientation to human rights advanced by the WCC by focusing on direct community engagement. This approach was the outgrowth of a newly evolving theology, "the mission of God" (*Hananim ŭi sŏn'gyo*). First professed by the Dutch theologian J. C. Hoekendijk, *missio Dei* gained increasing influence in world churches during the 1960s. In January 1969, NCCK general secretary Rev. Kim Kwan-sŏk introduced this theology in South Korea. Kim declared that unlike traditional evangelism (*chŏndo*), mission (*sŏn'gyo*) did "not try bringing nonbelievers into churches for their conversion." Instead, conversion took place "through the political salvation directly executed by God" without "necessarily [being] intermediated by churches." Another ecumenical leader Rev. Pak Hyŏng-gyu clearly noted that in contrast to the traditional theological orientation of churches directed at "individual salvation," mission aimed at "total salvation, embracing the entire range of societal issues." In initiating social engagements in urban poor areas, ecumenical activists called their work "the mission for the poor or slum dwellers" (*pinmin sŏn'gyo*) rather than "the evangelism for the poor" (*pinmin chŏndo*).[64] Thus, rather than calling people to the churches, ecumenical leaders and activists went out into the communities where people were suffering.

To build a bottom-up, maximalist engagement in the secular sphere, these ecumenical activists also adopted the theological and pragmatic concept of "fields." O Chae-sik, a leading lay activist, wrote on a blank piece of paper one English word—"presence"—when I interviewed him about how ecumenical activists could promote human rights campaigns in the 1970s democratization movements. This word had informed Christian engagement in the South Korean secular sphere since its articulation at the World Student Christian Federation in 1964. O Chae-sik translated the term into Korean secular parlance as *hyŏnjang*, connoting fields or working places. To elaborate its embedded meaning, he offered the powerful example of the American missionary Rev. George Ogle, who had pioneered an urban industrial mission (UIM) in the industrial area of Inch'ŏn in the early 1960s. O Chae-sik noted that Christian student activists would say that Ogle "entered into working places (or fields)" (*hyŏnjang e tŏlŏ katta*). In the same vein, Rev. Pak Hyŏng-gyu proclaimed to college student activists that "presence" required their "participation" in the "concrete reality" of society.[65] By taking part in various fields, ecumenical activists created momentum for secular-religious solidarity.

To translate these two theological concepts of mission and field into practice, ecumenical communities modeled their action programs on Saul Alinsky's concept of community organization, which he had pioneered in 1930s Chicago to empower local communities for civil action. With the support of Rev. George Todd, director of the WCC Office for Urban and Industrial Mission, O Chae-sik played a critical role in transplanting this program to South Korea. In 1966, as a Yale Divinity graduate, O Chae-sik participated in an ecumenical training program for community organization in African

American communities. In 1969, he initiated a two-year youth training program for community organization in South Korea, the Social Development Service Corps. Working under the leadership of Rev. Pak Hyŏng-gyu, he ran this program with the support of Rev. Herbert White, who had participated in Alinsky's intervention during the black community riots in Rochester, New York, in 1966.[66] In seeking to cultivate future "leaders of people's organization," these ecumenical leaders embedded young activists in various fields, such as urban squatter settlements and apartment houses, where they learned to manage concrete communal issues, including improved water supply, garbage collection, and land rights. In publishing his post-training report in 1973, White noted that this program provided future activists for democracy and human rights with practical opportunities to experience various "mass-based organization[s] of people, by and for the people."[67]

By teaching local activists how to organize local actors for communal issues and rights, this pioneering program sought to materialize Alinsky's interpretation of Alexis de Tocqueville's concept of participatory democracy based on localized community engagement. This concept of "local community" was not new to the history of Korea.[68] As historian Bruce Cumings illustrates, in the wake of liberation in August 1945, Koreans organized a mushrooming number of "people's committees," a form of self-government at the level of township, county, and province whose goal was the realization of democracy and social justice.[69] In reviving this sense of civic empowerment, one trainee, who had participated in a squatter area of Seoul, attested to the pioneering program's contribution to democratization movements: "The church certainly has a responsible role in its mission to participate in a wide range of activities such as the civil and labor movements, economic and social development, and politics, in order to realize social justice in this society. . . . We now define the community organization training . . . as a similar type of civil or democratic movement. . . . Democracy can only be matured by the will of the people."[70] With this remark, the trainee also grasped Tocqueville's comment about the fragility of democracy, which Alinsky had included in the prologue of *Rules for Radicals*: "Unless individual citizens were regularly involved in the action of governing themselves, self-government would pass from the scene."[71] Democracy devolved into dictatorship.

This training program also held a one-year seminar that produced a text that served as the guide for Christian student activism on democracy and human rights throughout the 1970s. The German theologian Gerhard

Breidenstein, who worked as a study secretary for the Korea Student Christian Federation (KSCF) and who in late 1969 had initiated the campaign for an AI national section in South Korea, led the seminar.[72] In leading the seminar, he utilized liberation theologies, such as "theology of secularization" (Friedrich Gogarten and Arend van Leeuwen), "theology of revolution" (Harvey Cox and Richard Shaull), and "theology of hope" (Jürgen Moltmann) to catalyze a discussion on social engagement in the secular sphere.[73] Breidenstein incorporated social, political, and economic subjects, such as poverty, social justice, and fair distribution of wealth during economic development.[74] In 1971, based on this collaborative and action-oriented workshop, Breidenstein published *Christians and Social Justice*, which was published in Korean as *Haksaeng kwa sahoe chŏngŭi*.[75]

Like the training program, ecumenical activists' campaigns in various fields of urban industry facilitated pragmatic learning and sensibility; it also encouraged denominational transcendence as well as religious-secular solidarity. As O Chae-sik illustrated, the activists Rev. Cho Sŭng-hyŏk, Rev. Cho Hwa-sun, and Rev. Cho Chi-song belonged to different denominations, but in working together on a mission in the mid-1960s, they discovered that they shared the same ideas about social justice.[76] This sense of solidarity was not confined to those representing different denominations. To illustrate, O Chae-sik recounted the reaction to the death of Chŏn T'ae-il, a garment worker. In November 1970, Chŏn died after setting himself on fire to call attention to inhumane working conditions in the industry and to demand the implementation of the Labor Standards Law. At the hospital mortuary, both ecumenical student trainees and nonreligious college student activists gathered. There they realized their common ground; O Chae-sik called this moment the "manifestation" of fields.[77]

Pope John XXIII's 1963 encyclical *Pacem in Terris* (Peace on Earth) and the Second Vatican Council (1962–65) also had a profound influence on ecumenical and secular-religious campaigns for human rights. *Pacem in Terris*, written in the wake of the 1962 Cuban missile crisis, combined a call for peace in the nuclear age with a systematic statement of the Catholic Church's commitment to human rights. As J. Bryan Hehir notes, the encyclical also provided the "baseline" for two conciliar documents—the Declaration on Religious Freedom, *Dignitatis humanae* (Of the dignity of the human person), and the Pastoral Constitution on the Church in the Modern World, *Gaudium et spes* (Joy and hope)—that addressed human rights. With *Dignitatis humanae*, the church overcame its centuries-long reluctance to recognize religious freedom. By providing a fully developed theological argument for religious freedom, *Dignitatis humanae* resolved concerns in religious and secular circles about the church's willingness to embrace this principle. Thus, it established the foundation for interreligious dialogue, cooperation, and activism. *Gaudium et spes*, J. Bryan Hehir explains, "provided theological legitimation for an activist ministry in the world in support of the human rights set forth in *Pacem in Terris*." This religious ministry should be carried out "in a way which fostered four significant secular objectives: the defense of human dignity, the advancement of human rights, the fostering of the unity of the human family, and the provision of meaning to human activity.[78]

In South Korea, the council made possible the indigenization of rituals and practice as well as introduced a greater role for laity that resulted in the church's increased engagement with society. In 1967, the Catholic Bishops' Conference of Korea (CBCK) launched the Catholic Commission for Justice and Peace (CCJP). Priests, bishops, and laypersons joined the mission led by organizations, including the Young Catholic Workers' Association, for the poor and the suppressed.[79] Religious-secular solidarity also developed in the early 1970s, as evidenced by multiple campaigns co-launched by religious and secular groups in support of democracy and human rights. In the early 1970s, poet and dissident Kim Chi-ha was baptized by Bishop Chi Hak-sun after expressing his interest in Catholicism and its social justice teachings. The two men worked together to revitalize Catholic ministry in the community and to connect religious networks with social movements for democracy and social justice.[80]

In September 1971, several Catholic and Protestant church groups launched the ecumenical action organization Metropolitan Community Mission Committee. This organization soon confronted difficulties when the regime labeled its field activists as "pro-Communists." This development, which occurred against the backdrop of the establishment of the Yushin Constitution in October 1972, introduced new challenges for those working in "fields"; and these challenges in turn ushered in a new form of political engagement. For Rev. Kim Tong-hwan, who worked with slum dwellers in the area of Ch'ŏnggye in Seoul, the government's actions against activists made clear that the order of operation needed to change: "Political liberty is a prerequisite to the freedom of mission." Rather than pursuing social engagements in poor villages, these ecumenical activists began turning to a

mission of "awaken[ing] Christians," calling upon the slogan of "no freedom, no love."[81]

On April 22, 1973, under the guidance of Rev. Pak Hyŏng-gyu, a group
of ecumenical activists staged an anti-regime protest in Seoul. During an Easter worship service, they attempted to distribute flyers that declared: "The
revival of democracy is the liberation of the people." In recalling the so-called
1973 Easter Incident, Pak labeled this protest as the moment at which there
was a clear transition from "mission" to "political salvation." In truth, an
overwhelming police presence had prevented protesters from distributing
many flyers. That said, two months later, when Pak and other key organizers
of the 1973 Easter Incident were arrested on conspiracy charges, these events
contributed to the emergence of a transnational human rights campaign.[82]

Also, in April 1973, ecumenical student activists affiliated with KSCF were
participating in a yearlong seminar series on global "human rights" struggles.
Linda Jones, chair of the Monday Night Group, a missionary group for social
engagements in South Korea, led this seminar that sought to "enlighten" activists about "the universality of the fight for human rights." By October 1973,
the seminar had turned to the topic of the struggles of the poor and oppressed
people in the Global South. For example, participants discussed the inequality
behind Brazil's economic miracle and poverty under American social reforms. Jones also planned to cover the Chilean president Salvador Allende's
progressive programs and the latest military coup.[83] As the topics of this seminar indicate, ecumenical activists developed local activism based on a deep
awareness of global human rights discourse and activism.

In early spring 1973, ecumenical activists also began working with a group
of female textile workers at the Taehan Mobang Company. After Ko Sŏng-
sin and three other workers were fired, the four women had sought shelter
and support from the Yŏngdŭngp'o UIM. This mission had held a ten-month
training program on laborers' "human rights" in 1971; the program had been
made possible through the support of German social activist Erick Holtze,
who was the Korean branch head of the Friedrich Ebert Foundation, a political foundation associated with, but independent from, the Social Democratic
Party of Germany. Like Gerhard Breidenstein, Holtze was also actively involved in efforts to establish AI Korea.[84] Schooled in workers' human rights,
this small group of ecumenical activists mobilized the language of human
rights on behalf of the women, describing the actions of the company as a
"violation of workers' human rights" and as "disregard of human dignity."[85]

In roughly early April 1973, the company attempted to break up this worker–ecumenical activist coalition by putting pressure on the umbrella church organization that funded the mission. Given widespread pro-regime, pro-business, and anti-Communist sentiment within Korean Christianity, ecumenical activists had reason for concern. At roughly the same time that they were advocating for these women, the Park regime had given its full support to the Korea '73 Billy Graham Crusade. This event drew millions of Christian evangelists to Seoul in late May 1973. To counter company pressure and gain the moral support of church leaders, ecumenical activists, as a vocal but small group within Korean Christianity, responded by amplifying their calls for the "protection of workers' human rights."[86] They also initiated a signature campaign for the fired workers.[87] In May 1973, having exhausted all other avenues of government labor offices available through the Seoul Regional Labor Administration and the Seoul Regional Labor Relations Committee, the female workers filed a suit against their employer with the Seoul District Prosecutor's Office. As the title of their appeal—"Breach of the Labor Standards Law and the Violation of Workers' Human Rights"— clearly indicates, the women articulated their grievances against the company utilizing the language of human rights.[88]

The "human rights" campaign of these women did not bring immediate results, but it did serve as an example for other socially and politically suppressed individuals and groups in various fields on how they might appropriate the language of human rights for their cause. In summer 1973, a group of protesting street cleaners in the provincial city of Ch'ŏngju echoed the "human rights" language by building a similar coalition with UIM activists. These activists helped them translate their suffering into "human rights" issues. The cleaning workers succeeded in realizing their demands, where the female textile workers had not.[89]

In tandem with the evolution of human rights talk and activism in the fields, ecumenical activists also had an impact on transnational human rights activism. In reaction to the regime's crackdown on those who waged the Easter protest in June 1973, O Chae-sik, then secretary of the Urban Rural Mission of the Christian Conference of Asia in Tokyo, organized a group of international delegates, including George Todd, secretary for the UIM in the WCC.[90] The delegates campaigned "to seek information concerning arrests because of reports of serious violations of human rights and of the possibility of increasing repression of the Christian Church in Korea." They met with church leaders as well as with government authorities, including Prime Minister Kim Chong-p'il.[91] Thus, this action prompted a transnational human rights intervention into a domestic dispute on democracy.

The First Indigenous Declaration of
Human Rights in South Korea

On October 2, 1973, college students held the first explicit anti-regime protest since President Park established the Yushin system in 1972. Two days later, the NCCK, the leading umbrella organization for ecumenical churches in South Korea, decided to hold a national consultation on human rights as part of the WCC's global human rights initiative. This consultation produced the first indigenous declaration on human rights. Against the backdrop of escalating pro-democracy protests and government repression, this declaration translated the concrete social, economic, and political issues faced by South Koreans into human rights issues.

Once the NCCK decided to hold its consultation on human rights, it made clear that the agenda would not be limited to the question of religious freedom. Instead, in keeping with the new orientation introduced by the WCC in 1968, the Research Committee explained that the consultation would address the general situation of human rights in South Korea. The NCCK also noted its disappointment with the international community, which had not made any significant progress in protecting or promoting human rights since the adoption of the UDHR in 1948.[92] Rev. Kim Kwan-sŏk, the consultation leader, asserted that the time had come to formulate a theological definition of "human rights" for the sake of "mission."[93] In November 1973, one week prior to the consultation, the NCCK released a translated excerpt from the 1973 WCC consultation guidelines.[94]

On November 23, 1973, the NCCK held a two-day meeting, "Faith and Human Rights" (Sinang kwa inkwŏn), at the Pundo Catholic retreat house in Seoul. Of the fifty experts invited to this consultation, thirty took part. The majority of participants were *chaeya* movement leaders, who also worked closely with AI Korea, including Kim Chae-jun, Ch'ŏn Kwan-u, An Pyŏng-mu, and Han Sŭng-hŏn. Several participants were ecumenical field activists. The participants, each a specialist in a particular area, such as church, women, media, labor, academia, and law, took part in lectures and discussions on human rights that approached the topic from various perspectives such as theology, media, academia, and women's issues. AI Korea chair Rev. Kim

Chae-jun presented a lecture on "total humanity" for the "liberty of human beings." At the end of the consultation, the participants produced the "Declaration of Human Rights" (*Inkwŏn sŏnŏn*). This declaration defined human rights as "the earthly value" granted by God to humans who are created in "the image of God." It proclaimed the establishment of human rights as the foundation for individuals' survival and for the progress of society.[95]

In developing a general framework for human rights, the declaration took as its starting point the concrete issues that these experts had witnessed first-hand in their respective fields, as well as the root causes of the problems. Based on the problems and their causes, the attendees specified a list of concrete human rights. At the bottom of the declaration, they enumerated "urgent" human rights problems for each field: academia (surveillance and suppression of students and professors), women (inadequate rights protection and sexual tourism), labor (lax implementation of the Labor Standards Law and the lack of a "minimum wage" and social security system), and media (job insecurity, secret inspections, and censorship). The declaration also demanded that the constitutional protection of people's sovereign rights be restored. To save "human beings from 'structural evils,'" it called on churches to institute internal reforms to promote "individual salvation" and "social salvation." It also advocated for continued solidarity among world churches.[96]

This first indigenous declaration of human rights realized the maximalist, bottom-up orientation to human rights outlined in the WCC's 1973 guidelines. In doing so, it presented an alternative human rights course that contrasted sharply with the minimalist and top-down expansion of human rights pursued by AI in South Korea and elsewhere. However, the emphasis of ecumenical activists on developing a framework for religious-secular collaboration as well as the overlap in personnel between the ecumenical network and AI Korea would contribute to both human rights networks becoming entangled in pro-democracy struggles in South Korea.

The Entanglement of Human Rights in
Democratization Movements

During the last three months of 1973, human rights discussions and activism became closely tied with democratization movements. AI Korea experienced significant growth, and the NCCK's "Declaration of Human Rights" achieved widespread dissemination. As pro-democracy protests intensified, human rights increasingly became a language of protests as well as a medium through which democratization movements and both human rights networks became entangled.

From the time of its inauguration in March 1972 until October 1973, AI Korea focused on conducting international human rights campaigns. During its first year, it sent over three thousand petitions on behalf of thirty-five international POCs. In the summer of 1973, it joined AI's global anti-torture signature campaigns and received positive recognition from AIIS for its collection of ten thousand signatures. In addition, between 1972 and 1973, AI Korea added more than 130 new members.[97]

But in October 1973, AI Korea abandoned its exclusive focus on international human rights campaigns. In the wake of the arrest of student protesters, AI Korea decided to cooperate with a coalitional committee to assist students taken into custody by the government. This committee had been initiated by an ecumenical student group to support arrested KSCF members; however, the group quickly expanded, as it embraced Catholic and nonreligious activists, who also had been arrested. On November 19, AI Korea announced in a joint statement with the committee and the families of the imprisoned students its intentions to provide judicial and financial aid to the student protesters in custody. As an action program for the protesters, AI Korea brought together a group of lawyers that included Han Sŭng-hŏn and Hwang In-ch'ŏl; from this group emerged the so-called human rights lawyer group of the 1970s and 1980s.[98] In addition to this program, AI Korea started a relief fund for the imprisoned students. It provided 200,000 won in assistance to three imprisoned students by using monies from the relief fund that Breidenstein in conjunction with his denomination in Germany had helped establish the previous May. This humanitarian aid program developed into AI Korea's principal program in the 1970s.[99]

At roughly the same time that AI Korea began intervening in domestic disputes, ecumenical groups also expanded their human rights campaigns, particularly through events organized around International Human Rights Day. In December 1973, the NCCK held its first weeklong human rights event, "Church and Human Rights Week." Through this event, it spread news of the first declaration of human rights, thereby creating additional momentum for ecumenism, especially between Catholics and Protestants.[100]

A driving force behind this ecumenical cooperation was the Korean Christian Action Organization for Urban Industrial Mission (KCAO-UIM), the first ecumenical organization bringing together Catholic and Protestant action groups in South Korea. In 1971, under the leadership of Rev. Pak Hyŏng-gyu and Rev. Cho Sŭng-hyŏk, this organization created a united and coordinated mission for the poor and oppressed in various fields.[101] As it had done for field action, this organization developed and led the events scheduled for the Human Rights Week and would continue to do so each year throughout the democratic struggles and beyond.

The Human Rights Week event (December 6–10, 1973) focused on translating specific local demands of ecumenical mission fields into human rights claims. Each day, the event focused on a specific "cause for human rights work": for example, students, laborers, the common people, farmers, and women. Prior to the event, the NCCK had sent to three thousand churches nationwide a packet of supportive materials; the packet included a series of sermons and liturgies authored by various field activists. In engaging in the "struggle for social and political salvation," the event highlighted social problems "neglected during the process of modernization," as well as political struggles for a "democratic" and "autonomous" system. The last day of the event was an ecumenical worship service, jointly presided over by Cardinal Kim Su-hwan and Rev. Kim Kwan-sŏk. In denouncing President Park's "absolute power," Cardinal Kim insisted that "the basic rights of citizens must be institutionalized." In commenting on the ineffectiveness of the United Nations in protecting human rights, Kim Kwan-sŏk reaffirmed the WCC's latest resolution that the people must engage in "independent" and "organized" protests for "human rights within their own state." At the end, five hundred participants read the indigenous "Declaration of Human Rights."[102]

During the event, the NCCK also accepted the recommendation of the first human rights consultation to establish a permanent human rights organization. In April 1974, one week after President Park enacted Emergency Decree No. 4 that illegalized student organizations and activism, the NCCK's Human Rights Committee, made up of representatives each active in different social sectors such as church, academia, labor, women, media, and law, was launched. In emphasizing Christian responsibility, the committee spelled out its objectives for "the rights of mission" and "the protection of human rights for the sake of human dignity." It envisioned its role as one of research, education, and networking on human rights issues in and across South Korea. The WCC subsidized two-thirds of the first-year budget.[103]

As human rights gained ascendancy, AI Korea and ecumenical groups, despite their distinctive approaches to human rights advocacy, built a variety of coalitional ties in order to respond to local causes. By December 1973, groups belonging to the *chaeya* movement launched a nationwide campaign to revise the Yushin Constitution, which, in turn, provoked President Park to enact a series of emergency decrees. Against this backdrop, human rights served as the frame through which democratic struggles in South Korea became internationalized.

Vernacularized Globalization of Human Rights

Human rights talk and activism continued to grow in South Korea in tandem with the global rise of human rights. During the 1970s, AI's POC campaign provided global publicity for AI. However, the term "prisoner of conscience" presented linguistic and cognitive challenges for AI Korea that took many years to overcome. Following his 1969 mission to Seoul, Ivan Morris carefully distinguished between "prisoners of conscience" and "political prisoners" in making his strategic recommendations for AI's future engagement in South Korea. As already noted, he described individuals arrested for advocating violence or carrying out a violent action as ineligible for POC status; additionally, those arrested for espionage did not meet the criteria. But despite his careful distinction, the founding members of AI Korea had difficulties grasping the concept for several reasons. First, although the words "conscience" (*yangsim*) and "prisoner" (*suin*) exist in Korean, linguistically no precedent existed for combining the two terms. So rather than referring to *yangsim suin*, AI Korea members used the English abbreviation "P.C." For example, in 1974 when AI Korea held its first International POC Week, they called it "P.C. chugan."[104]

Conceptually Koreans also had difficulty grasping the distinction that AI drew between political prisoners and prisoners of conscience. In fact, during the 1974 POC Week, AI Korea members often used the term "political prisoners" (*chŏngch'ibŏm*) when referring to POCs, despite the clear distinction drawn by AI. This confusion stemmed in part from another legal concept in circulation in South Korea at that time—"prisoners of conviction" (*hwaksinbŏm*), defined as individuals whose primary motivation for committing a crime is their religious or political convictions. According to Han Sŭng-hŏn, this concept, first expounded by German legal scholar Gustav Radbruch (1868–1949) in the 1920s, gained credence in Korean legal circles in the 1970s. Until the mid-1970s, lawyers frequently used *hwaksinbŏm* to mean prisoners of conscience. However, this older term, based on the person's motives, could not encompass the distinction between POCs and political prisoners drawn by AI based on the nature of the criminal act.[105]

But as AI gained international acceptance, the term "conscience," or POC, gained acceptance in South Korea, albeit its usage did not always correspond with that of AI. In 1974, knowing his arrest under Emergency Decree No. 4 was imminent, Bishop Chi Hak-sun read a "declaration of conscience," in Korean and English to an audience of national and foreign correspondents. In this statement, he declared his opposition to the Yushin Constitution and his resistance to government suppression. He was a leading figure in the *chaeya* pro-democracy movement and in AI Korea.[106] In 1975, poet Kim Chi-ha also wrote a "declaration of conscience" while in prison. Translated into English and smuggled out of Korea, this declaration helped Kim gain international support for his release from prison.[107] In 1976, the Family Association for Political Prisoners changed its name to the Family Association for Prisoners of Conscience in South Korea. Given their family members had been charged with espionage and treason, their understanding of the term was obviously incompatible with AI policy at the time.[108]

Like the POC policy, AI's political neutrality policy also took a thickening and convoluted turn. As we have already seen in this chapter, AIIS spent two years instilling in local promoters the importance of this policy before allowing the founding of AI Korea. At its inauguration in March 1972, AI Korea approved this policy in its statutes. However, as with the POC policy, AI Korea confronted a similar problem of indigenization. Although linguistically and conceptually the neutrality policy posed few issues, culturally the policy contradicted customs and mutual assistance practices in South Korea. In April 1974, when the regime cracked down on pro-democracy activists, this contradiction created a moral, political, and organizational crisis for AI Korea. Seeing friends and neighbors imprisoned by the government, AI Korea members asked: Why do we assist distant strangers, but do nothing for our neighbors? The AI Korea leaders found themselves in the difficult position of trying to provide an acceptable answer to this question. In his effort to explain, Yi Pyŏng-rin, a lawyer and chair of AI Korea, spoke of *p'umasi* (literally, an agricultural society's custom of exchanging labors). Yi described AI Korea's international POC campaigns as an "international exchange of labors [*p'umasi*]" with other AI national sections.[109] During the 1970s, AI Korea utilized this phrase extensively to try to clarify the policy to its members.[110]

However, behind this seemingly smooth indigenization, a discursive and institutional contestation developed within AI Korea. According to the original promoter Han Sŭng-hŏn, the phrase connoted an action of "working for others." Yet, in proposing an alternative version, *kungnae hwaldong kŭmji ŭi wŏnch'ik* (literally, the principle of banning members' activities on domestic issues), Yun Hyŏn rejected the dominant version, because *p'umasi* implied that one would work for others in exchange for their help, while also working one's own land.[111] In making this point, he was arguing against the revitalization of "double purpose," which some AI Korea members had never abandoned. For example, in 1975, many of AI Korea's leading members attempted to revise the article on political neutrality in its statutes to allow for engagement in democratization movements.[112]

This contentious indigenization in South Korea, as well as challenges made by other national sections, catalyzed AI to codify its neutrality policy. In 1974, Huib Leewnberg, a member of the Dutch Section, also called into question "neutrality."[113] By March 1976, AI had commenced the task of clarifying "what rules already exist[ed]—either in written form . . . or 'in spirit.'" In 1977, when AI Pakistan and AI East Germany mobilized their publications for domestic politics, it created additional motivation for this codification.[114] In 1991, after years of revising and fine-tuning, AI completed the codification of the "Work on Own Country" (WOOC) rule (*Chaguk chohang*).[115] Meanwhile, AIIS continued to caution AI Korea about its engagements in pro-democracy struggles; these cautions culminated in the closure of AI Korea, owing to some members' involvement in the Kwangju Uprising in May 1980. In 1992, AI Korea was revived under new leadership; the changed political order also meant that AIIS had few immediate concerns about the section violating the stipulation of political neutrality.[116]

Ecumenical field activism in South Korea and elsewhere also led to the creation of a forum through which the periphery could influence global human rights talk. In 1970, Rev. George Todd, secretary of the WCC Office for UIM, established a global information center for ecumenical field activism through the Chicago-based Institute of the Church in an Urban Industrial Society (ICUIS). The center was designed to facilitate communication between local groups rather than "passing the information from the center to the periphery." O Chae-sik's Documentation for Action Groups in Asia in Tokyo served as the Asian information center.[117] This organization's monthly bulletin had a subject index, publishing abstracts of thirty to fifty information and research articles, sent by about five hundred local groups from around the world. In August 1971, the term, "civil rights" (and sometimes "civil rights movements") began appearing in the index, but only in connection with articles on US domestic issues. In January 1974, the term "human rights" began to appear in the index, but the articles in question focused strictly on "civil rights." Afterward, the index began utilizing "civil rights" to index articles covering political repression and social movements outside America. In January 1975, another notable transition took place; under "civil rights" the index included the simple notation "See human rights."[118] In short, the globalization of human rights norms, policy, and discourse evolved through global-local interactions that entailed multidirectional courses of consent, contestation, and/or reconfiguration.

Conclusion

This chapter addressed the emergence of "human rights" as a protest language for pro-democracy movements in the early 1970s. It focuses on local pro-democracy actors' interactions with two global human rights initiatives led by AI and the WCC respectively. Against the backdrop of global protests and détente as well as local industrialization, urbanization, and Park's authoritarian turn, the chapter traced the development of the first human rights organization in South Korea, AI Korea. In doing so, the chapter highlighted contestations between local promoters and AIIS that resulted from their different visions for AI Korea. Local promoters imagined AI playing a critical role in local democratic struggles; in contrast, AIIS wanted AI Korea to maintain its neutrality policy. As political conditions deteriorated in South Korea, AI Korea began providing legal and financial assistance to arrested democratic protesters, thereby entangling AI in local pro-democracy struggles.

AI Korea's involvement in these struggles also resulted from many members' involvement in the other international human rights network active in South Korea, that is, the WCC. Unlike AI, the WCC adopted a maximalist, indigenous, and political approach to human rights activism. The NCCK, with the support of the WCC, held its first human rights consultation that focused on translating the concrete social, economic, and political issues faced by South Koreans into human rights issues. At the end of this consultation, the participants produced the "Declaration of Human Rights," based on local economic, social, and political needs. Ecumenical activists also recognized that human rights activism required local political engagement as well as building coalitions with nonreligious activists. In short, it represented an alternative model for the globalization of human rights. As local activists interacted with AI and WCC, they developed a framework for translating their disputes on social, political, and economic issues into global human rights issues. But as the chapter shows, this translation, appropriation, and adaptation of human rights norms, talk, and policy also affected the landscape of human rights at the global center. Thus, rather than a smooth unidirectional diffusion, the globalization of human rights developed as part of multidirectional and convoluted processes, in which non-state actors at the periphery played constitutive roles.

CHAPTER 2

Transpacific Politics

Emerging Transnational Human Rights
Actions and Counteractions

On January 8, 1974, President Park Chung-hee issued Emergency Decree No. 1 banning all criticism of the constitution. Written in October 1972, the Yushin Constitution—translated as "revitalizing reforms"—had despite its nomenclature institutionalized Park's authoritarian rule. Yet, this institutionalization failed to eliminate anti-regime protests. By December 1973, a nationwide campaign seeking to invalidate the constitution had achieved substantial momentum, and on December 10, 1973, AI Korea and the NCCK publicly celebrated International Human Rights Day for the first time. Disturbed by these and other developments, Park moved to consolidate his power by instituting a series of emergency decrees. Yet, even this crackdown did not end the confrontations between the regime and protesters. Instead, they escalated as democratization movements increasingly mobilized the language of human rights as part of their protests against the unlawful suspension of South Koreans' constitutional liberties and rights.

Four months after Decree No. 1, Park proclaimed Decree No. 4, which targeted college students, the most active resistance force. By July 1974, roughly one thousand people had been arrested for their alleged affiliation with the National Democratic Youth and Student Federation (NDYSF, Minch'ŏng Hangnyŏn) and/or the People's Revolutionary Party (PRP, Inhyŏktang). Of those, two hundred stood trial. On April 9, 1975, the government executed eight prisoners charged with espionage in the PRP case. Just one day prior to the executions, Park issued Decree No. 7, which dictated the indefinite closure of Korea University. The following month, the regime enacted its most repressive measure, Decree No. 9, which banned all criticism of the regime. Decree No. 9 remained in place until Park's death in October 1979. Through these decrees, Park systematically outlawed all opposition voices.[1]

Yet, the decrees failed to eradicate oppositional forces. Instead, pro-democracy movements expanded and increasingly challenged the regime in words and in actions. What can account for this paradoxical phenomenon? At a lecture on December 10, 1974, hosted by AI Korea in honor of the 1974 International Human Rights Day, Ham Sŏk-hŏn, a well-respected Quaker and honorary president of AI Korea, suggested that the answer was the transformative power of human rights: "What an awful year, such as we have never before experienced! It is the NDYSF incident that we will be unable to forget. However, a repercussion of this incident is that the traditional sense of the national border has vanished from our mind. Our understanding of the state has accordingly changed. Now we think of human rights violations, even those occurring elsewhere, not as some other country's affairs, but as our own."[2] Echoing Ham's points, AI Korea's executive director Yun Hyŏn called for "a united struggle of all people, transcending national boundaries" for human rights. Yun cogently labeled the 1974 emergency decrees as "a living source for human rights movements."[3]

With their remarks, these two leading AI Korea members captured the underlying mechanism through which pro-democracy movements in the era of emergency rule advanced their cause. Through the formation of human rights networks and protest actions, Korean activists succeeded in linking local pro-democracy protests to international politics. Rather than complying with AI's apolitical campaigning methods, local activists in South Korea and Japan pragmatically adapted international human rights campaigns to the local situation to create momentum for democracy. Such bottom-up engagements entangled transnational contestations on human rights with US-Korean diplomatic relations and in the process remade transnational human rights movements.

This chapter is divided into two parts. The first traces the emergence of a transnational human rights coalition in South Korea against the backdrop of the implementation of the emergency decrees. It opens with an analysis of AI's 1974 fact-finding mission to South Korea. It shows how this fact-finding mission resulted in a reorientation in AI's apolitical mobilization model in response to local geopolitical considerations. It argues that these same local geopolitical considerations played an important role in shifting AI's locus of action from the UN to the US Congress. Finally, it details the constitutive role of local actors and ecumenical activists in advancing a bottom-up, transpacific human rights activism.

The second part of the chapter focuses on the reaction of the Park regime and the Nixon/Ford administrations to these transnational human rights campaigns, that is, their mobilization of counteractive human rights policies. It analyzes how the Park regime utilized the Cold War frame to reinforce the regime's legitimacy and gain concessions from the United States. It also examines how US officials devised a strategic approach—namely, "quiet diplomacy"—in response to US–South Korean diplomatic relations becoming entangled with transnational human rights campaigns in South Korea. In short, this chapter illustrates the process through which South Korean domestic conflicts over democracy developed into transpacific politics on human rights.

An Uncharted Journey: AI's Strategic Shift

On June 28, 1974, following the South Korean government's crackdown in late April, the renowned American human rights lawyer William J. Butler arrived in Seoul to conduct a ten-day fact-finding mission for AI. At first glance, Butler's mission appeared no different from other classic AI fact-finding missions. Sparked by allegations that AI Korea had violated AI's neutrality policy, the mission took an uncharted turn when an intense debate developed between center and periphery over the mission's goals. At issue was who should be allowed to link South Korean domestic disputes to international politics and how it should be done. AIIS wanted to uphold the neutrality policy because it believed maintaining this policy created the conditions most conducive for winning human rights concessions from the Park regime. It also believed that the UN was the only appropriate venue for addressing international disputes on human rights.

In contrast, local activists supported self-determination and thus moved to engage in South Korean democratization struggles; they also viewed the situation in South Korea pragmatically, recognizing that geopolitics, most notably US Cold War policies, influenced South Korea's political and economic trajectory. Through an analysis of internal AI discussions about the fact-finding mission and its repercussions, this section demonstrates the entangled development of global human rights activism and pro-democracy struggles in South Korea as well as local actors' constitutive roles in shaping the direction of transnational human rights campaigns.

William J. Butler and AI's Fact-finding Mission

Butler's mission was an outgrowth of an AIIS proposal that was made shortly after the enactment of Decree No. 1 in January 1974. This first proposal focused exclusively on the possibility that AI Korea members' involvement in domestic affairs would undermine AI campaigns in the region. It made no mention of the victims of the regime's crackdown. In early February 1974, Peter Harris, an Asian specialist working out of London, noted the "increasingly troubling" AI Korea situation. Since October 1973, Harris asserted, AI Korea had assumed an active role in the mounting pro-democracy and anti-regime struggles. Since then, regular correspondence from Seoul had ceased, and four leading AI Korea members had been placed under house arrest multiple times for "actively opposing the [Yushin] Constitution." Harris shared his concerns with AIUSA chair Ivan Morris, who, as we saw in Chapter 1, had been involved in the founding of AI Korea. Consequently, he was aware of the four members' past involvement in the 1960s *chaeya* movements and had in fact expressed concerns about this affiliation at the time of AI Korea's founding.[4] On February 12, 1974, based on information garnered from a Japanese clergyman who had recently visited Seoul, AI Japan sent Harris an update on AI Korea.[5] With this information in hand, on February 15, Harris composed a "confidential" mission proposal. In it, he described a worst-case scenario in which the Korean regime would "stop Amnesty [from] protesting all political cases in South Korea" because of local AI members' disregard for the neutrality policy.[6] By March 20, Harris's cautionary memo had become a top item on AIIS's agenda. Stephanie Grant, head of the Research Department in London, succinctly summed up the stakes: "The problem we face is essentially one of deciding whether AI Korea can continue to exist as a viable Amnesty unit."[7] The issue became more critical following the crackdown on student activists under Decree No. 4.

After AIIS made AI Korea's future a priority, AI Japan intervened on AI Korea's behalf. On April 12, 1974, AI Japan's secretary-general Toshio Shimizu wrote AIIS secretary-general Martin Ennals to express his opposition to AI Korea's closure. When Ivan Morris visited Tokyo, Shimizu reiterated the devastating consequences for South Koreans, if the section were closed: "The Amnesty organization is the last resort for the people and a pipeline of

information for the country."[8] AI Japan's intervention seemingly influenced AIIS. On April 17, Morris, now back in New York, sent his recommendations to Ennals. After speaking with various figures, including AI Japan
members with firsthand knowledge of the South Korean situation, Korean
and Japanese leaders, and South Korean embassy officials, Morris recommended three actions: (1) write AI Korea's chair to stress the importance of
adhering to the impartiality policy; (2) organize a ten-day mission to Seoul;
and (3) postpone the decision to close AI Korea until after the mission.[9]

In elaborating these three interrelated action plans, Morris emphasized
the importance of maintaining AI's political neutrality. He believed that
the involvement of AI Korea's leaders, including Ham Sŏk-hŏn and Kim
Chae-jun, in domestic affairs "gravely impaired" AI's "present and future
effectiveness" in South Korea. However, he realized that it would be "unre-
alistic" to expect Ham to "restrain" from publicly criticizing the Park regime. Morris suggested that Ennals encourage AI Korea's executive director
Yun to increase efforts at clearly delineating AI Korea's official positions
from the personal positions of Ham and other activists in AI Korea. Morris
also believed that a South Korean mission should serve two purposes, rather
than just the one initially proposed. In addition to assessing AI Korea's
"continued viability," it should provide updated information on the situation of political prisoners in South Korea. Morris also requested that AIIS
send American delegates, because Japanese delegates might rekindle past
colonial antagonisms. To ensure the mission's neutrality, delegates should
prepare by studying the current situation in South Korea and AI's current
and past research on North Korean POCs. He assumed that the South
Korean government, as during his 1969 mission, would be more likely to cooperate, if Amnesty advanced a balanced approach.[10] Although Morris did
not recommend permanently closing AI Korea, he stressed that maintaining political neutrality was the most effective mechanism for handling the
crackdown in South Korea and the actions of AI Korea members.

Yet even as Morris reaffirmed political neutrality, AI Japan and other activists in the region continued to present AIIS with indigenous perspectives
on AI in South Korea. Ironically, Peter Harris, the Asian specialist who first
recommended disciplinary action against AI Korea, became the conduit
through which local perspectives reached AIIS. Since his initial proposal,
Harris had moved from London to Tokyo. On April 19, 1974, he wrote Ennals
to insist that AIIS maintain its strategic silence, that is, it should issue no
public statements criticizing the Park regime. Yun and other AI Korea

members, Harris noted, feared that "students and others working with the Amnesty movement in Korea will be rounded up if Amnesty is publicly identified with criticism of the Emergency Measures." Harris also advised against compiling "case sheets" on prominent political prisoners, such as Paek Ki-wan and Chang Chun-ha. Moreover, AIIS should make "no public statements or publicity or intervention on their behalf in the name of A.I." However, his opinion on closing AI now echoed that of AI Japan: "To close the [Korean] Section down or even give public expression of doubt about its work would be the height of folly."[11]

Harris also urged that AIIS take a more substantive role in South Korea. On May 31, he wrote his successor in London Cheng Huan and advised, "If the Secretariat really thinks it can get these people out of trouble, then it should be ready to do whatever it thinks suitable but sending postcards to President Park, as Mr. [Masahiko] Kurata remarked to me this afternoon, is an utter waste of time." In addition, Harris supported AI Korea's request, relayed by AI Japan, that an AI delegate observe the upcoming trial of the fifty-four prisoners indicted under Decree No. 4. In making this request, he backed AI Japan's position that to "secure an entry into the courtroom," AI should send a "high level legal observer" from the United States. Unlike Morris's vague reference to colonial antagonisms, Harris's rationale for sending a high-ranking American drew on the geopolitical strategies favored by local activists.[12] By mid-June, Harris still had not received any response from London, prompting AI Japan secretary-general Shimizu to write London again.[13]

The Tokyo-London communications seemingly changed the contours of the mission. Although upholding that the neutrality policy remain sacrosanct, AIIS made concessions to local expectations for the mission. One week prior to the mission's scheduled start date of June 28, AIIS selected the American lawyer William J. Butler for the mission (Figure 2). At the time, Butler was the UN representative for the International Commission of Jurists (ICJ) and chair of the New York City Bar Association's Committee on International Human Rights. He was also well known for his long-term working relationship with ACLU founder Roger Baldwin.[14] In a letter from June 21, Ennals instructed Butler to have a firm talk with AI Korea's leadership about maintaining political neutrality and to "observe the trial of 54 people." To emphasize the former, Ennals quoted AI's statute—"No section works for prisoners in their own country"—and enumerated specific actions by AI Korea that violated the policy, for example the "individual distribution of

Figure 2. AI's fact-finding
mission in 1974.
Clockwise from front row right,
Yi Pyŏng-rin, William J. Butler,
Ham Sŏk-hŏn, Yun Hyŏn, Han
Sŭng-hŏn, and Pu Wan-hyŏk.
Courtesy of Amnesty Interna-
tional Korea. © Amnesty
International.

relief to families" and local "observers at trials." As for AI Korea's future, he
specified options that ranged from preserving the status quo to closure.[15]

Before heading to Seoul on June 28, Butler visited Japan where he began
preparations for his mission. There, in conversation with an AI Japan
member, Butler announced his plan to "push" the US Embassy to pressure
Korean authorities "to let him observe the Emergency Court Martial of 54
[prisoners]." Butler worked diligently to enhance AI's image of neutrality—
from the selection of his interpreters to the information that he acquired on
political prisoners in North Korea.[16] However, as the mission proceeded, local interventions tipped the scale in favor of a more geopolitical approach,
which in turn was reinforced by growing liberal internationalist sentiment
in the US Congress.

The First US Congressional Hearing
on Human Rights in South Korea

On July 30, 1974, two weeks after completing the AI fact-finding mission in
Seoul, Butler testified at the first US congressional hearing on human rights
in South Korea. His testimony on behalf of AI introduced a new setting for
international contestations on human rights. This new site would become
critical for South Korea during the democratic transition and later for North
Korea in the post–Cold War era. Yet, ironically, prior to Butler's testimony,
AIIS had not considered the US Congress a viable theater of action, because
it was "too peripheral." The United Nations was the "competitive forum" in
which AI would have to make its case for a world premised on human rights
and defeat its ideological rivals.[17]

But contingent developments—the worsening plight of political prisoners in South Korea, the UN's failure to respond to the situation, and efforts
by the US Congress to restore the United States' reputation as a world moral
leader—forced AI to rethink its strategy. On July 4, 1974, AI's Research Department sent the national sections a report, "Violations of Human Rights
in South Korea." The report utilized UN human rights bills as the yardstick
to assess the legality of measures taken by the South Korean government, that
is, emergency decrees, restrictions placed on civil liberties, court-martial
trials, and death-penalty practices. Finding that these measures constituted
a gross violation of international human rights law, the report called on the
UN to take action. Aware that the South Korean regime might respond to
these charges by citing Article 2.7 of the UN Charter recognizing a state's exclusive rights over the domestic jurisdiction, the report preemptively countered this claim by citing the UN's right to intervene in domestic affairs if "a
consistent pattern of gross violations of human rights" exists. The report also
rebutted the argument that as a non–UN member, South Korea was under
no obligation to comply with UN human rights standards. It argued that the
UN Charter represented "the common opinion of the overwhelming majority of the international community" and consequently took precedence over
national sovereignty.[18] The report exemplified AI's humanitarian apolitical
model. Rather than taking direct action, the report sought to publicize human
rights violations, in hopes that the regime would voluntarily grant amnesty
or reformative amelioration.[19] The idea was to avoid any confrontational action that could potentially backfire and lead to the government taking more
repressive measures.

A week after Butler's mission, on July 13, 1974, the Korean regime sentenced eight of the fifty-four prisoners to death; this action prompted AIIS
to issue immediately a news release to urge its members to appeal to Korean
authorities to commute the sentences. AIIS also circulated guidelines for this
campaign to national sections and coordination groups. The guidelines, authored by Cheng Huan, a Research Department staff member, called for a
cautionary campaign "at the level of enquiries and appeals" to lift the death
sentences. Any other action, AIIS feared, would "endanger members" of AI
Korea.[20] At this point, AI apparently did not consider a geopolitical strategy
targeting politicians in Washington, DC, an option.

Yet by August 1973, human rights were in vogue on Capitol Hill. Rep.
Donald Fraser (D-MN) and other liberal internationalists in the US Congress
utilized human rights mandates to legitimize US foreign policy that had been

badly damaged by the Vietnam War as well as by political scandals on the home front. In fall 1973, the House Subcommittee on International Organizations and Movements, led by Fraser, held fifteen hearings on the international protection of human rights. On December 17, 1973, Congress approved Section 32 of the Foreign Assistance Act of 1973, which read: "It is the sense of Congress that the President should deny any economic or military assistance to the government of any foreign country which practices the internment or imprisonment of that country's citizens for political purposes."[21] Section 32 ended the decade-long practice of allowing the executive branch to determine US foreign policy based on perceived national security interests without any significant congressional input. In March 1974, the US Congress called on US administrations to assume global "leadership" in advocating for victims of human rights violations. Congress also urged the State Department to make the promotion of human rights the touchstone of US-Soviet relations.[22] On December 30, 1974, Congress amended the Foreign Assistance Act to include Section 502B, which required the suspension of US security assistance if recipient countries showed "a consistent pattern of gross violations of internationally recognized human rights," unless the president certified the existence of extraordinary circumstances or that the rights situation had significantly improved.[23] In theory, at least, these legislative interventions made human rights a substantial component of US foreign policy.

The changed mood in Washington and the worsening situation of the political prisoners in Seoul led Butler to supplement AI's traditional recourse to the United Nations with new interventions that entangled AI's human rights campaign with US congressional politics. On July 11, 1974, four days after returning from Seoul, Butler offered Ennals a summary of his preliminary report. In it, Butler clearly stated that the South Korean decrees violated UN bills of human rights and therefore should be rescinded. He advised AI to recognize all those imprisoned by the Park regime under Decree No. 4 as POCs, because they had been arrested for "political opposition" and did not "constitute a 'communist threat.'"[24] A few days after the eight PRP prisoners had been sentenced to death, he telephoned Stephanie Grant to propose a concrete plan of action. In this conversation, Butler summarized for Grant the "long and detailed" mission report, which he insisted AI should give "top priority." He began by emphasizing his opposition to closing AI Korea; AI Korea members had not flagrantly violated the neutrality policy; their sole "irregular" activity was providing legal aid to the students on trial. Next, he recommended organizing a team of international legal experts—a "joint

Amnesty/ICJ mission"—to observe the trials of the fifty-four prisoners in order to "place considerable pressures" on the regime. The next strategy that Butler recommended targeted the US Congress. Given the unlikelihood of any executive action, Butler urged pressuring Congress to arrange hearings "as soon as possible." To exert pressure on Congress, he advocated for an orchestrated "public opinion" media blitz. He recommended two Harvard alumni as potential leaders of this campaign: Gregory Henderson (former US Embassy counselor in Seoul and Tufts University professor) and Edwin Reischauer (former ambassador to Japan and Harvard University professor). Following this discussion, Grant authorized Butler to testify at any future US congressional hearing as AI's "representative." They agreed that AIIS should conduct a final review of the report before acting upon it; until completion of that review, the report's findings should remain confidential.[25]

AIUSA also encouraged AIIS to consider utilizing the US Congress as a platform for promoting human rights interventions in South Korea. Soon after Butler's call, Grant received a message from Arthur Michaelson, a member of AIUSA Board of Directors, concerning AIUSA's plan to campaign for the eight prisoners recently sentenced to death. In particular, AIUSA wanted to pressure the US Congress to issue a public condemnation of the Korean regime on this issue. Grant consented to the proposal, and AIUSA immediately launched a "telegram tree," a tactic in which "large numbers of cables are sent to individual [congressmen]."[26] In another correspondence to Michaelson from July 19, Grant reiterated that she thought the telegram campaign was "an excellent action." In addition, she sent Ennals a memorandum summarizing her conversation with Butler, including her approval of his proposals. In the memorandum, she highlighted AIIS's ultimate authority over how Butler's mission report was used: "As soon as we [AIIS] have his report, we will decide how and when it should be publicly used." She added that in the event of an urgent situation in South Korea, such as if the regime carried out any "executions" before AI's appeal, Butler would give an immediate public response. She also confirmed that Butler would act as AI's official representative at any US congressional hearings.[27]

Despite these assertions of AIIS's final authority, once Butler received permission to testify before Congress, he seemed increasingly to act autonomously. On July 20, the US Congress announced that on July 30, 1974, it would hold the first hearing on human rights in South Korea. Before sending Ennals a copy of his final report draft on July 25, Butler sent a copy to the US Congress in preparation for the upcoming hearing. The final version of his report included a list of recommendations that the AI representative should present to Congress. For example, the AI representative should "urge the suspension of all economic and military aid to the Republic of Korea pursuant to Section 32 of the Foreign Aid Law of 1973–1974."[28] In making this type of recommendation, Butler had largely disregarded AI's neutrality policy; instead, he activated a new geopolitically oriented approach that would challenge the mechanism of US Cold War policy toward South Korea.

Butler also recommended that AI file a complaint with the UN Sub-Commission on Prevention of Discrimination and Protection of Minorities. In making this recommendation, he referred to Resolutions 1235, 1503, and 728–F of the UN Economic and Social Council that allowed for UN intervention in domestic affairs in cases of human rights violations.[29] In fall 1974, he bypassed AIIS and submitted his mission report directly to the director of the UN Human Rights Division.[30] However, he received no response. In April 1976, AI submitted another petition to the UN; this petition included the mission report from 1975. When by 1979 the UN had still taken no action on the April 1976 petition, AI decided to stop pursuing its appeal through the UN—a decision analyzed in detail in Chapter 3. With the UN option proving ineffectual, AI increasingly deployed a geopolitical strategy aimed at building coalitional campaigns with the US Congress.

By October 1974, Butler had learned that there had been some improvements in the practices of the Korean regime. In a two-page update to his original report, he noted that the Korean government had "accepted" some of his original recommendations, such as "the alleviation of the use of torture by Korean police and military authorities." However, instead of softening his critical stance, he advocated for introducing more geopolitically oriented tactics. In particular, he targeted the US military's presence in South Korea. In doing so, Butler challenged a crucial mechanism of the Cold War security consensus, namely, what the historian Bruce Cumings labeled the "archipelago of military bases" that in effect buttressed the regime: "The United Nations, under whose flag foreign military forces stationed in Korea serve, and the United States, which provide[s] enormous military and economic aid to the Korean nation, should seriously consider withdrawing their support which is being used to perpetuate the tyrannical and repressive measures of a dictator with an insatiable appetite for autocratic power."[31] Butler added that his call for US and UN withdrawal from South Korea echoed the current campaigns of other international non-state groups involved in the international debate on the UN-ROK relationship.[32] Since Nixon's 1969 Guam Doctrine, which called for Asian allies to take charge of their defense, Washington had reconfigured the presence of US military forces in South Korea. This reconfiguration became one of the most controversial issues in US-ROK relations. Around 1971, Washington began withdrawing US forces from South Korea and assisting South Korea's military modernization programs. In addition, Butler's criticism and that of other NGOs emerged in the context of global détente, especially the Sino-US rapprochement.[33]

Butler's geopolitical advocacy diverged from AI's classic apolitical formula. In September 1974, Cheng Huan in AIIS proposed a few campaign options for South Korea, such as a campaign to repeal decrees (officially suspended on August 23 but which in practice continued) and an anti-torture campaign based on Butler's report.[34] But in keeping with AIIS's July 1974 guidelines, these campaigns would be initiated through the United Nations.

By fall 1974, the situation in South Korea had become a standing issue at the UN; however, UN engagement did not concern human rights. During Nixon's 1972 visit to the People's Republic of China (PRC), the United States and China issued a diplomatic document, known as the Shanghai Communiqué, pledging to work toward the normalization of relations between the two countries. As part of this normalization, the PRC called for the dissolution of the UN Commission on the Unification and Rehabilitation of Korea and withdrawal of the UN Command (UNC) from South Korea. The abolition of these institutions had been on the UN agenda off and on since the 1950s; however, the 1970s international atmosphere of détente meant that more nations were pressuring the UN to take action. Against the backdrop of these international developments, as well as those in South Korea and the United States, the battle escalated between those who wanted to utilize such geopolitical issues to advance democracy and human rights in South Korea and those more interested in ensuring the Cold War security consensus even at the expense of human rights.

Espionage Case and Self-Internationalization

AI's pioneering intervention in the April 1974 crackdown, especially Butler's fact-finding mission, had by the summer of 1974 produced a breakthrough in the international campaigns for human rights in South Korea. This internationalization generated another wave of transnational human rights campaigns in fall 1974, which in turn enhanced AI's developing cooperation and collaboration with US congressional human rights advocacy. Ironically, the eight prisoners whom AI had not supported because the South Korean government accused them of being Communist saboteurs would play a critical role. Unable to obtain support from AI, these prisoners and their families reached out to the ecumenical community for assistance. The introduction of this supportive community, I argue, enhanced the coalitional framework for international human rights politics that AI had built with the US Congress.

AI refused its official support to any political prisoner charged with espionage as well as to any political prisoner who committed violent acts or advocated violent means. However, in 1964, the latter of these two disqualifying conditions experienced a serious international challenge, when AI refused to recognize Nelson Mandela as a prisoner of conscience, because he did not completely uphold his faith in nonviolence.[35] However, the other disqualifier— the charge of espionage—remained unchallenged. For example, when in 1969 Ivan Morris conducted an AI fact-finding mission to Seoul with reference to prisoners sentenced to death in connection with the so-called German and European espionage cases, he never seriously questioned the veracity of the charges. Instead, AI actions on behalf of the prisoners entailed condemning the death penalty on humanitarian grounds. In fact, few histories of global human rights have tackled the issue of espionage. Yet, in the Cold War context, repressive regimes, such as the South Korean one, utilized false allegations of espionage to shutdown domestic opposition and to circumvent interventions by international advocacy groups.

This section analyzes how the wives of the eight prisoners sentenced to death for espionage in the 1974 PRP case utilized the discourse of impartiality to resist the marginalization of their husbands by the pro-democracy community and to challenge the veracity of the charges. These women's appeals via ecumenical activists working in South Korea, I argue, led to the intensification of the ongoing bottom-up internationalization of human rights as well as to the increased imbrication of US–South Korean foreign policy with transpacific contestations on human rights in South Korea.

Beginning in July 1974, families and supporters of political prisoners incarcerated under Decree No. 4 held a weekly prayer meeting campaign at the Korean Christian Building in Seoul. Despite a nationwide ban on protests, scores of Christians and non-Christians attended these Thursday Prayer

Meetings over the course of that summer. Yet, despite this show of solidarity within the movement for democracy and human rights, the organizers of this campaign were sharply criticized, when on September 19, 1974, the wives of the eight PRP prisoners spoke up: "We have attended many such meetings. However, not once were our husbands' names mentioned in the prayers." This silence, they reasoned, "may be due to the fact that our husbands are accused of being Communists."[36] In fact, the PRP prisoners numbered among the "54 prisoners" that Butler's fact-finding mission for AI had highlighted. In his report, Butler stated that none of these prisoners committed acts of espionage. Yet, in reality, neither pro-democracy nor international human rights advocacy groups were eager to include in their campaigns those charged with espionage. The "54 prisoners" encompassed only the student prisoners charged in the NDYSF case.[37]

The wives' remarks prompted an internal discussion on AI's impartiality policy; this discussion in turn led to counteractions by the regime. After hearing the wives' appeals, two AI Korea leaders assured the women that AI's impartiality policy meant that their husband's plight would not be ignored. Honorary president Ham Sŏk-hŏn declared, "We should not limit our prayers to only Christians but should include Communists." Executive director Yun Hyŏn confirmed AI's commitment to the PRP prisoners; the women's husbands, he explained, had been included in the August 1974 international postcard campaign for the "55 defendants."[38] This declaration of support resulted in Yun being detained by KCIA officers immediately after the meeting. According to the officers, AI was only "permitted to function in South Korea on condition that it did not work for communists." By financially "assisting communist[s]," AI Korea had violated the law. This allegation was based on the fact that AI Korea had provided aid to PRP prisoners through its relief fund program for political prisoners and their family members. The entire situation—from the public speeches to Yun's detention—heightened AIIS's anxiety over AI Korea's stability.[39] Fearing further suppression, the AI Korea Board decided to stop supplying relief funds to the families of the PRP prisoners. This action, they hoped, would allow them to continue supporting NDYSF prisoners, who vastly outnumbered the PRP prisoners.[40]

As a result, the wives lost the support of AI Korea, one of the few available advocacy groups at the time. In May 1974, a new group, the Human Rights Committee of the NCCK, emerged in a hurried reaction to the crackdown under Decree No. 4. But it did not yet have the resources or organizational structure needed to conduct a campaign on behalf of the PRP prisoners. The only assistance the PRP wives now received came from the Association of Prisoners' Families (founded in September 1974); some of its members chose to disregard the ideological allegations made against their husbands.[41] As yet, no advocacy group challenged the credibility of the espionage charges in the PRP case.

This changed on October 10, 1974, when at the Thursday Prayer Meeting, Rev. George Ogle, an American Methodist missionary affiliated with the Monday Night Group, declared during his sermon that the KCIA had provided "little evidence" that the PRP prisoners had Communist ties and "no crime [is] worthy of death." He urged participants to pray for the PRP prisoners and their families. Ogle, also known as O Myŏng-gŏl in Korea, was one of the pioneers of the Urban Industrial Mission (UIM) programs established in South Korea in the 1960s.[42] Ogle's sermon, as AI acknowledged in 1975, was "the first time" that anyone "dared" to mention "these alleged communists."[43]

Ogle's unprecedented declaration was set in motion by the wives' last-ditch effort to save their husbands. At roughly the same time that the wives appealed to AI Korea leaders for assistance, they also approached Ogle for help. They told Ogle that the government's allegation that their husbands were Communist was false. This prompted Ogle and his missionary colleagues in the Monday Night Group to investigate.[44] Father James Sinnott and Walter Durst took the lead in this investigation. They were aware that three of the eight prisoners in the PRP case had previously been arrested and tried for the same charges in the so-called "first" PRP case in 1964 and 1965. Sinnott and Durst began their investigation by surveying newspaper articles on the first PRP case. This survey revealed that Sin Chik-su, the KCIA chief and lead prosecutor in the 1974 PRP case, had also been the prosecutor in the first PRP case, for which he failed to gain a conviction. Based on their investigation, Sinnott and Durst concluded that the men were innocent, as their wives claimed; the regime had fabricated the charges against the men in the PRP case. The missionary group then decided to publicize their findings, which led to Ogle's declaration at the Thursday Prayer Meeting.[45] One month after his sermon, the missionaries smuggled a copy of their findings out of Seoul to American media reporters in Tokyo.[46] On November 26, the *New York Times* released a half-page article that recapitulated the missionaries' findings.[47]

The Korean regime responded quickly to the missionaries' findings and actions. Just ten hours after his speech, KCIA officers took Ogle into custody on the grounds that he had violated the Anti-Communist Law. At headquarters, they interrogated him: "What right do you have to pray for the release of criminals?" However, because he was a foreigner, an American one at that, the interrogation did not last long, and he was released shortly thereafter. As a condition of his release, the Korean authorities demanded that he write a statement in which he admit to his wrongdoings and promise never to take such actions again. Instead, Ogle released a statement declaring that he had acted in accordance with the tenets of his faith.[48] Ogle had no intentions of backing down.

The day after his arrest, Ogle and sixty-one other American missionaries sent a joint letter to President Gerald Ford, who was scheduled to visit Seoul in November 1974. In the letter, the missionaries described the death sentences given to the eight PRP prisoners as "drastic violations of human rights," because the government had provided no evidence that any "so-called conspiracy" had "ever existed." They also asserted that "the welfare and development of Korea and its people" were in jeopardy and urged Ford to express "strong disapproval" of the regime's current socioeconomic and political policy, especially its program of military modernization and citizens' forced compliance. They asked that Ford pressure the Park regime to release all political prisoners and to rescind repressive laws. The missionaries also noted that the letter-writing campaign reflected "a shift in U.S. public opinion" on US foreign policy and warned of "the grave disadvantages of the U.S. continuing its unconditional support of the Park regime." Finally, they requested that Ford or one of his aides meet with them to discuss these issues. An American friend immediately smuggled the letter out of South Korea. One month later, on November 5, the National Security Council (NSC) in Washington, DC, found it and placed it in a file, labeled "many signers."[49]

While waiting for a response from Washington, the missionaries continued their campaigns in Seoul. Linda Jones, chair of the Monday Night Group, proposed to her colleagues that they deliver the same letter to the US ambassador in Seoul. On the surface, this letter appeared no different from any other ordinary communication between American citizens and their government. Yet it stemmed from a global and geopolitical perspective. In her letter bearing the title "Where Are We Now?," Jones made clear that the letter's goal was to inform the US ambassador of "the reality in Korea," which they had "seen and heard." In leading this campaign, she considered this action as a way to "make the US Government budge." Although Jones was scheduled to return permanently to the United States in a few weeks, her words clearly indicated that she would continue the fight for human rights in South Korea from her home in Chicago. Sinnott also noted, "The US Government must change first, then the realities in Korea will change."[50] In focusing on the impact of US geopolitics on South Korea, the missionaries understood the entangled relationship between US foreign policy and transnational human rights campaigns and proceeded accordingly.

In early November, Ogle and four other delegates met Richard Sneider, the US ambassador to South Korea, at his house. Sneider had invited them to his house rather than the embassy to avoid any possible allegations by the Park regime of "meeting with political activists." At the meeting, Ogle read a statement, in which he exposed two false claims made by the South Korean regime to justify its repressive system. First, he declared that the North Korean "threat" had "certainly declined" since 1968; therefore, the 1972 Yushin Constitution institutionalizing Park's authoritarian rule was unwarranted. Second, based on the economic records from the two pre-1972 five-year economic plans, Ogle demonstrated that the positive correlation that the Korean regime drew between repressive rule and economic development was "spurious." He concluded his presentation by demanding that President Ford intervene on behalf of human rights in South Korea. In response, Sneider merely reiterated the ever-present threat from North Korea as the central reason for Ford's visit to Seoul. Sneider also refused to grant the missionaries' request to meet with President Ford, citing the US principle of noninterference in domestic affairs.[51]

Sneider had hoped to avoid calling any public attention to the missionary's demands. However, in the context of Ford's upcoming visit to Seoul, the growing pro-democracy protests on the streets and the missionaries' campaigns had caught the attention of New York Times special correspondent Fox Butterfield. In his reporting, Butterfield stressed the unprecedented intersection between South Korean domestic politics and US foreign policy, especially on human rights issues. Against this backdrop, Butterfield astutely identified "the first anti-American sentiment" in a country that for years had been "ardently pro-American" and "dependent" on the United States.[52] The South Korean regime, highly sensitive to such criticisms in the US media, quickly responded.

In choosing to respond, the South Korean regime catalyzed local and international coverage, thereby fueling transpacific contestations on human rights. On November 8, South Korea's foreign minister Kim Tong-jo, who was in New York for the UN General Assembly, warned that foreign missionaries were "likely to be deported" if they "continue these illegal activities." He later denied making this remark.[53] However, the next day, Prime Minister Kim Chong-p'il repeated the same warning at a morning prayer meeting. Denouncing the foreign missionaries' "deviation" from their proper mission, he insisted that they should abide by Korean law, and, as "visiting guests," they should focus on the missionary work for which they had been granted entry into the country. He also highlighted the "strict protection of people's rights to live [*saengjonkwŏn*] safe from aggressors" as an essential condition for the "genuine guarantee of human rights." In making this claim, he reinterpreted Romans 13:1–2 of the Bible, in which the apostle Paul called for submission to authority: "Those who hate or fear the democratic government whose authority is established by God are committing an evil act."[54]

This warning did not deter the missionaries' ongoing campaigns for the eight PRP prisoners. Quite the contrary, on November 21, just one day prior to Ford's arrival in Seoul, the missionaries along with thirty family members of the prisoners staged a public demonstration (Figure 3). After the Thursday Prayer Meeting ended, they marched to the US Embassy and into its courtyard. When three hundred Korean riot police surrounded the protesters, Sinnott pointed at the police tear-gas masks that were clearly labeled "Made in the USA" and shouted that he was "ashamed" of his country. The protesters wore sashes that read: "Free my husband" or "Free my child." They also carried placards that demanded: "President Ford! Can you overlook injustice?" and shouted: "We won't leave here until the release of prisoners of conscience in celebration of the US-Korean summit." The South Korean police dragged all the protesters out of the embassy courtyard and arrested them.[55]

On December 6, the Korean government decided to make good on its threat to deport missionaries involved in the human rights campaigns. The assistant foreign minister No Sin-yŏng notified the US Embassy of the Korean government's decision to deport Ogle. As justification for this action, he cited the October 10 speech on behalf of the PRP prisoners as well as another speech. Both speeches had been secretly recorded by the KCIA. The South Korean government gave Ogle an ultimatum: Issue an apology by December 9 or accept the consequences. But as already noted, Ogle chose instead to make a declaration of conscience: "My sermons are not political. I am not politically motivated. . . . My sermons are a witness to the teachings of Scripture as regards salvation, justice, and human rights."[56] On December 14,

Figure 3. Wives and mothers of political prisoners protesting in front of the
US Embassy in Seoul in November 1974.
Placards says "We can't stand it anymore! Free political prisoners!" and "Ford,
are you supporting the Yushin dictatorship?"
Source: https://archives.kdemo.or.kr; Serial No. 00718700. © Kyŏnghyang
sinmun.

Ogle became the first person deported from South Korea for engaging in
transnational human rights activism (Figure 4).

Ironically, by deporting Ogle, the South Korean regime advanced human
rights activism on Capitol Hill. Back in the United States, Ogle testified
before Congress about his experiences in South Korea. At the hearings on
human rights, chaired by Congressman Fraser, Ogle again declared that
his actions were not political; rather, they derived from his duty to God.
His faith required him to speak out when "workers and others have been
denied their legal and human rights." In rejecting the regime's label of "political agitator," he asserted that a "political system that violates the basic
rights of human beings is likely to perceive such a moral judgment as a political act."[57]

Figure 4. Rev. George Ogle leaving for the United States after being deported in December 1974.
Source: https://archives.kdemo.or.kr; serial no. 00722862. © Kyŏnghyang sinmun

After Ogle's deportation, the deportation of other missionaries, including Sinnott in April 1975 for his involvement in the same PRP case, soon followed. The Korean government also responded to transnational human rights activism by passing the Anti-Slander Law in March 1975. This law, in effect until the late 1980s, made any communication between a Korean and a foreigner that expressed criticism of the regime illegal. Yet, despite its best efforts, the South Korean regime could not contain within its sovereign-territorial boundaries the nation's democratic disputes. Both

Butler's fact-finding campaign for AI and the Korean wives' efforts on behalf of their husbands had set in motion an internationalization of the Korean democratic struggle that effectively mobilized the language of human rights. Once this internationalization began, the transpacific politicization of human rights pioneered by Butler continued to develop. But the barriers that the PRP prisoners' wives faced also reveal a little-discussed point in the history of human rights. In insisting on political neutrality, AI inadvertently contributed to the escalation of political repression. Wanting to avoid third-party interventions, the South Korean regime manipulated AI's policy to its advantage by making false charges of espionage and Communist ties. However, once the bottom-up mobilization of human rights took hold, this tactic backfired. Ecumenical activists exposed the government's manipulation of espionage charges and increasingly mobilized geopolitical tactics in their campaign. Just as these tactics provoked counteractions by the Korean regime, they also provoked counteractions by US administrations.

The Emergence of Kissinger's Quiet Diplomacy

The internationalization of human rights issues in South Korea increasingly entangled US administrations with transnational contestations on human rights. It did so when the US Congress emerged as a locus for coalitional campaigns to politicize human rights issues in the context of Cold War geopolitics. Political scientist Rosemary Foot shows that the evolution of global human rights politics during the Cold War had a critical connection with international powers' dual policies in mobilizing for and against the promotion of human rights.[58] Yet, the current literature on the global politics of human rights during the 1970s tends to focus on the activism and strategy of advocacy groups, while portraying Nixon, Ford, and their top foreign policy advisers as passive actors or bystanders at large.[59] In contrast, I argue that the Nixon/Ford administrations actively deployed a counteraction policy on human rights to safeguard the Cold War security consensus, to alleviate domestic and international pressure on the White House to advance human rights abroad, and to ensure the stability of an undemocratic ally.

The emergence of a counteraction coalition acted as another engine for the development of transpacific politics of human rights. In this section, I examine how Kissinger, during the Nixon/Ford administrations, designed a

realpolitik strategy, namely, "quiet diplomacy," in response to the liberal internationalist vision of foreign policy set forth by the US Congress during
the July 1974 congressional hearings on human rights in South Korea. I then
analyze how the Ford administration deployed quiet diplomacy to counter
the first transnational contestation on human rights in South Korea, prompted
by Ford's scheduled visit to Seoul in November 1974.

Publicizing Kissinger's Quiet Diplomacy

Since the second half of 1973, liberal internationalists in Congress had been
challenging the conventional approach of US foreign policy on human rights.
Instead of confining human rights to the domestic sphere, they called for
US global moral leadership. They flatly rejected quiet diplomacy on the
grounds that "private inquiries and low-key appeals" to governments committing human rights violations had few, if any, "desirable effects."[60]

On June 30, 1974, during the opening session of the first congressional
hearing on human rights in South Korea, leading members of Congress advanced liberal internationalist viewpoints in contradistinction to realpolitik
perspectives and practices. Fraser, chair of the Subcommittee on International
Organizations and Movements, openly challenged Kissinger's assertion, made
one week earlier during his testimony before the Senate Foreign Relations
Committee, that continuing "economic and military assistance" to South
Korea was "crucial to the security of the East Asian area." The greatest danger to regional security, Fraser countered, did not arise from "external aggression but from the oppressive nature" of the Park regime. Since this hearing
was in connection with US foreign aid bill, Fraser called for reducing or sus-
pending US military assistance to South Korea in reaction to the Park regime's refusal to uphold "internationally recognized human rights." Robert
Nix (D-PA), chair of the Subcommittee on Asian and Pacific Affairs, expanded on Fraser's demands, insisting that the US government withdraw all
38,000 troops stationed in South Korea, because there was "no evidence" of
an increased military presence in North Korea. He also believed that the $37
billion of US assistance provided to South Korea from 1946 to 1973 gave the
United States the right to intervene in South Korea's domestic affairs.[61] Thus,
liberal internationalists on Capitol Hill refused to accept the efficacy of quiet
diplomacy in promoting human rights.

Meanwhile, to counter liberal internationalists on Capitol Hill, the Nixon
and Ford administrations enhanced their realpolitik policy. For example, to

discredit the approach of liberal internationalists, Robert Ingersoll, assistant secretary of state for East Asian and Pacific Affairs, outlined in a letter to the chairman of the Foreign Affairs Committee, Thomas Morgan, dated June 27, 1974, what quiet diplomacy entailed. Expanding on earlier testimony before the committee, he challenged the wisdom of Section 32—the cornerstone of liberal internationalists' "policy and tactics." Cutting off assistance to nations with poor human rights records, Ingersoll maintained, was not "the most effective or appropriate response to violations of human rights in other countries" because such a "cut-off" was "a one-time thing." He also pointed to "the difficulty of formulating such a general rule as well as the difficulty of defining who is a political prisoner." One month later, on July 28, Ingersoll sent another letter to Morgan, in reaction to the upcoming hearing on human rights in South Korea. In the letter, he reaffirmed his belief that quiet diplomacy was more effective in promoting human rights than cutting aid.[62]

In July 1974, multiple high-ranking members of the Ford administration testified at the hearings of the Senate Foreign Relations Committee on human rights in South Korea and expressed the Ford administration's opposition to Section 502B of the Foreign Assistance Act. According to Pat M. Holt, the Foreign Relations Committee chief of staff, Kissinger gave an "impassioned plea not to tie his hands, that progress in human rights was best promoted through 'quiet diplomacy.'" But Kissinger's plea fell on deaf ears, because, as Holt noted, "the prevailing mood [in Congress] with respect to almost anything out of the White House was one of cynicism."[63]

On July 30, together with Ingersoll's two letters to Morgan, Arthur Hummel Jr., acting assistant secretary of state for East Asian and Pacific Affairs, delivered his testimony—the first official and most comprehensive presentation of the Nixon/Ford administration's foreign policy on human rights in South Korea. In September 1974, this policy appeared in the State Department's bulletin as "Special Report: Human Rights in the Republic of Korea." In acknowledging human rights as a core value of US foreign policy, Hummel presented the realpolitik policy line, especially by illustrating the policy and practice of quiet diplomacy. To highlight the administration's assurance for the crucial value of human rights, he cited an address made by Nixon on June 5, 1974, in Annapolis, Maryland. In that address, Nixon had stated that US foreign policy must reflect "our ideals and purposes" and thus could never "acquiesce in the suppression of human liberties." Based on Nixon's statement, Hummel insisted that the manner of intervention should be "through diplomatic actions" rather than "through hundreds of eloquent public speeches." Behind-the-scenes negotiation, he contended, would result in more positive outcomes. Reiterating Kissinger's remark from the October 1973 *Pacem in Terris* conference, Hummel asserted that quiet diplomacy would "avoid extremes—obsession with stability, excessive pragmatic policies or excessive moralistic ones." In so doing, he discussed the recently convicted South Korean prisoners (most likely the PRP prisoners sentenced to death) and confirmed that they had been sentenced for "acts of espionage" rather than for political offenses. In making this claim, he apparently utilized AI's criteria for defining POCs, which by this time had achieved significant global acceptance. Then, without questioning the credibility of the charges, he claimed that no explicit violations of human rights had taken place in South Korea, although he did admit that there had been institutional transgressions since the establishment of the Yushin Constitution in October 1972.[64]

Ironically, during the congressional hearings, the South Korean government echoed Hummel's assertions and reasoning. In fact, even though the regime received no official request to attend the hearings, it actively engaged in the process. On July 20, 1974, when the first hearing was announced, the regime commuted the death sentences of five prisoners in the NDYSF case, including Yi Ch'ŏl, Yu In-t'ae, and Kim Chi-ha. As rationale for this decision, the defense minister Sŏ Chong-ch'ŏl cited (falsely) the "deep repentance shown during their trials" by the five prisoners. But this public relations move did not go unchallenged. The *International Herald Tribune* acerbically noted that the Park regime was "bowing to international public opinion."[65]

The Korean Embassy in Washington also submitted to Congress a statement on human rights in South Korea. The statement marked the Korean government's first official international presentation on the topic. In addition to stressing its respect for religious freedom and its rejection of torture, the statement claimed, "No political prisoners are now being tried." It delineated "two distinct categories of offenses to investigate and to prosecute." The first concerned "a group of known communists" that had violated the National Security Law. The second group, albeit "not communists," had participated "in insurrection and rebellion." In making these claims, the Korean government relied heavily on Cold War containment policy, echoing the emphases of Hummel and other White House officials. The report highlighted the potential threat from North Korea, especially its tactical launching of a "peace offensive" in the context of global détente. To combat this potential threat, it emphasized the importance of "stable leadership," that is, the continuation of authoritarian rule for the sake of Cold War security and economic development.[66] On August 4, shortly after the hearing, Prime Minister Kim reasserted this point: "We must insure our economy and our national security before we can develop democracy."[67]

In September 1974, as news of Ford's upcoming November visit to Seoul escalated transpacific contestations on US human rights policy, US administration officials who favored quiet diplomacy remained firm in their position. In response to every domestic or international inquiry about US human rights policy, the State Department enclosed a copy of the bulletin outlining the rationale of quiet diplomacy. In October 1974, after a Korean daily newspaper published a translated version of the bulletin, the South Korean debate on US foreign policy's impact on democracy in South Korea intensified.[68] By December 1974, quiet diplomacy was under constant attack; reports of human rights abuses in Chile had prompted the US Congress to pursue even more liberal internationalist policies. At this point, one of Kissinger's aides even recommended compromise, but Kissinger refused on the grounds that if he budged, Congress would only demand more: "There isn't going to be any end to it." As Barbara Keys has argued, this remark became his "defin[ing] position that would last until the end of his office."[69] Kissinger would continue to strengthen his realpolitik perspective until the end of his tenure. But the policy of quiet diplomacy did not end with Kissinger. As we shall see in subsequent chapters, it continued to serve as an important framework for foreign policy during the Carter and Reagan administrations.

Ford's 1974 Visit and the Transpacific
Politicization of Human Rights

On September 21, 1974, the White House and the Korean Presidential Office, called Blue House, jointly announced that Ford would pay a state visit to Seoul in November 1974. Ford would be the third US president to visit Seoul in the post–Korean War era.[70] The visit, a twenty-four-hour stopover, was largely symbolic. Nevertheless, from the scheduling to the summit, it entailed an unprecedented transpacific politicization of human rights in South Korea. In this politicization, Kissinger initiated quiet diplomacy as a human rights counteraction policy.

Upon learning of President Ford's upcoming visit to Tokyo, the Korean regime had signaled its willingness to institute some democratic reforms if Seoul was added to Ford's itinerary. For example, on September 5, during a visit to the US Embassy in Seoul, Prime Minister Kim Chong-p'il had volunteered that his government would take care of all of the "domestic political obstacles" prior to such a presidential visit.[71]

Ironically, at this point in time, the Ford administration was much less interested in South Korea's domestic political affairs than it was in alleviating tensions between Tokyo and Seoul caused by two issues: the August 1973 kidnapping of opposition leader Kim Dae-jung from Tokyo by South Korean authorities and the August 1974 assassination of Park Chung-hee's wife by a Korean Japanese man. James Hodgson, the US ambassador to Japan, had recently warned of a possible "rupture of diplomatic relations."[72] Thus, Washington utilized a possible visit by Ford to Seoul as a bargaining tool to arbitrate the Seoul-Tokyo relationship. On September 17, Richard Sneider, former NSC staff member and newly appointed ambassador to South Korea, received directions to suggest to Seoul that a visit by President Ford was contingent upon the South Korean regime modifying its attitude toward Japan. One hour later, Sneider cabled back to Washington, "I left Fomin Kim [Tong-jo] dangling on Presidential visit, stating [that] it [is] under consideration but we [have been] awaiting outcome [of] ROK-GOJ discussions."[73] Thus, rather than embracing the Korean regime's voluntary proposal of domestic democratic reforms, the Ford administration utilized a possible presidential visit as a bargaining tool for strengthening the tripartite alliance in East Asia.

However, once publicized, Ford's visit to Seoul catalyzed transpacific contestations on human rights. On the day of the announcement, Senator Edward Kennedy (D-MA) insisted that Ford express US concern about human rights violations in South Korea. Representative Fraser warned that Ford's visit would damage US credibility if Ford failed to speak out in favor of human rights in South Korea.[74] In a lengthy article published in the *New York Times Magazine*, Harvard professor Edwin Reischauer seriously questioned, "what might be the damage done to other national interests by disregarding our basic [moral] principles?"[75] The *New York Times*, as noted earlier, highlighted the growing number of pro-democracy protests in South Korea since the repeal of Decrees Nos. 1 and 4 the previous August. And press coverage focused considerable attention on the possibility of political liberalization in South Korea.[76] The US Congress also took action. On September 24, the International Relations Committee passed a bill to cut one-third of the $161 million that the Ford administration had designated for US military assistance to South Korea. In leading the charge for this sanction, Fraser cited the necessity of supporting the restoration of political rights in South Korea.[77]

Against this backdrop, transpacific contestations, especially via the media, intensified. The State Department, wanting to take public pressure off the Korean regime, called attention to Prime Minister Kim's promise of political reforms if Ford visited. On September 27, one senior official, speaking before a group of reporters, stated that the Korean government's official promise had critically influenced the final decision. *Tonga ilbo* journalists immediately translated and published the US official's remark, in an effort to pressure for media freedom in South Korea.[78] On September 30, South Korea's foreign minister Kim Tong-jo reportedly signaled to Kissinger that his government had considered "a set of appropriate measures" (*mojong chŏkchŏlhan choch'idŭl*) to improve political conditions. However, shortly thereafter, he denied that the government had any plans to release political prisoners.[79] Nevertheless, in an effort to counter congressional demands that US foreign aid to South Korea be decreased or stop, the State Department continued to interpret the prime minister's remark favorably.[80] The *New York Times* also emphasized a positive link between Ford's visit and political liberalization in South Korea. Korean newspapers instantly translated and published such news stories.[81] For the next two months, the media tied Ford's visit to Seoul to the political and human rights conditions in South Korea.

Yet, the Ford administration never mentioned human rights issues during the US-Korea summit. Instead, it emphasized safeguarding the stability of the Park regime. South Korean officials had recently announced that discovery of a North Korean underground operational military tunnel; this unprecedented discovery seemingly set the stage for an anti–North Korea summit, at which Park could defend his authoritarian rule on grounds of national and Cold War security.[82] And in fact, Park spoke at length about security threats, economic downturn, and inter-Korean and regional disputes, which required "strong leadership" in order to ensure the "peace and stability" in and around the Korean peninsula. In making this argument, he displayed before his audience "a small-scale model of the tunnel" and highlighted the herculean efforts it had taken to find the tunnel, including the use of sophisticated oil drilling techniques. However, Park's heavy tone stopped when Kissinger joked, "You will probably end up finding oil." Ford's remarks also centered on security concerns in the region, although he did briefly acknowledge "problems with Congress," including a request to advise Park on how to handle domestic affairs. However, after this ambiguous statement, he "reaffirm[ed]" US support for "the [military] modernization program" and emphasized that he had "no intention of withdrawing U.S. personnel from Korea." Furthermore, he affirmed the importance of Park's "continued strong leadership" for the promotion of peace and stability in and around South Korea.[83]

Ford's failure to mention human rights reflected Kissinger's leading role in developing his talking points for the summit. Ten days earlier, Kissinger had summarized the nature of the summit: "We don't want anything from them, and they basically don't want anything from us except support." Then, he outlined to Ford what should be communicated to Park in a more private setting: "I would have a small meeting with Park and give him the sense that you are behind him. Overthrowing him could lead to incalculable consequences. You could quietly tell him he could make it look a little better."[84]

Within this general frame, Kissinger recapitulated to President Ford other security issues that he should address, for example, the abolition of the UNC and the renewal of the armistice agreement on the Korean peninsula. As for the long-promised assistance with military modernization, Kissinger noted, "There is not much we can do about it." He recommended that Ford "tell him [Park] frankly we have let him down militarily but we will do our best."[85] During the summit (Figure 5), Kissinger held a quiet meeting with Park to talk with him about using more caution in handling human rights issues.[86] Kissinger's recommendations to Ford and his behind-the-scenes meeting with Park illustrate how he and others in the State Department would utilize quiet diplomacy to draw public attention away from human rights issues and to safeguard US Cold War security interests.

After the summit, the US and Korean news media continued to play an important role in shaping transpacific contestations on human rights. A Korean newspaper printed in bold letters Ford's remarks on the United States' commitment to the security of South Korea. The same paper also noted that two high-ranking diplomats, the US assistant secretary of state Philip Habib and the Korean ambassador to the United States Ham Pyŏng-ch'un, had failed to answer two of the reporters' questions: Had Ford expressed concern about human rights violations in South Korea and demanded the release of political prisoners? And would the US Congress suspend US security assistance to South Korea if the prisoners were not released?[87]

In reporting on the summit, the Korean press focused on security policy and did not mention US human rights policy. In contrast, American journalists such as Richard Halloran of the *New York Times* did address the

Figure 5. *From left*, Secretary of State Henry Kissinger, President Gerald Ford, and President Park Chung-hee during the US-ROK summit in Seoul in November 1974.
Source: https://archives.kdemo.or.kr; serial no. 00716815. © Kyŏnghyang sinmun.

question of human rights. In one of his articles, Halloran quoted Habib as saying that Ford had "affirmed that we would seek to fulfill the military modernization program, while pointing out that that, of course, required the support and assistance of funds from the Congress."[88] Although Habib's comment was typical diplomatic rhetoric, Halloran had maximally interpreted it to mean that Ford had linked Korea's continued receipt of US aid to the improvement of political conditions in South Korea. Halloran's account suggesting positive human rights developments at the summit received significant attention in the South Korean press, which at that time was struggling to assert its right to freedom of expression. By describing Halloran's article as representative of the international view of the event, the South Korean press was able to broach a topic that until that point had not been addressed by the Korean media. Thus, Halloran's article and others like it created momentum for human rights discussions in South Korea.[89] Both the

US and South Korean media through their coverage of the event facilitated the transnational politicization of human rights.

Against the backdrop of the growing attention given to human rights by the media, the Ford administration, as part of the state visit to Seoul, scheduled a meeting with nine of the American missionaries who had written the Ford administration and whose letter had been filed away under "many signers." On November 23, the day that Ford and his entourage left for Vladivostok, one NSC senior official, Richard Smyser, stayed behind to speak with the nine missionaries. Both the timing and last-minute announcement of the meeting was deliberately orchestrated by Kissinger so as to call minimal attention to the event.[90] An unenthusiastic Smyser focused on taking notes for a presidential memorandum. Ogle and the other missionaries realized the meeting would probably have no immediate "influence" on Ford. Still, they utilized the meeting to deliver a realistic assessment of political life in South Korea.[91] The deliberately low-key tone of the meeting, however, did not assuage the anxiety of the Park regime. Speaking to the National Assembly, the foreign minister insisted that it was a routine meeting between the US government and its citizens; it did not concern South Korea's internal political affairs. Still, some politicians overreacted, calling for the deportation of the missionaries for violating Korean laws.[92] Given that the Ford administration had done everything in its power to downplay the significance of the meeting, the Korean reaction appeared extreme. Still it had set a precedent for direct meetings between US authorities and non-state actors on the issue of human rights in South Korea.

Conclusion

This chapter detailed how democratic struggles survived and even thrived in the mid-1970s, despite the Park regime's crackdown on opposition. It showed how local activists in South Korea and Japan adapted and vernacularized the language of human rights to create momentum for the local democratic struggle. It analyzed the historical development of AI's fact-finding mission and the resulting first human rights hearing in the US Congress. In doing so, it demonstrated how the internationalization of human rights developed through the convoluted and constructive effects of vernacularization at the periphery in the context of the Park regime's crackdown. Specifically, it showed how the interventions of local activists transformed AI's minimalist and apolitical approach to human rights and contributed to Washington becoming the new locus of international activism on human rights in South Korea. It also showed how the PRP wives, via ecumenical missionaries, contributed to the increasing geopolitical orientation of human rights, by exposing how the Korean government misused the charge of espionage to marginalize political prisoners and obfuscate human rights violations.

The chapter also traced the emergence of a second engine of global human rights politics—"quiet diplomacy"—that operated in parallel with transnational human rights campaigns. It showed how confrontations between these two transnational coalitions—one advocating a universalist approach to human rights and the other a relativist position that prioritized the Cold War security consensus over human rights—facilitated the emergence of a transpacific politics of human rights, one that would persist into the 1980s and 1990s.

CHAPTER 3

Washington

Emerging Epicenter for Transnational Human Rights Politics

In February 1975, in the face of unrelenting anti-regime protests, President Park Chung-hee held a national referendum on the Yushin Constitution and granted amnesty to scores of political prisoners. However, rather than consolidating his government's legitimacy, these measures backfired. Two days after being released, student activist Na Pyŏng-sik told Peter Hazelhurst of the London-based newspaper *The Times* that he had been tortured in order to extract a false confession that he was involved in the NDYSF, which the regime had spuriously labeled a Communist organization. The *New York Times* also reported that another student activist Kim Chŏng-gil had been forced by Army Security Command to profess his support for North Korea's founder Kim Il-sung. The Seoul daily newspaper *Tonga ilbo* prominently featured these stories of torture. Two months later, AI sent a fact-finding delegation to investigate. This intervention developed in tandem with US congressional campaigns addressing US foreign policy and human rights in South Korea.[1] Thus, the measures introduced by President Park to consolidate his power inadvertently triggered an unprecedented cascade of social justice actions on torture in South Korea that transcended national borders and contributed to making Washington the epicenter for transnational contestations on human rights in South Korea and elsewhere.

This chapter illustrates how transnational debates on human rights and democracy in South Korea became contentious topics on Capitol Hill. It details the complex and convoluted actions and counteractions of the Ford administration, the US Congress, the Park regime, and local and transnational actors to advance their respective political, economic, and security agendas. It argues that East Asia, and more specifically South Korea, largely did not experience the so-called "Helsinki effect." The new "modern methods," touted by Kissinger at the 1975 US-Japan summit as the only means of containing the Soviet Union in the era of global détente, did not materialize in East Asia, where US foreign policy aimed at advancing US security interests frequently impeded the progress of pro-democracy and human rights activists. In fact, the United States blocked the creation of an Asian version of the Conference on Security and Cooperation in Europe (CSCE), because it conflicted with the Nixon and Ford administrations' desire for a rapprochement with China. Without a regional multilateral or multinational mechanism for security and human rights, the standardization and institutionalization of human rights norms that unfolded in Europe did not occur in East Asia. Consequently, one sees proponents and opponents of democracy in South Korea mobilizing the language of human rights to advance their respective global agendas in Washington, DC.

While it would be easy to interpret this shift in locus as the product of US-ROK bilateral relations, it would be a mistake to do so for two reasons. First, such an interpretation cannot account for factors such as the role of internal divisions in US foreign policy (White House versus Congress), the agency of non-state actors (local and transnational), or even the way in which the Park regime, despite its position of weakness vis-à-vis the United States, influenced US foreign policy and gained strategic concessions. Second, this shift in locus for transnational contestations on human rights was not limited to South Korea.

Thus, only through a bottom-up, periphery-to-center analysis can we understand how local disputes over democracy in South Korea in the mid-1970s developed into global human rights contestations by way of Washington politics. This chapter first analyzes the role of the normative terms "conscience" (*yangsim*) and "torture" (*komun*) to show the evolution of pro-democracy protest repertoires and techniques that allowed for the linking of local disputes with international campaigns on human rights. The analysis focuses on AI's intervention and the role of the US Congress. Next, the chapter examines the regime's contingent deployment of repression, that is, the abrupt execution of eight prisoners charged with espionage, in order to make a diplomatic deal with the Ford administration. Last, it analyzes why and how two transnational human rights groups emerged in the aftermath of the

Helsinki Accords: the North American Coalition for Human Rights in Korea (NACHRK) and the AI Washington Office.

Protest Repertoire: "Conscience" and "Torture"

As examined in Chapter 1, AI introduced South Korean society to human rights principles and terminology. AI Korea's establishment in March 1972 resulted in the translation and indigenization of human rights concepts such as "conscience" (as in "prisoners of conscience"). Yet this development did not immediately result in pro-democracy movements mobilizing the language and politics of human rights. Only after the Park regime's massive crackdown in 1974–75 did pro-democracy activists translate these terms into protest repertoires that allowed them to maximize their nonviolent resistance against the strong South Korean state.

Campaigns Utilizing Conscientious Objection

In July 1974, honorary president of AI Korea Bishop Chi Hak-sun introduced a new protest tactic. Immediately prior to his arrest for funding student activists, he read a "Declaration of Conscience" (*Yangsim sŏn'ŏn*) to a group of national and international reporters. In his declaration, he stated that his "conscience and the justice of God" required him to disobey the military tribunal's summons and that any conclusion of the tribunal did not reflect his "true will." He readily admitted his financial "support of oppressed Christian-minded students," but denied charges of "instigating a revolt." In making this statement, he made clear his opposition to the Yushin Constitution and the emergency decrees, describing them as flagrant violations of "the most basic and essential rights of the people" and of "fundamental human dignity."[2] Within six months, declarations of conscience became a critical nonviolent protest tactic for pro-democracy and human rights activists in South Korea.

Against the backdrop of these protests, President Park, as noted earlier, called for a vote of confidence on the constitution and on his leadership. This announcement prompted the National Council for the Restoration of Democracy (NCRD), a representative *chaeya* group, to propose a boycott of the popular referendum. In response, the regime warned that anyone participating in the boycott would be arrested. On February 3, 1975, NCRD chair Father Yun Hyŏng-jung recommended that boycott participants write "declaration[s] of conscience," either before or after their arrest, to "nullify any statement or memo" written under duress. He believed that the declarations represented "a nonviolent" form of protest that allowed participants to express their conscientious objection to a regime that utilized the nation's security apparatus to suppress its citizenry. He referenced Bishop Chi's statement as an exemplary model.[3] On February 10, fourteen pro-democracy groups, including the NCRD, described the writing of declarations of conscience as an essential dimension of the boycott campaign. On February 12, the day of the referendum, protesters held prayer vigils and masses demanding the restoration of human rights and democracy.[4]

At first glance, the referendum appeared highly successful; 79.8 percent of voters participated, and, of those, 73.1 percent expressed confidence in the constitution and the regime. Yet both participation and pro-government support had declined significantly since the 1972 constitutional referendum, when 91.9 percent of Koreans participated of whom 91.5 percent endorsed the Yushin Constitution. Moreover, several declarations of conscience exposed nefarious voting practices. For example, in his "declaration of conscience," Hŏ Hŏn-gu, a rural schoolteacher in Kyŏnggi Province, called attention to the illegal practice of proxy voting at educational institutions. Similarly, Kim Chin-hwan, a rank-and-file member of the ruling party, confessed to illegally casting twenty-seven votes. Another rank-and-file party member, Kim Mu-gil, also admitted to participating in illegal voting practices, as did a local party leader in Ch'ungch'ŏng Province, who confirmed that voting notifications in the area had been taken down early to prevent voter turnout.[5]

Two months after the election, a group of pro-democracy activists adopted this tactic to save the life of one of the most prominent POCs, the poet Kim Chi-ha. In April 1975, Park announced that because of South Vietnam's fall to Communist forces, the regime must crackdown harder on dissidents. Pro-democracy activists, including Cho Yŏng-rae and Kim Chŏng-nam, interpreted this announcement as a signal that the prosecutors in the poet Kim's case now planned to seek the death sentence. Kim Chi-ha had previously been released from prison as part of the February 1975 amnesty, but was rearrested after publishing an essay exposing the regime's use of torture to extract false confessions of espionage. Kim's supporters feared that Kim would be forced to confess that he was an anti-government Communist agent, thus allowing for his legal execution. Six days after his rearrest, this fear became reality. Under duress, Kim signed a statement admitting that he violated the anti-Communist laws, endorsed Marxist ideology, and had ties to the North Korean government. To nullify this confession, over the next month Kim's supporters worked in secret with the imprisoned poet to produce a declaration of conscience. Upon completion, the declaration was smuggled out of prison and transported to Japan by a Japanese clergyman affiliated with the CCJP. On August 4, 1975, Bishop Soma Nobuo, who belonged to the Japanese CCJP, held a press conference in Tokyo to announce Kim's declaration. Reporters were provided copies of the declaration that had been translated into English and Japanese. Addressed "to all those who cherish justice and truth," the declaration rebutted the allegations of sedition. It also included an in-depth discussion of Kim's thoughts on resistance and democracy. By December 1975, the declaration had appeared in the *New York Times* and been translated into four other languages.[6]

This transnational campaign to save Kim's life gained additional momentum thanks to a group of Japanese intellectuals (Figure 6). In June 1975, Masao Takenaka, a professor of Christian ethics and sociology of religion at Doshisha University, and several of his colleagues, including Hachiro Yuasa, Hiroshi Suekewa, and Etsuji Sumiya, recommended Kim to the Nobel Prize Committee.[7] This effort elicited an immediate response from the Park regime. On August 16, 1975, Foreign Minister Kim Tong-jo was instructed to prevent Kim Chi-ha from receiving the nomination by any and all possible means. In a memo to the South Korean ambassador to Norway, Minister Kim advised, "To prevent the nomination, if necessary, you may hint that in your personal view Kim's death sentence will not be executed." The ambassador informed Minister Kim that he thought it was highly unlikely that the poet would receive the award; still, this secret correspondence continued through April 1976.[8] Although it cannot be known for certain if the AI Dutch Section was aware of the regime's hypersensitivity on this issue, the following year they too contemplated recommending the imprisoned poet for the Nobel Prize as a strategy to save his life.[9] By mobilizing the language of human rights, both the conscientious objection movement and the Nobel Prize campaign garnered the attention of international audiences.

Prisoners' Articulation of Torture

As discussed in Chapter 1, when AI Korea was established in March 1972, it immediately identified the use of torture as a human rights violation. That

Figure 6. A transnational campaign poster in 1976, "Free Kim Chi-ha."
Courtesy of Edward Baker. Photo taken by the author.

same year, it launched a nationwide anti-torture petition drive. This campaign collected over ten thousand signatures and undoubtedly contributed to increased awareness of the Park regime's systematic use of torture against political opponents. Yet, such awareness did not mean that pro-democracy communities in South Korea immediately made the government's use of torture part of their protest repertoire. Although in the early 1970s both AIIS and AI Japan investigated the South Korean government's use of torture against political dissidents, pro-democracy activists in South Korea paid little attention.[10] Even William J. Butler's 1974 fact-finding mission and subsequent testimony before the US Congress about government-sponsored torture in South Korea did not make anti-torture activism a critical modality for expressing pro-democracy sentiment. Only in February 1975, following the release of 148 political prisoners arrested under Emergency Decrees Nos. 1 and 4, did pro-democracy activists begin incorporating anti-torture activism into their campaigns.

For the Park regime, the February 1975 amnesty most likely had a twofold purpose. First, it allowed the regime to demonstrate to the nation and the world that it exercised moderation in dealing with political opponents. Second, by releasing only those prisoners affiliated with NDYSF and not the twenty-one PRP prisoners, the regime hoped to create an internal fissure within the pro-democracy community.[11] But these intended objectives proved illusory, because immediately after their release, the former prisoners spoke out about their personal experiences of torture while in police custody and challenged the veracity of the espionage charges in the PRP case. Thus, they added their voices to those of George Ogle and a small group of ecumenical activists. As noted in Chapter 2, because of the stigma of Communism attached to the PRP case, most advocacy groups shied away. By late March 1975, two hundred former prisoners had organized the Council of Prisoners for the Restoration of Democracy to advance anti-torture and pro-democracy activism.[12]

Spurred by the amnesty, pro-democracy groups also joined the released prisoners in demanding the cessation of government-sponsored torture and in challenging the allegations of espionage in the PRP case. On the day of the amnesty, the Catholic Priests Association for Justice (CPAJ) demanded fair and public trials for the PRP prisoners. On February 19, the Association of Prisoners' Families (APF) provided proof that the government fabricated the espionage charges in the PRP case. The KSCF called for an investigation into human rights violations against the PRP prisoners and for the closure of the KCIA, the agency responsible for the PRP prisoners' abusive treatment. Father Ham Se-ung, a spokesperson for the *chaeya* NCRD, also advocated for fair public hearings for the PRP prisoners.[13]

On February 24, 1975, the CPAJ released its findings on the PRP case. According to their investigators, many of those charged in the PRP case had no knowledge of their alleged coconspirators' level of political activism and in some cases those charged had never met one another prior to their arrest. Thus, the government's claim that these individuals conspired to create an anti-state organization, that is, the PRP, was unfounded. Justice Minister Hwang San-dŏk unilaterally rejected the CPAJ findings. However, his rejection did not deter the CPAJ and the APF from calling for a truth commission to investigate the NDYSF and PRP cases. The commission, they contended, should include government officials and *chaeya* group members.[14] On March 3, 1975, the *chaeya* NCRD expanded this demand, asking that the government establish a truth commission to investigate allegations of torture and other human rights violations; and that the commission members should include politicians, lawyers, journalists, and clerics.[15]

Even as these local anti-torture campaigns gained momentum, pro-democracy and human rights activists also pursued campaigns at the transnational level. On February 20, 1975, Professor Yi U-jŏng, the Korean branch president of the international ecumenical action group Church Women United (CWU), made a public appeal to AI that appeared in *The Times*: "The Christian community would like AI to send a team of observers from London to investigate these horrific stories of torture." This same message was also sent to the UN Commission on Human Rights (UNCHR). Although the UN office did not respond, AI took notice of the appeal and began organizing a fact-finding mission to Seoul.[16] On February 28, 1975, the French daily newspaper *Le Monde* reported that twelve former members of South Korea's National Assembly claimed that following the adoption of the Yushin Constitution in 1972 they had been "tortured in various manners including waterboarding and beatings." This media report also caught AI's attention and thus contributed to the growing internationalization of local South Korean disputes.[17]

At roughly the same time as the article in *Le Monde*, Kim Chi-ha published a three-part essay in *Tonga ilbo*. The essay "Kohaeng—1974" (Asceticism—1974), written shortly after Kim's release from prison as part of the February amnesty, offered a graphic account of his exchange with Ha Chae-wan, one of the PRP prisoners. In this exchange, Ha described his suffering at the

hands of his interrogators as well as that of other PRP prisoners: "My intes-
tines had come out of my belly and broken up. . . . Yi Kang-ch'ŏl, a college
student at Kyŏngbuk National University, stated unambiguously in court
that he was electrically tortured in the presence of the prosecutor because he
denied any knowledge of the PRP, of which, in fact, he had never heard." Ha's
vivid testimony and that of other PRP prisoners, delivered indirectly by Kim,
was the first such account published in South Korea. The 1974 Butler report
included accounts of torture but made no direct reference to PRP prisoners'
experiences. In publishing his testimony, Kim delivered Ha's testimony to
the CPAJ, which at that time was investigating the veracity of the charges
in the PRP case. Kim's essay fueled contestations on torture and on the
PRP case, but, as noted earlier, it also returned Kim to prison.[18]

As local pro-democracy actors became aware of global anti-torture campaigns, such as AI's 1975 campaign, they began utilizing these campaigns to
create international awareness of local grievances and to link their causes
with transnational human rights activism. Journalists in South Korea, despite severe restrictions on what they could publish,[19] tried to facilitate local
awareness of these campaigns. For example, in November 1974, the South Korean daily newspaper *Han'guk ilbo* reported that the UN General Assembly
had passed a resolution outlawing torture. In January 1975, the monthly magazine *Sindonga* highlighted AI's declaration calling for the abolition of torture, and in March 1975, *Tonga ilbo* published an article boldly titled, "AI
Believes Torture Is the Enemy of Humanity."[20]

These transnational communications on torture and on human rights
also developed in response to local demands. On February 21, 1975, shortly
after Professor Yi U-jŏng asked AI to investigate torture in South Korea, AI's
regional specialist for Asia informed AIIS in London of the appeal.[21] Four
days later, *The Times* reported that AI was considering such a mission. South
Korean media outlets, such as *Tonga ilbo* and Tongyang Broadcast Service,
also reported news of the proposed mission, as did AI Korea in its monthly
bulletin.[22]

The proposed mission quickly took shape; by March 5, the Research and
Campaign Department had presented AI secretary-general Martin Ennals a
detailed draft memo outlining the goals and objectives for a ten-day mission.
According to this memo, AI delegates (British lawyer Brian Wrobel and Danish
surgeon Erik Karup Pedersen) would visit Seoul at the end of March to "collect evidence from released prisoners" on the Park regime's use of torture.
They should also "intervene on behalf of seven individuals who are still

under sentence of death." Finally, the memo noted plans to coordinate AI efforts with those of the office of the US congressman Donald Fraser who also planned to visit Seoul to investigate reports of human rights violations.[23]

In calling for close coordination with Fraser's office, AI seemingly demonstrated an astute understanding of changing geopolitical considerations. As discussed in Chapter 2, developments following the 1974 fact-finding mission had introduced a shift in the locus for international contestations from the UN to the US Congress. Thus, it only made sense that in 1975 AI would mobilize its congressional connections to facilitate its upcoming mission and its human rights goals. On March 6, in anticipation of Fraser's written communication to the Korean Embassy in Washington, DC, supporting the AI mission, Wen-hsien Huang, head of AI's Asian Research Office, sent Fraser's top aide John Salzburg background documents prepared for AI's mission to South Korea; these documents became the basis for the upcoming three-member congressional mission on human rights violations in South Korea and the Philippines.[24] A week later, AI and Fraser's office began discussing how best to publicize mission findings and advance human rights advocacy; proposed post-mission plans included US congressional hearings on human rights violations in South Korea.[25]

Amnesty's 1975 Fact-Finding Mission

AI's planned anti-torture mission to Seoul in March 1975 facilitated the transformation of local pro-democracy disputes into international human rights politics. However, this internationalization did not always follow the trajectory that AIIS envisioned for the mission. As with William J. Butler's 1974 mission, local and indigenous non-state actors played a significant role in reshaping AI's 1975 mission. Most notably, the primary venue for publicizing the post-mission report became the US Congress rather than the UN, owing once again to geopolitical considerations taking precedence over impartiality and normative tactics. Thus, I argue, AI's 1975 intervention represented a continuation of the 1974 mission in that it reinforced the shift in locus for transnational contestations on human rights from the UN to Washington, DC.

The proposed March 1975 anti-torture mission, in fact, was not the first mission that year taken under advisement by the London AIIS office. In early January 1975, AIIS had received another mission proposal from Lynn Miles, an American missionary working with AI Japan. Since 1973, Miles had helped AI Korea to secure financial aid and to disseminate information outside of South Korea. He proposed a mission focused on the twenty-one PRP prisoners charged with espionage. As discussed in Chapter 2, AI did not categorize those charged with espionage as POCs and so provided them with only limited support. In November 1974, the Appeals Court handed down harsh sentences to the PRP prisoners, including the death penalty for eight of those charged. Given the harsh sentences and Ogle's expulsion for assisting these prisoners, Miles feared for the PRP prisoners' safety. However, AIIS believed the most pressing concern was AI Korea's continued involvement in local pro-democracy struggles. Thus, rather than a mission centered on the PRP case, AIIS proposed a "well-prepared mission" as "a follow-up to William Butler's 1974 mission." On January 13, Secretary-General Ennals informed AI Japan of this alternative mission.[26]

AI Japan's response highlights the growing internal tensions within AI about the organization's human rights strategy in South Korea. On March 14, 1975, AI Japan's assistant secretary-general Masahiko Kurata sent a three-page reply criticizing the proposed alternative mission and endorsing the mission proposed by Miles. Kurata insisted that because of its local contacts, AI Japan had "detailed and up-to-date knowledge" about the South Korean situation that AIIS should not ignore. Moreover, AI Japan members were becoming "fed up with and losing confidence in London's decision-making process" because of AIIS's continued insistence on separating the PRP case from the proposed anti-torture mission.[27] This response, however, had little effect on the final mission format. On March 17, 1975, the Research Department in London held a "confidential briefing" for the two mission delegates. At the briefing, the delegates were told the mission's objectives in order of priority: investigate allegations of torture, look into prison conditions, and try to obtain an "official court transcript of the court martial proceedings" or, alternatively, "unofficial transcripts" in the PRP espionage cases.[28]

The briefing also pointed to lingering tensions between AIIS and AI Korea on the organization's impartiality policy. London criticized AI Korea for working as "an independent, entirely Korean-based civil rights movement" and for acting as "a rallying point for the lawyers and churchmen defending people imprisoned for political reasons." This criticism echoed a recent on-site report by Gottfried Schmitz, former leader of the Korea Coordinating Group in Germany: "The confusion between a full-blown civil rights organization and an orthodox Amnesty International National Section can lead at times to difficulties." He urged that "confidential" efforts be made to "find a way to separate the two roles."[29] On January 8, 1975, Ennals reminded AI Korea of the importance of respecting AI's principle of "impartiality and political non-involvement."[30]

On March 19, 1975, AI announced the mission, describing it as a "direct response to a plea by leading South Korean citizens who have asked for an independent, international inquiry."[31] That same day, just hours before the announcement, the Korean National Assembly passed the Anti-Slander Law (*kukka modokchoe*); under the new law, South Koreans could be imprisoned for up to seven years for criticizing the government or constitution to foreigners.[32] The new law, Father James Sinnott and other missionaries in the Monday Night Group in Seoul conjectured, was intended to undermine their group's planned cooperation with three scheduled foreign interventions: AI's fact-finding mission, Congressman Fraser's mission, and a BBC documentary.[33] On hearing of the new law, Stephanie Grant, head of AI's Research Department, immediately thought that Fraser's upcoming visit was fortuitous, as it would provide an "important protection for those who testify" and thus prove "the key factor" for the mission.[34] Concerned that the new law might have dampened local support for the mission, AIIS made last-minute phone calls to Rev. Kim Kwan-sŏk and Professor Yi U-jŏng, both leaders in the South Korean Christian community; the two leaders confirmed their continued support. Similarly, Fraser's office contacted Rev. George Ogle in Georgia, who also expressed strong support for the mission.[35] On March 27, 1975, the first day of the AI mission, Deputy Secretary of State Robert Ingersoll warned Foreign Minister Kim Tong-jo that the Anti-Slander Law could be counterproductive, because it was likely to spark vocal criticism from the US Congress and the American press. Minister Kim dismissed the warning; after all, the Korean government had invited Congressman Fraser to visit.[36]

Any lingering doubts about the appropriate direction of the mission were put to rest when the regime without warning executed the eight PRP prisoners at dawn on April 9, 1975—the final day of AI's mission. The executions caught AI off guard because only twenty-four hours had elapsed since the Supreme Court announced its decision upholding the death penalties; the appeals process that should have followed never took place. Shocked by this sudden development, AIIS telephoned the organization's delegates in Seoul and changed the mission's priorities: "The emphasis should be PRP death sentences, condition of wives, assault on mission, in that order of emphasis and priority."[37] Ennals then sent a cable to the Korean ambassador in London,

Kim Yong-sik, protesting the executions. In the cable, Ennals described the evidence in the espionage cases as "questionable" and stressed that the normal appeals process had not been observed despite "a personal assurance by the public prosecutor" to the AI delegate "that the [eight] men would not be executed before an appeal for clemency or re-trial as provided by the law."[38]

The PRP prisoners' sudden executions also prompted local and transnational activists to take more pragmatic and confrontational positions. Since early 1975, the wives of the PRP prisoners condemned to death had wanted to hold public demonstrations targeting the United States for its role in the regime's decision to execute their husbands. Twice, Father Sinnott, an ardent supporter of the PRP families, had dissuaded the wives because he feared harsh retaliation by the regime. Each time, the women had countered, "No, we have to speak louder so that people, particularly Americans, will know. Only when Americans recognize it will the situation change." The executions eliminated all objections. One week after the executions, missionaries affiliated with the Monday Night Group staged a protest highlighting the role of geopolitics in the PRP case. Eight missionaries, donning black hoods and nooses around their necks, stood in front of the US Embassy in downtown Seoul. Rather than criticizing the Park regime's human rights record or its persecution of the PRP prisoners, the missionaries challenged US foreign policy that facilitated such actions, holding placards that read: "Is this the very outcome of quiet diplomacy?"[39]

Meanwhile, AI delegate Brian Wrobel returned to London. Working with the Research Department, he hurried to draft a post-mission report, whose findings he presented before the US Congress on May 22, 1975. In organizing the congressional hearing at which Wrobel testified, Congressman Fraser deliberately timed the hearing to coincide with the Ford administration's budget request for funding for South Korea.

"Transpacific Exercises" on Security and Human Rights in the Post–Vietnam War Era

In spring 1975, following South Vietnam's collapse, President Park Chung-hee enacted Emergency Degree No. 9 banning all criticism of the regime. This decree ushered in what many dissidents and scholars refer to as the "dark era" or "Winter Republic," because pro-democracy activists were effectively silenced.[40] Yet, as sociologist Paul Chang demonstrates, this period in which pro-democracy protests plummeted witnessed a diversification in the tactical repertoire of protesters and in the "discursive challenges that dissidents raised against the Yushin government." One of these "discursive challenges" was human rights; consequently, in this period we see human rights organizations becoming active participants in the pro-democracy movement.[41] In this section, I extend Chang's argument beyond South Korea's national borders, demonstrating how the language and politics of human rights were strategically mobilized outside of South Korea by pro-democracy protesters to overcome their limited ability to advance pro-democracy struggles at home. In making this argument, I pay attention to how anti- and pro-regime forces utilized the US media, turning it into a contentious interactional sphere in which each side made its case on the appropriate relationship between security, democracy, and human rights in South Korea to a transnational and local audience.

The PRP Prisoners' Execution

In April 1975, President Park Chung-hee introduced a series of extraordinary measures to suppress mounting pro-democracy protests. On April 8, the same day that the Supreme Court upheld the eight PRP prisoners' death sentences, Park enacted Emergency Decree No. 7, which empowered the minister of defense to close Korea University indefinitely. One month later, the regime proclaimed Emergency Decree No. 9, ushering in the "Winter Republic," which lasted until Park's assassination in 1979.

Yet, the unusual strength and pervasive presence of the South Korean state, as sociologist Hagen Koo highlights, never completely stifled the subversive, combative character of Korean civil society. This failure meant that the "asymmetrical relationship between the state and society, which has mostly been the norm, has required extra vigilance and shows of coercive power on the part of the state in order to maintain it, and many times in modern Korean history, this vertical relationship has been overturned by sudden eruptions of social force."[42] Given the simultaneous presence of a strong state and a strong contentious civil society, the regime's decision to target the PRP prisoners for abrupt execution at first glance makes little sense: Why would a strong state that must contend with a contentious civil society risk the escalation of domestic conflicts by taking such sudden and harsh actions against a group that posed little threat to the state? The answer, I believe, requires a closer look at transnational power dynamics, in particular the complex relationship between the White House, Congress, transnational advocacy groups, and the South Korean regime.

In its diplomatic interactions with the United States, South Korea was militarily and economically the weaker actor; however, the South Korean government was not without leverage. Both Park and his successor Chun Doo-hwan effectively mobilized the dynamic relationship between transnational human rights advocacy and domestic repressive measures to advance the regime's agenda. Here, I briefly consider how this dynamic informed the regime's decision to execute the PRP prisoners. While an exhaustive explanation is beyond the scope of this book, it is important that we briefly consider the role of this dynamic in the PRP case, because as discussed in later chapters, this dimension will take on critical importance in both propelling and impeding South Korea's democratization.

The veracity of the charges against the PRP prisoners and the legality of the judiciary proceedings remain contentious historical topics. In 2002, based on oral testimony, the Truth and Reconciliation Commission of the Republic of Korea (TRCK) released a report stating that the KCIA fabricated the allegations of espionage and that President Park was aware that the charges were false. In 2007, based on these findings, the Seoul Central District Court overruled the 1975 decision and declared the PRP prisoners innocent.[43] In 2012, the family of To Ye-jong, one of the executed prisoners, released documents showing that the prison facility received confirmation of the executions prior to the Supreme Court's decision. The victims had been denied due process under the law; a "judicial murder" had taken place.[44] That same year, however, against the backdrop of President Park's daughter Park Geun-hye running for president, Yi Ki-ch'ang, a former secretary for Park Chung-hee, forcefully declared: "President Park did not order the execution." The justice minister, Yi asserted, made the final decision.[45]

Yet, Yi's assertion does not align with what Prime Minister Kim Chong-p'il told the US ambassador Richard Sneider on April 10, 1975. Sneider reported that at this meeting, conversation quickly turned to recent developments in Vietnam, the implications for South Korea, and President Park's domestic decisions. Kim asserted that given Vietnam's collapse, the Park regime's top priority was to defend itself from North Korean aggression. In this line, Kim explained that the prisoners' execution was necessary "to unify the country and prevent opposition from fomenting unrest." Kim said that President Park knew that the executions were likely to produce an adverse reaction in the United States but derided American "idealists" for failing to recognize the reality of the North Korean threat. Kim went on to explain that Park's "decision" to execute the prisoners had been made "at [a] rump session of [the] Cabinet." Kim added that because he had been "ill," he had not been directly "involved" in overseeing the executions or in dispatching troops to Korea University. Kim only learned of the executions after the fact. In addition, Kim gave Sneider his assessment on why President Park ordered the executions. These "tougher internal measures," Kim explained, reflected Park's "sense of isolation and frustration" with US-Korean diplomatic relations; Park carried out the execution because he perceived a lack of "American support for the stability of his regime." Thus, Kim did not attribute Park's "tough repressive internal measures" solely to domestic causes. Instead, he portrayed the executions and other repressive measures as a diplomatic signal to the Ford administration in the context of South Vietnam's fall to Communism.[46]

Sneider's records of his conversation with Kim offer a critical vantage point for revisiting Park's role in the extraordinary measures taken in the PRP case as well as the diplomatic motivations behind the decision. As discussed below and in Chapter 4, understanding Park's actions against dissidents requires looking beyond the domestic context. The regime strategically utilized repressive domestic measures to advance its diplomatic agenda. By taking advantage of tensions between US Cold War security interests and transnational human rights politics, the regime could gain concessions from its stronger ally, despite its weak international position.

Vietnam's Fall and Emergency Decree No. 9

The enactment of Emergency Decree No. 9 escalated transnational contestations on US foreign policy. Yet even as these contestations played out on Capitol Hill, diplomatic relations between the Ford administration and the Park regime did not deteriorate. Quite the contrary, the massive political crackdown in Seoul seemingly solidified ties between the two governments. But why would the introduction of repressive measures in South Korea improve the Park regime's diplomatic position vis-à-vis the United States? Although, at first glance, this might seem counterintuitive, it is important to remember that the White House believed that its Cold War security interests on the Korean peninsula were best served by supporting Park's regime. Any action by the Park regime that catalyzed transnational human rights campaigns and prompted congressional scrutiny of the administration's foreign policy was perceived as a threat to US security interests. Thus, the United States mobilized Kissinger's quiet diplomacy to constrain the Park regime and to counter transnational campaigns highlighting human rights violations in South Korea. In "quietly" constraining the Park regime, the United States also conceded to some regime demands, such as postponing US troop withdrawal and increasing economic investment.

In late April 1975, in view of "declining ROK confidence in US commitment," US ambassador Richard Sneider appealed to the White House for an urgent review of US policy on South Korea. Concerned by this loss of confidence and by the resulting "more self-reliant" ROK moves, Sneider recommended a long list of measures aimed at reassuring Korean officials that the United States remained unwavering in its commitment to South Korea. These measures included postponing any reduction in US troops, providing more weapons and economic support, and devising a contingency plan for deploying US air and naval assets in the event of a serious threat of a North Korean attack. These proposals, he believed, would allay the Park regime's concerns and offset the "thrust of public and Congressional criticism of ROK domestic policies." As for South Korea's domestic policies, he contended that the United States had only "limited" influence. The White House, he continued, should abstain from commenting on human rights violations. Such public comments, he explained, would be seen by Park as an attempt to "undermine" his rule, which, in turn, could result in "an even more repressive policy."[47]

On the day that South Vietnam fell, President Park spoke with Sneider about the US-Korean security alliance. He told Sneider: "[South] Korea must be prepared for a rainy day." Thus, his nation must develop its missile capacity now, because "it would be too late" to do so at the point that the United States "informs the ROKG that it plans to withdraw its forces." Park also voiced concerns about the Nixon Doctrine's goal of reducing the US military presence in Asia. Park wanted US troop withdrawal postponed. He also brought up the State Department's strong opposition to South Korea purchasing from the American Lockheed Corporation propellant plant manufacturing facilities and advanced missile technology. He reassured Sneider that his regime had "no plans to develop nuclear weapons." However, he made clear that with or without US support, he planned to improve South Korea's "self-reliance" through a military build-up program.[48]

In the weeks to come, this diplomatic discussion of external security issues turned to the question of internal security, specifically Emergency Decree No. 9. Just as in the PRP case, the Park regime tied this repressive domestic policy to US-Korean diplomatic politics. On May 12, 1975, one day prior to the decree's enactment, Foreign Minister Kim Tong-jo gave Sneider a copy of the decree, making clear that the Korean government was not seeking a "consultation." In the past whenever the regime planned to introduce extraordinary domestic measures (for example, the Yushin Constitution in 1972), the regime contacted the US Embassy either formally or informally so that the White House would be prepared for any possible domestic repercussions. In reading the decree, Sneider immediately identified two recent international events—South Vietnam's collapse and Kim Il-sung's visit to Peking—as the rationale for tightening internal security to safeguard national security. But Sneider also realized that the decree was intended to "control students and media" and "to prohibit criticism of [the] constitution." Knowing that this repressive measure would generate public outrage and charges of US complicity, Sneider asked that the South Korean government clearly state that the United States had played no role in this decision.[49]

On June 20, 1975, Sneider sent Washington a nineteen-page policy review on South Korea's domestic situation. Sneider initiated the review to assess the likelihood that South Korea would become "another Vietnam." One of the major causes of Vietnam's collapse, he stressed, was "internal weakness," that is, the lack of a strong central government capable of commanding popular support. South Korea, he claimed, differed significantly from Vietnam owing to its "national cohesion and pro-American orientation." He highlighted the ROK regime's "highly refined system" of governance, the military's loyalty, and the nation's strong economy. Moreover, regime opposition was "poor," and the South Korean public had a strong anti-Communist orientation. Thus, in all probability South Korea would not follow the path of Vietnam; that said, he believed that the continued presence of US forces in South Korea was vital for the nation's future development.[50]

Sneider's rationale for keeping US troops in South Korea did not focus solely on the military containment of Cold War enemy states. Instead, he also viewed US troops in South Korea as a means of constraining the Park regime. Specifically, he worried that if the United States withdrew troops, as critics demanded, that it would lead Park and his hawkish supporters to pursue "measures, including the possible development of nuclear weapons, designed to achieve 'self-reliance.'"[51] Moreover, although he considered pro-democracy forces in South Korea weak, he worried that without the Ford administration's continued support, the stability of the Park regime (and consequently US security interests on the Korean peninsula) could be jeopardized by the growing connection between strong transnational advocacy groups and pro-democratic forces in South Korea. Thus, rather than the traditional concept of containment policy, as articulated by John Lewis Gaddis, Sneider's rationale for the continued presence of US troops, was more in line with what Bruce Cumings has described as a dual containment policy, that is, an effort to contain the communist enemy as well as to constrain the capitalist ally.[52]

The implementation of Sneider's recommendations, however, soon faced serious challenges from Congress. On June 19, 1975, Secretary of State Kissinger spoke in favor of US foreign assistance to East Asian ally states. But Section 502B of the Foreign Assistance Act of 1974 had made aid dependent upon an ally state's human rights records. Thus, the Ford administration needed to find a way to reconcile South Korea's dismal human rights records with the act's provisions before the scheduled testimony of Philip Habib, the assistant secretary for East Asian and Pacific Affairs, before Congress on June 24, 1975. As noted earlier, Congressman Fraser deliberately timed the hearings on human rights in South Korea to coincide with the administration's foreign aid spending request. On the same day that Habib was scheduled to testify, Father Sinnott, who had recently been expelled from South Korea for supporting the PRP prisoners, was also slated to testify on human rights abuses in South Korea.[53]

Determined to resolve this issue, the Ford administration mobilized Kissinger's quiet diplomacy. Three days before Habib's scheduled appearance, Kissinger sent Ambassador Sneider in Seoul a "personal instruction." He advised Sneider to arrange a private meeting with Park. At this meeting, Sneider should remind Park of his previous promise to Kissinger to "inform" him "if his internal actions" would create "US problems." Sneider should also emphasize that the Ford administration had "deliberately avoided public criticism" of his regime and that for the 1976 fiscal year, the administration planned on asking Congress to provide "substantial" military and humanitarian aid to South Korea through the Military Assistance Program (MAP) and Public Law (PL) 480. Only once these points were made, Kissinger instructed, should Sneider suggest that it would be helpful for US-Korean relations if President Park phased out rule by decree and desisted from making any "long-term effort to implement" Emergency Decree No. 9. Finally, Sneider should explain that human rights issues, such as poet Kim Chi-ha's death sentence and the imprisonment of church leaders, might compromise the administration's efforts to secure congressional funding.[54]

After relaying Kissinger's message, Sneider reported that President Park "calmly" rejected Kissinger's suggestion to rescind Emergency Decree No. 9. Park told him that the decree "would not continue forever and would be ended when [the] situation sufficiently stabilized in [the] ROK." Park also defended South Korea's current ruling system by reiterating that Western-style democracy was inappropriate for "less developed countries," such as South Korea, with no past history of "ideal democracy." As proof, he characterized the period between 1960 and 1961 in which South Korea had democratic rule as marked by "confusion and divisiveness." If Park imposed US standards, as American critics demanded, it would jeopardize South Korea's national security. Instead, he planned to "build democracy" through a "step by step" process that took into account national divisions. Thus, rather than lifting rule by decree, Park stated that he must "do his best to persuade the American critics," who "lacked an understanding of the true situation in Korea."[55]

Ironically, when Habib testified before Congress on June 24, 1975, he tried to persuade American critics, as Park had suggested. Although Habib repeatedly acknowledged that "the issue of human rights" in South Korea was a "continuing concern," he asserted that "our security relationship [with South Korea] contributes importantly to the peace and security of Northeast Asia and is so recognized by our allies, including Japan." It was essential, therefore, that US "support and assistance" be delivered "where it has been promised" despite rights violations.[56]

That same day, Sneider sent Kissinger a telegram recapping his previous arguments for "a continued long-term US military presence." US troop withdrawal would create "uncertainties" that would push Park to enact more repressive domestic measures and increase the likelihood that he would pursue a nuclear weapons program. The United States, he argued, should abandon "the outdated view of Korea as a client state" and develop "a long-term conceptual program."[57] Hence rather than weakening US-ROK relations, Emergency Decree No. 9 actually strengthened them. The White House's rationale for continued support neatly aligned with Park's situational understanding of democracy and his justification of repressive domestic measures.

Transpacific Disputes on Security:
Park Chung-hee v. Kim Dae-jung

In September 1975, Richard Halloran, a *New York Times* correspondent in Asia, astutely observed that the US press had become a "regular part of South

Korean politics" in that "all sides try to use it not only to influence American, especially Congressional, opinion, but also to sway political views in Korea." In this "transpacific exercise," Halloran explained, relevant stories from American media outlets, such as the *New York Times, Washington Post, Wall Street Journal,* and *Los Angeles Times,* are transmitted to South Korea by South Korean news agencies and reporters. These reports, however, are subject to censorship, as the South Korean government wants only those stories printed that advance their objectives. Yet, this censorship, Halloran noted, often backfired because, as one South Korean explained, "One of the joys of life in Korea . . . is knowing a secret. If we see a censored magazine, we ask foreign diplomats or travelers what was in the uncensored version." Consequently, regime opponents tried "just as hard as Government officials" to advance their objectives through American press coverage. As one opponent explained, "The American press has the credibility to transmit what we want said back home."[58] Given this dual mobilization, it is worth examining how two adversaries—President Park Chung-hee and political dissident Kim Dae-jung—mobilized the US press to advance their views on security and democracy in the post–Vietnam War era.

The Park regime actively utilized the American media to influence public opinion at home and abroad. One common method was through letters to editors. For example, on August 18, 1975, in a letter to the editor, National Assemblyman Chin Hwan Row condemned the US media for its "unfair news and commentaries" on ROK policies. Row, a member of the ruling party and recipient of a doctoral degree in international politics from the University of Pennsylvania, utilized his credibility as an American-trained academic to defend the Park regime. He highlighted the media's ignorance of Korean tradition and of the current political situation. He noted the "total absence of a tradition of a loyal opposition" in South Korea and the government's moral commitment to avoiding war despite North Korea's constant threats. In making this claim, he shrewdly praised Park for maintaining "a delicate balance between individual freedom and collective responsibility."[59]

The regime also extended invitations to prominent journalists for exclusive interviews with President Park. For example, on August 20, at the regime's invitation, *New York Times* correspondent Halloran conducted a two-hour interview with Park. In the resulting article, Halloran reported that Park described the withdrawal of US forces from South Korea by 1980 as a plausible goal. He acknowledged that harsh internal measures had led his American critics to demand an immediate reduction in US assistance to South Korea. However, he disarmed these criticisms by referencing the Communist commitment to North Korea: "But we must not lose sight of the fact that the North Koreans have military alliances with both Communist China and the Soviet Union." In this way, he played on American fears that South Korea would become another Vietnam, while linking US troop withdrawal to continued US funding of South Korea's military modernization program. Furthermore, he placed the onus on North Korea for repressive domestic measures. Park explained that if North Korea abandoned its objective "of uniting the whole of Korea by means of force and violence, and if they accepted peaceful coexistence with us, then I would immediately repeal the emergency measures I have taken, and I would take much more liberalized policies." The "absolute majority of our people," Park continued, "understand the necessity of the regime's restrictive measures," subtly implying that American critics lacked basic knowledge of the geopolitical situation in South Korea.[60]

But Park was not alone in utilizing the American media to advance a political agenda; Kim Dae-jung, who nearly defeated Park in the 1971 presidential election, did so as well. In June 1975, Sneider and other US officials described Kim as the most influential political opposition leader in South Korea, despite having been under house arrest since 1973. They assumed that Park would "do all within his considerable power" to squelch Kim's influence.[61] Thus, no one was surprised when on September 12, 1975, the Park regime announced that it was reopening the trial against Kim for allegedly violating election law in 1967 and 1971. For these alleged infractions, the prosecutor asked the court to sentence Kim to five years of imprisonment.[62] On September 22, shortly before the court's scheduled ruling, Kim Dae-jung's interview with Halloran, the same *New York Times* journalist who had interviewed Park the previous month, appeared in print. In the interview, Kim challenged Park's rationale for demanding the populace's complete obedience. He described Indochina's collapse as a "godsend" for President Park, because it allowed him to capitalize on South Korean fears of a North Korean attack and on US security concerns to suppress his political opponents.[63]

Three days after the first article, the *New York Times* published another article based on a memorandum written by Kim Dae-jung on August 11, 1975, and smuggled out of South Korea by Congressman Stephen J. Solarz (D-NY). In the document, Kim stated, "I don't believe that our present situation is the same as the Vietnamese situation. But if we don't change the suppressive and corrupted rule early, we can't avoid the fate of another Vietnam." He then challenged Park's assessment that the "absolute majority" supported his measures: "I believe most people in this country are becoming skeptical about fighting against Communism under the present dictatorial rule, [as they are] disappointed with the big gap between the haves and the have-nots and angry with the extent of corruption and the luxurious life of the privileged class. Their loyalties to the nation are eroding day by day."[64] In short, through the *New York Times*, Kim offered a radically different economic and political assessment from that presented by President Park. For Kim, national stability and security required democracy, and real economic growth had to be accompanied by social justice.

On September 26, the court announced its decision to postpone Kim Daejung's sentencing. For the moment, at least, this "transpacific exercise" had spared Kim from imprisonment, although he remained under house arrest until March 1976.[65] The US media emerged as a critical sphere in which South Korean dissidents and their opponents promoted their respective interests and agendas to a domestic and transnational audience. As congressional debates on the implications of US foreign policy for human rights in South Korea escalated, so too did this instrumentalization of the media.

Human Rights as Linchpin for US Aid

Since 1973, Congress had made a concerted effort to infuse human rights objectives into US foreign policy. In fall 1975, Congress introduced another critical advance. On September 10, the House of Representatives approved a $2.87 billion two-year foreign aid authorization. For the first time, this authorization included no military aid, and its adoption came after the House approved an amendment that would deny assistance to any country "engage[d] in a consistent pattern of gross violations of internationally recognized human rights." The House did not name any specific country during the authorization process. However, at that time, Congress was holding hearings on human rights violations in South Korea and the Philippines.[66]

In October 1975, the Senate Foreign Relations Committee and the House International Relations Committee drafted a bill that would "phase out" over a two-to-three-year period the military program under which the United

States since 1949 had given its allies an estimated $40 billion in arms, am-
munition, and advice. To compensate for the termination of military grant
aid, the new bill provided for a temporary increase in military credit sales.
However, it also imposed stringent controls on the military sales program.
South Korea, along with the Philippines and Turkey, had been a principal
beneficiary of the giveaway program. *New York Times* diplomatic correspondent Leslie H. Gelb recognized the significance of congressional action, noting that the new bill went "well beyond present Congressional control of the
sales program" as it gave Congress "actual prior policy control of all sales programs, including commercial sales." Foreign assistance bills, Gelb concluded, had become "the vehicle for historic struggles between Congress and
the President." This struggle pitted "realism" in the tradition of George F.
Kennan against internationalist "idealism" in the tradition of President
Woodrow Wilson.[67]

Liberal internationalists' efforts to change the realist orientation of US foreign policy provoked counteractions by the Ford administration. On October 30, Ford requested that for the current fiscal year Congress endorse a $4.7
billion foreign aid budget. The proposed budget would double the amount of
military aid provided to Asia for the previous fiscal year: Korea ($200
million), Taiwan ($80 million), the Philippines ($20 million), and so on.[68]
On November 18, 1975, the Ford administration refused to comply with the
congressional mandate requiring the administration to specify which nations
receiving American military assistance had questionable human rights practices and to outline for Congress any "extraordinary circumstances" that
might justify continuing aid for such nations. Although two weeks earlier, as
required by law, the State Department had drafted one-to-two-page reports
on each country's human rights practices, Kissinger ordered the State Department to submit to Congress instead a more generalized report asserting:
"Repressive laws and actions, arbitrary arrest and prolonged detention,
torture or cruel, inhuman or degrading treatment . . . are not extraordinary events in the world community." Consequently, the revised report
claimed it made no sense to single out any one nation, given there was "no
adequately objective way to make distinctions of degree between nations."
The administration also claimed that a "quiet but forceful diplomacy," rather
than public pressure, best served the promotion of security and human
rights abroad.[69]

The administration's refusal to comply with the Foreign Assistance Act's
provisions, prompted Congress to introduce additional initiatives. Senator

Alan Cranston (D-CA) described the revised report as "a cover-up" and announced that Congressman Fraser and he planned to introduce amendments that would strengthen the human rights provisions, thereby giving Congress a voice in declaring which nations were in "gross violation" of human rights. Their proposed amendments would also make it mandatory for the president to reduce or end aid to such nations unless justification for continuance was provided.[70] On December 17, 1975, Fraser and Solarz cosponsored a new bill that called for the gradual withdrawal of US forces from South Korea. Under this bill's provisions, the US military presence in South Korea must be reduced substantially by no later than the 1978 fiscal year. The bill also stipulated the withdrawal of all US military personnel once South Korea's military modernization program was completed.[71]

In calling for the total withdrawal of US troops and hence the closing of the US military base in South Korea, congressional internationalists challenged the most fundamental mechanism of US global hegemony. The complex interactions between Congress, the White House, the US media, the Park regime, and various national and transnational non-state actors ensured that US foreign policy remained entangled with human rights and pro-democracy debates and that the Cold War security consensus was subject to growing scrutiny.

No Helsinki Moment in East Asia

The Helsinki Final Act (commonly known as the Helsinki Accords), signed on August 1, 1975, at the conclusion of the first CSCE, has been heralded by leading scholars such as Samuel Moyn, Sarah Snyder, and Daniel Thomas, as a catalyst for the global rise of human rights in the 1970s and as a leading factor in bringing about the Cold War's demise in the late 1980s.[72] In making this assessment, these scholars concentrate on US-Soviet relations and on human rights behind the Iron Curtain. Thus, the question of how the Helsinki Accords impacted the political situation in East Asia, particularly South Korea, is left unaddressed. This section demonstrates that the "Helsinki effect" did not extend to East Asian politics. Focusing on the Ford administration's foreign policy in South Korea, it shows how the absence of any regional multilateral or multinational mechanism for security and human rights prevented a triumph of human rights norms in South Korea comparable to that experienced in Eastern Europe during the era of global détente.

Interestingly, in Helsinki, it was the Soviet Union that took the initiative in calling for the accords to extend to Cold War politics in East Asia. On July 30, 1975, the Soviets proposed to Hirohide Ishida, Japanese Diet member and chairman of the Japan-Soviet Parliamentarians Friendship Association, a meeting to discuss the Soviet's 1969 proposal to create an "Asian Collective Security Conference" comparable to the European CSCE. At roughly the same time, Soviet officials in Helsinki also broached the topic with Henry Kissinger, the US secretary of state. The Kremlin apparently believed that Asia would "benefit from a similar system of security and cooperation."[73]

Both the outcome of the first CSCE and the Soviet's proposal for a comparable Asian system were topics of discussion at the US-Japan summit held at the White House just four days after the signing of the Helsinki Accords. The Ford administration, however, offered very different assessments of the Helsinki Accords and the proposed Asian system. On August 5, 1975, during the first summit session, President Ford broached the topic of the Helsinki Accords and how they advanced US foreign policy objectives vis-à-vis the Soviet Union. First, they "reaffirm[ed] borders agreed to in 1947, 1948 and 1971." Second, they added "an element of integrity and morality" that would prevent the Soviet Union from repeating "what it did in the cases of Hungary, Czechoslovakia and Poland." Ford described the accords' utilization of a moral framework to limit Soviet hegemony over the Eastern bloc as "constructive," because it offered Eastern Europeans unprecedented "protection." In a similar vein, he described détente as "a vehicle" for easing tensions and avoiding confrontations, although he acknowledged that détente was not "a solution to all the world's problems."[74]

Secretary Kissinger echoed Ford's points, noting that thanks to the Helsinki Accords, there were now "no contested frontiers in Europe." This progress, he noted, had been achieved through "diplomacy" rather than "military force." In fact, Kissinger argued, in the age of global détente, diplomacy was the only way "to weaken Soviet political influence in Eastern Europe, not confirm it." To illustrate the power of "modern methods" in this "entirely new" setting, Kissinger stated, "If the President can be welcomed by tens of thousands as he was in Warsaw, Bucharest, Kracow, and Belgrade, this weakens the Soviet Union." In this line, he anticipated containing the Soviet Union without "aim[ing] at hegemony."[75] Although Kissinger, unlike Ford, never spoke of the accords infusing "an element of integrity and morality" into US foreign policy (preferring instead to speak of "modern methods"), they both characterized the human rights provision of the Helsinki Accords as an effective means of containing the Soviet Union.

However, when discussion turned to the Soviet proposal for an Asian CSCE, all summit participants expressed grave reservations about how such an entity would affect the balance of power in the region. Prime Minister Takeo Miki of Japan worried that the proposal would jeopardize Japan-China negotiations on a treaty of peace and friendship by exacerbating China's fears of "any third nation hegemony." Negotiations had already stalled because China objected to inclusion of a hegemony clause. The proposed security system, Miki observed, was viewed by the Chinese as an attempt by the Soviet Union to "encircle them." Kissinger immediately commented that the Chinese "were right." Therefore, he continued, "we will not cooperate with the Soviets in any anti-Chinese maneuver in Asia. It was for that reason that we signed the Shanghai Communiqué, with its hegemony clause. We knew what we were doing and made it explicit."[76]

The Ford administration's opposition to the Soviet proposal was consistent with its planned Sino-US rapprochement—the goal of which was to drive a wedge between the two Communist powers, thereby creating a new tripolar power configuration. In June 1969, Leonid Brezhnev, general secretary of the Soviet Communist Party, introduced the idea of an Asian CSCE. Two months later, President Nixon rejected this initiative in a handwritten note to the NSC: "Condemn Brezhnev's Asian collective security pact vigorously." According to Kissinger, Nixon "startled his Cabinet colleagues by his revolutionary thesis (which I strongly shared) that the Soviet Union was the more aggressive party and that it was against our interests to let China be 'smashed' in a Sino-Soviet war."[77] This stance became the foundation for the Nixon administration's opening to China. In June 1972, Kissinger told Premier Chou En-lai that the United States would not support an Asian collective security conference. In November 1974, Kissinger also told Vice Premier Teng Hsiaoping that the Soviet initiative was "really aimed at dividing and controlling the countries of the area." Kissinger added that the initiative was "ridiculous" and that the Soviet Union could not rewrite history "by sentences in a treaty."[78] One week after the US-Japan summit, Kissinger also told Ambassador Huang Chen of China that he had privately informed Brezhnev of his opposition to the proposal.[79]

The establishment of an Asian CSCE had been derailed by US containment policy, which aimed at stopping Soviet expansion. In the absence of any regional multinational security mechanism, the Shanghai Communiqué became the basis for US geopolitical and strategic policy for security and stability in the region. But the Shanghai Communiqué, unlike the Helsinki Accords, did not have an explicit pro-democracy or human rights orientation. Consequently, US foreign policy in East Asia maintained its realist orientation until the late 1980s, and the application of human rights policy remained at best selective.

On August 6, 1975, during the second session of the US-Japan summit, Prime Minister Miki observed that "a continued United States presence" was "absolutely essential to maintain stability" in South Korea. President Ford agreed wholeheartedly but warned that "the question of alleged domestic repression," raised by "some elements in Congress" prior to his state visit to Seoul in November 1974 remained "a problem." He expected President Park to be cognizant of "the difficulties" that would develop under "his present hard line." However, when discussion turned to democracy's future in South Korea, Ford and his top aides clearly defended Park's policy in the name of "realism":

> *Secretary* [Kissinger]: As the Prime Minister suggested, we can
>   appeal to President Park to be more lenient, but . . . if we press
>   too hard, they could be demoralized and we would have
>   another Vietnam situation. Therefore, we have to keep our
>   pressure below a certain threshold.
> *President* [Ford]: If a Vietnam situation were to develop in the ROK,
>   it would invite North Korea to undertake military operations.
>   Thus, we are on the horns of a dilemma. Maybe I'm wrong, but
>   I have the impression that there is not the same kind of public
>   opinion in the ROK as a year ago.
> *Secretary*: That's because they suppress it better.
> *Hodgson* [US ambassador to Japan]: There does seem to be a greater
>   degree of realism about possible adventurism on the other side.
> *Secretary*: From the historical point of view democracy does not
>   seem to be the normal course of governments in South
>   Korea . . .
> *President*: Or North Korea.
> *Secretary*: South Korea has had only two years of democratic
>   government in the post-war period, and they were chaotic. We
>   should keep this in mind in assessing the possibilities.[80]

The Ford administration remained firmly committed to Ambassador Sneider's realist assessment that Park's repressive system of rule was a source of stability. Moreover, in defending Park's authoritarian regime, Kissinger actually reiterated Park's unfounded claim that, historically, democracy had only engendered chaos in South Korea—a claim that Park earlier used to justify his refusal to acquiesce to Kissinger's demand for the rescission of Emergency Decree No. 9. Now Kissinger employed the same false narrative to advance the US Cold War security consensus. While the Helsinki Accords ushered in global détente in Europe, Cold War rivalry continued to define East Asian politics.

Washington as the Global Center for Transnational Human Rights Contestations

Even though the "Helsinki effect" did not extend to East Asia, local and transnational actors worked to translate domestic disputes in South Korea into global human rights issues. The emerging locus of these struggles was Washington, DC, rather than London (AI headquarters), New York (UN headquarters), or Geneva (WCC headquarters). Washington's ascendancy was not predetermined by the vast geopolitical influence of the United States or by US-Korean relations. Instead, it resulted from a series of transnational interactions that were contingent upon local and international political developments. This section focuses on two such interrelated developments. The first of these developments was the disappointing performance of the UNCHR, which led transnational activists in the mid-1970s to seek a new forum in which to promote their global campaigns for human rights. The second is the emergence of two Washington-centered human rights organizations— the AI Washington Office and the NACHRK—during this time frame. Both would become deeply involved in the internationalization of human rights issues in South Korea.

AI's Report to the UNCHR

For many international advocates and local protesters at this time, the UNCHR was the first institution that sprang to mind for publicizing and politicizing human rights issues on the international stage. In 1974, AI mission delegate William J. Butler sent the UNCHR his mission report but received no response. In 1976, AI tried again, submitting to the UNCHR its April 1975 mission report with an updated two-page preface. This time, the UNCHR made the report an official item on its agenda.

The Korean government responded to this news by denying the veracity of all claims in the AI report. In November 1976, the KCIA, the Foreign Ministry, and the Justice Ministry met to discuss how the government should respond to the UNCHR inquiry. A participant from the KCIA, called Mr. Hwang, reiterated President Park's instruction that in light of Jimmy Carter's election as US president and his commitment to human rights, their response should not create any unnecessary anxiety. However, given South Korea's "increasing state power" and the US decision to end "free economic aid," the regime should not "succumb to any pressure from the US administration." In short, the instruction recommended taking "a diplomatic and political approach" rather than engaging in "a legalistic dispute."[81] The response paper of the South Korean government maintained that the judicial authorities in the PRP case had upheld the requirements of due process under South Korean law and that, as a sovereign state, it had the right to make laws without external interference. Thus, AI's claims were "groundless."[82]

At the UNCHR inquiry, US officials backed the Park regime, despite Jimmy Carter's campaign promise to promote human rights abroad. On February 3, 1977, Edward Hurwitz, the US State Department's country director for Korea, informed a South Korean diplomat stationed in Washington, DC, that the State Department had directed US delegates to the United Nations to highlight to the UNCHR South Korea's non–UN member status. Based on this status, the delegates would question the appropriateness of a UNCHR review of AI's report. Hurwitz also assured the Korean official that the United States would support a motion to dismiss the proceedings.[83] Three weeks later on February 25, 1977, the UNCHR decided to "continue to study" South Korea's human rights situations "as a whole in light of the new information" AI provided.[84] The decision to postpone, while better than a dismissal, disappointed human rights advocacy groups that had hoped for prompt action.

The UNCHR's subsequent actions also disappointed transnational human rights advocacy groups. In accordance with ECOSOC (Economic and Social Council) Resolution 1503, the UNCHR maintained strict confidentiality; the South Korean inquiry was not made public until March 1978. While some close observers viewed the 1978 announcement as a "historic" development, most did not. The announcement merely named South Korea as one of nine nations under review for human rights violations. It provided no specific details about the case. Ten days after this announcement, AIIS "advised" AI's UN representative in New York that, "for various reasons," it no longer considered the UN an effective venue for pursuing human rights cases involving non–UN member states, such as South Korea.[85] In May 1979, the UNCHR notified the South Korean government that it could respond to the allegations in the AI report. The Park regime chose not to respond so as to avoid additional public scrutiny.[86] On this note, the South Korean case effectively ended.

Given this lackluster result, it is not surprising that transnational advocates for human rights in South Korea concluded that the UNCHR was not an effective forum for advancing human rights. An alternative forum for globally publicizing human rights abuses had to be found.

The NACHRK, 1975

The harsh measures introduced by the Park regime in 1974–75 prompted ecumenical communities in North America to establish an organization capable of maximizing the impact of transnational human rights campaigns. This grand scheme came to fruition with the establishment of the NACHRK in November 1975. In launching this group, the promoters employed the maximalist understanding of human rights championed by ecumenical groups since the late 1960s. As discussed in earlier chapters, this maximalist approach included social and economic rights as well as civil and political rights and took into account geopolitical factors and indigenous perspectives. Because ecumenical groups understood human rights violations in South Korea as deeply entangled with US hegemony in the region, the NACHRK considered Washington, DC, the best forum for publicizing and politicizing indigenous suffering as a human rights issue.

Around June 1975, ecumenical communities in North America established an ad hoc group that initiated a pilot project called the "Korea Human Rights Project."[87] In the context of this project, Edwin M. Luidens submitted a proposal to the Korean Joint Action Group of the National Council of Churches of Christ in the United States (NCCCUSA). In this proposal, Luidens stipulated that the group's primary concern should be "political repression and economic exploitation" under Park's regime. His proposal also emphasized the importance of incorporating local South Korean perspectives. He cited the 1973 indigenous human rights statement that the NCCK developed in concert with the WCC. He also referenced the 1948 UDHR and the human rights statements of other local and transnational advocacy groups. In citing these statements, Luidens stressed that understanding human rights violations in South Korea and in other Third World countries required a careful consideration of the "prevalence of United States' political, military, and economic power."[88]

The following month, based on its geopolitical understanding of human rights abuses in South Korea, the ad hoc group clarified where and how human rights issues in South Korea should be promoted. On August 18, the ad hoc group took under advisement a working paper that proposed the creation of an organization based in Washington, DC, that would provide the US Congress with up-to-date indigenous perspectives on the South Korean situation as well as present testimony before Congress. The Washington, DC, location would also allow the group to pressure the State Department to modify its foreign policy so that it did not facilitate the regime's human rights abuses.[89] The paper described the Chicago-based Coordinating Committee for Human Rights in the Republic of Korea, led by Linda Jones, the former chair of the Monday Night Group, and Dr. Richard Poething, the director of ICUIS, as an excellent model for how to mobilize resources and execute human rights actions.[90]

On November 19, 1975, the envisioned Washington-based advocacy group was launched as the NACHRK. With its maximalist, bottom-up orientation, the NACHRK strongly appealed to local South Korean activists struggling for democratic self-determination. Increasingly, these local actors looked to the NACHRK as a resource for globally publicizing indigenous suffering as human rights violations. Because the NACHRK prioritized geopolitical conditions that led to human rights violations in South Korea, it chose Washington, DC, rather than the UN, as the primary site for its advocacy, thereby standardizing the approach pioneered by AI in 1974.

AI Washington Office, 1976

In spring 1976, AIIS began exploring how it could best utilize the ties that it had developed with Congressman Fraser's office to attract international publicity for its human rights campaigns.[91] Around March 1976, Stephanie Grant sent Andrew Blane, an IEC and AIUSA member, a memo in which she outlined guidelines for AI's engagement with Washington's political mechanisms. In this memo bearing the caveat "personal opinion," she described

Fraser's subcommittee hearings as "the main fora for publicizing AI's information in Washington" and underscored the need to consult with Fraser and his aide John Salzberg concerning "the countries on which publicized testimony could be the most influential and the witnesses who should be invited to appear." Additionally, she noted that Section 502B, which made the receipt of US foreign assistance contingent upon a nation's human rights practices, created new opportunities for AI and other human rights organizations. Specifically, she believed that it would dramatically increase requests for information from Congress, other nongovernmental organizations, and the media. This new demand for information, she predicted, would make AI reports "the yardstick by which to measure the accuracy of the official position."[92]

Over the next months, AI held various discussions on the nature and direction of AI's organizational development in Washington, DC. On June 12, 1976, AIUSA's board of directors created an ad hoc committee to develop precise guidelines for the relationship between AIUSA and the US government offices. On September 7, the ad hoc committee presented to AIIS a working paper by Thomas Jones. In the paper, Jones argued that the opening of an office in Washington needed to be more than simply an expansion of AIUSA; the new office should fulfill a "special function" as an "A.I. pressure point." After a months-long discussion with Jones, AIIS expressed "no objections" to formalizing this arrangement. On September 20, Jones chaired the first meeting of the Washington committee that "identified the need for Amnesty International to develop a strategy for its relations in Washington." Out of this meeting emerged the Washington Office's "mandate" to engage with Congress by providing dossiers and reports that congressional members could use to critically assess State Department human rights country reports. In effect, this engagement policy allowed AI to informally coordinate congressional activity on Section 502B.[93]

By mid-1977, AI's Washington Office was utilizing the political structures and mechanisms in Washington, DC, to engage human rights across the globe. In August 1977, the acting director of the AI Washington Office, Ginger McRae, detailed to AIUSA the activities of the Washington office by continental regions and countries, highlighting the pivotal channel that Fraser's subcommittee had become for the AI Washington Office and the burgeoning requests for AI information.[94] In fact, the State Department's 1977 Country Reports on Human Rights relied almost exclusively on AI information. As a result, the reports focused on rights violations that fell within AI's mandate;

social and economic rights received no attention.[95] AI's minimalist definition of human rights had become the normative standard as Grant had predicted.

Conclusion

This chapter detailed how Washington, DC, in the mid-1970s became the central locus for transnational contestations on human rights issues in South Korea. It traced the conflicting and constitutive process through which human rights advocates and opponents mobilized human rights issues, thereby maximizing their respective objectives in international politics. In the context of Indochina's denouement and global détente, both parties assigned contradictory significances to Washington, which in turn shaped transnational politics of human rights.

The mobilization of the normative terms "conscience" and "torture" helped local dissidents to wage anti-regime, pro-democracy protests. Once local dissidents linked their struggles to AI's global anti-torture campaigns, they were able to transform domestic disputes into international human rights issues. AI could publicize its fact-finding reports in cooperation with the US Congress. In parallel with this emerging mechanism of resistance, the Park regime instituted repressive counteractions, such as the abrupt executions of the PRP prisoners and the enactment of Emergency Decree No. 9. Through these measures, the regime sought to capitalize on the Ford administration's unwavering commitment to US Cold War security assistance, especially against the backdrop of South Vietnam's collapse. This commitment placed the Ford administration at odds with the US Congress, the media, and transnational advocacy groups that were calling on the administration to hold ally states accountable for their human rights practices. In an effort to quell mounting moralist opposition, the Ford administration employed and defended quiet diplomacy as the best way of promoting human rights in South Korea. The rationale of quiet diplomacy was also utilized by the Ford administration to justify Park's relativist understanding of democracy. The end result was the strengthening of US-ROK relations.

Although the Helsinki effect did not extend to East Asia, local and transnational actors developed protest repertoires and techniques that allowed them to internationalize their campaigns. They utilized the American media to reach foreign and local audiences. When the UNCHR failed to act on AI's 1975 report, they took advantage of moralist sentiment in the US Congress and aired their grievances at US congressional hearings. This development became more pronounced with the emergence of two Washington-based human rights organizations, the AI Washington Office and the NACHKR. In short, Washington became the epicenter for human rights debates on South Korea. There, two transnational coalitions with contrasting understandings of the appropriate relationship between security, democracy, and human rights continuously engaged one another. As we shall see in the next chapter, these transpacific interactions and contestations intensified yet again following Jimmy Carter's 1976 election as president.

CHAPTER 4

The 1976 March 1 Incident

A Transnational Human Rights Issue and a US-ROK Diplomatic Quandary

President Park Chung-hee's rule under Emergency Decree No. 9, which outlawed any criticism of the regime, faced a critical challenge by early 1976. A small group of dissidents staged an unannounced pro-democracy protest at the Myŏngdong Catholic Cathedral in downtown Seoul. On the night of March 1, 1976, the anniversary of the 1919 people's uprising against Japanese colonial rule, Yi U-jŏng, a professor of theology, stood before a crowd of roughly seven hundred people gathered for mass and read "The Declaration for the Democratic National Salvation" (Minju kuguk sŏnŏnsŏ). The declaration had been signed by ten *chaeya* and ecumenical leaders, including former presidential candidate Kim Dae-jung and Rev. Mun Tong-hwan. It outlined a comprehensive vision for democracy and human rights in South Korea. Like the Charter 77 manifesto in Czechoslovakia, this declaration catalyzed pro-democracy campaigns. Every year until Park's death in 1979, protesters released an updated declaration. The 1976 March 1 Incident catalyzed an international human rights campaign and created a diplomatic quandary for US-Korean relations during the Gerald Ford and Jimmy Carter administrations.[1]

This chapter examines the transnational developments associated with the 1976 March 1 Incident (also called the 1976 Myŏngdong Incident). This incident coincided with the 1970s global human rights boom. Yet, few scholars reference this incident, and those who do, such as historian Kang Man-gil, reference it as one of many significant pro-democracy protests against the Park regime.[2] In contrast, I argue that this incident catalyzed transnational contestations on human rights in South Korea. In examining the incident, I focus on contentious interactions between protesters who mobilized the language of human rights to promote democracy in South Korea and US and ROK government officials who also mobilized the language of human rights, but who did so in order to ensure the Cold War security consensus.

In analyzing these interactions, I offer a reassessment of US human rights diplomacy, particularly during the Carter administration. To date, human rights historians, such as Samuel Moyn and Barbara Keys, have portrayed President Carter's human rights advocacy as a significant factor in the global rise of human rights activism in the 1970s.[3] In making this claim, they draw on the conclusions of US foreign policy scholars, such as Gaddis Smith and Tony Smith, who characterize foreign policy under Carter as a departure from the realpolitik policy of previous administrations. Carter, they posit, advanced a "Wilsonian" or idealist approach to human rights.[4] In highlighting this departure, these scholars frequently point to Carter's self-described status as a "born-again Christian" as a key factor for understanding the formation of his human rights agenda.[5] Although most of these scholars recognize that the Carter administration's foreign policy measures did not always diverge from those of earlier administrations, they see these instances as inconsistences in his approach, rather than as a continuation of the realpolitik of earlier administrations.[6] Thus, they utilize the binary of realism versus idealism to assess Carter's human rights diplomacy and security initiatives, including the withdrawal of US forces from South Korea.[7] With an eye to this scholarship, I draw attention to the policy and practice of the Carter administration on human rights issues in South Korea, comparing it with that of the Ford administration as well as with Carter's campaign rhetoric. Through this analysis, I show that in response to escalating transnational campaigns for human rights in South Korea, the Carter administration consistently deployed a realpolitik approach—that is, "quiet diplomacy"—to neutralize transnational human rights campaigns and ensure the US security agenda.

The 1976 March 1 Incident and the Transnational Politics of Human Rights

In 1970, the idea that human rights should be an integral part of foreign policy and international relations would have been considered radical. Yet, six years later, the reading of the March 1 declaration immediately triggered a series of events in Washington that entangled US-ROK diplomatic relations with transpacific human rights campaigns. This rapid ascendancy of human rights politics in the mid-1970s has largely been explained using the model advanced by political scientists Margaret Keck and Kathryn Sikkink that focuses on the pivotal role played by the post-1945 emergence of transnational advocacy networks in redefining the boundaries of sovereignty and community.[8] Yet, this advocacy-oriented model does not suffice to explain the dynamic developments surrounding the 1976 March 1 Incident. The role of Christian actors in transnational activism, especially ecumenical groups, has not received adequate attention. Moreover, the regime's repressive measures, especially against Kim Dae-jung, have been treated as domestic issues rather than as internationally embedded actions affecting human rights advocacy on the global stage. Moving beyond the advocacy-oriented model, I advance an interactive model in which it is the actions and counteractions of advocacy actors, the South Korean regime, and US administrations that contributed to the shaping of transpacific human rights politics in South Korea.

The 1976 March 1 Incident was not without precedence in terms of leading figures and protest repertoires; it reflected the strong ties that existed between pro-democracy movements and Korean Christians.[9] On January 23, 1976, during Church Unity Week, scores of ecumenical leaders, Catholic and Protestant, in the Wŏnju diocese in Kangwŏn Province held a prayer meeting for the restoration of democracy and human rights at which they presented a jointly signed statement. This statement offered the first comprehensive criticism of the South Korean government since the enactment of Emergency Decree No. 9. However, the government did not respond by initiating an immediate crackdown. Perhaps because as a religious event, it had not included any prominent secular activists; moreover, the event took place in a remote provincial city. Still, South Korea's repressive atmosphere meant that it took two weeks for the New York Times correspondent in Tokyo to access and publish the statement, which had been smuggled out of the country.[10]

As the anniversary of the 1919 March 1 Uprising drew near, there were three ongoing efforts to write a comprehensive, human rights, pro-democracy statement. Rev. Mun Ik-hwan, a Protestant minister who participated in the January 23 prayer meeting, wrote a statement supporting democracy in South Korea. According to Mun, he wrote this statement after having dreamed of his close friend and anti-regime protester Chang Chun-ha who had died under suspicious circumstances the previous August. In conjunction with student activists, two additional statements were prepared—one by Kim Dae-jung and another by former president Yun Po-sŏn. These three statements provided the foundation for the final declaration read at the 1976 March 1 Incident. Unlike the Wŏnju meeting, this action involved significant political figures and took place in the capital city.[11]

The final declaration called for comprehensive democratic reforms and criticized "the violations of human rights" and "the deprivation of freedom" under the Park regime. Based on these violations, it called for "institutions and policies originating from the people," the restoration of legislative and judiciary bodies, the reexamination of economic policy, and a democratic commitment to national unification. It envisioned South Korea as a peaceful nation of "justice and human rights" that acted as an honorable member of the international community. Like the Charter 77 manifesto, over time it drew the attention of national protesters and international actors, so the number and scope of signers grew with the release of each annual update. By 1979, workers and farmers, whose voices had largely gone unheard in the early 1970s, had joined the campaign.[12]

The reading of the March 1 declaration triggered an immediate crackdown by the regime, which in turn catalyzed ecumenical groups to launch transnational campaigns for human rights in South Korea (Figure 7). Shortly after returning from the protest at the cathedral, Professor Yi U-jŏng was arrested at her home. Over the next ten days, an additional nineteen Christian signers and supporters were also arrested; all were charged with violating Emergency Decree No. 9. After Yi's reading, a copy of the declaration was given to Edward W. Poitras, an American missionary, for translation into English. Anticipating her arrest, Yi contacted Dorothy Wagner the night before the protest to put in place an emergency action plan; Wagner belonged to the CWU—a principal member group of the NACHRK.[13] On March 3, the *New York Times* published the first of a series of articles informing the public about the March 1 Incident, the resulting arrests, and the actions being taken on behalf of those arrested. As chair of CWU Korea, Yi was recognized as "a prominent human rights activist," and the CWU organized campaigns directed at the South Korean Embassy in Washington and the US Congress.[14] These campaigns along with media reporting ensured that the public and the US administration took notice of events in South Korea.

International and local advocacy groups highlighted in their campaigns geopolitical factors that contributed to human rights abuse in South Korea. American Christian communities, including the American Friends Service

Figure 7. A transnational campaign poster in 1976, "Free! All Prisoners of Conscience in South Korea!"
Courtesy of Edward Baker. Photo taken by the author.

Committee and the Board of Global Ministries of the United Presbyterian Church, insisted that the US government reassess its aid programs to South Korea based on its human rights record.[15] According to Ku Ch'un-hoe, a Korean American ecumenical activist in New York, approximately 250 Korean Americans and Korean Canadians demonstrated in Washington; it was the largest US demonstration to date advocating for democracy in South Korea. To put direct pressure on the Park regime, the WCC organized an international conference on human rights and peace to take place in Seoul in November 1976. The international media, including the *New York Times*, the *Washington Post*, and the *Christian Science Monitor*, kept the story in the news, publishing regular updates on events surrounding the 1976 March 1 Incident.[16]

As these transnational human rights campaigns developed, the Park regime took steps to involve the Ford administration in this domestic dispute. On March 10, at a press conference, Sŏ Chŏng-gak, head of the Prosecutors' Office in Seoul, described the peaceful prayer meeting as an "instigation to overthrow the government" and labeled Kim Dae-jung as the ringleader.[17] According to previously classified US diplomatic documents, a few hours before the government's announcement, the prosecutor briefed an informant working for US ambassador Richard Sneider. The informant told Sneider that Kim Dae-jung wrote a "freely confessed" statement admitting to subversion. The briefing had been ordered by President Park after learning of Kim's written confession. Shocked by this update, the informant requested a copy of the confession, which the prosecutor refused to provide. Despite having produced no proof,[18] Park utilized Kim's alleged confession to his advantage in US-ROK diplomatic negotiations.

Why did the Park regime target Kim Dae-jung? Historian Kang Man-gil and others have attributed the excessive measures against Kim to a personal vendetta by Park against the man who almost defeated him in the 1971 presidential election.[19] Upon winning the election, Park institutionalized his authoritarian rule by establishing the Yushin system in 1972, and Kim traveled to the United States and Japan, where he continued to advocate for democratic rule in South Korea. In August 1973, KCIA officials kidnapped Kim while he was in Tokyo; the plan was to murder him. However, at the last minute, US authorities intervened, and Kim's life was spared. Although Kim was not released from custody, he continued to position himself as an ardent promoter of democracy. In April 1975, the Ford administration's "Country Team for Korea" commented that because of Kim's status as the most powerful

opposition leader, Park would "do all within his considerable power to prevent" Kim from challenging him again.[20] Hence, beyond any personal
vendetta, Park might have realized that no one was better positioned than
Kim Dae-jung to leverage US-ROK relations.

The Ford administration's involvement in South Korean domestic affairs
coincided with increased criticism of the Park regime on Capitol Hill. On
March 13, 1976, Kissinger instructed Sneider to withdraw the request for a
copy of Kim's confession. Instead, Sneider should highlight to Korean officials his "concerns about [the] impact" recent developments in South Korea
might have on the US Congress.[21] A few days later, anxious about the "seri-
ousness and sensitivity" of the issue, Kissinger sent a stronger instruction to
Seoul, in which he flatly stated that Park "should not proceed with a trial of
Kim Dae-jung and others."[22] In opting to make such a sudden and deep intervention into South Korean domestic affairs, Kissinger may have been influenced by the upcoming hearings of Fraser's Subcommittee on International
Relations. On March 17, US congressional members were scheduled to hear
testimony on the Park regime's suppression of South Korean critics in America and on the regime's illegal lobbying of members of the US Congress to
win political favors, including continued economic and military aid. Given
this already tense situation, Kissinger's intervention may have been aimed at
preventing further damage to US-ROK diplomatic relations.

Yet, Kissinger's strong intervention prompted an equally strong response from the Park regime. On March 18, 1976, Park's chief secretary
Kim Chŏng-yŏm offered Sneider a "fully prepared" response to Kissinger's
intervention. Kim began by citing "national security" and "national survival" as justification for the arrests. Then, under the caveat that this was his
personal view, Kim defiantly dismissed possible US congressional action,
noting that the South Korean government was "prepared to accept cut[s] in
military assistance and [the] loss of some US bank credit as [the] price of
maintaining domestic stability." He disparaged transnational human rights
activism as a "possible conspiracy between anti-government elements in [the
United States] and Japan, particularly Koreans, but also some Americans,"
aimed at "overthrow[ing] the Park government."[23] A few days later, Foreign
Minister Pak Tong-jin approached Sneider and complained about a recent
Washington Post op-ed, in which President Park was labeled "South Korea's
most dangerous man" because of his actions against the dissidents involved in
the March 1 Incident. Shortly after making this complaint, Minister Pak appealed to the Ford administration for "patience and understanding for three

or four years," so the regime would have sufficient time to achieve economic consolidation and political stability.[24]

For the next ten days, the Park regime made no further response to Kissinger's demand, and State Department officials assumed the trial would proceed. In a March 27 telegram to Washington, Sneider stated, "The only area of uncertainty is [the] timing of the trial." He discussed Park's underlying motives for the trial—from Park's personal animosity toward Kim Dae-jung to his desire to "seek a 'greater American understanding' of the need for tight internal controls" in the post–Vietnam War era. Sneider fully recognized that unless Washington was prepared to reshuffle the status quo, there were no tactical options.[25]

Seoul's delayed response to Kissinger's demand confirmed the complexity of the issue. On April 1, at the request of the Korean Embassy in Washington, Philip Habib, assistant secretary of state for East Asian and Pacific affairs, met with Ambassador Ham Pyŏng-ch'un. Ham spoke in an "extremely low key, almost apologetic fashion," as he reiterated President Park's unchanged stance on the arrested dissidents. Ham stressed that "any moderate approach" by the Korean government would likely "intensify" dissident opposition. In response, Habib highlighted that the crackdown had become a human rights issue, which in turn posed a challenge for US-ROK relations: "ROKG actions against its critics would be judged in the U.S. in human rights terms. Executive Branch for its part is not trying to embarrass ROKG. However, we have pointed out the likely consequences in years of reactions here if Kim Tae Chung [Kim Dae-jung] and others are brought to trial and sentenced." At the end of the meeting, Habib realized that despite Ham's "very soft line," President Park remained steadfast in his position.[26]

The March 1 Incident became an open diplomatic issue when the US Congress intervened. On April 2, Fraser, Senator Kennedy, and 119 other congressional members sent a joint letter to President Ford demanding that he give "strong public signals" that he opposed the Park regime's actions. In evaluating the repressive measures instituted by the regime, the letter's authors pointed to violations of "internationally recognized standards of human rights" and insisted that the administration uphold the principles that they claimed originally informed US containment policy, that is, that recipients of US aid have a "credible commitment to democracy."[27] A week later, the US Congress pushed the Ford administration even further, asking that it clarify US foreign policy goals vis-à-vis South Korea. On April 8, during his testimony before the Senate Subcommittee on Foreign Assistance and Economic Policy, Habib had to explain the diplomatic quandary. In defining the crackdown as "an issue between President Park and his domestic critics," he differentiated the domestic issue from the "basic security relationship" between the United States and South Korea. In doing so, he rejected any connection between "the Korean human rights situation" and US foreign policy, thus reaffirming the Park regime's position as well as the Ford administration's realpolitik policy. He asserted what Park might have anticipated hearing: "No present plans for significant force reduction in Korea."[28]

On hearing Habib's public support, the Park regime maneuvered to gain the unqualified support of the Ford administration in the face of continuing pressure from the US Congress. On the same day that Habib testified, Foreign Minister Pak informed Sneider that President Park was "quite satisfied" with Habib's statements. Then, Minister Pak added that Park was not prepared "to bow to" congressional critics; rather he was "prepared to react very strongly and not acquiesce should [the] Administration 'join Congressional critics.'"[29] The Park regime also actively called for the Ford administration's "greater understanding of Korea's 'unique' situation." To underpin the political peculiarity of the situation, a week later, on April 15, Chief Secretary Kim highlighted President Park's belief that, as in 1960, student protests would result in the regime's collapse and Kim Dae-jung would "create [a] 'fireball' with students" as an influential "agitator." In fact, it was President Park who positively acknowledged the 1960 student uprising right after his coup in 1961. Thus, Sneider was reassured that the Park regime would "stand fast on pressing their case against" Kim Dae-jung and other dissidents involved in the March 1 Incident.[30]

Confronted by this policy dilemma, the Ford administration reasserted its existing policy line. On May 19, President Ford clearly opposed a pending bill, Section 413 of H.R. 13680, imposing a $175 million ceiling on Title I assistance to South Korea under Public Law 480 (often designated "Food for Peace") for the fiscal year 1976–77. In early June when the bill failed, Ford thanked Rep. Edward Derwinski (R-IL) for leading the effort to prevent the "drastic cut" in US aid and military programs. Ford added that the bill would have "prove[n] counterproductive in its intended objective of improving the human rights situation in South Korea."[31] Meanwhile, an incident in August 1976 provided Ford with circumstantial evidence that his view was correct. At that time, North Korean forces killed two US soldiers in the demilitarized zone (DMZ). The so-called Korean ax murder incident, one of the highest security alerts in the post–Korean War era, most likely contributed to the heavy sentences meted out to the political prisoners of the March 1 Incident at the end of that same month.[32]

The March 1 Incident had quickly morphed into a major US-ROK diplomatic issue. The rapid internationalization of the incident points to the emergence of an effective transpacific human rights campaign that culminated in the active involvement of the US Congress. At the same time, it highlights the impact of the Park regime's strategic use of repressive measures against dissidents, especially Kim Dae-jung, to advance its security objectives for US-ROK relations. This manipulation, in turn, contributed to escalating tensions over human rights between liberal internationalists on Capitol Hill and the Ford administration. This tension did not dissipate under the Carter administration, but rather intensified.

Nixon-Kissinger-Ford Security Rationales in the Transition to the Carter Administration

In demystifying Carter's human rights advocacy, historian Barbara Keys in her book *Reclaiming American Virtue* highlights Carter's late and reluctant adoption of a "human rights" agenda during his 1976 campaign: "Only in the final two months of the campaign did Carter fully embrace human rights, spurred by the clear resonance the issue had among the public."[33] However, the South Korean case offers a vantage point from which to observe how early and eagerly Carter incorporated "human rights" into his campaign in order to challenge the Ford administration's grand security policy. As part of his human rights advocacy, Carter called for the withdrawal of US forces from South Korea, thereby challenging a crucial mechanism of the US national security state. In this section, I highlight that Carter's commitment to human rights developed through contestations with the Ford camp; yet, his embrace of human rights provoked strong reactions from US security-concerned officials, even within his own circle.

In early spring 1976, Carter, as the Democratic presidential candidate, enumerated his human rights policy and linked it with US security assistance programs for South Korea. His advocacy clearly contradicted the Ford administration's realpolitik policy. At this time, Secretary Kissinger reasserted before the US Congress the administration's policy toward South Korea: "The Korean human rights situation is an important element in our policy considerations. We have strongly made known our views to the Korean Government. . . . [However,] at the same time, we cannot lose sight of our basic concerns over the security situation on the Korean peninsula."[34] In contrast, on March 21, Carter announced his intentions, if elected, to "remove all atomic weapons from Korea" as well as to withdraw US troops in a gradual four-or-five-year-long process. Two months later, on May 10, Carter expanded on the rationale behind his policy: "Park is much too autocratic and has very little concern about human freedoms and human rights. Our commitment is not to Park. Our longstanding commitment has been to the people of South Korea. I think to reduce our land forces in South Korea gradually over a period of years would be an appropriate action to take. The South Koreans would have a competitive force with that of the North."[35]

A favorable institutional and political setting allowed Carter to continue promoting human rights agendas. In June 1976, confronted by increasing pressure on the Hill to champion human rights, President Ford finally endorsed the International Security Assistance and Arms Export Control Act of 1976. Under Section 301 of the act, Congress safeguarded the mandatory implementation of Section 502B of the Foreign Assistance Act of 1974 limiting security assistance to those governments that showed a consistent pattern of violating human rights.[36] In July, Carter also advocated for utilizing US security programs as "a lever to fight repression" in South Korea, Chile, and Brazil. By early September, the Democratic Party platform supported phasing out US military forces and the withdrawal of nuclear weapons from South Korea.[37] At this time, as the Democratic presidential nominee, Carter delivered a so-called "human rights speech."[38] Historian Barbara Keys regards this speech as "a key step in the evolution of Carter's efforts to define a new foreign policy."[39] In the speech, Carter insisted that the United States should use "our tremendous influence to increase freedom," particularly in South Korea, Chile, and other countries that have "depend[ed] on us for their very survival."[40]

Still, Ford and his administration maintained its realpolitik orientation. On October 6, during a presidential election debate, Ford defended his practice of quiet diplomacy: "I have personally told President Park that the United States does not condone the kind of repressive measures that he has taken in that country." However, in the same debate, Ford also defended the Park regime, stating, "in all fairness and equity," the genuine security issues faced by South Korea must be taken into consideration.[41] Ten days later, in a conversation with Kissinger about Carter's security policy on South Korea, Ford expressed his exasperation with his opponent's approach: "Is he [Carter] going to defend it [South Korea] or not?"[42]

However, Ford's perspective was out of step with the mood of the national electorate in 1976. As an NSC staff member under the Carter presidency recalled in 1981, "In the wake of Vietnam and Watergate, the American electorate was demonstrably in search of a foreign policy emphasis that would again reflect what most Americans consider their deepest political values—values many felt had been muffled during the Nixon-Kissinger-Ford years."[43] A week before the election, in line with Carter's advocacy, 154 members of Congress sent an open letter to President Park criticizing his suppression of political opposition groups.[44] Thus, Carter's foreign policy perspective during the presidential campaign that linked human rights advocacy to US security/military policy in South Korea stood in direct opposition to the Ford administration's realpolitik policy.

On November 2, Carter won the presidential election. But Carter's foreign policy approach soon came under attack from security-concerned officials of the Ford administration as well as from some members of his incoming administration. Three days after being elected, an eight-page paper entitled "US Forces in Korea" was brought to the attention of the incoming administration. Michael Armacost, the author, was a State Department staff member specializing in East Asian affairs. In the paper, bearing the notation "personal thoughts," Armacost argued that the presence of US forces overseas was the crucial mechanism for ensuring US global hegemony and that the presence of US military forces in South Korea was "instrumental" in promoting "US interests." He opposed the liberal internationalist position that the continued presence of US forces in South Korea should be contingent upon South Korea ending domestic political repression, arguing that "an issue between Park and his domestic critics" should not influence "our basic security relationship" with South Korea. In short, rather than endorsing President-elect Carter's foreign policy approach on South Korea, Armacost reaffirmed the efficacy of the Ford administration's realpolitik perspective.[45]

Secretary of state nominee Cyrus Vance also publicly opposed Carter's foreign policy on South Korea. On November 30, 1976, Vance, who had served as deputy secretary of defense during the Johnson administration, identified Carter's position on US military forces in South Korea as misguided: "A special problem for our Asia policy would be the president elect's campaign commitment to pull American ground forces out of South Korea." In objecting to Carter's plan to withdraw military personnel, Vance outlined the rationale that in a few months would guide his actions as secretary of state: "We do nothing without the closest consultation with Seoul and Tokyo, and ... in any event, troop withdrawals should take place only in carefully planned stages." He also rejected Carter's liberal internationalist tendency to link security programs with human rights: "We [should] continue to press hard on this [human rights] issue, but not ... tie it to our economic or military assistance," because of South Korea's geopolitical locus in East Asia.[46] Like Armacost, Vance's perspective was more in keeping with the Nixon-Kissinger-Ford rationales than it was with those advanced by Carter during his campaign. In his appointments, President-elect Carter perhaps underestimated how ideological differences within his administration might impact future policy directions.

Wanting to safeguard the realpolitik mechanism for US global hegemony, Ford and officials in his administration continued to voice their opposition to President-elect Carter's foreign policy on South Korea until the very last days of Ford's presidency. By November 30, 1976, the Ford administration had completed a research memorandum on US defense forces in South Korea, NSSM 246.[47] On December 15, 1976, during the last NSC meeting of Ford's presidency, this memorandum became a topic of discussion. In this context, Ford firmly stated his realpolitik perspective: "We are going to stay in Korea. .... If Carter cuts Korea, he is cutting off from what I would do. We are going for a responsible worldwide capability that we have endorsed." Kissinger wittily supported Ford: "You can say that in your valedictory." Kissinger added, "You can say you see the need for building up regional forces against an increasing danger, but this is a 10-year program. We can't go through peaks and valleys." Ford echoed, "I favor keeping forces in Korea. And I favor regional capability."[48] Beyond simply opposing Carter, Ford and Kissinger envisioned the role of US forces in South Korea as part of a global US strategy.

During the transition period between White House administrations, the future direction of US-ROK relations became more uncertain because of an outstanding diplomatic issue. Coinciding with congressional hearings on South Korean officials' illegal activities in the United States, the *Washington Post* revealed in October 1976 that the Korean regime illegally lobbied (to the point of bribery) ninety US government officials and congressional members; the media dubbed the scandal "Koreagate," evoking the recent Watergate affair. The total expended by Korean officials was estimated at between five hundred thousand and one million dollars.[49] Historian Bruce Cumings notes the complex origins of Koreagate, tracing it back to Nixon's disengagement policy in Asia in 1969. To "reverse Nixon's troop withdrawal policy," the Park regime had reacted by illegally distributing one-hundred-dollar bills to Democrats on Capitol Hill in an effort to win influence. The 1976 election of the Democratic candidate Jimmy Carter further complicated the situation.[50]

In parallel with increasing diplomatic tensions, the issue of human rights emerged as a diplomatic démarche. In early December, Sneider opined in a cable to Washington that Koreagate should not be an agenda item. Instead, "more fundamental issues," such as "nuclear-missile development, human rights issues, and possible troop reduction" should be the primary focus. With reference to human rights, Sneider seemed to suggest that the March 1 Incident might be an issue on which the new administration and South Korea could find common ground. Reflecting on a recent confidential dialogue with former prime minister Kim Chong-p'il, Sneider drew attention to Kim's admission that the Park regime from the outset had "mishandled" the March 1 Incident—an admission that no other South Korean official had made. While Kim noted that President Park "opposed" making an "early gesture to the new administration" by releasing Kim Dae-jung, he made clear that Park "kept [it] under consideration." Consequently, Kim Chong-p'il considered this issue as possibly a viable option "to repair and strengthen [the US-ROK] relationship." Neither Kim Chong-p'il nor Sneider believed at that time that there was any political opponent "prepared to move against Park" or to "replace him."[51] Thus, when Carter won the 1976 presidential election, the stage seemed set for a new direction in US foreign policy; however, within the Carter administration, there were contradictory views on security and human rights. The most noticeable internal tension involved Richard Holbrooke, the author of the "human rights speech," who, as illustrated below, would reorient the Carter administration's foreign policy to a realpolitik course on human rights issues in South Korea once he became the top aide for East Asian affairs.

The Carter Administration and the Politics
of Quiet Diplomacy

During the first month of his presidential term, Carter—from the perspective of his aides—made a "zealous" effort to link security and human rights issues in South Korea; yet, despite these efforts, Carter never succeeded in getting his administration officials to adopt a consistent and coordinated diplomacy that emphasized human rights.[52] As noted earlier, secretary of state nominee Vance publicly challenged Carter's liberal internationalist orientation, championing instead "a pragmatic approach" for the sake of "American security interests."[53] Yet Carter remained committed to linking the two foreign policy objectives, human rights and security. One week after his inauguration, Carter hastily instructed the NSC to put together a presidential review memorandum (PRM). The resulting memorandum, PRM 13, called for a comprehensive review of US foreign policy in South Korea, including a reduction of US conventional forces. According to journalist Don Oberdorfer, Carter simultaneously informed Vance of his de facto resolution. The only issue would be "how to withdraw" US ground troops from South Korea, not "whether" to do so.[54]

To Michael Armacost, who joined the NSC staff in January 1977, Carter seemed determined from the moment he assumed office to fulfill his campaign promises, acting like "a Sunday School teacher, checking off boxes of honor pledges" rather than giving serious thought to the positions of his aides, who were unsure of the origins of the policy to withdraw US troops and had serious reservations about Carter's approach. In 2010, Armacost described the early days of the administration as a "very confusing time." In roughly the second week of the new administration, Vice President Walter Mondale went to Japan to inform the Japanese government of the White House's decision to remove US troops from South Korea. Prior to his departure, Carter instructed Mondale to ask the Japanese government to relay a message to President Ferdinand Marcos of the Philippines: "If he didn't improve human rights records, we will pull out of the Clark Air Base." While on board the plane to Japan, Mondale discussed the instruction with Richard Holbrooke, the assistant secretary of state nominee for East Asian and Pacific affairs, and NSC staff member Michael Armacost who considered it "crazy." Mondale did not deliver the message to the Japanese government.[55] Over time, this initial confusion developed into a serious rift within the administration on policy toward South Korea.

Like Vance, National Security Adviser Zbigniew Brzezinski favored a realpolitik approach over Carter's moralist one. On February 7, 1977, Brzezinski opposed a draft bill to cut US security aid for South Korea that had been prepared by NSC staff member Jessica Tuchman.[56] Instead, Brzezinski endorsed an NSC initiative that would continue US security assistance to South Korea. He noted the "difficulties of expressing in practical terms what a human rights policy ought to be." When the administration initiated an interagency group on human rights, the "Christopher Group," he continued to advocate for a realpolitik approach to South Korea.[57] He also informed Carter that he did not believe that the Park regime would pursue political liberalization in the near future.[58]

Despite his top aides' lack of support for a new foreign policy direction, Carter tried in his first presidential letter to Park Chung-hee to launch his human rights diplomacy. In the letter dated February 14, 1977, Carter cautiously, but clearly, recapitulated his campaign commitment to human rights, while largely ignoring his top aides' recommendations. He began by reassuring Park of the US security commitment to South Korea; he confirmed that South Korea would receive $275 million of foreign military sales (FMS) for the next fiscal year. He then informed Park that he planned to withdraw US military personnel gradually from South Korea. In making this move, Carter emphasized the human rights issues that Congress and the American public had repeatedly raised. Specifically, he highlighted concerns about "personal liberty, due process and imprisonment" in South Korea. He then moderated his tone: "It is not directed towards reordering particular political structures." Yet, this concession aside, he clearly connected security agendas with human rights mandates, just as liberal internationalists on Capitol Hill had done: "Just as we intend to defend our relationships with your country, particularly in the security field, I request that you give consideration to what can be done in [the] human rights area in Korea." Thus, Carter placed human rights at the top of the US diplomatic agenda alongside security issues.[59]

Carter sent a separate instruction to Ambassador Sneider in Seoul clarifying his human rights policy. Carter expected the letter to become the basis for initiating a diplomatic dialogue with South Korea at the highest level. Among the human right issues that Carter identified were Kim Dae-jung's arrest and the imprisonment of others involved in the 1976 March 1 Incident. Yet, Carter told Sneider that, if necessary, he could deny "linking [the] security relationship to [the] human rights situation" and emphasize instead the "realities of U.S. Congressional and domestic opinion as well as Carter's own personal concern about human rights matters."[60]

As Carter anticipated, his letter ushered in a top-level diplomatic dialogue on human rights in South Korea. In his reply dated February 26, 1977, Park showed no signs of backing down from his earlier position. He opened the letter by requesting that Carter consult with his advisers prior to making any decision on withdrawing US forces from South Korea. Then Park bluntly asserted, "Human rights issues do not exist in Korea." In so doing, he stressed the legality of the Yushin Constitution, its legitimate enforcement, and his government's observance of due process in prosecuting those who violated the laws. He also underscored cultural differences between the United States and South Korea as well as the Korean peninsula's peculiar security environment.[61] Additionally, on February 28, Park communicated through Sneider that "American pressure" could provoke greater domestic dissent. Thus, Park warned that this intervention would hinder the release of any dissidents.[62]

Park's recalcitrance prompted the Carter administration to take a firm stance. On March 4, Vance instructed US officials in Seoul to "speak out on [the] human rights problem in Korea."[63] On March 5, as the first official diplomatic meeting with South Korea approached, Carter left a handwritten memo for Brzezinski and Vance not to back down:

I will see the South Korean Foreign Minister next week. Park must understand
a) American forces will be withdrawn. Air cover will be continued.
b) US-Korean relations as determined by Congress and [the] American people are at an all[-]time low ebb.
c) Present military aid support and my reticence on [the] human rights issue will be temporary unless Park voluntarily adopts some open change re[garding] political prisoners.[64]

The tone and content of this memo were consistent with his 1976 campaign rhetoric. Carter clearly tied human rights mandates to security assistance programs and allowed for no compromise with reference to reducing US forces in South Korea.

Ironically, Carter's decision to make human rights the crux of US diplomatic efforts in South Korea increased internal tensions within the Carter administration. As journalist Oberdorfer succinctly observed, Carter's aides initiated not "a battle for the president's mind" but "a battle against the president's mind."[65] Carter's human rights diplomacy produced "bruising confrontations" within the administration, especially between Patricia Derian's Human Rights Bureau and the State Department's regional offices in East Asia and Latin America.[66] This team, historian Barbara Keys notes, "worked to keep such references [to human rights] from impinging on major security interests."[67] In working as an East Asian liaison official to the Christopher Group, William Gleysteen emphasized the significance of the ROK regime's "political stability." Gleysteen also noted that senior officials of the administration "grasped the danger" of any policy that "personally and publicly" attacked President Park and thus "never experimented with major sanctions" against Park.[68] Against this backdrop, Carter's security-concerned officials began deploying a realpolitik approach on human rights, that is, quiet diplomacy.

Carter's March 9 meeting with Foreign Minister Pak Tong-jin revealed a major shift in his administration's foreign policy direction. His personal approach stressing human rights advocacy had been replaced by his security-concerned officials' realpolitik approach. At this meeting, Carter did not recapitulate his March 5 message to President Park. Instead, Carter carefully repeated the "talking points" that Brzezinski had handed to him the day before. The meeting focused on human rights in South Korea, specifically what actions the Park regime needed to take so that the US Congress and the public would support additional US security assistance programs in conjunction with a reduction in US military personnel. When Korean officials continued to deny that there had been any human rights violations in South Korea, Carter patiently explained how this stance aggravated negative opinions of the regime in the United States. Carter also stated that in criticizing the Park regime, he had not intended to "embarrass President Park." Carter wanted to avoid any image of interference in South Korea's domestic politics. Carter highlighted the symbolic value of any voluntary reform actions by the regime: "Even small gestures [by Park]—if properly publicized—could pay rich dividends." Carter added that Park's preemptive gestures would end speculation that reforms were the product of US public pressure.[69]

The talking points, especially the reference to "gestures," signified a strategic shift to quiet diplomacy. In authoring the memorandum for Brzezinski, NSC staff member Armacost emphasized that Carter should ask Park to make "some visible gesture" that would indicate a commitment to human rights in South Korea. This "gesture," he noted, would allow the South Korean regime to salvage its image before the US Congress and the American public. In recommending that Carter pursue a behind-the-scenes request for a "gesture," Armacost, in accordance with Brzezinski's directions, set a course of quiet diplomacy. In the talking points, Armacost described Park's political stability as a principal condition for political liberalization. As discussed below, Armacost presented a strategic tactic to lessen American congressional and public criticism of the Park regime, while at the same time assuring the stability of the US Cold War security alliance with South Korea. Armacost also proposed that together with Carter's meeting with Minister Pak, Sneider should hold a subsequent "quiet dialogue" with the Park regime.[70]

This was a critical moment for the Carter administration's human rights diplomacy toward South Korea; the diplomatic course, designed by Arma-cost and Brzezinski and carried out by Carter, marked a clear departure from Carter's human rights advocacy during his 1976 election campaign and a return to the "quiet" diplomatic talks of earlier administrations. This de-velopment did not go unnoticed by liberal internationalists on Capitol Hill. In fact, Congressman Fraser and other advocates did not disagree with quiet diplomacy per se as long as the Carter administration embraced and real-ized "the deep-seated desire of the American people" to promote human rights. What they rejected was the previous administration's use of quiet diplomacy, because its only achievement had been the preservation of "con-tinued military assistance."[71] However, by March 1977, Fraser began criticiz-ing the Carter administration's human rights policy for "replicat[ing] the Nixon-Ford-Kissinger line" in South Korea.[72] While Fraser's criticism may have been premature, given the Carter administration had only been in of-fice for two months, it highlights that very early on the Carter administra-tion began to advance a realpolitik policy through quiet diplomacy rather than putting into practice Carter's campaign promise.

Pursuing Human Rights Behind the Cloak of "Quiet Diplomacy"

In April 1977, Secretary of State Vance publicly acknowledged "quiet diplo-macy" as one tactic available to the Carter administration for pursuing human rights diplomacy.[73] In 1979, Patricia Derian, assistant secretary of state for human rights and humanitarian affairs, described quiet diplomacy as "our preferred approach," although the previous administrations had given it "a bad name" by "saying virtually nothing" to the countries about human rights. She highlighted that quiet diplomacy made it "easier" for a country "to make changes in its practices without seeming to be knuckling under to outside pressures."[74]

In contrast to this positive assessment, political scientist Jack Donnelly noted in the context of the Reagan administration's explicit adoption of quiet diplomacy that in principle and practice quiet diplomacy did "not address the systemic character of the violations" and thus failed to "cure the disease itself . . . focusing primarily on prisoners of conscience." In other words, quiet diplomacy essentially pursued diplomatic "concessions" without challenging fundamental causes.[75] Bearing in mind Donnelly's points, I analyze the ramifications of the Carter administration's use of quiet diplomacy for human rights in South Korea, focusing specifically on how the dissidents of the March 1 Incident became bargaining chips in US-ROK diplomatic relations. Behind closed doors, US administration officials negotiated the release of the political prisoners; however, as we shall see, the behind-the-scenes nature of the negotiations allowed Park to take public credit for the releases as human rights improvements without making any real changes to his authoritarian rule. Thus, I argue that the Carter administration's practice of quiet diplomacy did more to safeguard the Cold War security consensus than it did to advance human rights.

"No Action" as Active Action

After Carter's first diplomatic meeting with Minister Pak in March 1977, the Carter administration continued to practice quiet diplomacy against the backdrop of increasing transnational pressure to actively intervene in South Korea. On April 1, Fraser delivered to Carter a letter written by the March 1 Incident dissidents and their families. In so doing, Fraser insisted that Carter should actively intervene on behalf of Kim Dae-jung and other prisoners, just as he had done for Soviet dissidents, such as Aleksandr Solzhenitsyn and Andrei Sakharov. In making this request, Fraser highlighted the unparalleled influence that the United States had in South Korea: "In the USSR our leverage is limited—our leverage in Korea is at least 1,000 times greater if we ever decide to use it."[76] Fraser's claim was reminiscent of Carter's 1976 campaign rhetoric that had been critical of the Ford administration's policy. It also contradicted the viewpoint of Carter's security-concerned officials working in East Asia. In the words of William Gleysteen, who replaced Richard Sneider as ambassador to South Korea in 1978, the United States had "massive entanglement" but "marginal influence" in South Korea.[77]

Although the Carter administration was eager to gain the release of Kim Dae-jung and other prisoners, it opted not to pursue a liberal internationalist course, choosing quiet diplomacy instead. On April 6, when handling Fraser's letter, NSC staff member Armacost suggested that Carter's aides should "discourage him [Carter] from speaking out" on the grounds that public criticism of the Park regime by Carter would be "counterproductive." Armacost recommended "private approaches" to Park. In making this recommendation, he pointed to Carter's previous cautious approach during his recent meeting with Minister Pak as well as Carter's consistent effort to abstain from publicly criticizing Park. Upon reading Armacost's memo, Deputy National Security Adviser David Aaron summarized Armacost's suggestion in the margin as follows: "No Action." Brzezinski copied these points to Carter.[78]

At roughly the same time that Washington became focused on garnering the release of the dissidents, the Park regime moved to utilize their imprisonment as a diplomatic bargaining tool.[79] On April 8, President Park met with Sneider privately. But rather than focusing on US troop withdrawal—ostensibly the reason for the meeting—Park concentrated solely on the March 1 Incident. At first, he seemed intent on reiterating his justification for the crackdown. But then, he indicated a possible condition for release, namely, that the imprisoned dissidents should express repentance for their actions so as to prevent any future social unrest. Park's remarks, given his past resistance to any release, prompted Sneider to consider how the Carter administration might capitalize on Park's apparent openness to negotiation. Thus, after this private meeting, Sneider contemplated what Park's "first and foremost" condition of release would be. Sneider believed that Park feared that US "pressure to release Kim Dae-jung" was a "prelude to [a] move by USG [the US Government] to oust him [Park] personally."[80] Thus, he advised the Carter administration to utilize quiet diplomacy to defuse these concerns, so as to win the prisoner's release without escalating tensions between the United States and its undemocratic ally.

As transnational human rights advocates continued to call for Carter to criticize the Park regime publicly, realpolitik advocates in the Carter administration intensified their use of quiet diplomacy. On April 11, Fraser sent another letter to the White House, in which he enclosed an appeal on behalf of the March 1 dissidents by Edward W. Poitras, an American missionary working in Seoul. Poitras urged Washington to utilize the ongoing Japanese investigation of Kim Dae-jung's 1973 kidnapping from Tokyo as leverage against the Park regime. In echoing this appeal, Fraser noted that the United States had at its disposal "far more leverage" than deployed. Fraser also criticized Vance's policy for prioritizing security over human rights. Thus, he hinted at a legislative action to block further military assistance to South Korea if the administration failed to take action.[81] In handling this letter, Armacost proposed that Brzezinski respond to Fraser by telephone, rather than by letter, on the premise that any written response might find its way to the press. Armacost believed that if Park perceived the administration as exerting any type of public pressure, he would be "less likely to make conciliatory gestures." Armacost insisted that the Carter administration should "give quiet diplomacy a fair chance."[82] Hence, quiet diplomacy became the means through which the Carter administration countered pressure from transnational human rights campaigns.

The Carter administration's consistent practice of quiet diplomacy yielded a positive signal from the Park regime. On April 25, Ham Pyŏng-ch'un, the former ambassador to Washington, told Sneider that the Park regime acknowledged the Carter administration's restraint in voicing public criticism; President Park would release Kim Dae-jung on condition that his "release would be credited to the strength of Park and not solely as the consequence of U.S. pressure." Upon receiving the message, Armacost astutely paid less attention in his analysis to Park's request for "credit for Kim's release" and more to his demand for "assurance that Kim, if released, will not resume an active political role." After reading Armacost's memo, Carter consented to the terms by writing on the memo "Will be glad to do so."[83]

Thus, Carter acquiesced to the Park regime's gesture, accepting the release of Kim without requiring any fundamental political changes in South Korea. This symbolic gesture alleviated public pressure on the Park regime, and it allowed the Carter administration to claim that its human rights diplomacy was effective. In turn, it reinforced the regime's stability.

Staying Quiet for Mutual Interests

By April 1977, the Carter administration also turned to quiet diplomacy to handle other significant foreign policy objectives, including the withdrawal of US military forces from South Korea. Although Carter had advocated for troop withdrawal during his presidential campaign, many of his high-ranking aides did not support this objective and utilized the framework of quiet diplomacy to argue against any reduction in the US military presence in South Korea. American historian Charles A. Beard's 1934 description of the moral nature of US foreign policy seemed increasingly germane: "Moral obligation as employed in American foreign policy is not . . . a transcendent point of reference far above national interest practically conceived. It is admittedly secular and utilitarian."[84] In discussing the realpolitik nature of quiet diplomacy during the Carter administration, I call attention to how Carter and his security officials, despite differences in views on military withdrawal, consistently utilized quiet diplomacy to uphold the US security consensus in East Asia.

In late April 1977, against the backdrop of Carter's insistence on the withdrawal of military forces from South Korea, Carter's security-concerned officials paid greater attention to this issue. On April 26, Armacost pressed Brzezinski to remind Carter of "the danger" of speaking out on human rights abuses in South Korea and also emphasized the adverse repercussions of the troop withdrawal policy. Armacost reasoned that in the absence of a comparable call for a reduction in North Korean military forces, other states in the region might misinterpret Carter's proposed "unconditional withdrawal" as a "punitive move" against Park's repressive rule. Armacost also warned that the military withdrawal would diminish US "leverage" in the region as well as provoke a nationalist reaction by Park that might further exacerbate the political crackdown in South Korea. Armacost also cautioned Carter to offer no public criticism of Park's politics since Park would view it as a conspiracy by those who were "encouraging a change of regime." Armacost described such a regime change as "what people like Don Fraser want" to accomplish from the campaign to have Kim Dae-jung released. Armacost warned that without the current military presence, "we can no longer preserve our security arrangements with him [Park]." In presenting Armacost's points to Carter, Brzezinski explained "the disadvantages and risks" of US military withdrawal.[85] Thus, Carter's security officials utilized the rationales of quiet diplomacy for Carter's initiative for US military withdrawal as well as any public moral criticism of the Park regime.

It is notable that Carter and his aides differed on the issue of troop withdrawal, but in general, they did not try to jeopardize the stability of the Park regime. On April 27, at an NSC meeting, most officials called for flexibility in the timing of troop withdrawal and in the method of withdrawal. Defense Secretary Harold Brown insisted on the continuation of military assistance regardless of human rights conditions in South Korea. Rather than accepting the aides' recommendations, Carter instructed Vance to send a special emissary to Seoul to commence a detailed consultation on the issue. Carter noted that the emissary should "quietly reiterate U.S. concerns on human rights issues," which "should not be the primary focus."[86] Two days later, in handling Fraser's letter, Armacost reassured Brzezinski that the administration had no intentions of undermining Park's authority: "If Park were removed from power, he would undoubtedly be replaced by another military man. That his successor would inevitably be more benign is wild conjecture and wishful thinking."[87] Likewise, both Carter and his security officials sought to safeguard the stability of the Park regime through the practice of quiet diplomacy.

A month later, the Carter administration succeeded in using quiet diplomacy to secure a promise from the Park regime to release the March 1 dissidents from prison within the next few months. On May 21, 1977, five days before the arrival in Seoul of Carter's special emissary of US military withdrawal, Undersecretary of State Philip Habib, Carter had fired Major General John K. Singlaub, US chief of staff in South Korea, after he publicly voiced his opposition to Carter's plan to withdraw US ground forces from South Korea.[88] News of Singlaub's dismissal escalated the internal and external disputes in which the Carter administration was embroiled and potentially jeopardized Habib's meeting with President Park. However, at the meeting, human rights issues eclipsed the military issue. Habib informed Park that any reforms on the part of his government would be "very helpful" to Carter in "eliciting the necessary Congressional support" for military assistance. Per Carter's instructions, Habib made clear: "No public statement will be made about human rights." Habib also moderated his tone when Park refused to recognize the March 1 Incident as a "human rights" issue, calling it instead a "political problem in [the] U.S., which affects our mutual interests." In response, Park proposed a striking deal. He would take positive action on this matter if the Carter administration would observe "a period of quiet" in which "U.S. pressure was not publicly evident . . . in this context, a period of several months."[89] His remark confirmed Sneider's earlier communication to Washington that Park's public announcement on the release of the March 1 dissidents would be "only months" away. Until that time, silence needed to be maintained to ensure the mutual interests of the Carter administration and the Park regime.[90]

The deal made by Habib and Park ushered in a two-month quiet period, in which White House officials made no public comments on human rights issues in South Korea. During this period, the topic of human rights was only broached once in US-ROK diplomatic relations. In late May, Sneider held a reception at the US Embassy in Seoul for Christian leaders and several participants in the March 1 Incident. This unusual event caused some disgruntled rumblings from South Korean officials and the state-controlled media.[91] Nevertheless, Washington and Seoul maintained the diplomatic agreement to remain silent so as to protect their mutual interests. The Carter administration hoped through this silence to secure the release of the still-imprisoned March 1 dissidents, thus ensuring US congressional support for security assistance to South Korea. The Park regime also achieved its goal of securing US military assistance without having to introduce any real changes in its repressive system. Thus, it was realpolitik considerations, not human rights, that informed Carter's use of quiet diplomacy.

The Politics of Amnesty

At the crux of US-ROK relations on human rights was Park's granting of political amnesties. For authoritarian regimes, the granting of political amnesty may signify a new orientation toward promoting human rights. Political scientists Margaret Keck and Kathryn Sikkink consider the number of released political prisoners as a positive indicator of the effectiveness of transnational human rights advocacy and networks, as well as an indicator of changed political conditions in the concerned country.[92] However, any short-term assessment of the effectiveness of amnesties risks misreading the situation, given that in authoritarian regimes amnesties can occur in tandem with deteriorating human rights conditions. I argue that the political meaning of amnesty, as set forth by the Carter administration, contributed to President Park being able to pursue on the international stage the granting of amnesty as a mechanism for ensuring the stability of his undemocratic regime; it also allowed the Carter administration to realize US Cold War security consensus.

By late July 1977, two months into the diplomatic agreement requiring the United States to remain silent on human rights conditions in South Korea, the Carter administration advanced a politics of amnesty vis-à-vis US military withdrawal policy. Once more, in the frame of quiet diplomacy, the Carter administration advised the Park regime that if it pursued reform measures, the US Congress would be more likely to approve funds for security and economic assistance programs. This recommendation occurred against the backdrop of three congressional committees investigating Koreagate. On July 14, ten days prior to the first Security Consultative Meeting to discuss details for the military reduction, Carter instructed Secretary of Defense Brown to address at the meeting the value of Park's timely liberalization action. Carter anticipated that said action would save military assistance programs pending on Capitol Hill.[93] The next day, Armacost insisted that Brzezinski reassure Seoul that if the political prisoners from the March 1 Incident were released, the White House would make no public statements attributing the release to "U.S. pressure."[94]

The Park regime promptly responded to the Carter administration's signals. On July 17, South Korea's Constitution Day, Park announced the release of fourteen political prisoners. This low number reflected the fact that the regime made amnesty contingent upon prisoners declaring their repentance in a written statement. Yet, the amnesty granted these fourteen prisoners received significant attention in US-ROK diplomatic circles, because it included two prisoners involved in the March 1 Incident.[95] Following this first announcement, the regime strategically announced a series of political amnesties. Forty-seven political prisoners in total were freed: fourteen in July, seventeen in August, and sixteen in December. Each amnesty announcement was timed to coincide with a date of special significance in Korean history; the last five prisoners held in connection with the March 1 Incident were released on December 31, 1977. Ten days earlier, on December 19, Korean authorities relocated Kim Dae-jung to a hospital ward at Seoul National University, where he continued his detention, but now with little public criticism.[96] Thus, by the end of 1977, none of the prisoners associated with the March 1 Incident remained in jail.

The international response to these amnesties clearly demonstrates the motives of the US government and the Korean regime. In January 1978, the State Department publicly described the amnesties as human rights actions.[97] Spotlighting the latest amnesty, Vance recognized the prisoners' release as "one of our important objectives" and recommended that Carter send a presidential letter to Park.[98] The next month, Armacost similarly asserted that the amnesties legitimized the US humanitarian/security-related aid program Public Law 480, which hinged on the recipient country's human rights conditions. Brzezinski concurred with Armacost's interpretation. Thus, the Carter administration justified continued US economic and military assistance to South Korea by pointing to the release of the March 1 dissidents.

Although the dominant view, Armacost and Brzezinski's positive assessment of the amnesties was not the only perspective being advanced within the NSC. At the same time that they hailed the amnesties as human rights actions, NSC staff member proposed that the United States discontinue providing PL 480 funds to South Korea due to human rights violations. This proposal was rejected by Armacost and Brzezinski, who characterized it as advocating for "globaloney." However, the existence of such diametrically opposed viewpoints and proposals within the same organization, Brzezinski acknowledged, clearly indicated that the Carter administration had not yet developed a consistent human rights diplomatic program.[99] One anonymous NSC staff member tersely captured the problem: "We had a policy but not a program." On February 17, 1978, the Carter administration released the Presidential Directive on Human Rights. Despite Carter's considerable efforts to move the directive in an internationalist direction, the final version apparently was too vague to uproot the realpolitik approach to which US security officials were deeply attached and which had informed US Cold War foreign policy for years.[100]

In the wake of the amnesties, the 1976 March 1 Incident faded from the diplomatic landscape, but not from that of pro-democracy movements that continued to struggle against President Park's unchanging repressive rule. On March 1, 1978, the anniversary of the 1976 March 1 Incident, democratic activists released an updated statement on democracy and human rights in South Korea. This public statement triggered the immediate arrest of two of the initiators, Ham Sŏk-hŏn and Mun Ik-hwan, who also participated in the 1976 March 1 Incident. In fact, Mun had only recently been released from prison for his part in the 1976 protest.[101] Another dissident was also reimprisoned, after he published an open letter to Carter in which he asserted that the State Department's annual human rights report was wrong in its assessment that human rights conditions had improved in South Korea. Some of the arrested dissidents' wives also wrote to First Lady Rosalynn Carter to update her on recent suppressions.[102] In May 1978, Kim Dae-jung's wife, Yi Hŭi-ho, wrote a letter to Brzezinski, in which she described the prison-like cell in which her husband was confined at the hospital ward. Like others who participated in this letter-writing campaign, Yi received no response from the Carter administration. Instead, Brzezinski delivered to Park a letter from Carter praising the recent amnesties. Later, in mid-June, Brzezinski sent a brief reply to Yi, in which he reiterated the cliché of nonintervention in other countries' domestic politics.[103]

At roughly the same time as the above actions, realpolitik advocates in Carter's administration moved again to derail the planned withdrawal of US military troops from South Korea. In March 1978 when the first scheduled phaseout of troops seemed unlikely to proceed due to procedural delays on Capitol Hill, they called for revising or canceling the plan. In April 1978, Brzezinski convened an ad hoc meeting, at which, among others, Vance, Brown, Holbrooke, and Armacost were in attendance. At this meeting, they discussed the repercussions of Koreagate on the current planned military withdrawal. Summarizing the conclusions of this meeting, Brzezinski stated that the current initiative might have been "the wrong decision," but Carter "could slow down the pace of withdrawing the first brigade."[104] Two weeks later, Carter accepted this suggestion together with an entirely revised policy.[105] This decision marked the actual end of the initiative, although the issue would briefly come up again when Carter visited Seoul in July 1979.

Overall, in reacting to transnational human rights campaigns in and for South Korea, realpolitik advocates in the Carter administration turned to quiet diplomacy. Rather than challenging the fundamental causes of political repression in South Korea, they sought to induce President Park to make symbolic gestures, so as to neutralize the pressure exerted by transnational human rights groups and to ensure the Cold War security consensus. As a crucial mechanism of quiet diplomacy, they adopted the politics of amnesty, especially for Kim Dae-jung and other prisoners associated with the 1976 March 1 Incident. Yet, the continued arrests of pro-democracy actors reveal that the Carter administration's quiet diplomacy was in practice a pseudo–human rights policy.

Conclusion

This chapter detailed the transnational human rights contestations that developed in response to the little historicized 1976 March 1 Incident. It examined how this South Korean version of the Charter 77 campaign developed into a transnational human rights issue and a US-ROK diplomatic quandary during the Ford and Carter administrations. Through a comparative analysis of US foreign policy during the Ford and Carter administrations, it pointed to continuity between the two administrations' foreign policy, despite Carter's campaign commitment to a fundamentally different foreign policy approach that prioritized human rights. Specifically, it showed how realpolitik advocates in the Carter administration shifted the direction of Carter's human rights diplomacy, so that its main goal became avoiding transnational moral pressure on the Park regime and safeguarding US security interests in East Asia.

This shift, I argue, had negative consequences for human rights in South Korea, as it allowed the regime to make symbolic human rights gestures without introducing any fundamental changes in the political system. Because the underlying goal of US diplomatic negotiations was ensuring the stability of the Park regime and maintaining US Cold War hegemony, both US officials and the Park regime championed the regime's granting of political amnesty as human rights improvements. This characterization allowed the Carter administration to secure funding from Congress for the economic and military assistance programs needed to maintain the stability of its undemocratic ally. But the arrests of democratic protesters in South Korea continued and the letter-writing campaign launched by pro-democratic actors ensured that the Carter administration was acutely aware of the lack of real democratic reform in South Korea, as even those released under the amnesty program soon were reimprisoned. However, the US response was to label these developments domestic affairs in which it could not intervene. Thus, the human rights failures of the Carter administration were not the product of policy inconsistencies, as much existing scholarship claims, but rather reflected its consistent practice of a realpolitik policy, that is, quiet diplomacy.

CHAPTER 5

People's Protests

Economic Rights as Human Rights

On August 11, 1979, across South Korea, the following caption appeared on black-and-white television screens: "Arrest of All Female Workers Protesting at the New Democratic Party (NDP) Office: One Female Worker Dead." Three days earlier, 187 former female workers of the YH Company, a wig-making firm, recommenced their protests against the company's corrupt labor practices and closure five days earlier. The protest, previously at the company, had been relocated to the opposition party's headquarters, in hopes that there the women could make their voices heard without risking violent suppression. But more than one thousand riot police attacked the protesting women, killing twenty-one-year-old Kim Kyŏng-suk. The picture accompanying the story showed female workers in worn-out work uniforms being dragged by police officers from the headquarters. One placard hung outside NDP headquarters read: "We are dying of hunger! Give us food!" This scene contrasted sharply with the sanitized images that appeared in the press of President Park Chung-hee's daily visits to the developing heavy industrial areas and the shining high-rise skyscrapers in downtown Seoul that highlighted the South Korean "economic miracle."[1] The protest and the young female worker's resulting death sparked a groundswell of people's (*minjung*) protests for democracy that utilized the language and politics of human rights. These protests unfolded on both domestic and international stages.

This chapter examines the politicization and mobilization of human rights in people's protests for democracy between 1977 and 1979. As noted in the Introduction, to shed new light on the role of human rights in people's struggles and the relationship of these struggles to transnational human rights movements during the democratic transition, this chapter focuses on groups that previously existed on the margins of pro-democracy struggles, that is, low-income workers and farmers. Specifically, I address how these protesters appropriated "the right to subsistence" (*saengjonkwŏn*) to articulate their economic and political needs and demonstrate how a claim to this right became a substantial sphere of engagement for democratization movements and transnational human rights campaigns. This chapter also illustrates the internationalization of local disputes that incorporated demands for socioeconomic justice as well as for civil and political rights. This maximalist human rights trajectory, as discussed in the Introduction and Chapter 1, departs from the dominant historiographical narrative of human rights in the 1970s that emphasizes the global rise of human rights groups, campaigns, and policies in the West that advanced a minimalist orientation, such as Carter's human rights diplomacy and AI's global campaigns. Yet, recent inquiries, such as Brad Simpson's study of human rights advocacy in Indonesia, show that local human rights discourses and activism "gave eloquent voice to a far broader conception of human rights" that "emphasized the social and economic dimensions of the problem."[2]

Consequently, this chapter emphasizes the impact of local labor disputes on domestic and international affairs as well as the geopolitical significance of internationalized disputes on human rights issues, especially in the context of US Cold War policy. It argues that people's protests for democracy and human rights were embedded in international political and economic systems underpinned by US Cold War hegemonic policy. In making this argument, the chapter first examines how low-income workers, farmers, and their supporters appropriated the term "right to subsistence" to consolidate their democratic struggles. Next, it focuses on how the translation and mobilization of human rights activism in labor disputes became contestations on US Cold War policy. Finally, the chapter examines how local and transnational protesters utilized President Carter's 1979 Seoul visit to challenge the Carter administration's policy on democracy and human rights in South Korea. In sum, the chapter highlights how ordinary people at the local level came to reassess the impact of US Cold War policy on their daily lives and use that knowledge to create local and transnational campaigns for economic justice and democracy in South Korea.

The "Right to Subsistence" in "Fields"

The Park regime utilized the term *saengjonkwŏn*, that is, the "right to subsistence," long before pro-democracy protesters mobilized and politicized it. Following the establishment of the Yushin Constitution in 1972, the regime employed the term to emphasize the need to prioritize the collective good over individual rights and human rights. For example, on March 1, 1974, the anniversary of the 1919 independence movement, President Park urged the protection of the "national [*minjok*] right of subsistence" in the context of the international oil crisis and North Korea's security threats.[3] In October 1974, against the backdrop of strong local and international opposition to President Ford's visit to Seoul because of the regime's human rights records, Park highlighted the critical importance of his government's anti-Communism campaign for protecting the national right to subsistence. This national right, he explained, was the "foundation" for "individual rights." Thus, South Koreans "should voluntarily restrain or reserve individual liberty" in the interest of national security and the collective right to subsistence.[4]

Park's usage of the right to subsistence closely approximated that employed by the Chinese government following the 1989 Tiananmen Square Massacre that left the government's international reputation and its domestic legitimacy severely damaged. To counter these developments, the Chinese government released the 1991 white paper that described the right to subsistence as the "single most important right for the Chinese people." This collective right to subsistence, it claimed, had been jeopardized by foreign actors that wanted to harm China utilizing the false premise of human rights. Thus, as historian Marina Svensson notes, the white paper implicitly justified the state's actions at Tiananmen Square.[5] In much the same way, the Park regime in the 1970s mobilized the term "right to subsistence" nationally and internationally to legitimize its relativist understanding of human rights—a tactic that the South Korean pro-democracy movements did not take for granted.

From the early 1970s onward, pro-democracy activists in South Korea understood that economic rights as well as civil and political rights were an integral part of human rights. The first indigenous declaration of human rights in South Korea, initiated in 1973 by the NCCK in concert with the WCC, enumerated laborers' rights. As examined in Chapter 1, this first declaration placed particular emphasis on workers' right to a minimum wage. In September 1974, in addition to championing civil and political rights, the CPAJ articulated a right to a "minimum standard of living and welfare" (*ch'oesohan ŭi saenghwal kwa pokchi*). One month later, at the 1974 Synod of Bishops on "evangelization and the contemporary world," the universal church affirmed this maximalist understanding of human rights, declaring that the "rights most threatened today" were "the right to life," "the right to eat," "social and economic rights," "political and cultural rights," and "the right to religious liberty."[6]

But the relationship of economic rights to political and civil rights remained a topic of contention in South Korea. Following the launch of the *chaeya* organization NCRD on January 6, 1975, Father Yun Hyŏng-jung, the group's chair, criticized the regime's economic policy for endangering the people's right to subsistence.[7] A few days later, Pak Se-gyŏng, a NCCK Human Rights Committee lawyer, offered a theoretical critique of the regime's concept of that right. In a daily newspaper column, Pak wrote that because human rights were natural rights, the relationship between the right to subsistence and civil and political rights (*chayukwŏn*) was complementary, not "hierarchical." Together, they encompassed the totality of human rights. Pak also pointed to similarities between the Park regime's rhetorical practices and those of the Soviet Union during the first two decades of the Cold War to defend its prioritization of social and economic rights over civil and political rights. This relativist advocacy of human rights, he added, had been criticized by the United States, that is, South Korea's political ally.[8] In challenging the regime's human rights rhetoric, pro-democracy and human rights activists in South Korea employed a maximalist definition in which economic rights were inseparable from civil and political rights.

In fall 1977, as discussed below, theoretical and practical debates on the right to subsistence developed in tandem with the global resurgence of human rights advocacy and with the local revitalization of pro-democracy movements. Previously voiceless victims, such as low-income workers and farmers, began to articulate their social, economic, and political problems utilizing the language of human rights. In addition, human rights became a lens for envisioning a future democratic society in South Korea. In a series of public statements, newly emerging and existing organizations employed the language of human rights to raise fundamental questions about Korean government and society: Whose responsibility was it to protect and promote human rights? And when human rights violations occurred, who should be held accountable and by whom? As various groups grappled with these questions in the field, the territorial, socioeconomic, religious, and/or ideological divisions in South Korean society began to erode, thus expanding and deepening the sphere of contestation.

Laborers, Farmers, Youth

In the early months of 1977, local pro-democracy groups in South Korea began producing human rights statements that addressed the socioeconomic and political rights denied particular sectors of Korean society, most notably low-income urban workers, farmers, and youth. The emergence of these statements coincided with the global upsurge in human rights advocacy that followed Jimmy Carter's election as president on a platform that promised to make human rights the touchstone of American foreign policy; however, these statements did not advance the minimalist human rights orientation of the Global North. Instead they drew on local understandings of human rights, making these the foundation of pro-democracy struggles.

On March 10, 1977, the pseudo–Labor Day (Kŭlloja ŭi nal) instituted by the Syngman Rhee regime in 1958 to disassociate the holiday from proletarian activism,[9] ecumenical pro-democracy and labor activists released one of the earliest labor-specific human rights statements, "The 1977 Declaration of Laborers' Human Rights" (1977-yŏn nodongja inkwŏn sŏnŏnsŏ). This statement grew out of earlier campaigns by democratization movements that attempted to link local struggles to global human rights campaigns. For example, the KCAO, which organized the first Human Rights Week in 1973, also played a leading role in developing the 1977 statement.

Like earlier advocacies, the 1977 statement advanced concrete demands for socioeconomic and political rights.[10] It opened by calling for the recognition of "three basic rights" for workers: the right to organize, the right to bargain collectively, and the right to take collective action. It described the abolition of the 1971 National Security Act as a prerequisite for realizing these rights. It also denounced the Factory Saemaŭl (New Village) Movement—a program introduced by the Park regime in 1970 to promote rural development and later expanded to include the development of urban areas—for forcing workers to "work overtime without pay." In censuring starvation-level wages, the declaration demanded that the government pass a minimum wage law that guaranteed workers thirty thousand won per month. In addition, it insisted that multinational companies operating in South Korea recognize the rights of indigenous employees. In short, the declaration rejected the idea that the pursuit of "national security and economic development" justified the violation of workers' rights.[11]

In addition to these renewed public protests, pro-democracy communities launched a new coalitional organization in 1977—Human Rights Council for the P'yŏnghwa Market Workers (P'yŏnghwa Sijang Kŭlloja Inkwŏn Munje Hyŏbŭihoe). As noted in Chapter 1, the workers at P'yŏnghwa Market established a democratic union shortly after a worker, Chŏn T'ae-il, set himself on fire in November 1970 to protest inhumane working conditions there. After his death, Chŏn's mother Yi So-sŏn took the lead in building a strong union and worker solidarity primarily through the union-run Ch'ŏnggye Labor School. In 1977, Yi was arrested during a crackdown on the labor school, prompting union members to form a coalition with a broad circle of pro-democracy communities, including religious groups, students, journalists, lawyers, and the families of prisoners of conscience. The Council for the P'yŏnghwa Market Workers called for Yi's release, the school's reopening, and the abolition of the 1971 National Security Act.[12]

Over the next two months, the council became a vehicle for translating the specific sufferings and needs in various fields into a universal human rights agenda on labor. On November 1, 1977, the council published "Korean Laborers' Charter for Human Rights" (Han'guk nodong inkwŏn hŏnjang). This charter raised fundamental questions, such as: "Who benefits" from "ten billion dollars in exports" and from the "high economic growth?" and "Why have laborers been unable to escape their miserable reality?" In challenging the regime's developmental policy, the charter advanced a universalist agenda grounded in local realities. Thus, it called for a minimum wage, an eight-hour workday, safe working conditions, free and autonomous trade unions, and an equitable distribution of income.[13]

A development that paralleled the emergence of worker-oriented human rights was the mobilization of human rights discourse and activism by farmers working in concert with other pro-democracy groups to articulate their struggles for the right to subsistence. In 1972, the Catholic Farmers Association became the first national farmers' organization in South Korea in the post–Korean War era. In 1976 in a southwestern rural area of Hamp'yŏng County, a watershed moment for farmers' rights developed after the government-controlled agricultural cooperative broke its promise to purchase newly harvested sweet potatoes. On behalf of the farmers who suffered huge economic losses because of the government's broken promise, the Hamp'yŏng Catholic Farmers Association initiated an investigation that exposed government corruption and sought recompense for 160 households in nine villages. For over a year and a half, the authorities ignored the protesting farmers' appeals for justice. Frustrated by government inaction, protest leaders organized a large public forum. On April 24, 1978, hundreds of farmers gathered at a Catholic church in Kwangju, a southwestern provincial city and historically a center of peasant revolts. This was the first mass protest by farmers in the 1970s. The banners at the gathering made clear that the farmers wanted more than compensation for their losses and the punishment of corrupt officials; they also sought the democratic reform of the government-run cooperative and the release of farmers imprisoned under Emergency Decree No. 9.[14] In short, the farmers were realizing that real change required challenging the root cause of their suffering, that is, the repressive political-economic system.

At the rally, the farmers sang two protest songs: a popular local protest song from the 1940s "The Farmers' Song" ("Nongsa hyŏngje," later called "Nongmin'ga") and the American civil rights movement anthem of the 1950s and 1960s "We Shall Overcome," known as *"Uri sŭngri harira."*[15] Through these songs and their demands, they connected their current protest to past unfulfilled demands for democracy and for land reform from the mid-1940s and to people's movements beyond their national borders in which the call for human rights took center stage. As one anonymous eyewitness attested, one farmer demanded that the state implement the "justice of land ownership" that it promised in 1949. Because land reform had not been fully realized then, many of the farmers protesting in 1978 did not own the land on which they toiled. These farmers could not help but see parallels between their plight under Japanese colonial rule and the hardships they faced under US Cold War hegemony. The importation of domestic food grains, such as wheat through the US aid program PL 480, kept prices artificially low, thereby minimizing any improvements in farmers' income. Thus, Sŏ Kyŏng-wŏn, one of the leaders of the protesting farmers, criticized both the South Korean government and PL 480 for making "Korea and Korean peasants worse and worse off in economic and social terms." Already frustrated by the government's failure to resolve the problem, the presence of riot police drove the participants to take additional action. Seventy farmers still at the cathedral instituted a hunger strike in an effort to have their right to subsistence recognized.[16]

On April 28, the fourth day of the hunger strike, to show their solidarity and support, representatives of various advocacy groups, such as the CPAJ and Writers for the Practice of Freedom, met to organize a nationwide ad hoc preparatory committee for "farmers' human rights." Also, among the 340 ad hoc committee members were leading members of the Kwangju Chapter of AI Korea, including Father Cho Pi-o, Yi Ki-hong, Hong Nam-sun, and Rev. Ŭn Myŏng-gi.[17] These AI members chose to take part even though their participation contravened AI's impartiality mandate and the economic and social aspirations of these farmers exceeded AI's focus on civil and political rights. As discussed in Chapter 1, the boundaries established by AIIS were not always observed at the local level. As a result, AI's approach to human rights became part of a broader indigenous orientation to human rights.

Three days later, on May 1, a second rally was held. In attendance were forty Catholic and Protestant clergy members, five hundred farmers, as well as other participants. This second rally also marked the inauguration of the National Committee for Farmers' Human Rights (Chŏn'guk Nongmin Inkwŏn Wiwŏnhoe), an outgrowth of the ad hoc committee established after the first rally. In its inaugural statement, the National Committee for Farmers' Human Rights connected the economic and political plight of farmers to that of workers. Specifically, it drew parallels between the suffering experienced by farmers due to the government's policy of maintaining artificially low prices for agricultural products and the plight of workers who labored long hours for low wages. In short, the statement linked two heretofore disparate communities behind a shared agenda of realizing human rights and democracy in South Korea. The following day, the government agreed to compensate the farmers for their losses and release the imprisoned farmers.[18] After twenty months, the farmers had achieved a partial victory; the cooperative's democratization would have to wait until democracy in South Korea was realized.

This campaign's partial success led other provincial farmers' groups to appropriate the language of human rights to articulate their suffering. For example, in Ch'ŏngju, farmers organized a prayer meeting for "the restoration of farmers' human rights." This protest was followed by a one-hundred-day prayer meeting and a fast in support of imprisoned ecumenical activist Rev. In Myŏng-jin, who had been arrested for giving sermons that condemned the regime's low-income policy. This prayer meeting also served as a discursive forum in which some farmers invoked human rights to describe their various sufferings. This protest action gained the support of two ecumenical activist groups, the National Committee for Farmers' Human Rights and the Coalition for Human Rights Movements in South Korea, a newly formed

nationwide human rights group.[19] This nationwide solidarity group helped
both farmers and workers articulate their right to subsistence as part of
pro-democracy struggles.[20]

At roughly the same time that farmers and workers mobilized the language of human rights, youth (ch'ŏngnyŏn) in South Korea also began building solidarity groups based on human rights advocacy. A crucial stimulus
behind their actions was the April 1978 incarceration of two young activists,
Kim Pyŏng-gon and Kim Pong-u, for helping the protesting Dong-il textile
workers to publicize and politicize their grievances against the company.
Their imprisonment sparked one hundred students to launch a hunger strike,
which in turn led to the formation of the Democratic Youth Council for
Human Rights (Minju ch'ŏngnyŏn inkwŏn hyŏbŭihoe) in May 1978.[21] Its
members included students previously imprisoned or dismissed from college
for participating in democratization movements. Instead of creating field-
specific human rights demands, the Democratic Youth Council for Human
Rights advanced a comprehensive rights agenda; it supported the right to subsistence and called on the Park regime to desist from using torture and other
repressive measures against pro-democracy protesters. Because this was not
an underground movement, it soon came under attack by the Park regime.
By mid-1979, the group had removed "human rights" from its name to appeal to a broader base, becoming the Democratic Youth Council (Minju
ch'ŏngnyŏn hyŏbŭihoe).[22]

In short, this grassroots expansion of human rights solidarity organizations for laborers, farmers, and youth in 1977–78 occurred in tandem with
the revitalization of democratization movements in South Korea and with the
global rise of human rights. However, this human rights talk ranged far beyond the civil and political rights advanced by global human rights groups
established in the West, incorporating also social justice, economic rights,
and developmental policy. Thus, its content was not crafted simply by translating universal human rights norms into vernacular form; rather these
groups drew on lived local experiences and traditions. Thus, to speak of a unilateral diffusion of human rights talk from center to periphery cannot fully
capture the dynamics in South Korea.

The Uniting of Human Rights Organizations

During the second week of December 1977, the NCCK organized its annual
Human Rights Week. As clearly indicated by the title—"Christ Coming to

the Fields of Human Rights" (Inkwŏn ŭi hyŏnjang e osinŭn Kŭrisdo), the focus was on human rights in the field or workplace. A sample sermon highlighting the indivisibility of civil, political, social, and economic rights was distributed to 1,500 churches. The sermon made clear that the "fields of human rights" (*inkwŏn hyŏnjang*) guaranteed that "freemen" (*chayuin*) deserved "the right to eat and live" (*mŏkko sal kwŏlli*) as well as "the right to see, hear, and speak" (*pogo tŭkko marhanŭn kwŏlli*).[23] As a result of this event, fifty representatives from various social sectors agreed to establish a united human rights organization. Two weeks later, on December 29, 1977, twenty human rights and people's rights groups established the Coalition for Human Rights Movements in Korea (Han'guk inkwŏn undong hyŏbŭihoe) to investigate human rights violations and offer legal aid to victims.[24] For the first time, one organization represented the human rights interests of multiple fields; cross-sectional solidarity was beginning to take shape.

In February 1978, the Coalition for Human Rights Movements in Korea held its first lecture series. The regime reacted by placing two of the lecturers under house arrest and incarcerating one staff member. In response, the coalition issued two statements: "The Realities of Our Human Rights" (Uri ŭi inkwŏn hyŏnsil) and "The Korean People's Human Rights Declaration" (Han'guk kungmin ŭi inkwŏn sŏnŏn). The first statement pointed to multiple ways in which the government violated the political and socioeconomic rights of Koreans. For example, it referenced the government's use of torture during interrogations and its labeling of protesters as Communists. It also noted the government's failure to safeguard the three basic rights of laborers and its policy of keeping agricultural prices artificially low. The second statement rejected the legitimacy of any government that failed to safeguard the human rights of the people. It asserted that in cases in which the government passed laws that violated the human rights of its citizenry, those citizens "possess[ed] the right to form a new government capable of ensuring their human rights and happiness." Both statements appealed to Koreans and to "friends throughout the world" to abolish the "evil laws and systems" perpetrated by the Park regime and "establish a new democratic constitution."[25]

In addition to calling out the Park regime for its blatant violation of political, civil, and socioeconomic rights, the two statements also criticized the policies and actions of the Carter administration. In referencing the government's use of interrogation and labeling of protesters as Communists, the statements made clear that the 1978 human rights report, recently released by the US State Department, did not offer an accurate assessment of conditions in South Korea. The report's claim that "trials are public, and . . . the legalities of the trial itself are observed" was not borne out by the experiences of the political prisoners who had taken part in the 1976 March 1 Incident. These prisoners recently granted amnesty by the Park regime also wrote an open letter to Carter objecting to the report.[26]

By June 1978, the Coalition had grown substantially. Initially composed of 32 promoters, it now had 118 central committee members as well as a new executive committee. Over half of the leading members of this group also held leading positions in AI Korea. For example, the chair and the vice-chair of the new executive committee, Ham Sŏk-hŏn and Rev. Mun Ik-hwan, were prominent AI Korea leaders. On June 9, the coalition announced its new platform "The Human Rights of Fifty Million People" (Och'ŏnman ŭi inkwŏn) describing both Koreas as oligarchies in which pronounced divisions existed between the haves and the have-nots. According to the platform, safeguarding human rights began with ensuring the people's right to subsistence; this entailed a right to be free from hunger, "the right to work in accordance with his or her own capability," and the right to be fairly compensated. The platform also included civil and political rights. It called on people to use their "moral power" (todŏngnyŏk) to fight the "enemies of human rights," including "dictatorship," "statism without people's sovereignty," "nationalism without concern for people," and "violence of power and money." The platform also established the goal of institutionalizing human rights.[27] Meanwhile, pro-democracy groups within the chaeya circle increased owing to the foundation of the National League for Democracy (Minjujuŭi kungmin yŏnhap) in July 1978.[28]

Human Rights and Cold War Labor Diplomacy

By spring 1978, industry-specific field disputes on democratic unions, low wages, and unpaid overtime work had evolved into state-society conflicts and into transnational human rights contestations. This section focuses on two labor disputes, one at the Dong-il Textile Company and the other at the Taehyup Company. In doing so, it advances a threefold goal. First, it traces the emergence of transnational solidarity movements for socioeconomic and political justice. Second, it demonstrates that the above development was accompanied by the formation of a transnational countercoalition that consisted of South Korean state corporatist actors (regime authorities, corporate

management, and company-controlled unions) and US actors in labor diplomacy (the national security community, multinational corporations, and
labor organizations). Finally, it unpacks the hidden mechanisms through
which this countercoalition advanced its anti-labor agenda—what I call "Cold
War labor diplomacy." Thus, I contend that local disputes on economic justice developed into transnational contestations on human rights due to their
entanglement with international labor politics under US Cold War hegemony.

Dong-il Textiles and the AFL-CIO

In March 1978, the NACHRK circulated a leaflet in English, which at the top
in bold handwritten letters proclaimed: "S.O.S.!!" The leaflet stated that more
than one hundred workers fired by Dong-il Textiles had launched a two-week
fast to protest the company's actions and the regime's accompanying crackdown. One month earlier, on February 21, the company hired outside agita-
tors and bribed male workers to thwart union elections scheduled for that
day. When the female union workers approached the ballot box, they were
attacked by the men, who threw "human excrement" at them and smeared it
on their faces (Figure 8).[29] When the women cried out for help, neither the police officers on-site nor the representatives of the National Textile Union who
had been sent to observe the elections intervened to help.[30] The union leaders
were later dismissed from their posts. Ten days after their dismissal, the National Textile Union president sent out the following memorandum to all
local unions and to the other textile and garment factories: "Attached is a list
of workers who were fired from Dong-il Textiles because they had left their
jobs and were engaged in violent behavior under the direction of external
forces. So, please take proper precautions."[31] The National Textile Union in
concert with the KCIA made sure that this "blacklist" prevented the dismissed women from finding employment elsewhere.[32]

Anti-labor violence, such as that experienced at Dong-il Textiles, has received extensive attention in studies of labor activism in South Korea. For
example, studies, such as Hagen Koo's *Korean Workers* and Sohn Hak-kyu's
Authoritarianism and Opposition in South Korea, depict this violence as part
of a broader postwar history of violent confrontation and repression in
state-society relations.[33] But because such studies focus on the national
context, they seldom address the transnational roots of the violence. By
calling attention to this transnational dimension, I hope to shed new light
on the origins of this violence and address how this unprecedented and

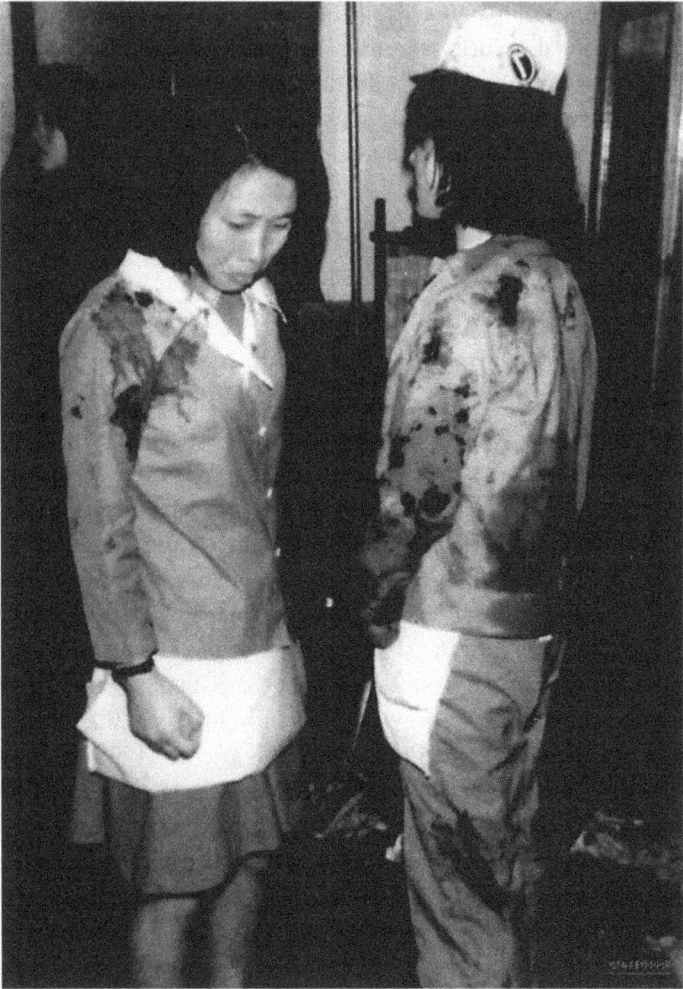

Figure 8. Two Dong-il workers assaulted by a group of male employees with human excrement in February 1978.
Source: https://archives.kdemo.or.kr; serial no. 00833204. Courtesy of the Korea Democracy Foundation and Yi Ch'ong-gak.

seemingly domestic violence shaped human rights activism and politics both within and beyond the borders of South Korea.

The NACHRK's prompt intervention transformed a local labor conflict into an international human rights dispute. At first glance, this transformation may seem to chime with diffusionist human rights narratives of the 1970s in which civil and political rights radiate from the West outward to the post-colonial world. However, the NACHRK's timely intervention was not based on the minimalist understanding of human rights advocated by President Carter or AI, the 1977 Nobel Peace Prize recipient. Instead, the NACHRK acted in response to local needs. In January 1978, its guidelines highlighted the importance of prioritizing "the problems of labor in relation to human rights," especially considering "the context of the present Korean economic model." It also approved Congressman Donald Fraser's request for "expert testimony" on South Korea's labor situation.[34] In contrast, both AIIS and the AI Washington Office declined Fraser's request because labor issues did not fall within the organization's mandate.[35] Likewise, the NACHRK had strategically shifted to economic rights.

The SOS leaflet, distributed by the NACHRK, included a copy of a letter that they had sent to President Carter, the State Department, Congressman Fraser, and George Meany, president of the American Federation of Labor and Congress of Industrial Organizations (AFL-CIO), among others. In the letter, the NACHRK condemned the regime for falsely characterizing UIM, an ecumenical group that helped the Dong-il workers organize, as a Communist organization. The letter also suggested that the social and economic injustice experienced by Korean laborers could jeopardize national stability and made clear that if the United States did not support workers in their struggles, it would indicate that "the United States' interests are strongly connected with that of the labor policy of the Park government."[36] One might assume that the NACHRK selected the AFL-CIO as one of the recipients because it considered the organization an ally. But this assumption would be wrong. Although Korean workers received some limited support from international labor federations, such as the International Textile, Garment and Leather Workers' Federation, as documented by labor activism scholar Soonok Chun,[37] the AFL-CIO, the largest American labor organization, did not support workers in South Korea. As this section shows, many pro-democracy and transnational human rights actors during this period suspected the AFL-CIO of aiding and abetting the South Korean government's efforts to control labor.

In March 1978, Kim Kwan-sŏk, general secretary of the NCCK, sent a letter to Philip Potter, general secretary of the WCC, calling for "ecumenical joint action." Kim wrote, "We are discovering" that the US government and the AFL-CIO are behind the "violent strategy" to discredit Dong-il workers and the UIM groups. Enclosed with the letter was a paper (no author given) that claimed that the Asian American Free Labor Institute (AAFLI), an AFL-CIO affiliate and US aid recipient, had played a role "in determining the labor strategy of the Korean government." The paper suggested that the AAFLI was "an organ of the American CIA" that was being used to influence the government-controlled National Federation of Korean Trade Unions (FKTU). According to the paper, the FKTU with AAFLI support was utilizing the Organizing Activities Troupe (OAT, Chojik haengdong-dae)—an FKTU agency established in 1971—to carry out its anti-labor strategy. The paper also claimed that in February 1978, a two-hundred-man OAT team had been mobilized to "suppress" self-reliant workers' unions at Dong-il and at other companies. It also noted that the AAFLI provided the FKTU with financial support; however, the extent of this support could not be determined, because the FKTU only made a small percentage of its 1978 budget public. Thus, Kim's letter suggested that to protect its Cold War security interests, the United States actively aided government-sponsored anti-labor organizations in South Korea.[38]

In the wake of Kim's letter, the NACHRK began an investigation of the AAFLI's alleged collaboration with the FKTU to suppress Korean workers and UIM groups. In April 1978, Mike McIntyre, director of the NACHRK Washington office, visited AFL-CIO headquarters to interview officials and review documentation. His research revealed the "pro-management, pro-government and anti-UIM" attitudes of the AFL-CIO. McIntyre was not alone in his suspicions that the allegations contained in Kim's letter were true. Rev. Pharis Harvey noted that many of "our friends" would be "surprised" by the AAFLI's actions since they regarded American labor organizations as "potential allies."[39] In June, George Ogle, a pioneer of the 1960s UIM campaigns in South Korea, wrote Meany to inform him that the AAFLI was "tightly in the hands of the KCIA." Thus, the AFL-CIO was "in the ironic position of supporting an oppressive labor union organization." Ogle also explained that the AAFLI had subsidized a FKTU booklet written by the KCIA. The booklet, falsely labeling ecumenical groups as Communist organizations, was used by the FKTU as a textbook in "worker education" programs. Ogle concluded the letter by requesting that the AFL-CIO investigate the AAFLI for collaborating with the KCIA and with the FKTU to suppress worker activism in South Korea.[40] Two weeks later, in early July, the AFL-CIO denied Ogle's allegations against the AAFLI, claiming that its investigation had found no grounds for the charges.[41] Despite this denial, McIntyre continued to investigate the AAFLI. With the help of Congressmen Fraser and Abner J. Mikva (D-IL), McIntyre obtained some information about monies received by the FKTU from USAID and the AAFLI. However, by March 1979, McIntyre acknowledged that he had found no definitive proof of collusion. Still, he believed that Kim's "informed speculation" was "probably true."[42]

Several years passed before the allegations against the AAFLI became a subject of scholarly inquiry. In 1989, the political scientist Jang Jip Choi examined the close connections between the AAFLI and the FKTU in his study *Labor and the Authoritarian State*. Choi found that through the AAFLI, the AFL-CIO had worked closely with the FKTU to devise policies on labor welfare services and to educate FKTU officials. In particular, Choi notes, the AAFLI played a leading role in the top-down mobilization of the Factory Saemaŭl Movement, whose programs facilitated state corporatism's establishment in the 1970s. In theory and practice, state corporatism gave the government control over the industrial labor sector and prevented workers from challenging the status quo.[43]

Historian Im Song-ja confirms that the OAT attacked the Dong-il workers. Im argues that by 1972 the OAT had become an anti-labor and anti-democratic organization. In January 1974, FKTU President Pae Sang-ho called upon the OAT to emulate the ultra-right Korean Democratic Youth League (KDYL, Taehan minju ch'ŏngnyŏn tongmaeng), which in 1945 had attempted to destroy the National Council of Labor Unions (often called Chŏnp'yŏng), a left-wing labor organization. Kim Yŏng-t'ae, president the National Textile Workers Union, part of the FKTU, had been a leader in the KDYL, and in 1978 he played a leading role in ordering the OAT to attack the Dong-il workers.[44]

In 2003, Tim Shorrock, an investigative journalist, published an article in *The Nation* that also highlighted the AFL-CIO's willingness to collaborate with the FKTU, despite being fully aware of its penetration by the KCIA. In the article, Shorrock quotes from a 1971 report, written by AAFLI regional director Jack Muth, in which he described to AAFLI executive director Morris Paladino the control that the government exercised over the unions: "Undoubtedly, the US [Embassy] Mission is aware that the Korean

Government keeps a close watch on the activities of the unions." Muth continued: "Even during our visit, we were introduced to two Korean CIA agents who were attending the FKTU political seminars; they were introduced as CIA agents openly." Shorrock also learned from AFL-CIO archival records that Paladino repeatedly made negative comments about Christian groups that supported the independent union workers. For example, at the 1979 AAFLI board meeting, Paladino attacked UIM campaigns, because they "resulted in the diffusion of slanted and partial information in the United States and in Europe" about South Korea and the FKTU. In response, he told the board that the AAFLI had "attempted to keep the record straight and provide the facts to American affiliates of the AFL-CIO whenever requested." Based on such remarks, Shorrock concluded, "Paladino's goal, apparently, was to whitewash the image of one of Asia's cruelest dictatorships." Shorrock also notes that during the Cold War, the AFL-CIO pursued anti-labor actions in other Third World countries.[45] In fact, multiple scholarly studies exist now documenting US labor organizations' involvement in US Cold War foreign policy and anti-labor action abroad.[46]

The Dong-il workers' struggle points to transnational aspects of South Korea's democratization process. By mobilizing the language of human rights, local workers created a transpacific coalition of pro-democracy, human rights, and labor movements. In tandem with the development of this coalition, a countercoalition formed that linked ROK state corporatist actors with US security-related offices and labor organizations.

Cotton Politics and Public Law 480

The Dong-il Incident prompted the NACHRK to investigate systemic problems that led to labor and human rights violations. By November 1979, McIntyre had identified the Dong-il Incident as a "microcosm" that was "illustrative of the larger pattern of labor-problems" in South Korea. He reasoned, "Labor must be kept disorganized . . . and wages must be kept low if investment of outside capital is to continue." In detailing the causes of artificially low wages and the limited clout of independent workers' organizations, McIntyre advanced a twofold emphasis, which pointed to how the Park regime's domestic policies institutionalized this situation and how US PL 480 undermined workers' rights. He claimed that this aid program constituted "one of the most clearly correlated" modes of US involvement in "labor control" in South Korea. PL 480, he elaborated, was "a system of political favors and economically unjustified concessional sales," that served the interests of Korean textile entrepreneurs and underpinned the regime's "cheap wage" policy. This "US/Korea cotton politics," he concluded, required "close examination exactly because of the deprivation of human rights which ultimately issues from the policies involved."[47]

Numerous scholars have examined economic growth in South Korea and other Third World countries as examples of "late industrialization," a process in which a nation's industries learn from the innovations of earlier industrializing nations rather than introducing inventions themselves. These late industrializers, they argue, achieve sufficiently high productivity that allows them to compete in the world economy thanks to an interventionist state that deliberately distorts relative prices to stimulate investment and trade and excludes workers economically and politically from the growth process.[48] Yet in describing the violation of workers' human rights, these studies primarily focus on how the erosion of structural safeguards under state interventionist policies gives rise to human rights violations. In particular, studies of late industrializing nations have left largely unexplored the relationship between US Cold War humanitarian aid and human rights conditions in South Korea and other Third World nations. Although a significant number of studies on international relations examine the impact of US foreign aid on the human rights policies of recipient nations, most assume the domestic construction of human rights disputes.[49] To shed new light on the constitutive role of transnational factors in shaping local human rights disputes, this section analyzes the international dispute on PL 480 to demonstrate how US humanitarian aid influenced labor and human rights policies in South Korea.

Initiated in 1954 to dispose of surplus agricultural commodities and amended in 1966 to enhance its humanitarian dimension, PL 480 did not spark controversy in South Korea until the first half of 1977. According to a NACHRK paper "U.S.-Korea Cotton Politics" (circa June 1978), South Korea had received $390 million of raw cotton since the program's inception in 1954—thus accounting for 18.4 percent of all cotton shipments received through the program worldwide. The humanitarian justification for this aid was "to meet Korea's domestic textile needs." Yet, South Korea continued to receive raw cotton through the PL 480 program well into the 1970s despite having become one of the most competitive exporters of cotton commodities. From July 1976 to September 1977, South Korea received American cotton valued at $28.19 million (sold at a reduced rate of $339.68 per bale, as compared to the average market rate of $346.86).[50] Despite changes in South Korea's political and economic situation, PL 480 aid continued unabated.

However, in August 1977, President Carter's endorsement of the International Development and Food Assistance Act posed a fundamental challenge to South Korea's continued receipt of PL 480 program aid. The act, effective October 1977, specified that a country engaged in gross violations of human rights was ineligible to receive nonmilitary aid unless it could be shown that the aid would "directly benefit the needy people" of that country.[51] South Korea's continued receipt of aid was further complicated by the outcome of a 1971 trade dispute between Washington and Seoul over South Korean textile exports to the United States. After a year of contentious debates, mediated by US ambassador-at-large David Kennedy, South Korea agreed in 1972 to restrict the export of woolen and synthetic textiles to the United States. In return, Washington agreed to provide South Korea over a five-year period with approximately $776 million in aid in the form of agricultural commodities. At the time of the agreement, Congress was not informed, and the 1973 oil crisis delayed its implementation.[52] When the suspended agreement resumed in July 1977, all seemed fine. Congress, which by 1974 had learned of the deal, authorized the request for aid in the form of wheat (410 kilotons) to South Korea through the PL 480 program. However, in December 1977, after the International Development and Food Assistance Act went into effect, an additional request for barley (150 kilotons) did not go smoothly. Instead, it sparked a transnational contestation on the influence of US Cold War humanitarian aid on human rights in South Korea.

In an effort to ensure that South Korean aid remained unaffected by the new law, Ambassador Sneider asked the Park regime in December 1977 to include the phrase "will directly benefit the needy people" in its aid request. This wording, he reassured his South Korean counterpart in January 1978, was strictly a "legislative requirement." However, the Park regime took issue with the phrase's inclusion, because it contradicted the regime's repeated claims that there were "no human rights issues in South Korea." Moreover, South Korean officials worried that by acquiescing to the phrase's inclusion, it would signal their acceptance of other terms of the new act. Specifically, they did not want to be subject to an "unimpeded investigation of alleged violations of internationally recognized human rights by an international organization including the International Committee of the Red Cross or groups or persons acting under the authority of the United Nations or of the Organization of American States," as stipulated in Section 116C of the new law. After much stalling, Nam Tŏk-u, minister of the Economic Planning Board, stipulated in his statement that the aid would benefit "the poorest people."[53] In March 1978, the statement was submitted to Congress. But tensions remained high, as officials in both the White House and Seoul worried that the recent publication of an open letter to President Carter from former president Yun Po-sŏn and a group of recently released political prisoners, related to the 1976 March 1 Incident, might derail funding. The letter, which received extensive coverage in the *New York Times* and in the *Washington Post*, contested the conclusions on South Korea that appeared in the State Department's 1978 human rights report. Officials in both governments worried that the letter would prompt a congressional investigation.[54]

Yet, it was another crisis—the South Korean government's refusal to cooperate with the congressional investigation of the 1976 Koreagate scandal—that led Congressman Bruce Caputo (D-NY) in April 1978 to propose a bill reducing economic aid to South Korea by $56 million. By threatening to reduce economic aid, Congress hoped to pressure Ambassador Kim Tong-jo to cooperate with the investigation. Two months later, in June 1978, the US House passed the bill.[55] However, on August 10, 1978, the US Senate voted against deleting a legislative provision for $56 million in PL 480 food aid for South Korea, effectively nullifying the House bill. Meanwhile, Ambassador Kim resigned, and President Park publicly pledged that Kim would give his "complete cooperation" to the congressional investigation. It is also noteworthy that after the US House passed the bill in June 1978, the National Association of Wheat Growers expressed anxiety over the loss of the South Korean market. In October 1978, Carter endorsed the Senate's decision. South Korea continued to receive aid through the PL 480 program, even though the Park regime's authoritarian system remained unchanged.[56]

In short, the Dong-il Incident precipitated transnational and institutional disputes in which human rights and PL 480 took center stage. These contestations revealed a paradoxical connection between humanitarian aid and human rights promotion in the context of US Cold War policy. This paradox stemmed from US Cold War modernization policy that advanced industrialization, without also prioritizing democratic values or economic justice. As one leading liberal internationalist on Capitol Hill, Tom Harkin (D-IA), noted in February 1978, the "most 'successful' economic development programs in such countries as Brazil, Korea and Indonesia" had been "accompanied by both greater economic inequality and increased repression."[57] The NACHRK also articulated this sentiment in debates on the PL 480 program: "Obviously, cotton exports to Korea have not benefitted workers." Transnational "solidar-ity," the NACHRK maintained, was needed to press both Washington and Seoul for political and economic justice.[58]

Taehyup and Mattel

Established in 1971, Taehyup (Taehyŏp), a toy manufacturing company in Seoul, expanded rapidly. By 1975, it had secured a lucrative contract with the US multinational toy manufacturing company Mattel Incorporated, known for its Barbie doll line.[59] Yet, Taehyup achieved rapid growth at workers' expense. The advertised high wages that they claimed to pay em-ployees did not exist in reality. In fact, its female labor force was required to work overtime without compensation. On June 10, 1977, Taehyup work-ers appealed to the company to address these issues, but the company did nothing.[60] As Stephen Lavender, an Australian missionary and UIM activ-ist in Seoul, noted in a letter to George Ogle, the company had adopted a "wait and in a while, we'll fix it" approach. Given this response, Lavender asked Ogle if he would launch a letter-writing campaign in the United States to "prod them into action." In addition to requesting that letters be sent to Taehyup's management, Lavender also requested that letters be sent to Mattel and to US congressmen.[61] Lavender's request signaled the start of a transpacific dispute that clearly showed that in the context of authoritar-ian industrialization and the neoliberalist turn under US Cold War hege-mony, economic and social rights could not be divorced from civil and political rights.

The CWU also played a leading role in publicizing the plight of Taehyup workers beyond the borders of South Korea. They distributed leaflets through-out the United States that demanded economic justice for workers. Based on interviews with actual workers, they created a composite profile of the typi-cal Taehyup worker, which they used in a leaflet to graphically portray the everyday realities of factory life. The leaflet, "Worker Profile—Taehyup," writ-ten from the viewpoint of a sixteen-year-old factory worker, vividly de-scribed the low wages and brutal working conditions at the factory: "I work 6 days a week, nine hours a day and earn 26¢ an hour" by "sewing doll dress hems" for "about 3,000 [dresses] per day." This wage, the leaflet explained, "is a little over ½ what even the government says a single female needs to sub-sist." The leaflet ended with a poignant question: "What good is the saving of a country if its people are destroyed in the struggle?"[62]

The leaflet exposed a harsh reality. Although real wages in South Korea's manufacturing sector in the 1970s had increased dramatically compared with other countries such as Brazil, Turkey, and Taiwan, not all workers benefitted equally. As economist Alice Amsden notes, the increase in real wages "was unevenly distributed across firms of different size, industries of different capital intensity, and workers of different sex." The lowest paid (mostly women) worked in informal light manufacturing, while the highest paid (mostly men) labored in heavy industries.[63] This pattern of low wages in certain industries and of male-female wage disparity was the product of the regime's developmental policy and promotion of state corporatism.[64] For example, under the "Big Push" for heavy and chemical industrialization, the regime gave skilled male workers in these industries higher wages and benefits in exchange for their complete cooperation. In the case of the shipbuilding industry, as historian Hwasook Nam illustrates, this tactic transformed a male workforce that in the 1960s had been rebellious into a "quiescent" workforce in the 1970s.[65] But the wages in female-dominated light industries were kept artificially low through government-controlled unions and appeals to economic nationalism.

In 1976, Mattel's president visited the Taehyup factory in Seoul and presented the workers with "a solid-gold Barbie doll" in recognition of their hard work. But Taehyup workers wanted "more practical recognition, like a decent wage." Through the company-controlled union, the factory's management tried to control workers' expectations and demands. In August 1977, when workers demanded redress for their grievances, Taehyup's president told workers that they were "soldiers," and he was their "commander in the battlefield" for "production contracts." Through this military analogy, he signaled that failure to "obey his orders" was an act of treason that would lead to the company's and the nation's demise at the hands of its enemies (Mattel's affiliates in Taiwan, Hong Kong, and the Philippines). Because he acted "on behalf" of the nation, employees must "abide by his decisions on wage issues." But as the CWU's leaflet so poignantly demonstrated, victory at the expense of the people's well-being was a Pyrrhic one.[66] Thus, the workers rejected management's rationale, including their claim that Mattel was to blame: "The Americans won't pay more," because if they concede to workers' demands in South Korea, "workers in the Philippines and Hong Kong will want raises."[67]

At roughly the same time as the Taehyup workers' protest, three thousand workers at Signetics Korea—an electronics company owned by North

American Philips Company, which was owned by Philips N.V. of the Netherlands—began a hunger strike during wage negotiations. The workers demanded a 46.8 percent increase based on the average pay of thirty-nine cents per hour for a first-year contract worker. The company countered by proposing a 12–14 percent increase. After a one-week strike, workers received a 23 percent increase, but only 350 workers maintained their original positions. As a report written by Ed Kinchley of the Quakers International Affairs Program noted, the pay increase was not enough "to help keep Signetics workers in Korea ahead of inflation." However, in the first quarter of 1977, the North American Philips Company reported profits of $63.9 million—an increase of almost 53 percent over the same period of the previous year. A female Taehyup employee succinctly summarized the situation: "Signetics in the U.S. makes the profits, and all we Korean people get is low wages."[68]

In spring 1978, Taehyup gave workers free copies of the booklet "What Does the UIM Have Its Eye On?" (Sanŏp sŏn'gyo nŭn muŏt ŭl norina). This booklet, as noted earlier, claimed that ecumenical groups working in the field of labor pursued "Communist" activities with the financial support of the WCC.[69] But this government-sponsored smear campaign did little to deter Taehyup workers and their allies. The CWU organized a stockholder action, and Taehyup workers barraged Mattel with letters that demanded: "Now that Taehyup is exploiting workers, you must not import its products." Concerned by the letters, Mattel asked Taehyup to explain the complaints. In an effort to de-escalate tensions, the Korean minister of commerce and industry responded directly to Mattel.[70] Against this backdrop, at its annual meeting in June 1978, Mattel executives established "a company-wide labor standards policy" to guarantee "decent minimum wages and labor conditions" for workers at supplying/subsidiary factories in Third World countries. The success of this transnational campaign led one ecumenical observer to describe it as "a model for action against the exploitation of workers by multinational corporations."[71] NACHRK secretary-general Sang-ho Kim also described this action as "one model of a successful way of handling the Korean labor issue and economic rights."[72]

Yet, for Taehyup workers victory came at a price. Shortly after the dispute, Mattel terminated its contract with Taehyup and relocated its production to other Third World countries where such labor disputes were unlikely to occur. Without its Mattel contracts, Taehyup ceased to be profitable and by August 1980 had closed all its factories.[73] Still, as we shall see in Chapter 7, the Taehyup campaign became a model for similar labor struggles in the 1980s.

In demanding a living wage and better working conditions, workers' protests, such as those at Dong-il and Taehyup, exposed the corporatist mechanisms that the state utilized to subordinate labor to its authority. By articulating their suffering in the framework of human rights, workers and their allies transformed local labor disputes into transnational campaigns for economic justice. While this strategy allowed workers to gain a transnational platform for their cause, it also placed them on a collision course with US Cold War security interests. The transnational disputes on PL 480 thus illustrate the paradoxical intersection between humanitarianism and human rights under US Cold War hegemony.

People's Disputes on US Human Rights Policy

It is a common belief among historians that the invocation of anti-Americanism by pro-democracy movements in South Korea erupted in the aftermath of the May 1980 Kwangju crisis. However, prior to the 1980 eruption of such overt criticisms, pro-democracy activists had been accumulating experiences and developing awareness of how US foreign policy negatively impacted their efforts. To illustrate the growing unease with and resistance to the Carter administration's political and socioeconomic policies in South Korea, this section analyzes local and transnational opposition to the State Department's second annual human rights report and to President Carter's visit to Seoul in summer 1979 as well as the administration's subsequent response to post-visit developments.

US Annual Human Rights Reports

Section 502B of the Foreign Assistance Act of 1975 obliged the State Department to present its annual human rights report on US aid recipient countries to the US Congress. The first report came out in February 1977, shortly after Carter's inauguration as president. For pro-democracy and advocacy activists, this publication represented a critical medium for intervening in US foreign policy on South Korea. The annual publication of the report, I contend, created a transnational forum for human rights debates. As the years passed, these debates led to more comprehensive understandings of human rights that increasingly called into question US Cold War policy.

Shortly after the publication of the second annual human rights report in February 1978, a group of South Korean dissidents imprisoned for their involvement in the 1976 March 1 Incident challenged the report's accuracy. As discussed in Chapter 4, the Carter administration had utilized "quiet diplomacy" to convince the Park regime to free these dissidents. However, once released, these dissidents did not abandon their political protests; instead, they wrote an open letter to Carter in which they declared a more appropriate title for the 1978 human rights report was "Cover-up for the Korean Government That Tramples Human Rights." In particular, the dissidents took issue with the way in which the report utilized security concerns to minimize human rights abuses in South Korea: "No one will deny the report's statement that the division of the Korean peninsula and the continuing hostility of North Korea" made national security "a matter of life and death for Koreans. . . . However, it is clear from this report that it considers only military security, and fails to take seriously both human rights and issues of political stability." The dissidents reminded the White House that its failure to address these latter two issues in South Vietnam was what led to that nation's collapse despite a huge infusion of American aid. Political stability, the letter asserted, required that South Korea have a "strong democratic system in which human rights are fully respected and the will of the people is fully regarded." With the help of two ecumenical groups, the Japan Emergency Christian Conference on the Korean Problem (JECCKP) and the NACHRK, the prisoners garnered an international audience for this letter.[74]

Rev. Ogle and Father James Sinnott also offered rebuttals of the report. In particular, they objected to the report's characterization of the PRP prisoners' trials as fair. These prisoners, they asserted, had been summarily executed "without an appeals process." Although the report acknowledged AI's conclusion that the charges in the PRP case were "fabricated," the report minimized this finding: "The U.S. Government has never had sufficient evidence to make an independent judgment on the merits of the AI conclusions." Sinnott challenged this phrasing, noting that in April 1974, US officials informed him that the KCIA had "fabricated" the case to justify "the massive arrests of students, professors, [and] religious ministers." The State Department, he declared, cannot be allowed "to get away with this!"[75]

In March 1978, the NACHRK added its voice to those of local protesters, publishing a four-page review of the report, written by Mike McIntyre, the director of the organization's Washington office, and published in its bulletin *Washington Note*. McIntyre described the language used in the report as "misleading." For example, in lieu of "outright torture," the report spoke of "subtle forms of punishment." Moreover, the report, he claimed, ascribed too much significance to symbolic gestures by the regime, such as periodic amnesties given to political prisoners. These gestures, he noted, were often followed by the rearrest of those individuals. McIntyre also stated that the State Department used the Park regime's economic development policy as an "apologia" for human rights abuses. Yet, the growth of gross national product (GNP) per capita from two hundred dollars in 1968 to eight hundred dollars in 1977, he argued, failed "to reflect the reality" experienced by most workers, because it did not factor in "skyrocketing" inflation and the increased cost of living. He cautioned that the current model of "economic concentration" would "in all likelihood widen the gaps and create a greater rich/poor situation." In articulating his counterpoints, McIntyre identified economic rights as human rights and lamented the report's failure to address the "the relationship of economic policies, political repressions, and labor unrest."[76]

In describing economic rights as human rights, McIntyre was not introducing a new topic to the discussion, rather he was engaging the maximalist analytical framework introduced in the State Department's second report. He gave credit to Secretary of State Cyrus Vance for the second report's focus on "an amalgamation of both the civil, political rights and economic, social, and cultural rights" that had been absent from the first report. He noted that the newly issued report echoed "the themes of the two separate UN Covenants." But in the case of South Korea, an "honest analysis" had not materialized. McIntyre conjectured that the State Department's Korea desk had impeded such an analysis.[77]

One year later, human rights advocates and pro-democracy groups would not wait for the publication of the report before taking action. In January 1979, one month before the scheduled release of the State Department report, they created an ad hoc organization, the Task Force for Human Rights in Korea, that drafted a one-hundred-page counter-report. In March 1979, shortly after the State Department's report appeared, they published the prepared counter-report, "Report on the Situation of Human

Rights in the Republic of Korea, 1978." Mounting protests in South Korea accompanied this report's publication.[78]

President Carter's 1979 Visit to Seoul

By July 1978, tensions over Koreagate and Carter's proposed withdrawal of US ground forces from South Korea had dissipated significantly, prompting the US ambassador to South Korea William Gleysteen to "cautiously" pursue a Carter-Park summit for the "normalization" of US-Korea diplomatic relations. Having secured Secretary of State Vance's endorsement of a summit to "secure US security and other national interests," Gleysteen broached the topic with President Park on October 25, 1978. President Park responded favorably, and the summit was scheduled to take place in Seoul on June 30, 1979.

From almost the outset, the Carter-Park summit was plagued by controversy, despite Gleysteen's best efforts to avoid publicity during the planning stage. These efforts were foiled when in July 1978, a high-ranking Korean official publicly announced plans for a US–South Korea summit. Meanwhile, in the United States, the Carter administration remained silent on the topic until October 1978.[79] But the proverbial cat was out of the bag. Korean officials continued to publicize the summit, and scores of American missionaries stationed in South Korea mobilized against it. In September 1978, these missionaries wrote a joint letter to Carter, expressing their opposition to any presidential visit to South Korea that did not bring about "meaningful change." In their letter, they reminded Carter of the long-term "negative consequences" of Ford's 1974 visit that ultimately outweighed any short-term relaxation of repressive measures. This sentiment was echoed in another letter to Carter from NCCCUSA president Rev. William P. Thompson. Thompson informed Carter that Christian leaders in South Korea feared that Carter's visit would be interpreted as "approval of the unfortunate human rights record of the Park government" and for that reason opposed his visit.[80]

In response, Gleysteen invited a group of leading dissidents, including Rev. Mun Tong-hwan and Professor Yi U-jŏng, to meet with him on November 5, 1978. Also present at the meeting were the heads of the Korea desk and the Embassy Political Analysis Office. When the US officials asked about the dissidents' goals, they replied, "We are not striving for the release of political prisoners or the lifting of emergency decrees, but quite simply the resignation of Park and the establishment of true democracy in Korea." To achieve this goal, one dissident explained, all they wanted was the United States "to

remain neutral in the internal politics of Korea." On hearing this, US officials walked out of the meeting, prompting another dissident to shout that if
the US government maintained its current policy orientation, anti-American
sentiment and actions would grow.[81]

The following week, Gleysteen organized another meeting with ecumenical labor activists to hear their viewpoints. Two months later with the help
of Maud Easter, an American Quaker living in Tokyo, these activists shared
their opposition to the Carter visit with a transnational audience. In a nine-
page paper—translated into English and titled "A Criticism of Jimmy Carter
and a Message to the American People from South Korea"—they asserted that
"the US military-industrial complex" exercised undue influence over US political leaders, including President Carter. As result, the "disease" of "double
standards and indifference to human rights" was advanced in the name of
"America's 'national interests.'" As proof, they cited the Carter administration's recent offer of $250 million in "'emergency' teargas and riot equipment"
to the shah of Iran's regime.[82]

At roughly the same time that the above paper acquired a transnational
audience, the internationally renowned journalist known as "T.K.," who since
1973 had written a column on democratization movements in South Korea
for the Japanese political magazine *Sekai*, entered the fray. In his column
"Letters from South Korea" (Jap., "Kankoku kara no tsūshin"; Kor., "Han'guk
ŭrobut'ŏ ŭi t'ongsin"), he claimed that some embassy officials "interpret the
government's tear gas and riot police intransigence" in dealing with labor protesters "as evidence of the government's stability." The article called out one US
official by name, John Lamazza. In February 1978, T.K. explained, Lamazza
had approached union activists involved in the Dong-il Incident to gather information on "labor problems" and on how churches were helping workers.
According to the dissidents, rather than informing the US government of what
he learned, he went straight to the ROK government. Because of his anti-labor,
anti–human rights conduct, dissidents suspected that he was "most probably
an officer of the American CIA." T.K. concluded, "America has learned nothing from its failure in Vietnam. . . . It still aligns itself with and supports the
powers that trample upon the people in Korea, as it has in Nicaragua, Iran, and
South Vietnam." Thus, he opposed Carter's visit and censured the anti-labor
and reactionary orientation of the Carter administration's foreign policy.[83]

In early January 1979, three prominent *chaeya* leaders—Ham Sŏk-hŏn,
Yun Po-sŏn, and Kim Dae-jung—sent a letter to President Carter in which
they challenged the Cold War security concept on which US foreign policy

was based: "National security must presuppose and be based upon the safety of individual citizens." They insisted that unless democratic reforms were introduced prior to Carter's visit, the visit would be of "no significance for the Korean people." Instead, it would be "misused to legitimize the dictatorial and oppressive regime."[84] The letter outraged the Park regime, which was unwilling to tolerate any intervention by local dissidents in US-ROK diplomatic relations. To prevent further interventions, the regime deported thirty-seven American missionaries who had been involved in smuggling the letter out of South Korea. This mass deportation prompted the State Department to send a senior official to Seoul to address the growing controversy around Carter's upcoming visit.[85] But the controversy did not dissipate; in late April, Brzezinski's aide noted that petitions and letters from dissident groups expressing their opposition to the summit continued unabated.[86] Through these letter-writing campaigns, pro-democracy activists in South Korea interjected their voices into US-ROK relations.

Despite these transpacific challenges, Carter's top aides continued to utilize quiet diplomacy to advance policies designed to maintain the status quo in South Korea. In March 1979, Assistant Secretary of State Richard Holbrooke and Gleysteen delivered a clear message to President Park that "a successful summit required progress on human rights" and that "the most convincing signs" of such progress would be lifting Emergency Decree No. 9 and freeing political dissidents. However, this demand was not made a prerequisite for the summit. Gleysteen insisted that the State Department distance itself from Carter's "zealous" human rights agenda. Thus, Gleysteen opposed "a conditional invitation." Citing the recent release of Kim Dae-jung, he reasoned, "The incentive of a successful summit was the most powerful instrument to get what we wanted in human rights." Gleysteen also contended that the economic progress and security achieved under the Park regime deserved acknowledgment. He cautioned that any criticism of Park's presidency could be "seen as lifting the mantle of legitimacy from Park," and "the consequence could conceivably be another coup and another military leader, not necessarily more enlightened than Park Chung-hee." Based on this reasoning, Gleysteen advised Carter against meeting with Kim Dae-jung during his visit to Seoul.[87]

In June 1979, local and transnational protests of Carter's visit to Seoul intensified. In early June, a group of college students publicly expressed their opposition. They called attention to the Park regime's latest instrument of oppression, that is, the coercive conscription of student activists into the military. They condemned the Carter administration for supporting the Park regime and other regimes such as those in Chile and Iran that used coercion to control the population.[88] On June 11, family members of eleven political prisoners rushed into the US Embassy courtyard, where they held up placards in English that read: "How Can a Friend of the Korean Shah Talk About Human Rights?" and "Carter? Is He [a] Human Rights Cutter?"[89] In mid-June, Korean citizens living in the United States and Japan bought an advertisement in the *New York Times* to express their opposition to the visit.[90] On June 19, Congressman Harkin and scores of his congressional colleagues sent a joint letter to Carter that cautioned against "business as usual" with Park.[91] On June 21, Senator Kennedy delivered to Carter a list of three hundred political prisoners in South Korea compiled by the NACHRK.[92]

As the summit neared, the Park regime moved to quell protests. On June 15, 1979, the regime placed scores of *chaeya* leaders under house arrest. Yet on June 23, many *chaeya* leaders, including Yun Po-sŏn, attended a rally in downtown Seoul. The demonstrators carried placards that read: "Without Democracy, There Is No Security," and "NO Carter in Korea." Roughly one thousand Korea University students also held a rally to oppose Carter's visit, and two days prior to Carter's arrival, a group of college students burned down an arch in downtown Seoul welcoming Carter to Seoul. On June 29, the day of Carter's arrival, journalists from two newspapers (*Tonga ilbo* and *Chosŏn ilbo*) who had been fired for expressing their opposition to Carter's visit staged a sit-in protest at the office of AI Korea.[93]

Amid mounting protests, on June 28, 1979, Kim Dae-jung implored the White House to rethink its approach to US-Korea relations. The US government, he said, must recognize that security in South Korea required the restoration of democracy:

What we need from Carter is simply (1) to indicate his strong moral support for the people and their rights, and (2) to stop supporting repression in the name of military security or economic growth.

Recently I have been increasingly worried about . . . loyalty to the nation. . . . It's very simple: people won't die for military security itself; they might be willing to die for human rights and democracy. The longer we maintain the present oppressive order, the less we will be able to sustain this country in the face of the threat from the North.[94]

The NACHRK mailed an English transcript of Kim's remarks to Bruce Cumings, an American historian and supporter of democracy and human rights

in South Korea. In early November 1979, shortly after Park Chung-hee's assassination, Cumings forwarded a sizable excerpt of the transcript to Michel
Oksenberg, a senior NSC staff member responsible for overseeing issues involving China and East Asia, who Cumings had studied under as a doctoral
student at Columbia University. The timing of this transmission was no ac-
cident; given Park's recent murder, Cumings hoped that the letter would push
Washington to reconsider its approach to South Korea. Kim's prescient warning made clear that the regime's measures would lead to political unrest and
to a backlash against the United States.

On June 30, 1979, the summit commenced (Figure 9). During the second
session, Carter and Park met privately for thirty minutes to discuss their primary concerns. Given Carter's human rights platform, we might assume, as
journalist Don Oberdorfer did in his book *The Two Koreas*, that Carter prioritized human rights over security and defense issues during this private meeting.[95] However, according to the memorandum on the meeting, the opposite
was the case. During the first session, Carter had been frustrated because Park
utilized roughly half of their meeting to insist that the United States "discontinue ground force withdrawals until such time as tension on the Korean peninsula is reduced."[96] Thus, during the second session, Carter largely focused
on this unfinished discussion. Carter began by calling attention to the large
discrepancy between South Korea's defense budget and that of North Korea;
this gap was particularly glaring given South Korea's greater economic capacity. Carter broached this issue despite Gleysteen's warning that it would be
"unwise" to do so. Once Park agreed to increase South Korea's defense budget,
Carter then raised the topic of US forces in South Korea, specifically the continued presence of the Second Infantry Division in South Korea and the Combined Forces Command. Finally, Carter brought up human rights, but this
discussion followed the well-worn formula. Carter reminded Park that US
citizens had serious concerns about ongoing human rights violations, and
Park countered by highlighting South Korea's unique security situation that
required exceptional measures. Park gave Carter a vague promise but never
acknowledged Carter's request that he rescind Emergency Degree No. 9.[97]

YH Incident and Pusan-Masan Uprising

At the end of Carter's visit, some progress appeared to have been made on
human rights. On July 1, 1979, just before leaving Seoul, Secretary of State
Vance remarked at the final press conference that he had presented Foreign

Figure 9. President Jimmy Carter's visit to Seoul for the summit in June 1979. South Korean president Park Chung-hee, *left*, and US president Jimmy Carter. Source: https://archives.kdemo.or.kr; serial no. 00718089. © Kyŏnghyang sinmun.

Minister Pak Tong-jin with two lists of political prisoners (one compiled by AI and one compiled in Seoul) containing more than one hundred names. Having said that, he noted that the Carter administration had made no decision on withdrawing US forces from South Korea.[98] Shortly thereafter, Park sent KCIA director Kim Chae-gyu to Gleysteen with a message for Carter announcing that he would release, as promised, 180 political prisoners over the next six months.[99] On July 17, Constitution Day, Park granted amnesty to eighty-six dissidents found guilty of violating Emergency Decree No. 9.[100] In response, the White House prepared what one NSC staff member described as "the best possible message Park could receive." On July 20, Brzezinski read the prepared White House press statement declaring that plans to withdraw the Second Infantry Division of the US Army from South Korea had been suspended. The statement also explained that a reassessment of US forces in South Korea would take place in 1981 based on "the restoration of a satisfactory North-South balance" and "evidence of tangible progress toward a reduction of tensions on the peninsula."[101] Meanwhile, Carter informed opponents of the summit on Capitol Hill that he had met with dissidents during his visit and that Park had agreed to release hundreds of political prisoners.[102]

For the Carter administration, Park's amnesty announcement vindicated the summit. But in South Korea, the amnesty announcement neither quelled political unrest nor bolstered the regime's legitimacy. Thus, even as the Park regime fulfilled its summit obligation by releasing prisoners, it also launched a crackdown on dissidents. On July 25, the education minister refused to allow students granted amnesty to return to campus. Shortly thereafter, the police rearrested Father Mun Chŏng-hyŏn for hosting the "Seminar for Justice and Peace." In early August, there were reports that police and intelligence officers had kidnapped and tortured farmer activist O Wŏn-ch'un. The South Korean Catholic community reacted to this news by holding a rally to call attention to his suffering.[103] On August 9, as noted earlier, Kim Kyŏng-suk was killed when police attacked female demonstrators from the YH Company.[104] Once again, the regime falsely claimed that the union leaders were the pawns of the UIM, a Communist group pretending to be a religious organization.[105] On August 15, Liberation Day, against the backdrop of these suppressive actions, the regime announced the release of fifty-three more political prisoners.[106]

The regime's pseudo-liberalization strengthened the resolve of people's solidarity movements. Three nationwide human rights groups—the NCCK's Human Rights Committee, the CPAJ, and AI Korea—cohosted a memorial service for Kim Kyŏng-suk.[107] In September, college students returned to campus and made the YH Incident an integral part of their political agenda. As students, workers, and other sectors of society joined forces to protest the YH Incident, what had been a struggle by laborers for the right to subsistence (*saengjonkwŏn t'ujaeng*) morphed into an anti-regime political struggle (*chŏngch'i t'ujaeng*).[108] This coalescing of various social sectors around the YH Incident and the cascade of protests that followed also invigorated transpacific contestations on human rights.

On September 15, 1979, NDP chair Kim Young-sam did an interview with the *New York Times*, in which he criticized Carter for visiting Seoul: "We asked him not to come, precisely because it could encourage Park to strengthen oppression, and all this came true." On the verge of being arrested himself, Kim called upon the United States to use its political leverage to advance democracy in South Korea, rather than dictatorship: "The time has come for the United States to make a clear choice between a basically dictatorial regime, increasingly alienated from the people, and the majority who aspire to democracy. . . . In the long run only with more democracy, with more liberal institutions can the Republic of Korea serve American interests in this part of the world." He warned that if the United States did not intervene, the US Embassy in Seoul might meet a similar fate as that experienced at the US Embassy in Teheran.[109] The interview provoked a serious political backlash. The regime-controlled newspaper labeled his remark as "subservient" (*sadaejuŭi*) to the United States.[110] On October 4, at President Park's instruction, the National Assembly ousted Kim.[111]

The escalation of this conflict induced the Carter administration to make an unprecedented intervention into South Korean domestic affairs. The intervention was carefully planned so as to avoid endangering the regime's stability. On October 12, 1979, Secretary of State Vance publicly criticized the suppression and called Ambassador Gleysteen back to Washington for consultation. Meanwhile, Vance informed Carter that "the political fabric in Korea is not about to tear asunder," and thus "we should be careful not to imply that we are inviting a change in leadership or backing any particular challenger."[112] That same day, the NSC recommended that Vice President Walter Mondale not meet with Ham Sŏk-hŏn, a prominent pro-democracy Quaker leader, because the meeting might be "subject to exaggerated interpretations."[113] The next day, Carter sent Park a letter, in which he called on him to find a way "to resume a liberalizing trend."[114]

However, the spontaneously developing situation in South Korea was outside the routine bounds of political assessments and intelligence reports. On October 16, a massive anti-regime protest erupted in Pusan, South Korea's second largest city and Kim Young-sam's hometown. At 10 A.M., approximately one thousand students at Pusan University launched a demonstration on campus, shouting chants of "Abolish the Yushin Constitution" and "Down with the Park Regime." Within an hour, the students' numbers had swollen to more than eight thousand, and they began trying to break through the riot police line to spread their demonstration to other parts of the city. That night, as noted in trial records, hundreds of college students and thousands of low-income workers and citizens fought riot police throughout Pusan. Several police stations were attacked and cars bombed. The following day, the authorities closed the campuses of all universities in the vicinity.[115] It was the beginning of the Pusan-Masan Uprising (also called Pu-Ma Uprising), which many believed ultimately led to Park's assassination by KCIA director Kim Chae-gyu on October 26, 1979.

On October 18, 1979, the government declared martial law for Pusan and the surrounding area. But the political struggles had spread to the nearby city of Masan, which President Park had made the first Free Export Zone in 1970. There, students at Kyŏngnam University launched a major anti-regime protest. As in Pusan, this protest spread beyond the university; eventually roughly ten thousand citizens joined the anti-regime protests in Masan. On October 20, 1979, the regime used "airborne troops" to bring the Pusan-Masan Uprising under control.[116]

Student leaders, such as Chŏng Kwang-min of Pusan University, could hardly have predicted the magnitude or explosiveness of the protests that erupted that October. One common explanation given for what happened was that Pusan was Kim Young-sam's hometown. Yet, the leaflets distributed at the demonstrations made no mention of Kim Young-sam's situation. Instead, they focused on a broader reform agenda. For example, the "Declaration for Democracy," distributed on October 16, called for "freedom of the press" and "human rights" to realize "the restoration of democracy" and "national unification." Other slogans included "economic nationalism" (kyŏngjejŏk minjokjuŭi) and "the abolition of the Yushin Constitution." Another leaflet stressed the issues of the "equal distribution" of wealth and the situation of YH workers.[117] Another factor worth considering, given the absence for several years of a significant social movement or protest in the city, is the establishment of the Pusan Chapter of AI Korea in January 1978. Leading members of that chapter, including Professor Kim Chŏng-han, Father Song Ki-in, Rev. Ch'oi Sŏng-muk, and Kim Kwang-il, had by October 1979 developed a significant sphere of influence through lectures and networking. Many involved in these networks were also involved in the uprising.[118]

Historian Sŏ Chung-sŏk also points to the deteriorating living conditions of workers in the area as a reason for their spontaneous participation in protests, which escalated the protests' volatility.[119] This assessment was echoed by KCIA director Kim Chae-gyu, who traveled to Pusan on October 18 and later reported his observations to President Park at a meeting at which Kim Kye-wŏn, chief secretary, and Ch'a Chi-ch'ŏl, Security Service chief, were also present: "According to my eyewitness, they [the crowds] were inflamed not by subversive elements or behind-the-scenes political manipulators; instead, it was a people's uprising [minjung ponggi], led by solely ordinary citizens, who not only ran to bring beverages and beers to protesters but also offered shelter." In making his report, Director Kim stressed three points. First, the unrest in Pusan was a "people's revolt" (*millan*) against the Yushin system and state policies, sparked by public outrage about the high cost of living and dissatisfaction with the system of taxation. Second, he believed that the riots would spread to five major cities. Finally, the regime needed to "come up with fundamental countermeasures."[120]

In a statement given after the assassination justifying his actions, Director Kim claimed that the briefing infuriated President Park, who declared, "I will give the order myself to open fire if any incident breaks out as in Pusan. Who will execute me for this order?" Echoing Park's heated remarks, Security Service chief Ch'a added, "Look at the Cambodia case, the state remained intact despite killing five million people. If we kill one or two million protesters, it will not make any difference to us." Director Kim claimed that these frightful remarks reminded him of the massive casualties resulting from the 1960 student uprising and to prevent history from repeating itself, he killed Park and Ch'a.[121]

As riots erupted in Pusan and Masan, the Carter administration stressed that the US government would not interfere in South Korean domestic affairs. On October 19, after meeting with President Park and Ambassador Gleysteen the previous day, Secretary of Defense Harold Brown informed the press: "I do not believe that any attempt by the U.S. to manage the U.S. security role here to achieve some particular political objectives would benefit either our long-term strategic interests or contribute constructively to political developments in Korea."[122] At roughly the same time that Brown made these remarks, Carter wrote Park to reassure him that the United States would not act against the regime. On October 24, two days before President Park's assassination, NSC staff member Nick Platt praised Brown's remarks, calling them "the most incisive on the subject." Platt predicted that President Park "might be willing to ease off in an effort to gain political support."[123] In short, the Carter administration remained committed to preserving the status quo in South Korea, even if it meant supporting an authoritarian regime's suppression of pro-democracy forces.

Conclusion

As this chapter has shown, the dominant narrative of a unilateral diffusion of human rights from center to periphery cannot capture the complex local dynamics that informed invocations of human rights in South Korea.

Local activists did not accept the narrow definition of human rights advanced by AI or by Carter's human rights diplomacy. Instead, they drew upon local experiences and traditions to demand the protection of economic and social rights, as well as the civil and political rights championed in the West. Farmers and workers drew on the local concept of the right to subsistence that triggered a cascade of similar human rights campaigns. In exposing the economic rights violations that hid behind the so-called "economic miracle" vaunted by the South Korean government, their campaigns impacted the local human rights and pro-democracy landscape, while becoming entangled with US Cold War diplomacy.

This entanglement, linking local campaigns with transnational advocacy groups, catalyzed the formation of anti-labor countercoalitions, whereby state corporatist actors joined forces with US actors, intent on preserving US Cold War security interests on the Korean peninsula. At the transnational level, contestations between these two coalitions over economic rights exposed the paradoxical relationship between US humanitarian aid and human rights in South Korea, thereby calling into question US Cold War modernization policy in South Korea. These contestations, because they centered on economic rights and developmental policy and utilized the language of human rights, led to an expanded understanding of human rights. In short, local actors through the transnational networks that they developed exercised influence on Western understandings of human rights, introducing economic rights and social justice as integral parts of human rights.

CHAPTER 6

Kwangju

Democratic Struggles and Anti-Americanism

In the wake of President Park Chung-hee's assassination in October 1979, South Korea experienced a democratic opening, the so-called Seoul Spring (*Soul ŭi pom*). But like other such openings—the 1953 East German Uprising, the 1956 Hungarian Revolution, and the 1968 Prague Spring—the Seoul Spring ended in violence and without the desired political liberalization having been realized. In December 1979, a new military group, led by Chun Doo-hwan and Roh Tae-woo, moved to take power, and in May 1980, this junta completed its coup by massacring hundreds of civilian protesters in the provincial city of Kwangju. But this bloody crackdown did not mark the end of the anti-regime movement, rather it introduced within the resistance movement two new overlapping discursive themes: resentment of bloc hegemony and explicit anti-Americanism. As sociologist Gi-Wook Shin explains, "Anti-Americanism became a new form of nationalism that fueled South Korea's march for democracy, and Kwangju was the turning point."[1]

This chapter examines how and why anti-American sentiment developed in local and transnational protests for democracy and human rights in South Korea in the aftermath of the Kwangju Incident (*sat'ae*), which in 1995, the ROK government renamed the Kwangju Democratization Movement in honor of the protesters' contribution to the decade-long struggle for democracy in South Korea. Officially, this renaming ended the Kwangju Incident's stigmatization as a Communist provocation. Yet the topic of US involvement in the Kwangju Incident and the events that unfolded in its aftermath, especially in relation to the rise of anti-Americanism, remain contentious.[2] To this day, the US government insists that this tragedy was the outgrowth of a domestic conflict, and thus Washington's rule of nonintervention applied. Therefore, to speak of American "responsibility," in particular based on US authorities' military operation control over the ROK Army, is misleading. In upholding this position, veteran researcher William Drennan argues that anti-Americanism stemmed from "the myth of U.S. responsibility."[3] In contrast, a group of journalists, scholars, and activists, including Tim Shorrock, Bruce Cumings, Yi Sam-sŏng, and Namhee Lee, contend that when faced with looming regional instability and threats to American dominance, the United States prioritized its geopolitical interests over the mission of promoting democracy. The end result was the slaughter of hundreds of South Korean protesters at Kwangju, democracy's postponement in South Korea, and the rise of anti-Americanism.[4]

This chapter builds on the arguments of these scholars who emphasize the role of American geopolitical interests in shaping the US response to Kwangju. Through a comparative analysis of US policy on the 1980 Kwangju Incident and on the April Uprising in 1960, I point to striking parallels in US actions, thus demonstrating that the difference in the South Korean response in 1960 and 1980 did not issue from diverging US actions, rather it was the product of a process of demystification in which ironically the idealized collective memory of US actions in 1960 played a critical role. Once the mythic image of the United States as liberator and champion of democracy was shattered in 1980, a blowback against US policies aimed at preserving US hegemony in the region ensued. This blowback manifested locally and transnationally and was accelerated by the Carter administration's tepid public response to the arrest and trial of political dissident Kim Dae-jung.

The administration's response, in turn, exposed a deep divide between Carter and members of his administration on US foreign policy goals in South Korea and elsewhere. In keeping with his campaign promise of restoring morality to US foreign policy objectives, Carter favored proactive, public measures to save Kim's life; however, many within his administration did not. Their ultimate victory meant that the Carter administration, like its predecessor, utilized quiet diplomacy to ensure the US Cold War security consensus. This policy direction facilitated the

Chun regime's countermobilization of human rights politics to consolidate its power.

Seoul's Unseasonal Spring

Pro-democracy leaders had hoped that Park's assassination would usher in democracy, but within two weeks of his death, these hopes were crushed. On November 10, 1979, Ch'oi Kyu-ha, the acting president, announced that the new president would be elected at the National Council for Reunification, as stipulated in the Yushin Constitution. This announcement created immediate concern within pro-democracy communities. To protest this decision, the Minju Ch'ŏngnyŏn Hyŏbŭihoe (Democratic Youth Council), a pro-democracy organization led by students removed from campus for earlier protest actions, decided to host a fake wedding on November 24, since under martial law rallies were banned. Over one hundred pro-democracy leaders gathered for the wedding/demonstration to protest any presidential election under the Yushin Constitution. Immediately after the demonstrators read a statement denouncing the proposed election, the police raided the building and arrested all participants. As Kim Dae-jung noted in his autobiography, the interim government was using the same tactics as its predecessor: "The KCIA hadn't changed at all."[5]

Any lingering hopes for political change were dashed when General Chun Doo-hwan (Chŏn Tu-hwan) and his colleagues seized power from the civilian government in a military coup on December 12, 1979. Chun, a brigadier general and Park's former chief of army security command, arrested the army chief of staff, General Chŏng Sŭng-hwa, charging him with complicity in Park's assassination. Chun also purged from the military Chŏng's supporters. Although Ch'oi Kyu-ha was officially president, it soon became clear that Chun was the real power holder.[6]

Yet, in March 1980, there appeared again cause for optimism, when President Ch'oi announced that he would restore the political rights of 687 critics of the Park dictatorship, including Kim Dae-jung. The *New York Times* reported that "chances for a democratic future look[ed] brighter now" than they had in December when a new strongman appeared poised to take over.[7] But this wishful thinking proved false; in fact, tensions between the emerging military regime and pro-democracy protesters were propelling the nation toward a second round of people's uprisings, like those in Pusan and Masan in October 1979. It was a local conflict over democracy in which the United States from almost the onset had become embroiled.

On March 2, 1980, against the backdrop of watchful local and international optimism, the university academic year began. Pro-democracy student activists on campus concentrated their efforts on introducing changes in the educational system, rather than engaging in street demonstrations. For example, they sought to terminate military drill classes, abolish compulsory conscriptions targeting student activists, and replace paramilitary student organizations, namely, the Student Defense Corps, with democratic student bodies.[8] Former students and professors who had returned to campus thanks to Ch'oi's amnesty gave added impetus to the campaign to remove the remaining Park regime collaborators from campus.

March also witnessed the resumption of US security and economic aid to South Korea. Although politicians on Capitol Hill expressed concerns about the slow speed of political liberalization in South Korea, the House Foreign Affairs Committee approved the Carter administration's request for $225 million in military credits to South Korea for the 1981 fiscal year. In approving the aid package, Congress urged the ROK regime to lift martial law at the earliest possible time.[9]

Yet by mid-April, no obvious signs of political liberalization had materialized. Martial law remained in place and continued to play a substantial role in determining the sociopolitical landscape. For example, a group of seventy-nine political prisoners, charged with espionage under President Park's rule, remained in prison and faced secret trials.[10] Similarly, Kim Chae-gyu, President Park's assassin, was court-martialed in secret, despite public outcry for a fair trial and full disclosure of the truth surrounding Park's assassination. In the remote town of Sabuk, the government also took brutal and decisive action against miners protesting low wages.[11] Rather than using police or riot police to subdue the protesting miners as was typically the case, the government mobilized military troops against them. According to historian Pak Man-kyu, this was the first time that the newly emerging military regime used military forces trained for war situations to subdue protesters. Unlike police and riot police who were expected to use defensive nonviolent tactics to quell protests whenever possible, these military troops were trained to take an aggressive approach (ch'ungjŏng hullyŏn), that is, to employ offensive weapons and tactical skills against protesters. The tactic, developed in February 1980 as a mechanism for handling wartime social clashes, was used one month later against protesters in Kwangju with deadly results.[12] On May 9, Ch'oi Kwang-su, the president's chief secretary, told Ambassador William Gleysteen that he was "proud of the way" the mining riot had been handled and was also "pleased with the successful quashing of violence at four major industrial plants" in Seoul, Pusan, and Inch'ŏn.[13]

In addition to suppressing civil unrest, General Chun moved to consolidate his power. On April 14, 1980, he became acting director of the KCIA. Combined with his existing position as chief of the Army Security Command, he now controlled both the civilian and military domains. International critics and pro-democracy activists saw this as an ominous development and speculated that it might signal the regime's "determination to resort to tough measures to control social and political unrest," even if the government lifted martial law as promised in early June 1980.[14] In response to these concerns, Chun declared, "A time has come for the agency to make a fresh start as an organization modest and loyal to the people and dedicated to the nation's security." The KCIA would cease its "past interference with government and other organizations."[15]

This verbal nod to reform did not assuage student unrest; activists continued to demand on-campus democratization, and street protests for democracy gained new momentum. In early May, tens of thousands of college students staged daily nationwide rallies against Chun's "amassing [of] too much power." In calling for martial law to be lifted, they also demanded freedom of the press, freedom of political expression, a minimum wage, and the reinstatement of dismissed professors. On May 10, 1980, student protesters gave the regime an ultimatum: Lift martial law by May 15—one day before the anniversary of Park Chung-hee's military coup—or face massive street protests on May 16.[16]

Because of the growing tensions between the regime and college students, the Carter administration anticipated clashes in South Korea and responded accordingly. To address any volatile situation that might arise, the administration, as Tim Shorrock revealed, opened a top-level internal channel (NODIS CHEROKEE) between Washington and Seoul following Park's assassination.[17] On May 7, 1980, Gleysteen informed Washington that the ROK government had advised US authorities that the Thirteenth Special Forces Brigade of the ROK Army would be moved on May 8 to the Kimp'o Peninsula on the outskirts of Seoul, where the First Special Forces Brigade was already in place. The two brigades, totaling 2,500 soldiers, would respond, if any student demonstrations erupted in Seoul. Gleysteen also noted that General John A. Wickham Jr., the commander of US Forces in South Korea, was aware that the ROK First Marine Division in P'ohang might be needed in the area of Taejŏn and Pusan, two major provincial cities.[18] This division, Gleysteen continued, was under the operational control of the ROK-US Combined Forces Command (CFC) and would require "U.S. approval" to move. However, Gleysteen noted, no such request had been made, "but CINCUNC [Commander in Chief of the United Nations Command] would agree if asked." The correspondence between Gleysteen and Washington officials demonstrates that the White House possessed detailed knowledge about the regime's contingency plan for maintaining law and order if student demonstrations erupted and was willing to assist, if needed, to safeguard US interests.

At 8:57 P.M. on May 8, 1980, Deputy Secretary of State Warren Christopher responded to Gleysteen's cable to provide him with instructions for his scheduled meeting with Chun the following morning. Christopher noted that it was agreed that the United States "should not oppose ROK contingency plans to maintain law and order." However, Christopher apprised Gleysteen: "He should remind Chun and Choi of the danger of escalation if law enforcement responsibilities are not carried out with care and restraint." Washington also believed that President Ch'oi needed to "dampen rumors and cool tempers" before his scheduled departure for the Middle East on May 9, given he was not scheduled to return until after the student-imposed May 15 deadline. If decisive action was not taken immediately, Washington worried that the situation would "escalate to unhealthy proportions." Christopher also instructed Gleysteen to ask General Chun "what he believes is motivating student pressures toward confrontation."[19]

The next morning, as scheduled, Gleysteen met separately with General Chun and Chief Secretary Ch'oi. In his report to Washington, Gleysteen indicated that both meetings went well. He relayed that he had been able to communicate his points to Chun "without souring the atmosphere." In fact, he thought that Chun most likely found his attitude "sympathetic." His overall impression from this meeting was that the South Korean authorities had "adopted a sensible, prudent approach to the student problem" and were cognizant of the dangers of overreacting and using military force. This impression, he stated, was confirmed by his meeting with President Ch'oi. Even more than Chun, Ch'oi seemed "determined to go to great lengths to avoid using the army except as an instrument of last resort." As advised, Gleysteen reassured Ch'oi that the United States "would not obstruct development of military contingency plans," but warned against any "excessive" actions that might give "moderate students and men in the street" reason to sympathize with the ringleaders. Gleysteen also suggested that President Ch'oi release a statement clarifying his plans for liberalization. This latter advice was not well received, prompting Ch'oi to lambast dissident leaders Kim Dae-jung and Kim Young-sam for failing "to understand the danger of bringing the soldiers out of the barracks." There were, Ch'oi warned, "12,000 combat troops distributed throughout Seoul" as part of the contingency plan. Based on these two conversations, Gleysteen informed Washington that he planned to "caution" the two dissidents about the risks they ran if they continued to "fan the flames."[20] In short, Gleysteen had detailed knowledge of the contingency plan and in an effort to eschew or minimize the danger of the regime using military force, tried to act as mediator.

By this time, the South Korean situation had become one of the most pressing topics in the White House. On May 9, in his daily report to Carter, National Security Adviser Zbigniew Brzezinski highlighted a few points based on the previous day's memo from NSC staff member Donald Gregg. Brzezinski noted that the likelihood was high that the ROK government would have "a harsh military reaction" to the anticipated student demonstrations on or around May 15. He added that General Chun, who was "isolated, ambitious, and irritated," had already "moved two or three elite army units close to Seoul." Brzezinski noted that Gleysteen was scheduled to meet with Chun that day and would urge him "to defuse the problem of the students." Brzezinski also made a cryptic reference to "rumors" that Chun instigated the student unrest "in an effort to justify his seizing power" but offered no assessment of these rumors' veracity. In closing the report, Brzezinski suggested that Carter hold a meeting of the Special Coordinating Committee or of the Policy Review Committee on the situation in South Korea.[21] This suggestion resulted in the first and only meeting of the Policy Review Committee on May 22, 1980.

As the May 15 deadline neared, the confrontation between the regime and student protesters escalated. On May 14, more than fifty thousand students took part in a street protest in Seoul—the largest such demonstration, it was reported, in fifteen years. The students called for an accelerated plan of liberalization and demanded General Chun's resignation. That same day, rumors circulated that North Korea was poised to attack; these rumors, student leaders believed, were initiated by the ROK government to justify the use of military force against them. In fact, the ROK government had deployed military units and thousands of riot police in response to the May 14 student protests. However, these units had not opened fire on the students. South Korean authorities, it was reported, had reached an agreement with Ambassador Gleysteen "to refrain moving troops in to keep order." Meanwhile, Education

Minister Kim Ok-gil warned student protesters that any further action on their part would prompt the strict enforcement of martial law.[22] On May 16, student leaders decided not to act; they would wait and see what the government's next move would be. The crisis, it seemed, had passed.

In reality, it had only been postponed by one day. On May 17, 1980, Gleysteen informed Washington that an "all but formal military takeover" was underway in South Korea. Based on information that he received from unofficial sources, Gleysteen told Washington that the imposition of "extraordinary martial law" was imminent, and that under these circumstances, the appointed martial law commander would assume authority normally reserved for the minister of defense. To address this developing situation, of which the South Koreans had provided "no notification," Gleysteen recommended that the White House issue a public statement "decrying the action, urging restraint on the part of all concerned, and warning the North Koreans." In addition, he counseled sending a message to President Ch'oi and the martial law commander admonishing them that these measures threatened to "undermine the credibility of the legally constituted government, frustrate the people's hope for domestic evolution, raise the threat of civil strife, and seriously increase the danger of North Korean intervention." This message, Gleysteen believed, should be endorsed by Washington's "highest authority," that is, President Carter. Moreover, if the situation did not improve over the next few days, Gleysteen recommended imposing economic consequences, specifically postponing visits by international financial agencies, including the Export-Import Bank, to South Korea.[23]

Within a few hours of the telegraph being sent, Gleysteen's information was confirmed. That same day, prior to the proclamation of Martial Law Decree No. 10, riot police raided a campus building in Seoul where student dissidents gathered for a meeting. In multiple other major cities, military units occupied universities, taking scores of dissidents into custody in a preemptive action. Following the official announcement, the regime closed schools, prohibited outdoor assemblies, and instituted censorship.[24] As this political crackdown unfolded, both the ROK government and pro-democracy dissidents demanded that Washington clarify the role of US hegemony in South Korea.

The Kwangju Incident in May 1980

On May 18, 1980, as anticipated, tensions erupted, but the vortex of the maelstrom was the provincial city of Kwangju, not Seoul. Historically, Kwangju had been the site of numerous struggles against authoritarian rule, including the Tonghak Peasant Uprising at the turn of the century and the 1929 Kwangju Student Independence Movement.[25] Moreover, because of the uneven development of capitalism in South Korea, the socioeconomic situation in Kwangju and surrounding areas was dire; per capita income in the region was substantially lower than the national average and working conditions were extremely poor. These factors, along with the fact that the city was Kim Dae-jung's hometown, increased the potential for widespread anti-regime resistance. Moreover, as political scientist Jean Ahn notes, "The local small and medium sized entrepreneurs" had become "antagonist toward the existing forces in power, as they were discriminated against in both political and economic terms, even though they were a faction of the ruling classes."[26]

The conflict in Kwangju, however, did not remain localized; it became the symbol of the South Korean movement for democracy. Moreover, in contrast to two previous uprisings, one against the Syngman Rhee regime in April 1960 and one against the Park Chung-hee regime in October 1979, the unparalleled resistance at Kwangju catalyzed a debate on US geopolitics and on US-ROK relations.

Violent Crackdown and Washington's Low-Key Posture

At roughly ten o'clock in the morning on May 18, 1980, as planned, hundreds of college students gathered in front of the main gate of Chŏnnam National University in Kwangju to protest the university's closure and the institution of martial law. Shortly thereafter, riot police clashed with student protesters, and some protesters broke through the barricades and proceeded downtown. By early afternoon, the number of protesting students had tripled, and a sit-in was held in front of the Catholic Center in downtown Kwangju. Initially, the police responded to the protests, but around four o'clock in the afternoon, soldiers from the Special Forces Brigades took over. According to eyewitness accounts, these soldiers clubbed demonstrators and onlookers.[27]

In the United States, media coverage of the unfolding crisis in South Korea included few details on the escalating violence. On May 19, an article in the *New York Times* on the crisis only briefly referenced riots in Kwangju, reporting that an estimated five thousand students had "defied the new Government decrees and battled riot policemen and troops in the streets for several hours before a 9 p.m. curfew was imposed." No mention was made of civilian deaths at the hands of ROK troops. Instead, the article focused on the

government's schedule for "returning South Korea to full democracy."
According to the article, President Ch'oi remained committed to his "political evolution program" despite the imposition of additional martial law
orders the previous night.[28] On May 20, the *New York Times* supplemented its
earlier report, noting: "The State Department said today that it was 'deeply
disturbed by the extension of martial law throughout the Republic of Korea,
the closing of universities, and the arrests of a number of political and student leaders.'"[29]

Meanwhile, in Kwangju, the government's brutal response to protests did
not quell riots; instead, it fueled them. Enraged by the government's random
use of deadly force, ordinary citizens and workers joined the ranks of protesters. On May 20, 1980, thirty thousand protesters fought back, setting
fire to government-run and partisan television and radio stations to protest
their misleading coverage of the crisis. To counter the official narrative that
portrayed protesters as hoodlums, the Field Fire Night School (Tŭlbul ya-
hak) team and college students introduced the *Fighters' Bulletin* (*T'usa
hoebo*).[30] That same night, hundreds of taxis led a parade of buses, trucks,
and cars to the Provincial Office, where they protested the attacks on bystanders by ROK Special Forces paratroopers the previous day.

The next day, the violence continued to escalate. Protesters broke into police stations and armories, taking rifles, carbines, and even some machine
guns. By the evening of May 21, protesters controlled the city. Forced to retreat from the city, ROK troops cordoned off Kwangju in an attempt to iso-
late the protesters and prevent the spread of anti-regime demonstrations to
other locales. Yet, despite these measures, anti-regime protests expanded
to adjacent cities, including Mokp'o, Hwasun, and Chŏnju. The *New York
Times*, initially slow to the Kwangju crisis, now highlighted the unprecedented scale of the protests there. South Koreans, the paper reported, were
comparing the current situation to the October 1946 riots and to the people's
uprising in October 1979. The regime's inability to restore "domestic calm"
led several high-ranking cabinet members, including Prime Minister Sin
Hyŏn-hwak, to resign.[31]

Following these developments, the White House opted not to actualize
Gleysteen's proposals from May 17, 1980, which included economic sanctions
against the ROK government. Instead, on May 21, a few high-ranking officials in the Carter administration drafted strategic guidelines designed to
maintain the status quo in South Korea. According to the guidelines, White
House officials would support the regime publicly, but once the political

situation stabilized, it would pressure the regime from behind the scenes to introduce democratic reforms. At 9:00 A.M., NSC staff member Gregg sent Brzezinski a memorandum outlining a plan of action. Gregg began the memorandum by recapping an assessment of the situation that he had received overnight from Gleysteen. Gregg explained that both protesters and troops in Kwangju were heavily armed. The military, he continued, planned to withdraw troops from the city that night and negotiate a ceasefire with the protesters. He also reiterated Gleysteen's belief that anti-Americanism was "not too far beneath the surface within both the Government and anti-government camps." Thus, a real danger existed that "the [ROK] government may attack us for interfering, its opponents may feel equally strongly that we have done too little." It was critical therefore that the United States adopt a "low key posture." The Carter administration, Gleysteen and Gregg agreed, should issue a statement counseling "calm on the part of all parties in Korea." Although both men recognized that due to "heavy Korean censorship," the statement was unlikely to reach a broad audience," they still believed the statement was worth making.[32]

Gregg also outlined talking points for Brzezinski's lunch meeting with Secretary of State Edmund Muskie and Secretary of Defense Harold Brown. The Carter administration's three main objectives in dealing with the crisis should be: (1) "Maintain security on the Korean peninsula and strategic stability in Northeast Asia," so as not to "contribute to 'another Iran'"; (2) "Express a carefully calibrated degree of disapproval, public and private, towards recent events in Korea"; (3) "Once the situation clarifies work through Ambassador Gleysteen and General Wickham towards a return to political process, etc."[33] As these talking points clearly indicate, the ongoing Iranian hostage crisis, which already had resulted in the resignation of several high-level State Department officials, including Secretary of State Vance, was never far from the minds of policymakers tasked with defusing the Kwangju crisis.

On May 22, 1980, the first Policy Review Committee meeting on South Korea, proposed by Brzezinski to Carter on May 9, took place in the White House Situation Room at 4:00 P.M. All major US foreign policy actors, including Brzezinski, Muskie (Vance's replacement), Brown, CIA director Stansfield Turner, assistant secretary of state for East Asia and Pacific Affairs Richard Holbrooke, and NSC staff member Gregg, were in attendance. The one-and-a-half-hour discussion produced a general policy direction, of which the first priority was the restoration of order in Kwangju by ROK authorities using "the minimum use of force necessary without laying the seeds for wide disorders later." Once restored, the Carter administration should "press the Korean Government, and the military in particular, to allow a greater degree of political freedom to evolve." In addition to this general policy line, they also decided several specific issues. Brown would "prepare for 'worst case scenarios'" in the event North Korea intervened, and John Moore, president of the Export-Import Bank, would be allowed to visit Seoul. In contradistinction to Gleysteen's recommendation from May 17 (advice he no longer supported), the Carter administration would take no punitive measures against ROK authorities. The participants also agreed that no additional public statement on the situation was required. The Policy Review Committee would not meet again unless "the situation in Kwangju involves large loss of life." On May 30, 1980, President Carter signed off on the meeting's conclusions.[34] Despite hundreds of civilian deaths the following week, the Policy Review Committee never met again.

On May 22, 1980, Gleysteen asked Washington to issue a new statement, since "more and more people want to know the U.S. attitude" on this crisis. The new statement should be similar to the one released on May 21, 1980, which urged restraint on the part of all concerned parties in South Korea so that a peaceful settlement could be reached. The one addition Gleysteen recommended was that the new statement should also underscore that the US government would "react strongly in accordance with its treaty obligations to any external attempt to exploit the situation in the Republic of Korea." To alleviate concerns that the ROK regime would manipulate the new statement as it had the previous one, Gleysteen emphasized that the ROK government welcomed the new statement and that the military hierarchy promised to distribute the text "uncensored" and to take no aggressive action in Kwangju "for at least two days," unless the situation "completely soured."[35] On May 23, he met for the first time with the acting prime minister Pak Ch'ung-hun and expressed the United States' willingness "to contribute to the restoration of order." He referenced the State Department's May 22 statement and informed Chun that the US government had "agreed to 'chop' forces under CFC [US-ROK Combined Forces Command] to Korean authorities for use in Kwangju."[36]

With diplomatic negotiations now completed, the Carter administration turned its efforts to shaping public perceptions of the Kwangju Incident in South Korea and in the United States. This public spin campaign by the administration initially tried to shift the focus from the domestic situation, that is, democracy and political oppression in South Korea, to the geopolitical situation, that is, the North Korean threat and the Cold War confrontation. White House officials publicly confirmed that the US government would react strongly to any "miscalculation by external forces," that is, North Korea. In the same vein, Pentagon officials stressed that the aircraft carrier USS *Coral Sea* had been moved to a point off the coast of Pusan, that is, within striking distance in the event of North Korean aggression.[37]

Censuring Washington's Role in the Kwangju Incident

On May 22, 1980, the fifth day of the uprising, the military command and protest leaders met to discuss a truce but failed to reach any resolution that would end the conflict. Meanwhile, in downtown Kwangju over 100,000 citizens gathered for a peaceful rally.[38] One leading student group, the Committee for the Democratic Struggle of Chosun University, issued a leaflet that one week later would also be circulated outside of South Korea. The leaflet described the crackdown as "genocidal" and drew a direct comparison between the military's actions in 1951, when ROK soldiers massacred South Korean citizens, and the military's current actions in Kwangju. As in 1951, the leaflet claimed, the military was killing the citizenry rather than "defend[ing] the nation."[39] But the leaflet did not address implicitly or explicitly the role of US authorities in the Kwangju crisis. However, once the use of deadly force against protesters in Kwangju intensified to unparalleled levels, critical voices—both within and outside of South Korea—assigned substantial responsibility for the crisis to US authorities.

Linda Jones and Joyce Overton, both ecumenical activists who had been part of the Monday Night Group in the early 1970s, were among the most outspoken critics of the United States' role in the crisis. Now members of the Church Committee on Human Rights in Asia (CCHRA), based in Chicago, the two women sent a letter to the *Chicago Tribune* on May 21, 1980, in which they claimed that US authorities had "trained and equipped" the Korean riot police officers and paratroopers used to suppress the demonstrators in Kwangju. In doing so, they asserted, the US government had facilitated General Chun's "reign of terror and death." They urged Washington to stop all military aide to South Korea until the government lifted martial law. In making this demand, they compared South Korea to Chile, Nicaragua, El Salvador, and other nations, where Washington "has neglected the aspirations of the people" in the name of "military security and economic expansion." Two weeks later, the letter appeared in the *Chicago Tribune*'s op-ed section.[40] On May 23, Jones and Overton sent a similar letter to the *Chicago Sun-Times* calling for a critical reassessment of US foreign policy on South Korea. For the past decade, the two women asserted, the US government has supported "the powers of oppression" while claiming to champion democracy. The US response to the Kwangju Incident, they insisted, signified that current US foreign policy did not advance democracy in South Korea and should be reevaluated. This letter also appeared in print in early June.[41]

On May 23, 1980, an unidentified South Korean woman living in Kwangju mailed a handwritten letter to a foreign correspondent in South Korea. In the letter, she derided foreign journalists' "weak" and "superficial" coverage of the Kwangju Incident that made no mention of the horrors perpetrated by ROK military forces, such as those she and her family had witnessed. For example, she had seen paratroopers throw injured protesters off two-story rooftops. She recalled a young demonstrator beaten so badly that "his cerebral tissue" was "exposed." Yet, unlike the atrocities in Uganda and El Salvador, no Western journalist reported these criminal actions. She implored *Newsweek* and *Time* to "offer pages as many as possible" on these atrocities so that the American people would realize the magnitude of the crisis and answer their cry for help. In her letter, she also held US military authorities responsible for atrocities by ROK soldiers, noting that it was the American commander of the US-Korea Combined Forces who had "the right of commanding in this Republic." By May 26, 1980, the letter, thanks to a network of ecumenical activists in Tokyo and Washington that included the NACHRK, had gained an audience beyond South Korea's borders.[42]

Meanwhile, on May 25, 1980, South Korean national television broadcast a photograph of President Ch'oi Kyu-ha as the newscaster read the president's appeal to the protesters. The appeal promised "'maximum leniency' if the dissidents laid down their arms" and negotiated a peaceful settlement. Despite the seeming benevolence of the appeal, many South Koreans viewed the announcement as a bad omen of things to come. Ch'oi's conspicuous absence combined with the foreign ministry's advisory to foreign embassies to remove all nationals from the area triggered widespread speculation that military action was imminent.[43]

The following morning, Gleysteen met with Chief Secretary Ch'oi Kwang-su and reiterated a message that General Wickham had delivered earlier to the ROK military. Gleysteen insisted that "all realistic non-military options be exhausted" for handling the situation in Kwangju and that "any military operations be carried out with the greatest care." He also cautioned against distorting US policies. Specifically, he expressed displeasure with Korean media reports that asserted that "General Wickham had not only authorized the shift of troops to Kwangju but had also encouraged the movement of military forces to control the city." Such reports, he explained, would inspire anti-American sentiment and "nothing could be worse than to have a sizeable anti-American movement." After the meeting, Gleysteen cabled Washington to make officials there aware that the Korean military would begin operation to reoccupy Kwangju at midnight.[44] In keeping with decisions reached at the Policy Review Committee meeting, US authorities did not attempt to stop the military intervention; rather, they worked to minimize the repercussions of the operation on US interests.

In fact, the United States turned down a last-minute opportunity to prioritize the promotion of democracy and human rights. On May 26, student leaders, in addition to appealing to the Korean Red Cross, the International Red Cross, and any "human-rights organization" for humanitarian medical assistance, asked Gleysteen to act as "an intermediary to arrange a truce" so as to "bring an end to bloodshed."[45] The State Department rejected the request: "It is difficult to see how a foreign country can intervene helpfully in a situation such as that in Kwangju . . . we recognize that a situation of total disorder and disruption in a major city cannot be allowed to go on indefinitely."[46]

At 4:45 A.M. on May 27, 1980, one hour after the State Department refused the dissidents' request for mediation, the Martial Law Command launched its final operation to restore order in Kwangju. Armed with helicopters and tanks, the Seventh, Eleventh, and Third Airborne Brigades, along with the Twentieth Division, attacked positions held by citizen militias. The one-and-a-half-hour operation terminated the ten-day riot. Based on local accounts, the *New York Times* reported that 261 people—civilians and soldiers—were killed during the uprising and another 2,000 were injured.[47] For South Koreans, the myth that US interventions on the Korean peninsula advanced a twofold goal of maintaining security and promoting democracy and human rights had been shattered. The former, they now realized, eclipsed the latter, ushering in a new era of anti-Americanism.

In 1988–89, an investigation of the Kwangju Incident by the ROK National Assembly closely scrutinized US policy of nonintervention during the crisis. As in 1980, the US government justified its inaction by claiming it had no leverage over South Korean domestic affairs. In a written statement, the US government maintained that initially it was unaware of the "full extent of violence in Kwangju" and that it had played no role in authorizing the use of South Korean troops against demonstrators: "Neither troops of the SWC [Special Warfare Command] nor elements of the 20th Division, employed by the Martial Law Command in Kwangju, were under CFC OPCON [Operational Control], either at the time they were deployed to the city or while operating there. None of the Korean forces deployed at Kwangju were, during that time, under the control of any American authorities. The United States had neither prior knowledge of the deployment of SWC forces to Kwangju nor responsibility for their actions there."[48] This statement, as this section demonstrated, contradicts information contained in hundreds of cables between US officials in Washington and in South Korea that clearly indicate that the White House had prior knowledge of Chun's plan to deploy paratroopers against the civilian population. Moreover, on multiple occasions, State Department officials communicated to ROK authorities, including General Chun, that the United States would support the ROK government if it decided to mobilize troops against the protesters. The State Department's explicit support for the use of troops to restore order and its refusal to act as intermediary between dissidents and ROK officials reflected a cohesive and carefully calculated policy that prioritized preventing another Iran and preserving US Cold War security interests over the promotion of democracy and human rights.

Delayed Blowback, Anti-Americanism

The tragic ending of the Kwangju Uprising seemingly ushered in a wave of democratization movements that expressed anti-American sentiment and (re) acted against US foreign policy, often violently. Yet, compared to other Third World nations that expressed anti-American sentiment in the Cold War context, South Korea was a late bloomer. But once anti-Americanism erupted, it gained substantial popular support and had long-term ramifications for US-ROK relations.

As noted earlier, comprehending the roots of anti-Americanism in South Korea requires an understanding of how US geopolitical interests have shaped modern Korean politics. To illustrate, this section comparatively analyzes US policy during the 1980 Kwangju Incident and during the April Uprising in 1960. It shows that in both cases the United States failed to support democratic forces. In fact, significant parallels can be seen between the actions of the Eisenhower administration and those of the Carter administration. Specifically, both administrations authorized the release of ROK troops under US command to quell protests, and both worked to stabilize the existing regime at the expense of pro-democracy protesters. However, because the 1960 incident ended with Syngman Rhee's resignation, anti-democratic actions by US authorities remained largely hidden from public view. This veil of secrecy allowed for the perpetuation of the myth of the US military as the defender of the Korean people, which the 1980 Kwangju Incident shattered.

Kwangju: Mobilizing the Memory of the April Uprising in 1960

The day after the Kwangju Incident's tragic conclusion, Secretary of State Muskie in a meeting with senior staff members expressed his concerns about the "human rights aspects of the crisis" and reaffirmed the "American desire to see the trend toward liberalization" in South Korea. This concern, however, as Assistant Secretary Holbrooke promptly clarified, did not mean that the United States would issue any public statement condemning the actions of the ROK military generals. Both Ambassador Gleysteen and General Wickham, Holbrooke added, had "privately" communicated their concerns to the ROK government. The possibility that the crackdown in Kwangju might lead to virulent anti-Americanism, similar to that in Iran, was dismissed by one official, who stressed that "both the military and civilians in South Korea looked to the United States for support."[49] Thus, all parties remained cautiously optimistic that quiet diplomacy could ameliorate any fallout from the crisis.

But this optimism proved unfounded as local and transnational actors almost immediately attacked the US handling of Kwangju. On May 27, 1980, the NACHRK and two other advocacy groups sent a joint letter to President Carter claiming that Washington "betrayed both the American and Korean people" at Kwangju. It offered a detailed chronology of events, that clearly illustrated that the United States had supported the military junta at the expense of political liberalization. The letter denounced the Carter administration for failing to side with pro-democracy actors and demanded that it impose economic and military sanctions on South Korea.[50]

On May 29, at a New York memorial service in honor of those killed in the Kwangju Incident, Rev. Mun Tong-hwan, a Korean exile, censured the Carter administration for its "silence on the suppression of the rebellion." The US government, he explained, always claims that it cannot interfere in the domestic affairs of another country; yet "by their inaction, actually they are helping the dictatorial regime." As proof, Mun enumerated multiple occasions when the US authorities failed to use their substantial influence to prevent Chun's military actions. For example, when Chun took over as acting chief of the KCIA, General Wickham did not order Chun to leave his military post, thereby acquiescing to his control of civilian and military intelligence agencies. Similarly, when Chun requested more forces from the front line to combat the students, Wickham granted this request. This policy of acquiescence, Mun declared, contrasted sharply with the US decision in 1960–61, when the American CINCUNC rejected Syngman Rhee's request to release troops to quell student demonstrators. The consequence, he noted, was the collapse of Rhee's authoritarian regime, raising the question: "Why not this time, if the U.S. really wanted a more democratic government instead of a military rule?"[51]

On May 30, 1980, Horace G. Underwood, acting representative in South Korea for the United Presbyterian Church in the United States of America, echoed this sentiment in a letter to the New York headquarters of the church. In his letter, Underwood highlighted the contrast between General Wickham's approval of the military operation to reoccupy Kwangju and his "furious" reaction to General Chun's unauthorized troop mobilization for his coup in December 1979. This seeming policy reversal by the general undermined the long-held belief in South Korea that "whatever the actions of the 'government' . . . 'the army' was on the side of the people." This trust, he claimed, "arose largely from the failure of the troops to shoot in 1960." But the US military's response to the Pusan and Masan uprisings in 1979 and to the Kwangju Uprising changed this perspective; now the US Army was identified with "anti-popular forces." He viewed this changed state of affairs as "an extremely dangerous situation, breeding great instability and inviting further coups, Vietnamization, or Iranization."[52] In short, he feared that US authorities' failure to support pro-democracy actors would have harmful repercussions for US-ROK relations.

Yet, the sharp contrast, which critics such as Mun and Underwood drew between US reactions to unrest in 1980 and in 1960, did not in fact exist. By 1960, Syngman Rhee, the ROK's first president, faced widespread accusations of corruption and nepotism and was not expected to win reelection for a fourth term. Thus, his landslide victory on March 15, 1960, immediately prompted allegations of election fraud and catalyzed student and worker groups in the southern ocean city of Masan to launch protests that same day. During this protest, Kim Chu-yŏl, a local high school student, disappeared following an altercation between police and protesters. On April 11, 1960, a local fisherman recovered Kim's body from the water. The government claimed that the cause of death was drowning, but it soon was revealed that Kim had been killed by a police tear-gas cannister. This revelation combined with the government's attempt to cover up the incident outraged citizens in Masan, and over the course of the following week, this outrage grew into a nationwide movement for democratic change.[53]

The same day that the fisherman found Kim's body, the ROK Army chief of staff requested that acting CINCUNC General Emerson L. Cummings release South Korean troops to "restore law and order" in Masan. The actual use of troops in Masan, as Walter P. McConaughy, US ambassador to South Korea, later noted, proved "unnecessary except to guard a hydro-electric plant on the outskirts of Masan." However, over the subsequent week, the number of protesting students grew exponentially, and an increasing number of angry citizens joined the uprising as protests spread to other cities, including Seoul. On April 19, 1960, tens of thousands of protesters from area high schools and colleges gathered outside the presidential palace in Seoul, demanding to see Syngman Rhee. The police and military police responded by firing into the crowd killing more than one hundred protesters. This exchange prompted the ROK government to declare martial law and to request permission from General Cummings to move troops to respond. Cummings gave his "assent" to release the Fifteenth Division of the ROK Army. The unit would be used "to quell rioting and enforce martial law" in Seoul and surrounding areas. McConaughy "concurred" with this decision." Both Cummings and McConaughy "urged" Defense Minister Kim Chŏng-ryŏl to "exercise minimum force . . . avoiding at all acceptable cost any firing on civilians." McConaughy stressed that given the high number of civilian casualties on April 19, the mobilized South Korea troops should be used to maintain the "good will of people who seem to regard [the] army as their protector against police." Defense Minister Kim "agreed" to these stipulations.[54]

On April 25, 1960, the day prior to Rhee's anticipated resignation as president, McConaughy sent Washington a cable in which he outlined the South Korean public's reaction to the US decision to endorse the mobilization of ROK troops to suppress protesters: "So far as Embassy and CINCUNC [are] aware, there has been no public comment, adverse or otherwise, concerning US action in releasing troops [in] either instance."[55] In the absence of any significant media coverage, the intentions and decisions of US authorities in April 1960 remained largely hidden from public view, allowing a benevolent image of US involvement to remain intact even though US decisions in 1960 did not differ significantly from those of US authorities in May 1980. Rhee's resignation also postponed potential blowback because it created the immediate impression that democracy would soon be restored. In contrast, the 1980 Kwangju Uprising ended with the violent suppression of demonstrators and the consolidation of the anti-democratic Chun regime. From this very different ending emerged a pro-democracy movement that drew upon an idealized memory of US actions in 1960 to fuel its anti-American orientation.

Delayed Blowback: 1980 v. 1960

Following the Kwangju Incident, the State Department continued to advance policies aimed at stabilizing the military regime. This policy placed diplomats and grassroots activists on a collision course and gave rise to local and transnational campaigns for democracy and human rights in South Korea that challenged the morality of US foreign policy. The blowback against the United States, postponed in 1960, now reached a crescendo, as rumors that the United States was behind Chun's rise to power gained widespread circulation.

On May 30, 1980, the *Stars and Stripes* reported that Chun had established the Special Committee for National Security Measures and that over half its members were military officers. Upon reading this story, Horace G. Underwood in Seoul conjectured that this action was yet another step by Chun to "assume overt control of the Korean government." In a confidential memorandum to the United Methodist headquarters in New York, Underwood noted that various ROK and US sources indicated that the US government's response to these moves had fallen seriously short of expectations and thus sparked "a rapidly growing, very bitter anti-American sentiment." Underwood believed that it was critical for the US government to "publicly and repeatedly disassociate itself from the actions of the present military *junta*."[56]

One day later, the South Korean media reported that Chun now held multiple key government and military posts: acting director of the KCIA, head of defense security command, and chair of the Special Committee. This expansion of Chun's powers only intensified debates among local and transnational actors about US responsibility for the Kwangju Incident.[57]

On June 6, 1980, a group of women whose husbands had been imprisoned for their part in the Kwangju Uprising met with US embassy officials to express their anger over the United States' failure to side with pro-democratic actors and to protect human rights. But instead of listening to their grievances, Ambassador Gleysteen offered the women a thirty-minute defense of US policy, in which he repeated the well-worn refrain that the United States could not interfere in another nation's domestic affairs. As for the issue of human rights, he reassured the women that Washington was advocating for the humane treatment of arrested dissidents and for "public announcements of trials." He then scolded students and pro-democracy actors for taking advantage of "rumors" of persecution to manipulate the current political situation to their advantage and echoed a talking point of the Chun regime, namely, that "American style democracy" was "not desirable in South Korea." On this note the meeting ended.

Dissatisfied and outraged by Gleysteen's lecture, one of the women drafted a post-meeting statement, which the NACHRK circulated internationally. According to the statement, US authorities shared responsibility for the Kwangju Incident because, among other things, they had endorsed the use of military troops to suppress demonstrations. In supporting the regime, the women contended, Gleysteen had ignored the voices of countless workers, students, and human rights activists, who had been marginalized under the Yushin system. They warned that in a few years, South Korea would "end up another Vietnam or another Iran."[58]

That same day, in Washington, a group of Christian delegates met with Michael Armacost, deputy assistant secretary of state for East Asia. The delegation included Claire Randall, general secretary of the NCCCUSA, Edward Dougherty, member of the US Catholic Conference, Martha Edens, president of CWU, as well as two exiled dissidents, Rev. Mun Tong-hwan and Professor Yi U-jŏng. The delegates assigned Washington moral, political, and military responsibility for the Kwangju Incident and advanced talking points that mirrored those that the political prisoners' wives had tried to make to Gleysteen. They also criticized Washington's "business as usual" approach to South Korea. Specifically, they expressed outrage that John Moore's upcoming visit to Seoul to discuss loans to the regime had not been canceled. They urged Washington to take concrete action against the Chun regime, such as recalling Gleysteen or instituting economic sanctions.[59]

On June 25, Gleysteen met with Chief Secretary Ch'oi Kwang-su to arrange a meeting with General Chun for the following day. That same day,

Gleysteen cabled Washington to summarize his talking points for the meeting with Chun, which he also broached with Ch'oi at their meeting. He planned to inform Chun that the United States "would be watching carefully how and whether the new authorities achieved acceptance among the Korean people." He also raised concerns about "anti-American manifestations among some elements of the regime as well as in opposition/dissident quarters." Finally, he underscored to Chun that it would be a mistake if he and his colleagues "did not adequately appreciate the dangers to Korea of an erosion in friendly relations even while basic security ties bind us." In response, Ch'oi "urged" the United States to speak "quite bluntly to them in private" about these concerns. In public, however, the United States should refrain from criticizing the regime, because most likely it would "be misunderstood and create antagonism among the generals." He then reassured Gleysteen that while it was true that "among some younger military officers, a nationalistic reaction against 'U.S. meddling" had led to some undesirable behavior, "both the Blue House and the senior military authorities wanted to hold down the growth of anti-American sentiment and prevent any adverse consequences."[60]

Washington's defensive posture following the Kwangju Incident enhanced local and transnational activists' questions and concerns about US Cold War hegemony and the American government's betrayal of its democratic ideals. In July 1980, in an article published in the ecumenical journal *Christianity and Crisis*, NACHRK's executive director Pharis Harvey drew parallels between US inaction in 1919 when Koreans rebelled against their Japanese colonizers and its "timid" response to the Kwangju crisis. As in 1919, the United States, Harvey lamented, had failed to come to the aid of a popular movement that aspired to establish a democratic government in Korea: "Again, the beleaguered citizens appealed to the US to mediate. And once again, an American President who had been known for his commitment to moral values in foreign policy—like Woodrow Wilson 61 years before—turned a deaf ear to their cries, while, in the city of Kwangju, troops armed with US-supplied weapons wreaked sadistic havoc on the citizens." If the United States did not "redeem" itself by helping "restore the possibility of development toward genuine popular government," Harvey hinted, there might be serious political repercussions in South Korea and violent retaliation against the United States: "The failure of a moral and non-violent movement to throw off colonial rule in 1919 led directly to the formation of underground terrorist groups, based in Manchuria and committed to the violent overthrow of Japanese rule. . . . It is premature to judge what will logically follow from the tragedy of Kwangju." That said, Harvey left no doubt that the United States must abandon its realpolitik orientation in favor of advancing democratic causes in South Korea or risk "dishonor."[61]

These cautious moral indictments of US foreign policy prompted almost no reaction from the Carter administration. This lack of reaction created an atmosphere in which more sinister explanations of US actions emerged and thrived. For example, following a fact-finding mission to South Korea in August 1980, NACHRK chair Peggy Billings wrote a confidential memorandum in which she alleged that current US actions were "obviously part of a larger scenario" that began with the assassination of President Park in October 1979 or earlier. "It is clear," Billings continued, "that General Chun was the Pentagon's choice. It is also clear that the Pentagon has upstaged the Department of State in setting policies for Korea." As circumstantial proof that the Pentagon had "won out," she cited General Wickham's "return to Korea [after the outbreak of the crisis at Kwangju] rather than begin reassigned [after losing his post as the CINCUNC]."[62]

Although largely unsubstantiated at the time, this claim and others like it gained credence among local and transnational advocacy groups frustrated by the Carter administration's refusal to take public action against the new regime. Despite Gleysteen's dismissal of such claims as "rumors," they entered the public discourse and fueled suspicions about US motives, decisions, and actions. They also produced a sharp increase in violent actions against the United States (for example, arsons against US installations in South Korea).[63] Even today, many remain convinced of their veracity, and because so many documents concerning US policy at Kwangju remain classified, it is difficult to confirm or deny this assessment.

Yet, a document I uncovered in 2010 about US decisions in 1960 suggests that these "rumors" deserve further investigation for two reasons. First, this document shows that at minimum in 1960 the United States seriously considered taking steps to put a new military regime in place that would then introduce a gradual process of demilitarization and political liberalization. Second, this plan, whether deliberate or coincidental, became a reality; this reality in 1960 closely paralleled "rumors" about the course of events in 1980. Hence, it points to a possible pattern of continuity in US actions.

On April 21, 1960, two days after the anti-regime student uprising and the unprecedented crackdown in Seoul, CIA Senior Research Staff (SRS) members drafted an action proposal for the Eisenhower administration. The SRS chief, whose name has been redacted from the document, summarized

SRS members' discussion with the CIA director. The memo noted, "We should ease him [President Rhee] out of power altogether with his party lieutenants." Once the incumbent regime had been removed from power, Washington should take "deliberate resort to sponsorship of a quasi-military regime." This strategic maneuver assumed that as in some other Asian countries, "a responsible core of senior officers" would be "the soundest instrument for forging a true democracy." Once such officers were identified, a "guided and benevolent military coup" should take place. As for final step, the memo explained, "We should insist that the military . . . begin immediately the task of reconstructing democracy, setting a timetable of perhaps two or three years for its full restoration." During this step, Washington needed to eschew the "danger" of any scheme by the military regime "to perpetuate itself in power." Instead this "limited military dictatorship" must "assume the responsibility of truly 'guiding' the formation of democracy," as in the other "promising" cases, such as Pakistan and Burma. Overall, this proposal aimed at "containing Communism in Asia," while depicting such military leadership as "still universally craved" in the region and as a legitimate pathway to democracy.[64]

Whether the United States officially adopted and implemented this action proposal cannot be confirmed based on currently available documents; nevertheless, the existence of such a proposal points to serious contemplation on the part of high-ranking Washington officials about how the United States could shape the political destiny of an ally, which in the context of the Cold War, it viewed as a satellite state. This action proposal also corresponded exactly to what happened: On April 26, 1960, five days after the draft memorandum, Rhee announced his resignation; on May 16, 1961, Major General Park Chung-hee and Lieutenant Major Kim Chong-p'il staged a military coup; in October 1963, following two years of behind-the-scenes diplomatic disputes, the interim military regime held elections, and General Park became an elected president. Admittedly, this trajectory need not have resulted from implementation of the CIA action proposal. Yet there are some firsthand accounts that support US authorities' partial or full implementation, including that of the CIA chief in Seoul at that time, Peer de Silva. In his 1978 memoir, he indicated that US officials, such as US military adviser James Hausman, goaded General Park and Kim Chong-p'il to stage a military coup.[65]

Neither this action plan nor the US decision to release ROK troops was known in 1960. As a result, an idealized collective memory of the US military as champions of democracy took hold in South Korea. This memory came back to haunt US authorities in 1980, as repeatedly local and transnational pro-democracy activists utilized it to denounce US actions during the Kwangju Incident and to rethink US-ROK relations. As a group of nine American missionaries and students living in South Korea explained in a letter to President Carter dated June 6, 1980, anti-American sentiment was growing because South Koreans now understood that for the United States promoting human rights was only "a secondary policy goal dependent upon military security."[66] The image of the United States as liberator and promoter of human rights had been destroyed.

Kim Dae-jung Case

Despite local and transnational activists' pleas, the Carter administration did not proactively advance a human rights agenda following the Kwangju Incident. That said, Kim Dae-jung's arrest on May 17, 1980, on charges of sedition and the extensive international attention this arrest garnered owing to the assumption that Kim would receive the death sentence meant that the Carter administration could not ignore the issue of human rights, even as it continued to pursue US security interests in the region. As in 1976, when Kim was arrested for his involvement in the March 1 Incident, the Carter administration attempted to utilize quiet diplomacy to pressure the Chun regime to commute Kim's sentence. However, as this section shows, the administration's reliance on quiet diplomacy in these negotiations was marred by tensions between Carter, who preferred a proactive human rights approach in keeping with his campaign promise, and officials in his administration who rejected this approach. These negotiations also highlight how the Chun regime utilized human rights politics to gain concessions from the Carter administration (and its successor) in order to consolidate its power.

Carter's Quiet Diplomacy

Following the Kwangju Incident, the Carter administration meticulously avoided taking any action that might appear threatening to the Chun regime. In early July 1980, CIA director Turner noted that to "step up public pressure on Chun Doo Hwan to hand authority to civilians and step down from all positions of authority" would be one of several "possible policy options" for the anticipated transition in South Korea. However, the NSC immediately eliminated this option from the list.[67]

On August 14, 1980, Deputy Assistant Secretary Armacost convened a special meeting on the "Kim Dae-jung case" to decide the administration's reaction to the case and to the leadership situation in South Korea. The Kwangju Incident had made clear that although Ch'oi Kyu-ha remained the titular head of state, General Chun actually wielded the power. Gleysteen, who was in Washington at the time and present at the meeting, proposed that Carter send Chun a letter in which he acknowledged his status as the de facto leader of South Korea and broached the topic of clemency for Kim Dae-jung. This letter, Gleysteen believed, would have a positive influence on "reordering the command structure" in South Korea, that is, it would lend greater legitimacy to Chun's new military regime and thus safeguard US security interests. In making this recommendation, Gleysteen also emphasized the need for discretion to avoid public perception that Washington supported General Chun. This perception had already gained currency in the public arena owing to an interview with an unidentified US military official that appeared in the *Los Angeles Times* on August 8, 1980. The official had stated that South Koreans were not ready for "democracy as we know it." They require a "strong leader," whom, "lemming-like," they could follow. So "we will support him [Chun], because that, of course, is what we think the Korean people want."[68] The next day, Chun exposed the identity of this official when he told Henry Scott Stokes of the *New York Times* that he appreciated General Wickham's endorsement in the *Los Angeles Times*.[69] Given rising anti-American sentiment in South Korea and growing transnational criticism of US foreign policy, Gleysteen wanted to avoid adding any more fuel to the fire.

On August 27, 1980, following Chun's election as president, Carter sent the letter that White House officials had discussed on August 14. However, prior to sending it, Carter revised the letter, giving it a more moderate and respectful tone that acknowledged Chun's new status as president-elect. The phrase "Dear Mr. Chun" was replaced with "Dear President Elect Chun." He also struck from the letter any lines that might appear provocative to Chun. For example, the following sentence was deleted: "Certainly an execution would threaten our ability to maintain our vital security cooperation." Instead, the revised letter noted, "Mr. Kim's execution, or even a sentence of death, could have [a] serious repercussion"; however, it also assured Chun that all US appeals on this matter would be made "under conditions of total confidentiality."[70] In short, the letter reaffirmed Washington's commitment to employing quiet diplomacy in its negotiations with Chun.

On September 3, 1980, when Gleysteen met with Chun for the first time since the latter's election as president, he gave him Carter's letter. On September 8, Ambassador Kim Kyŏng-wŏn delivered Chun's reply to the State Department. In his reply, Chun stated that he planned to lift martial law prior to scheduled elections under the new constitution. As for the Kim Dae-jung case, Chun refused to give any "specifics" until after the court's ruling. This response prompted Muskie to suggest to Carter that he write Chun asking for commutation or amnesty "if Kim is given a maximum sentence."[71]

There were, in fact, deep divisions within the Carter administration about the appropriate course of action: Should the White House intervene immediately or wait for the court's decision? If the court sentenced Kim to death, what measures should the administration take? Carter favored an immediate response, including possible economic sanctions, but Brzezinski and his staff objected. On September 16, 1980, one day prior to the court's ruling, Brzezinski sent Carter a memorandum in which he advocated for a wait-and-see approach. Carter, he asserted, should take no action prior to the court's decision, and even once the anticipated guilty verdict was announced, Carter should give Chun sufficient time to develop a "positive" response during the appeals process. Describing Chun as "essentially a Confucian leader," Brzezinski argued that he would find his way to a "virtuous path" if given the chance. This esoteric argument he then supplemented with a more practical one, that is, that the economic sanctions, formulated by Secretary of Defense Brown at Carter's request, would not work. Citing a survey prepared by Turner, Brzezinski reminded Carter that military, economic, and political measures would be likely to lead to greater "instability" rather than Kim's release. Carter's only option was to "make a personal appeal to Chun, without threats." In an addendum to Brzezinski's memorandum, Gregg echoed this message: "Our reaction to Kim's initial sentence, whatever it is, should be low-key." But Carter was not yet willing to abandon more proactive measures and made a notation on Brzezinski's memo: "Hold options for possible use."[72]

On September 17, two days after the court's verdict, Carter made one last attempt to employ a direct approach. He proposed releasing to the public a short excerpt from Chun's September 8 letter, in which the military regime's "commitment to political development" was discussed. Presumably publicizing this excerpt would place pressure on Chun to release those arrested during the Kwangju Incident, including Kim Dae-jung, in order to demonstrate his regime's commitment to liberalization. This proposal, however, encountered stiff opposition from administration officials, who apparently informed Chun of Carter's proposal. Armed with this information, Chun communicated his displeasure through official channels, noting it would be "inappropriate to set the precedent of releasing the private exchange." In the absence of any support for his approach, Carter adopted the "low-key" attitude recommended by his advisers. Quiet diplomacy became the standard method of negotiation with the Chun regime for the remainder of Carter's presidency.[73]

When Washington did not intervene immediately on Kim Dae-jung's behalf, Yi Hŭi-ho, Kim's wife, wrote Carter and his wife a "confidential letter" in an effort to generate momentum across the Pacific in support of her husband. The letter—smuggled out of South Korea on October 1, 1980, by Robert Kinney, a longtime friend, retired federal employee, and recipient of the Medal of Freedom—reached Washington on October 6. Ten days later, Gregg informed Brzezinski of the letter, describing it as strategically "well written" and "calculated to establish a religious bond between Kim and the President." Although Kim Dae-jung was Roman Catholic, Yi was Protestant and repeatedly used religious references that would have appealed to the "born-again" Carter. For example, she opened the letter with the salutation "May God's abundant blessing be with you both," and multiple times she referenced praying to God for guidance in this crisis. Gregg advised Brzezinski against letting Carter see the letter: "I feel that we are now doing all we can (and in the most effective way) to save Kim's life."[74]

But Brzezinski made Carter aware of the letter on October 20, 1980. In it, Yi offered a vehement refutation of the government's accusation that Kim belonged to the overseas South Korea organization Hanmint'ong (Korean Congress for Democracy and Unification), which the ROK government labeled Communist. This organization, Yi explained, named Kim its chairman without his knowledge after he was abducted from Japan by the ROK government in August 1973. At no time had her husband had any "public or informal contact" with this organization. She then pleaded for the Carter administration to intervene on her husband's behalf: "The present Korean government may well call such an effort 'interference in domestic affairs,' but the United States has already sacrificed tens of thousands of American lives for the preservation of democracy. . . . Since Korea receives so much assistance and support, she cannot ignore the United States' views." In making this appeal, Yi also suggested that her husband would be willing to retire from politics if the Carter administration found "a way for Kim to leave Korea and come to the United States for study and medical attention." Brzezinski highlighted this suggestion that Kim might abandon politics if his life were spared as a possible negotiating point with the Chun regime in the letter that he attached to Yi's letter. He also reassured Carter that US officials were placing "heavy pressure" on the Chun regime, accentuating the possibility of "widespread protests from many groups from within the US" if Kim were executed and describing North Korea as the only beneficiary of such developments.[75]

On November 3, 1980, the appeals court upheld Kim Dae-jung's death sentence. The next day Carter lost his bid for reelection by a landslide. Despite his lame-duck status, on November 14, Carter once again broached the topic of employing more proactive measures to save Kim's life. This effort was prompted by a CIA report included in Carter's daily brief suggesting that the Chun regime might expedite or bypass the appeals process in Kim's case. Deputy National Security Adviser Aaron rejected this idea in a memorandum in which he advised Carter to maintain "the private pressure on the Koreans" through a "personal letter from you shortly before the Korean Supreme Court acts." This suggestion did not satisfy Carter, who noted on the memorandum: "I want more [pressure] very strongly when necessary." Aaron, however, proposed one other option to which Carter agreed, namely, reaching out to representatives of the incoming Reagan administration.[76]

On November 20, Carter followed up on this latter option, when he met with President–elect Reagan at the Oval Office to brief him on the current state of domestic and world affairs. Toward the end of this meeting, Carter mentioned the "special problem in South Korea with Kim Dae Jung possibly being executed" and expressed his thanks to the representatives of the newly elected president for speaking out on this issue. Reagan's responses apparently did not satisfy Carter, who wrote disapprovingly in his briefing report that Reagan's "only real original statement" was when he "described to me how envious he was of that authority that the President of Korea had."[77]

The Outgoing Carter Administration, the Incoming Reagan Administration, and Chun's Commutation of Kim's Sentence

The Carter administration, despite its lame-duck status, had no choice other than to escalate its efforts on Kim's behalf. On November 19, 1980, Mike

Mansfield, US ambassador to Japan, cabled the US State Department to make it aware of his conversation with Japanese chief cabinet secretary Kiichi Miyazawa on the Kim Dae-jung case. Miyazawa believed that once the Supreme Court announced its anticipated verdict denying Kim's appeal on December 10, there was a "ninety percent probability" that Kim's execution would be carried out shortly thereafter. The next day, Washington informed Mansfield of the measures that it would take in this event, including the imposition of economic and military sanctions, which the Carter administration had previously rejected as ineffective. Mansfield informed the Japanese foreign minister Masayosi Ito of this decision.[78]

Meanwhile in Seoul, Gleysteen spoke privately with Chun and his aide about the Kim Dae-jung case on November 20, 1980. He insinuated that the future of US-ROK relations hinged upon Kim's fate. "A humane resolution," Gleysteen explained, was needed to avoid "a long sour [diplomatic] period," such as that which took place between 1976 and 1978. To put additional pressure on the regime, he also hinted at a possible US–North Korea rapprochement. In a one-on-one follow-up talk with Chun, Gleysteen took a similar position, but he also reassured Chun that he was "not arguing about the facts of the Kim Dae Jung case," rather he was suggesting that the regime grant Kim amnesty as a humanitarian gesture.[79]

Even as the Carter presidency drew to a close, the internal debate on the Kim Dae-jung case continued. On November 24, 1980, the Carter administration held a one-week-long consultation on the Kim Dae-jung case at which Gleysteen was present. Wanting to amplify pressure on the regime, Carter instructed Secretary of State Muskie to assess the urgency of South Korea's need for rice imports from the United States and Japan, given its disastrous fall harvest. On November 26, Brzezinski opposed utilizing rice imports as a bargaining chip. Both Brzezinski and Muskie believed that the administration was already doing everything that it could to save Kim's life and additional pressures could backfire. That same day, Aaron also rejected the rice option. However, unlike his two colleagues, he believed additional pressure was needed: "Only pressure will save Kim. Everything we read indicates they want to kill him. There is no such thing as counter-productive pressure with the Koreans." Aaron suggested that pursuing a diplomatic rapprochement with North Korea was a more effective means of pressuring Chun than threatening rice imports.[80]

But the Carter administration was running out of time and options. On December 1, 1980, Carter took one of the few remaining options open to him, a personal letter to Chun, asking that he "reverse or commute the court martial findings."[81] This letter was followed up by a meeting between Secretary of Defense Brown and Chun in Seoul on December 13, at which Brown reiterated the Carter administration's position on the Kim Dae-jung case. After this meeting, Gleysteen praised Brown's performance as "well timed, authoritative, and formulated in the way most likely to impress Chun rather than antagonize him." There would, however, be no follow-up by Carter or any other administration officials.[82]

On December 31, 1980, twenty days before the Reagan administration took over from the Carter administration, the ROK Supreme Court denied Kim's appeal. Using the highly confidential NODIS CHEROKEE channel, Gleysteen informed the White House of the decision and tersely noted: "The only thing of which I am certain is that we have done virtually everything possible" to save Kim's life. Based on his sources, he feared that there was nothing more the Carter administration could do to prevent Kim's execution.[83] Six minutes later, however, Gleysteen sent a second cable informing the White House that Chun had decided to commute Kim Dae-jung's sentence. This new information, Gleysteen reported, had been gleaned from Edward Poitras, a missionary who was in touch with Rev. Kang Wŏl-lyong, a member of Chun's Presidential Advisory Council and president of the NCCK.[84]

The Carter administration was unable to claim credit for this victory for two reasons. First, the Chun regime did not make the decision public until three days after Carter left office. Second, the commutation, as Gleysteen admitted, resulted from behind-the-scenes negotiations between the incoming Reagan administration and the Chun regime. On December 6, 1980, Gleysteen had learned through a "usually well informed source" that Chun had sent his wife's uncle retired Major General Yi Kyu-hwang to Washington "to sound out directly the views of the emergent Reagan administration" on the Kim Dae-jung case.[85] This meeting marked the apparent beginning of the Reagan administration's reliance on quiet diplomacy in its negotiations with the Chun regime—a development that will be discussed in greater detail in the next chapter.

Conclusion

The Kwangju crisis and its aftermath ushered in a new wave of pro-democracy and pro–human rights movements that no longer believed in the benevolence of US hegemony in the region. Like the older generation of pro-democracy activists in the 1970s, this new generation of pro-democracy activists mobilized the language of human rights. But unlike their predecessors, they utilized their knowledge of human rights politics to critically reevaluate US foreign policy. Ironically, this negative reevaluation, in part, was facilitated by an idealized and inaccurate image of US actions in 1960. Local and transnational activists compared US actions in 1980 with what they believed the United States had done in 1960 and based on this comparison found the 1980 actions morally abhorrent. This negative assessment was reinforced by the Carter administration's failure to take proactive measures against the Chun regime following the Kwangju Incident—also ironic given Carter's campaign promises. Yet, Carter failed to follow through with his campaign promise to restore morality to US foreign policy by prioritizing the promotion of human rights and democracy. Instead, advocates of quiet diplomacy and the primacy of US security interests abroad ultimately determined his administration's foreign policy objectives. This policy direction, as shown in the next chapter, became more pronounced under Ronald Reagan.

CHAPTER 7

Aftermath

Human Rights Talk, Activism, and Politics in the 1980s Democratic Transition

In May 1980, human rights activism for social justice and democracy in South Korea experienced a devastating blow when military troops crushed the Kwangju Uprising. Yet, this crackdown did not end pro-democracy activism in South Korea. Instead, as this chapter shows, within various circles—labor unions, religious communities, student groups, and newly formed opposition political parties—the language and politics of human rights remained a vital tool for articulating local grievances, uniting local pro-democracy movements, and building transnational campaigns to promote democracy and human rights. As in the 1970s, local activists translated, appropriated, and transformed universal human rights norms to address the socioeconomic and political vicissitudes they confronted. These efforts centered primarily on two issues: deplorable working conditions in factories run by national and multinational corporations and the regime's brutal interrogation methods. Local pro-democratic activists utilized these issues to demand *saengjonkwŏn* (right to subsistence) and to denounce the regime's use of torture as a human rights violation. Local and transnational activists made clear that the only redress for these grievances was the democratization of South Korea. This solution placed local and transnational activists at odds with the Reagan administration, because it believed that US Cold War security interests on the Korean peninsula required bolstering the stability of Chun's authoritarian regime.

To demonstrate human rights' centrality for local and transnational contestations for democracy in 1980s South Korea, this chapter utilizes a threefold approach. First, it illustrates how the Reagan administration's foreign policy approach impeded and propelled transnational campaigns for human rights in the 1980s. Second, it traces the evolution of local campaigns in the 1980s that linked human rights issues to the campaign for democratic reform, highlighting how this focus gradually contributed to growing cohesion among disparate pro-labor and pro-democracy groups and advanced transnational campaigns in support of local demands. As these campaigns grew in strength, transnational and local activists were able to call greater attention to the United States' tacit support for the regime's repressive policies. Increased awareness of US complicity fueled anti-Americanism and resulted in transnational human rights organizations placing substantial pressure on the United States to side with pro-democratic forces in South Korea. Moreover, the harsh countermeasures of the regime emboldened liberal internationalists in the US Congress to challenge the efficacy of quiet diplomacy and to impose stiff economic sanctions on the Chun regime. Finally, the chapter examines how regime countermeasures, US foreign policy, and growing transnational campaigns for human rights and democracy collided, forcing the ruling party to make pro-democracy concessions. In tracing these developments in the 1980s, this chapter also points to continuities and discontinuities with the 1970s.

Quiet Diplomacy and Human Rights: The Reagan Administration

Following his inauguration on January 20, 1981, President Ronald Reagan immediately signaled his administration's departure from the Carter administration's foreign policy by inviting ROK president Chun Doo-hwan for a state visit. Chun viewed the visit as an opportunity to bolster the legitimacy of his regime. However, the Reagan administration made the visit contingent upon Chun commuting Kim Dae-jung's death sentence. As we saw in the previous chapter, the Carter administration made multiple attempts without success to secure Kim's release. Running out of options and time, it reached out to the incoming Reagan administration for assistance. Against this backdrop, Reagan authorized the behind-the-scenes negotiations that saved Kim's life and awarded Chun with the first official state visit of the new administration.

The success of these closed-door negotiations provided the perfect oppor-tunity for the Reagan administration to distinguish its foreign policy ap-proach from that of its predecessor. After all, the new administration's nascent quiet diplomacy succeeded where the Carter administration's human rights policy failed. However, as this chapter shows, the diplomatic approaches of the two administrations did not differ as sharply as the Reagan administra-tion claimed. In seeking to safeguard US Cold War security interests on the Korean peninsula, the Reagan administration, like its predecessor, pursued policies aimed at safeguarding the stability of its ROK ally. Consequently, the Reagan administration's quiet diplomacy reinforced, rather than challenged, South Korea's system of political repression. At the same time, its implemen-tation sparked growing transnational criticism of the Chun regime and a deepening awareness of the US government's complicity in the regime's re-pression of political dissent.

The Reagan-Chun Summit

Reagan's invitation, as noted above, went hand in hand with a series of closed-door diplomatic negotiations on Kim Dae-jung's death sentence, which at that time was under review by the ROK Supreme Court. On the day that Chun accepted the invitation, Foreign Minister No Sin-yŏng informed Ambassa-dor William Gleysteen of Chun's intention to commute Kim's sentence im-mediately following the Supreme Court's anticipated decision upholding the death sentence.[1] The commutation would be announced prior to Chun's de-parture for Washington. Minister No noted that Washington's "restrained" handling of the affair played a critical role in Chun's decision and expressed his hope that the administration would maintain this position during the "fi-nal stages" of negotiations, as many within the military and "certain intel-lectual circles" wished to see Kim's execution carried out. This message Gleysteen relayed to Secretary of State Alexander Haig.[2]

Gleysteen saw restraint as critical for improving strained US-ROK rela-tions. Just hours prior to Chun's decision, he told Haig that the administra-tion must avoid "complicating" Chun's decision by making any "unhelpful" public statements.[3] Gleysteen recommended that Reagan send Chun a con-fidential letter in which he welcomed Chun's decision but made no further comments on the charges against Kim Dae-jung. Pointing to the successful outcome of the closed-door negotiations, Gleysteen disavowed publicly lecturing Chun on human rights issues or on the regime's "political form."[4] In short, Gleysteen defined and articulated the rationale of quiet diplomacy toward Seoul.

On January 23, 1981, immediately following the court's decision, as promised, Chun commuted Kim's sentence to life imprisonment. The commutation was accompanied by a public statement in which Chun's accommodation of international "humanitarian" concerns was highlighted. The statement conspicuously avoided the issue of "human rights" and referenced a handwritten letter of "repentance" by Kim (years later shown to have been fabricated) for "endangering national security."[5] One day later, Chun lifted martial law, which had been in effect since May 1980.

In preparation for the February 2 summit, the State Department postponed the release of its annual human rights report to avoid embarrassing Chun during his Washington visit. The report, written during the Carter administration, contained a section highly critical of the ROK government's human rights record.[6] A top White House aide also advised Reagan to commend Chun for the "statesmanlike manner in which the Kim Dae-jung decision had been handled, thus facilitating our resumption of a normal relationship."[7] In short, the administration went to great lengths to defuse criticism of the Chun regime and ensure a successful visit.

These efforts were part of a larger strategy by the Reagan administration to assist Chun in consolidating power. One week prior to Chun's arrival, the NSC reviewed a twenty-page "private" paper enumerating the difficulties Chun faced in cultivating his political legitimacy. The paper noted, among other things, that within the military "the President is disposable," if perceived as a threat to "the security and well-being of the nation."[8] On January 29, 1981 National Security Adviser Richard Allen reaffirmed to Reagan that the summit would "validate" and legitimize Chun's leadership "in a way no other single event could." In the same memo, Allen noted that Reagan should reassure Chun that the United States had no plans to withdraw troops nor to make "any unilateral moves" toward North Korea.[9] For the Reagan administration, enhancing US-ROK security ties was the overarching goal of the summit, not promoting human rights.

The Reagan administration's quiet diplomacy, however, did not go unchallenged; the transnational networks of protest established in the 1970s responded by renewing their campaigns against a US foreign policy agenda that supported anti-democratic forces in South Korea. Upon hearing of the summit, the CWU immediately sent President Reagan a telegram urging him to demand the release of Kim Dae-jung and other political prisoners.[10] Shortly thereafter, Senator Tom Harkin and thirty other US congressional members sent Reagan a joint letter that labeled Kim's trial "a travesty of justice for the Korean people" and warned that failure to place explicit pressure on the Chun regime would increase "anti-American sentiment in Korea," thereby "making it difficult for the U.S. to carry out defense and security commitments there."[11] This sentiment was echoed in another joint letter sent by leaders of thirty US Christian communities, including the NCCCUSA and the NACHRK.[12]

Despite its public show of support for the regime, the administration harbored some concerns about South Korea's human rights record. In a pre-summit internal briefing, the State Department acknowledged the regime's "authoritarian" style and its use of force against political opponents, but opted to place greater emphasis on the commutation of Kim Dae-jung's sentence and the termination of martial law. The State Department concluded that in working with the regime, Chun "should be encouraged" to pursue political liberalization.[13]

The Reagan-Chun summit sought to bolster US Cold War modernization, that is, foster economic and military development in South Korea for the purpose of stabilizing the regime and promoting US security interests. When Chun arrived at Andrews Air Force Base on February 1, 1981, Haig noted that Chun's "only worry" was facing public pressure on the Kim Dae-jung case from the United States. On the drive from the airport, Haig reassured Chun that the Reagan administration would offer "no public advice" on such "internal affairs." And if such advice was deemed necessary, it would be given in "private." The administration, Haig explained, preferred to concentrate on "critical strategic interests," such as working with Seoul to facilitate South Korea's economic recovery. The United States would provide assistance through, among other things, FMS credits and PL 480 aid.[14]

Yet, ironically, Chun chose to make democracy and human rights the primary topics of discussion during his thirty-minute meeting with Reagan. Emulating his predecessor Park Chung-hee, Chun foregrounded the difficulties of transplanting American-style democracy to Asia, arguing that South Korea must implement its brand of democracy; he expressed appreciation for Reagan's view that each nation "exists under special circumstances." He suggested that the Carter administration's "lack of consistency" had undermined the development of Korean-style democracy. He then asserted, "Korea highly values human rights and morality," but it cannot afford to lose sight of the military situation, with North Korean forces "as close to Seoul as Andrews Air Force Base is to Washington." Here too, he made a thinly veiled criticism of the Carter administration for publicly criticizing South Korea's human rights record and complimented the Reagan administration for its discretion. In response, Reagan echoed Chun's points, identifying Communism as the real enemy and criticizing his predecessor's policy for ignoring "the greatest violators of human rights, most of whom are to be found behind the bamboo and iron curtains."[15]

The joint communiqué released after the Reagan-Chun meeting made few references to human rights and democracy in South Korea; instead, it spotlighted security, economic development, and military issues. The communiqué also noted that there were "no plans to withdraw US ground forces" from South Korea and announced the resumption of bilateral consultations.[16] A few days later, Allen, pleased with the positive US press coverage and the administration's adroit deployment of quiet diplomacy, labeled the summit a success: "There has been wide recognition that the Koreans are strong allies. . . . Our side avoided striking any notes of fulsome praise of Korea which would have brought heavy press criticism. Human rights survive as a concept, but in a broadened context."[17]

Despite this seeming success, the Reagan administration's foreign policy did not go unchallenged. In May 1981, Reagan nominated Ernest Lefever for the position of assistant secretary of state for human rights and humanitarian affairs—a position previously held by Patricia Derian, an ardent human rights advocate. Lefever, a vocal critic of Carter's "public preaching and punitive policies directed against friendly and allied regimes," had previously advocated for abolishing the office for which he was nominated.[18] A strident supporter of quiet diplomacy, Lefever during his Senate confirmation hearings stressed: "We must recognize that there are moral and political limits to what the United States Government can and should do to modify the internal behavior of another sovereign state." When strong opposition to his nomination materialized, Lefever accused his detractors of being part of a "Communist-inspired" conspiracy to thwart his appointment.[19] On June 5, Lefever's nomination was defeated when five of the nine Republicans on the Foreign Relations Committee joined Democrats in rejecting Lefever's nomination. This defeat, at least for some White House officials, signaled that "saying we don't care about human rights" was not a winning formula.[20] To sway recalcitrant internationalist members of Congress and the transnational human rights groups that saw Congress as the locus for advancing human rights causes, the administration needed to find a way to incorporate human rights language into its foreign policy.

On March 31, 1981, in a speech before the Trilateral Commission, a group of roughly two hundred leading businessmen and intellectuals from Western Europe, North America, and Japan, Haig provided the first hint on how the administration would accomplish the above goal. He reassured the audience that the new administration "resoundingly" believed that "a concern for human rights is compatible with the pursuit of America's national interest." However, in defending human rights, the United States must consider "the source of the violation and the impact of our protest on the violator." Specifically, the United States must distinguish between a "totalitarian" Communist regime and an "authoritarian" regime. The former, he explained, was "actively hostile to all we represent and ideologically resistant to political change." The latter "reserved for itself absolute authority in only a few politically sensitive areas," and thus was "more likely to change" than its Communist counterpart. Because the previous administration's policy had "not [been] informed by these principles," it had facilitated the collapse of anti-Communist regimes in Vietnam, Cambodia, Iran, and Nicaragua and risked "a world remade by others hostile to our deepest convictions."[21] In short, resisting Communism, even if it required supporting authoritarian regimes, represented the best way to promote human rights.

This ideological schema soon found concrete expression in South Korea. In June 1981, upon completing his three-year ambassadorship in Seoul, Gleysteen sent Haig his recommendations for future US policy on South Korea. These recommendations included maintaining US forces in South Korea and safeguarding the regime's cooperation with US nuclear nonproliferation policies. Gleysteen also maintained that long-term political stability in South Korea could be realized through "a gradual liberalization" and "a decent observation of human rights." In making this assertion, he underscored quiet diplomacy's utility: "We will be more effective if we keep our advice mostly private." He recalled that past public criticism "tended to embolden challengers and antagonize the authorities without effective result." Elaborating, he argued: "Our voluble public complaining during the Park era may have played some role in his demise; certainly, it misled opposition forces to the incorrect assumption that we would back them up even in their more extreme demands."[22] Gleysteen's recommendations, for at least the first half of the 1980s, defined the Reagan administration's policy toward South Korea.

But the development and implementation of quiet diplomacy in South Korea was not solely the province of the Reagan administration. The Chun regime also shaped quiet diplomacy by leveraging, among other things, the possibility of South Korea developing a nuclear arsenal to gain concessions from the United States. Immediately prior to the summit, Chun suggested to Haig that he might authorize a program to develop nuclear weapons in order to consolidate his regime's power. As a result, compliance with US nuclear nonproliferation policies became a negotiating point at the summit—one that Chun deftly used to ensure that the Reagan administration would follow through on its promises, that is, maintain US troops in South Korea and refrain from any public criticism in the Kim Dae-jung case. In fact, Chun would not take this bargaining chip off the table until four months after the summit's conclusion.[23] Thus, quiet diplomacy worked bilaterally to enhance security and military ties between Washington and Seoul.

Challenging the Totalitarian-Authoritarian Distinction of Quiet Diplomacy

Transnational advocacy groups moved quickly to challenge the White House's totalitarian-authoritarian distinction. In June 1981, the NACHRK sent President Reagan a letter, emphasizing the burgeoning number of political prisoners under the Chun regime and the regime's reliance on torture to secure false confessions from political dissidents. The NACHRK also enclosed a letter from family members of political prisoners. This second letter pointedly noted: "Our aspiration [for democracy] can become a reality if you do not prop up the military regime in Korea."[24] *New York Times* journalist Henry Scott Stokes also helped create international awareness of ROK anti-regime protests and of US complicity in the regime's oppressive policies. On August 25, 1981, he published a story about eleven South Korean women who were staging sit-in protests at NCCK headquarters. These women accused the US government of having played a central role in the Kwangju Incident. As one elderly participant explained, US actions in May 1980 had transformed how South Koreans viewed Americans: "People in Korea believed that Americans were angels. . . . We believed in America as a model of democracy. But suddenly your image changed overnight. You were Satan all of a sudden."[25]

The Reagan administration and the Chun regime worked together to combat anti-American and anti-regime criticism. In May 1981, at Ambassador

Gleysteen's suggestion, ROK National Security Planning (NSP) director Yu Hak-sŏng met with Senator Edward Kennedy, a vocal critic of quiet diplomacy and of South Korea's human rights record. At the conclusion of their Washington meeting, Yu invited Kennedy to visit Seoul.[26] Three months later, Kennedy's foreign policy adviser Jan Kalicki traveled to Seoul and met with the president's chief secretary Kim Kyŏng-wŏn. Kim reassured Kalicki that Chun would not seek reelection for another presidential term and would spend his current seven-year term advancing a program of "political modernization"; this plan included withdrawing security forces from university campuses and utilizing greater restraint in handling dissident demonstrations.[27]

Despite these promises, the regime continued to crackdown on dissidents, prompting transnational advocacy groups to launch a campaign aimed at calling international attention to the South Korea situation. In September 1981, the Japan Emergency Christian Conference on Korean Problems (JECCKP) and the NACHRK, in collaboration with *New York Times* journalist Stokes, exposed cases of inmates being subjected to "electric shock" and "beatings."[28] Two weeks later, citing the JECCKP's English bulletin *Korea Communiqué*, Stokes published another article describing the regime's illegal arrest and detention of 15,000 people at one of the so-called "purification camps" (or reeducation camps).[29] The regime quickly responded to these allegations. The ROK Embassy in the United States issued a statement claiming that none of those detained in the camps were political prisoners. They were "thieves, robbers, and other criminals."[30] Against this backdrop, Richard Walker, the US ambassador to South Korea, informed Haig in October 1981 that the Chun regime, like its predecessor, maintained domestic stability through comprehensive control over every sector of society. In sum, Walker saw no signs of political liberalization.[31]

Nevertheless, the Reagan administration remained unwavering in its commitment to a minimalist human rights orientation. In October 1981, the administration submitted a second nominee for the position of assistant secretary of state for human rights and humanitarian affairs—Elliott Abrams. Abrams, unlike Lefever, saw human rights advocacy as a valid foreign policy objective. In fact, he described it as "the very purpose of foreign policy." However, Abrams, a Cold War hawk, equated human rights promotion with the moral and ideological struggle against Communism. Although Abrams's avowal of human rights placated Congress and allowed for his successful confirmation, it did not fundamentally change the Reagan administration's foreign policy approach, as it reaffirmed the totalitarian-authoritarian distinction advanced by Haig and UN Ambassador Jeane Kirkpatrick.[32]

In fact, quiet diplomacy became an effective tool in diverting attention from human rights issues in South Korea. When the 1981 annual human rights report was finally released in February 1982, the report's tone, contrary to expectations, was quite mild in assessing human rights violation in South Korea. For example, it included no firsthand accounts of the torture of political prisoners. Instead, the report focused on the government's preparations for lifting martial law, noting that "the legislature enacted 189 laws that profoundly affected the political system."[33]

The Reagan administration, like its predecessor, spotlighted amnesties of political prisoners as proof that its foreign policy was contributing to liberalization in South Korea. To celebrate the one-year anniversary of Chun's inauguration, the ROK government announced "with much fanfare" the commutation of Kim Dae-jung's life sentence to twenty years' imprisonment. Another 297 political prisoners were also granted reduced sentences or amnesty.[34] Three weeks later during a visit to Seoul, Secretary of Defense Caspar Weinberger briefly noted the role of "private" discussions in fostering progress in human rights, before turning his attention to America's "unswerving commitment" to South Korean security.[35]

Pro-democracy advocates, however, were not impressed by the highly publicized amnesties, as it left the system of repression intact. In attacking the regime, they also targeted US complicity. In late March 1982, a group of theology students torched the American Cultural Center in Pusan to protest the US government's role in suppressing anti-regime demonstrations in Kwangju. In early June 1982, some female electronic workers of the Control Data Corporation, as illustrated below, held two Americans hostage for nine hours. The insensitive responses of American officials to protesters' demands only exacerbated the already volatile situation. For example, Ambassador Walker called dissidents "spoiled brats," and General Wickham derided them as "field mice." Such actions by US officials prompted Rev. Pak Hyŏng-gyu and scores of other ecumenical leaders in a letter to President Reagan to decry the administration's disregard for the democratic demands of the people.[36] A month later, at a breakfast meeting with Pak and other ecumenical leaders, Vice President George H. W. Bush chastised the attendees for focusing exclusively on human rights violations by authoritarian states friendly to the United States.[37] Yet, such remonstrations did little to staunch public criticism of US foreign policy. In a *New York Times* op-ed, historian Bruce Cumings succinctly captured the potential implications of this dispute for US hegemony: "The biggest loss, for Koreans and Americans, is the end of hopes that Washington would nurture the sprouts of democracy. Now there will be the devil to pay."[38]

This public dispute on US foreign policy in South Korea carried over to joint congressional hearings on reconciling strategic interests and human rights in Asia. In the opening session on August 19, 1982, former Ambassador Gleysteen testified that "only a minority" in Asia were worried about human rights, whereas "the majority of Koreans saw Kwangju as a threat, and they wanted it cauterized."[39] Former assistant secretary of state Richard Holbrooke also voiced opposition to incorporating human rights into US foreign policy; he called on Congress to cease publication of its annual human rights report, noting that "public attacks on friendly countries are unproductive and undesirable" for national interests.[40]

The hearings became more contentious in early September 1982 when Congress became aware that Commerce Secretary Malcolm Baldridge had approved the sale of high-voltage shock batons to the South Korean police. Several congressional members denounced the sale on grounds it violated Section 502B of the Foreign Assistance Act prohibiting, among other things, the sale of "crime control and detection instruments and equipment" to a gross violator of human rights. The strong congressional reaction along with negative press coverage and a call-in campaign to the White House forced the Reagan administration to suspend the sale indefinitely.[41] At a follow-up session on September 21, Don Bonker, a senior member of the House Foreign Affairs Committee and chairman of the Subcommittee on International Economic Policy and Trade, labeled the aborted sale further evidence of the Reagan administration's anti-human rights orientation. In his testimony, human rights scholar and activist Edward J. Baker argued that "quiet diplomacy" had done nothing to improve the political situation in South Korea. In making this assertion, he acknowledged that quiet diplomacy "can often ameliorate the situation of an individual or a small group of individuals" but "without public pressure, it is unlikely to bring about systematic improvement."[42]

Despite growing public disillusionment with quiet diplomacy, the Reagan administration made no adjustments to its foreign policy. Behind closed doors, the crux of its human rights efforts in South Korea centered on securing the release of Kim Dae-jung as proof of South Korea's commitment to political liberalization. In November 1982, Pharis Harvey of the NACHRK wrote Reagan demanding that his administration dedicate equal diligence to securing the release of political prisoners of authoritarian regimes as they did to those of totalitarian regimes. He cited the administration's recent success in securing the freedom of Polish dissident Lech Walesa and asked that the White House devote the same energy to Kim's case.[43] On December 20, 1982, the US deputy chief of mission in Seoul spoke with Kim's wife, Yi Hŭi-ho, about a plan to bring Kim to the United States. In this conversation, the deputy chief sought Yi's promise that Kim would "not make any political statements" and would abstain from anti-regime activities for a substantial period of time if allowed to leave South Korea.[44] Four days later, Kim Dae-jung was released and the State Department triumphantly proclaimed: "We believe the action embodies a spirit of reconciliation and will make a further contribution to political harmony in South Korea." The State Department credited the success to "many months of quiet yet intense pressure" and the regime's desire "to improve the political atmosphere."[45] In short, Kim Dae-jung's release was depicted as another victory for quiet diplomacy and for democratization in South Korea.

However, the successful resolution of Kim Dae-jung's case accelerated criticism of US foreign policy, since Kim utilized his newly acquired direct access to the American press to publicize South Korean grievances against the United States. In an interview with the *New York Times*, Kim insisted that the US administrations, including the current Reagan administration, "helped dictatorial regimes in the name of anti-Communism, security and economic rehabilitation."[46] On January 5, 1983, he repeated this accusation in a televised interview with CNN. Asked to comment on the State Department's assertion that quiet diplomacy was facilitating "a more liberal human rights stance" in South Korea, Kim tersely replied that quiet diplomacy was "not enough." The United States, he explained, "should advocate its human rights principles openly and strongly." He then clarified that he wanted only "moral support" from the United States, because the US government too often disregarded the wishes of the Korean people: "For example, after Park's assassination our people felt this is a chance to restore democracy. . . . And then America openly declared its attitude to support democracy. But once Chun staged the coup, America kept silent. And Korean troops . . . who were under American commanders' control massacred people."[47]

For two years, Kim continued to spread this message, giving speeches at universities such as Harvard and Emory, in which he attacked the accuracy of the State Department's human rights reports and called on the United

States to provide South Korea moral leadership. This message reached an even broader audience thanks to activist scholars such as Ch'oi Sŏng-il and Edward J. Baker who in concert with the NACHRK and the International Christian Network published his addresses in the ad hoc bulletin *Korea Scope*.[48] Yet Kim never felt that he had been fully successful "in persuading the American government to change its Korea policy."[49]

As a result, in November 1984, Kim announced his plans to return to Korea. Both Kim and his American supporters realized that by returning to Korea, he risked reimprisonment or execution. Efforts were made to convince the Reagan administration to intervene on Kim's behalf to ensure his safety. However, some of Kim's supporters, such as former assistant secretary of state for human rights Patricia Derian, held out little hope of such an intervention, noting the Reagan administration "swallowed the Aquino assassination with more equanimity than one would expect."[50] The obvious parallels between Kim's announced return and the ill-fated 1983 return of Philippine opposition leader Benigno Aquino Jr. only intensified the debate on US foreign policy and its support of authoritarian ally regimes.

This debate became more acrimonious when violence erupted shortly after Kim's plane landed on February 8, 1985. A thirty-eight-member delegation, including two US congressmen (Edward Feighan and Thomas Foglietta), former assistant secretary of state Derian, former US ambassador to El Salvador Robert E. White, and Professor Bruce Cumings, accompanied Kim to ensure his safety. According to the delegation, after the plane landed in Seoul, the South Korean police forcefully separated Kim from his protectors. In an interview with the *New York Times*, White recounted events: "They cut off the majority of our delegation. They tore me away and threw me to the ground." Foglietti added, "They just bodily picked up Mr. Kim to put him in an elevator. He resisted and they started kicking and punching him." Derian demanded that Washington cancel Chun's planned visit to the United States, because it was no longer tenable for the Reagan administration to "promote this country as a democracy."[51]

In response to these charges, the Reagan administration downplayed the ROK police's use of force and blamed the delegation for the incident. Ambassador Walker told reporters: "As I look on it, I cannot help but believe that leaders of the group wanted the confrontation and media event."[52] President Reagan cited "bad judgment on both sides" as the cause of the incident and lamented that it had detracted from "the great strides in democracy" made by the ROK regime. In an appearance on the NBC morning news show *Today*,

Secretary of State George P. Shultz dismissed the incident as a "scuffle" that stemmed from a "misunderstanding" over security arrangements.[53]

The Reagan administration's efforts to recast the incident in a more favorable light largely failed. Local opposition to the Chun regime grew as did debates on quiet diplomacy's effectiveness in bringing about systemic change. The New Korea Democratic Party (NKDP), an opposition party formed in January 1985, won an unprecedented 67 out of 276 seats in the February 1985 National Assembly elections. Yet, as William J. Butler noted in an interview with the *Washington Post*, this victory did not portend South Korea's imminent return to democratic rule. The constitution guaranteed that 57 percent of the deputies to the National Assembly belonged to the ruling party. When asked if the Reagan administration's quiet diplomacy advanced democracy in South Korea, Butler offered a measured response: "I've used it myself on many occasions and sometimes it works, but when it doesn't, you have to go public."[54]

Anti-American Arsons and Quiet Diplomacy

The Reagan administration also utilized quiet diplomacy to intervene in the death sentence cases of two South Koreans found guilty of setting fire to the American Cultural Center in Pusan. In January 1983, President Reagan received a letter from Pharis Harvey on behalf of the "NACHRK, its member churches and movements and all other organizations that have joined this effort." The letter included petitions, containing the signatures of 4,087 persons representing forty-one US states. As Harvey noted, although the language varied from petition to petition, there was a common theme: clemency for the two men accused of setting the fire in Pusan in March 1982. According to the letter, one of the men, Mun Pu-sik, confessed that he set the fire because he wanted the United States to realize its error in supporting dictatorship. Mun had "voluntarily surrendered." The other prisoner, Kim Hyŏn-jang, the letter stated, was falsely accused of participating in the arson. Harvey ended his letter by reminding the president that such cases fueled anti-Americanism: "Mr. President, we know you share our concern about the deteriorating attitudes of many Korean people toward the United States, and that our hope of justice tempered with mercy is your hope." Copies of the letter and accompanying petitions also were sent to Thomas P. O'Neill, Speaker of the House, Howard Baker, Senate majority leader, and Lew Byong-hyun (Ryu Pyŏng-hŏn), the ROK ambassador to the United States.[55]

Given the ongoing Kim Dae-jung case and congressional concerns about US support of anti-democratic regimes, the petition campaign garnered the Reagan administration's immediate attention. As with the Kim Dae-jung case, a sense of urgency prevailed because it was assumed that the ROK Supreme Court would uphold the earlier court's decision. On February 4, 1983, Shultz sent a priority message to Walker in Seoul authorizing him to approach the Chun regime "at any level you deem appropriate to seek commutation of those sentences." In the message, Shultz underscored that any discussions of this issue should be "entirely private" and that if the ROK government mentioned "legal aspects of the case," he "should demur." Instead, Shultz advised Walker to take a "political" approach. Specifically, he recommended leveraging past congressional hostility and the regime's desire for congressional approval of FMS credits: "While clearly there should be no link between the ROKG's handling of the Pusan arson case and congressional consideration of the most important Korea-related issue now before it, that of FMS funding, Koreans' concern with the latter issue may nonetheless have heightened their usual sensitivity to congressional attitudes."[56] On March 8, when the court as expected upheld the death sentences, Walker passed a "non-paper" position to Foreign Minister Yi Bŏm-sŏk.[57] On March 14, NSP director No Sin-yŏng informed Walker of Chun's plan to commute the sentences of the two arsonists. In this "confidential" message, Director No emphasized that Chun made his decision "in accordance with the non-paper [formula]" as well as "out of consideration for relations with 'UNCLE SAM.'"[58]

In commending Chun's "correct and courageous decision," Walker noted to Shultz that the decision "confirm[ed] the effectiveness of our quiet diplomacy in the human rights field" and "serve[d] to strengthen our relations."[59] Pleased with the outcome, Washington officials proposed that at his upcoming meeting with Foreign Minister Yi, Reagan should state that Chun's decisions in both the Kim Dae-jung case and the Pusan arson case had "greatly reduced criticism here" and had been "very beneficial for U.S.-Korean relations." Reagan should also reaffirm the administration's commitment to quiet diplomacy as the preferred approach to human rights issues.[60] At the actual meeting on May 3, 1983, Reagan extolled Chun's decision as a move in "the direction of greater participatory democracy."[61]

Although religious and intellectual dissidents urged Reagan to take "concrete" action for human rights during his scheduled visit to South Korea in November 1983, Reagan adroitly sidestepped these appeals by shifting the focus to recent incidents of Communist aggression.[62] Speaking before the ROK National Assembly, Reagan condemned the Russian government for offering "denials" rather than "condolences" to the families of the 269 killed on board the ROK jet that strayed into Soviet airspace. He, then, broached the Rangoon bombing by North Koreans that left nineteen South Koreans dead, including four top ROK officials, to draw a sharp contrast between the two Koreas: "North Korea is one of the most repressive societies on earth. It does not prosper, it arms. Let the world look long and hard at both sides of the 38th parallel and then ask: Which side enjoys a better life?" Only once this contrast was established did Reagan turn to the development of democratic political institutions in South Korea, describing it as "the surest means to build the national consensus that is the foundation of true security." Reagan modulated this assertion by recognizing how hard it was to make advances on this front "when, even as we speak, a shell from the North could destroy this assembly." He congratulated the Chun regime on its "farsighted plans" for the constitutional transfer of power in 1988; in fact, by June 1984, Chun and his few top aides reviewed a "top secret" document on measures to maintain his power in the post-presidency era.[63] By raising the specter of Communism, Reagan succeeded in downplaying the regime's suppression of political opponents and justified continued US military and economic support of South Korea.

Mobilizing Human Rights as the Language of Pro-Democracy Protests

Even as the Reagan administration touted quiet diplomacy's victories, local and international pro-democracy advocates were organizing campaigns to expose the lack of any significant progress toward democracy in South Korea. As in the 1970s, these campaigns drew on international human rights norms to give voice to local suffering. By translating, appropriating, and reimagining the human rights lexicon, local activists linked their campaigns to transnational human rights campaigns and won an international audience for local grievances. This section traces the emergence of two such campaigns: the campaign for *saengjonkwŏn* (right to subsistence) and the anti-torture campaign. It shows how these campaigns, at first localized and isolated within certain fields, came to provide the foundation for a pro-democratic, anti-regime transnational campaign that implicated US foreign policy in perpetuating dictatorship abroad and pushed South Korea in the direction of democracy.

Saengjonkwŏn Struggles and Human Rights Coalitions

By May 1982, the second anniversary of the Kwangju massacre, Chun Doohwan had firmly established a level of repressive rule that made it difficult for pro-democracy groups to wage an organized resistance campaign. The regime—a handwritten note acquired by the NACHRK in late 1981 explained—had established control over all religious assembly, implemented "press guidance" (podo chich'im), and silenced its opponents through torture.[64] Yet, workers from several labor fields continued to organize protest actions. In these actions, local protesters succeeded in garnering the support of transnational human rights advocacy groups by translating their socioeconomic struggles into human rights issues. These workers spoke of saengjonkwŏn, that is, the right to subsistence, and denounced the government's use of torture against those who called for better working conditions and challenged the existing political order. Although these labor protest actions did not reach critical mass until June 1987, they allowed local protesters to create transnational coalitions that brought international attention to the regime's human rights violations and to US foreign policy aimed at stabilizing Chun's authoritarian regime.[65]

On May 22, 1982, the Wŏnp'ung Textile Company, a subsidiary of the Kukje Company, a major international export manufacturer of shoes, targeted the company's democratically run female union. As one of the first independent unions organized in 1970s South Korea, it had been the target of repeated crackdowns by the company and the ROK government. On this occasion, the company mobilized male workers to block the union leadership from accessing union offices. When the women tried to enter the offices, the men sexually assaulted and threatened to kill the women. In mid-June 1982, the women staged public demonstrations at various subway stations to publicize the violent measures used by the company. The police stopped the protests, arrested the women, and forced them to admit their ties to the Yŏngdŭngp'o UIM, the ecumenical group that helped organize the women in 1972.

Following these arrests, the union chair, Chŏng Sŏn-sun, went to the CWU and asked for their assistance "to resolve human rights violations against female workers." By October 1982, eighty workers had required hospitalization for injuries sustained at the hands of company and government operatives. Another four hundred workers had sustained minor injuries, and most of the union's thirty-two executive union members had been forced into hiding to avoid arrest. The union also requested that the Yŏngdŭngp'o UIM appeal to the NCCK's Human Rights Committee for legal assistance for those arrested. In addition to providing legal support, Pharis Harvey of the NACHRK utilized the organization's transnational connections to publicize the female workers' plight in the United States and elsewhere. Harvey also wrote Arnold Hiatt, a spokesperson for the American shoe import industry, asking him to utilize his influence to persuade the president of the Kukje Company to desist from anti-union activities.[66]

At roughly the same time as the above incident, a Korean factory affiliated with the American-owned Control Data Corporation, also became the site of a transnational contestation on labor and human rights. In 1967, the company opened the first computer-tech factory in South Korea; by 1979, it had become $24 million export industry. As at the Wŏnp'ung Textile Company, UIM activists had helped the female employees establish an independent democratic union in the early 1970s; the union actively worked for better labor conditions and for greater worker solidarity. In May 1980, the new regime put in place so-called "labor union purification" to squelch labor disputes that had quadrupled during the Seoul Spring. Under this law, Control Data Corporation was forced to dismiss the union's leadership. In March 1982, amid growing internal tensions, the company fired the former union president Yi Yŏng-sun and five other union members. On June 4, 1982, when union leaders met with representatives from the Minnesota home office about having the fired workers reinstated, the South Korean police stormed the meeting on the pretext of rescuing the representatives from a hostage situation. Forty union leaders and members were arrested.[67]

The dispute, however, did not end with these arrests; the company working in conjunction with the regime continued to crackdown on union activity at the factory, arresting more union leaders. On July 16, a group of male employees assaulted acting union president Han Myŏng-hoe and other members, including several pregnant workers. Although a labor inspector and police officers were on-site, they did not intervene. The union issued a public appeal, describing the abuse that they suffered as "the deprivation of the right to subsistence" and as "human rights violations against female workers." They also accused the company and the ROK government of orchestrating the male employees' actions and drew parallels to the "human excrement incident" at the Dong-il Textile factory in February 1978. They demanded the cessation of government-sponsored violence in the workplace, the release of incarcerated union workers, and the cancellation of the company's plans to close the factory.[68]

National and transnational organizations utilized the incident to call attention to human rights violations under the Chun regime and to the US government's "unjust handling" of the incident. On July 26, six days after the factory's closure, CPAJ sent President Reagan a confidential letter, which accused the company and the Reagan administration of acting unfairly. The company, the letter stated, "enslaved the women workers" in its pursuit of "excessive profits." The US State Department exacerbated the situation by labeling the protesting union workers as "leftists," thus echoing the regime's ideological stigmatization of labor activism and of UIM groups. Such commentary, the letter continued, posed a "profound challenge to workers' right to subsistence" and constituted a "shameful blunder" that demonstrated contempt for the "spirit" of the UDHR. The letter cautioned the Reagan administration against making any other hostile interventions in pro-labor and pro-democracy actions in South Korea.[69] Roughly a week later, the NCCK's Human Rights Committee sent a similar letter to the US secretary of state.[70] The Chun regime responded to the internationalization of the dispute by reenacting the 1975 Anti-Slander Law.

The human rights grievances vocalized by union workers during these grassroots disputes were more fully articulated at the NCCK's annual consultations on human rights. In October 1982, participants first reaffirmed "the responsibility of the Church's mission" to uphold human dignity and human rights as "divine rights given by God." They decried the systematic oppression of laborers, farmers, and the poor, whose right to subsistence had been sacrificed to "the false [idol] of economic growth."[71] In 1983, the consultation "Public Welfare and Human Rights" (Minsaeng kwa inkwŏn) centered on how foreign debts, economic inequality, and anti-nuclear warheads on the Korean peninsula detracted from South Koreans' right to subsistence.[72] In December 1983, the NCCK's Human Rights Committee coordinated a ten-day prayer event in twelve South Korean cities to publicize recent human rights violations, including the regime's use of torture to extract false confessions from prisoners.[73]

The Korean Catholic community also campaigned for human rights, which they too defined as including socioeconomic rights. To celebrate the 1983 International Human Rights Day, the Catholic Bishops' Conference of

Korea (CBCK) organized "Human Rights Sunday." As part of the event, the Catholic Commission for Justice and Peace (CCJP) issued a statement in which they expressed concern about growing economic inequality and the government's use of the National Security Law to suppress opposition. They also called on the state to protect the "right to subsistence" of workers and farmers.[74] The following year's consultation "Assuring the Right to Subsistence" utilized Pope Paul VI's 1967 encyclical *Populorum progressio* (On the development of peoples) to define "development" (*kaebel*) and to delineate a healthy, balanced relationship between "economic development and right to subsistence." This emphasis on balance, they asserted, meant that income, growth, and utility did not suffice to measure "development"; individual opportunities, capabilities, freedoms, and rights were also important factors.[75]

The Christian churches' attention to human rights seemingly had an effect, as on the eve of Pope John Paul II's planned visit to Seoul, the Chun regime began loosening its controls over political dissidents. For a "good-size majority" in South Korea, this "liberalization gesture" (*yuhwa choch'i*) was nothing more than a strategy aimed at improving the regime's human rights image prior to the papal visit in early May 1984. Others attributed the liberalization to Chun's growing confidence in his control over the military and state bureaucracy, while yet another group argued that the liberalization simply reflected the regime's past inability to stop student protests through crackdowns. The CIA chief in Seoul posited that the liberalization was an effort to lower political tensions prior to national elections scheduled for early 1985.[76]

But whatever the cause, the liberalization measures set 350 student prisoners free, allowed another 1,300 expelled students to return to school if they agreed to abstain from political activities, and removed 200 dissidents from the political blacklist. The liberalization measures, however, introduced no change to the system of rule. Although newspapers appeared to have a slightly freer hand in reporting anti-government statements made during National Assembly debates, state-imposed guidelines about what could appear in print still applied. Similarly, the political blacklist remained intact, and 100 dissidents, including Kim Dae-jung and Kim Young-sam, remained on the list. "They're tinkering with the system," Kim Young-sam noted in an interview, "but the basic problems of achieving democracy remain."[77] And the CIA chief in Seoul predicted if students renewed their protests, the regime would suspend liberalization.[78]

Although the CIA chief's prescient warning ultimately proved true, this temporary liberalization opened a political space in which grassroots pro-democracy groups, particularly student groups, were able to articulate their socioeconomic and political demands as human rights issues. With the start of the academic year in March 1984, student activists eagerly took advantage of the government's liberalization to launch campaigns for campus liberalization (*chayurhwa*) or democratization (*minjuhwa*). The following September, the democratic student association (Ch'onghaksaenghoe) reopened. In 1980, the government shut down this association and replaced it with a paramilitary student organization (Hakto hoguktan). The returned students (*pokhaksaeng*) renewed their political activism, but their activism gained a new emphasis. As historian Namhee Lee shows, students began pursuing socioeconomic and political change through the creation of solidarity movements with farmers and workers. These efforts led to the emergence of the "student-labor alliance" (*nohak yŏndae*).[79] Renewed student activism also focused on the upcoming 1985 national elections. By February 1985, the Committee for Promotion of Democracy (Minjuhwa Ch'ujin Wiwŏnhoe), a nationwide student organization, had been formed. To mark the anniversary of the 1929 anticolonial protest, student activists called for Chun's resignation. Ten days later, 264 students staged a sit-in at the ruling party's headquarters to demand the revision of labor laws, the end of press censorship, the guarantee of the right to subsistence, and other pro-democracy measures.[80]

Other pro-democracy and anti-regime movements also gained momentum during this period. In spring 1984, former union leaders initiated a campaign to restore the P'yŏnghwa Market (Ch'ŏnggye) Clothing and Textile Trade Union dissolved by the government in 1981. As part of this campaign, they organized public forums, and in March 1984, an alliance of union leaders, students, and other labor activists organized two large-scale demonstrations in the streets of Seoul at which violent confrontations with police occurred.

Secret blacklists (*pŭllaengnisŭt'ŭ*), created by the government in 1978 to bar labor activists from employment, also came under attack.[81] In December 1983, Kim Yong-ja and Sŏ Ki-hwa, blacklisted for union activities at the T'aep'yŏng Textile Company and the Samik Musical Instrument Company respectively, issued "The Fired Workers' Declaration of Human Rights." By early 1984, fired workers had joined forces with *chaeya* and student groups to protest this policy. Their activism forced the Ministry of Labor in May 1984 to acknowledge publicly the clandestine policy of blacklisting.[82] At roughly the same time this campaign was underway, farmers were demanding improved conditions, such as the reduction of debt, stabilization of farm prices, and the democratization of farmers' associations. Young adult activism was also on the rise. In 1983, the National Youth Alliance for Democracy (NYAD) emerged. The following year, its women's bureau identified three basic rights denied female workers: (1) a right to a subsistence wage; (2) a right to a reasonable workday; and (3) a right to a work environment free from sexual harassment and abuse.[83]

In the mid-1980s, these grassroots human rights campaigns continued to develop in conjunction with pro-democracy protests. In April, the NYAD released an open complaint to the Minister of Domestic Affairs in which the group articulated the dire socioeconomic hardships experienced by workers due to low wages and long working hours. Seoul National University students organized a committee focused on "people's rights to subsistence," believing that pro-democratic actions must also take into account the economic well-being of the people.[84]

This emphasis on the relationship between development, economic rights, and democratic political reform was also highlighted by the NCCK. At its annual consultation on human rights in June 1985, 136 participants attended sessions on topics such as Third World activism and the struggles in the fields and on industrial development and the problem of air pollution.[85] In July, the NCCK's Human Rights Committee wrote the president of the Haet'ai Confectionery factory to protest the company's violent suppression of democratic union activity. The letter demanded the reinstatement of workers fired for participating in union activities; it also protested violence against female workers and the blacklisting of fired employees.[86]

Political tensions continued to grow as labor rights became a central issue in the struggle for democracy. By November 1986, Labor Minister Yi Hŏn-gi had ordered fourteen labor groups to disband as part of a concerted effort to weaken the connection between UIM activists and workers. Since the late 1960s, UIM activists had been organizing meetings at which workers could discuss low wages and long hours as well as learn self-advocacy skills. This alliance between secular workers and Christian labor organizations acquired a new dimension when student activists in the 1980s went underground as "disguised workers." As Namhee Lee demonstrates, "Their willingness to forego their middle-class futures and share the life of the

worker—the discourse of moral privilege—brought further societal attention
to labor, thereby shifting the terms and grounds of public debate on labor."[87]
Disguised student workers helped organize strikes, and when the government
arrested strikers, they smuggled out, copied, and widely circulated the testimony of imprisoned workers. In these circulated accounts, they emphasized
the correlation between democratic state building and worker protection. By
early 1987, they had succeeded in elevating local struggles on labor and the
right to subsistence into transnational contestations on human rights.

Anti-Torture Campaigns for Democracy

In tandem with the campaign for the right to subsistence, torture also became a central issue in the contestation for democracy in South Korea in the
1980s. As we saw in Chapters 1 and 3, in 1973, AI Korea actively participated
in AI's international anti-torture campaign and by 1975, pro-democracy
movements in South Korea regularly called attention to the government's
use of torture in violation of international human rights standards.
However, prior to the mid-1980s, these efforts received only limited national and international attention, in part because of US government action.
For example, when one of the defendants in the Pusan arson case discussed
earlier in this chapter alleged torture, the US State Department immediately looked into the allegations but opted for a "private approach" to assure
the "preservation of stability in Korea."[88] But by the mid-1980s, multiple
factors—the failure of the regime's liberalization gesture, the development of
worker-student solidarity, global attention on the region due to the 1986
Asian Games and 1988 Summer Olympics in Seoul, changing international political norms, and shifts in US foreign policy that national and
international protesters utilized to their advantage—had combined so
that now Korean pro-democracy struggles emerged front and center on the
international stage.

The first South Korean torture incident that developed into a major transnational human rights campaign began on September 4, 1985, when Kim
Kŭn-t'ae, the founder of the NYAD, was detained along with twenty-two
other South Koreans by the Police Anti-Communist Bureau for allegedly instigating protests and other activities against the government in violation of
the National Security Law. When Kim's wife In Chae-gŭn saw him at the
Prosecutors' Office on September 26, 1985, he told her that he had been
"beaten, tied up, given electric shocks, and forced to swallow water laced with

red peppers in salt" in an effort to force him to confess to being a North Korean agent—a crime punishable by death. His wife approached the NCCK about her husband's torture, and they addressed it at their Thursday Prayer Meeting, an event that since 1974 had focused on publicizing pro-democracy and human rights issues. By mid-October 1985, AI had launched an investigation into the regime's use of torture to secure false confessions. In a tape recording smuggled out of South Korea by a NYAD member, the relatives of other detainees made similar allegations.[89]

In October 1985, a host of pro-democracy and human rights advocacy groups, including the NCCK's Human Rights Committee, the CPAJ, the KSCF, and the NYAD, launched the Ad Hoc Committee Against Torture and the Fabrication of Spies (ACTS, Komun Kongdaewi). Together with the Council for the Promotion of Democracy and the NKDP, the ACTS issued a statement condemning the regime's use of torture to secure false confessions of espionage. To show its support, the Human Rights Committee of the Korean Bar Association sent a group of investigators to the Seoul Detention Center. A Korean-American media outlet reported and communicated this news to other media outlets and human rights groups in the United States.[90] In November 1985, 120 pro-democracy leaders, including South Korea's two most prominent opposition leaders, Kim Dae-jung and Kim Young-sam, took part in a three-day protest against the government's use of torture. The protesters issued a statement calling for the resignation of Home Minister Chŏng Sŏk-mo and for the cessation of torture.[91]

In December 1985, Kim Kŭn-t'ae testified at his trial that he had been tortured in the Anti-Communist Bureau Offices at National Police Headquarters in Namyŏng-dong. As evidence, he pointed to "a scab" and asserted that "the torture had been planned from the start," as part of a systematic effort to gain false confessions from political dissidents. AI, the NACHRK, and other international advocacy groups publicized his testimony.[92] American television outlets, such as CNN, provided extensive coverage of the case. However, the Reagan administration secretly prohibited the American Forces Korean Network from broadcasting this coverage in South Korea; this restriction would only come to light two years later.[93]

The campaign for Kim Kŭn-t'ae inspired other anti-torture campaigns. For example, in 1986 Kwŏn In-suk was arrested for falsifying job application documents. Kwŏn, a student activist, concealed her university background so that she could gain factory employment to help organize factory workers into a trade union. After her arrest, like many female detainees, she was subjected to sexual torture. To call attention to sexual torture by police investigators, she staged a hunger strike that gained the attention of other POCs and of various national and transnational advocacy groups. Through her lawyer, she filed a complaint against her interrogator for severe sexual abuse, and after an investigation, he was fired. However, the government refused to indict the police officer, claiming that she exaggerated her complaint for the purpose of "damaging the prestige of law enforcement agencies and abetting and escalating revolutionary anti-establishment struggles."[94] In December 1986, she was convicted and sentenced to eighteen months' imprisonment.

But Kwŏn's legal case did not end here. A group of 166 attorneys filed a petition with the Seoul High Court seeking reconsideration of her criminal complaint; their petition was rejected, but they appealed to the Supreme Court and won. This victory was achieved against the backdrop of government censorship of the press. For example, newspapers were required to publish the entire prosecutorial report. This report described Kwŏn's allegations of physical abuse and rape as groundless fabrications and part of a Communist plot. The guidelines also specified that "the details of accusations made by attorneys for the anti-government side or the NCCK, and the communiqué about the incident published by other women's associations, must not be reported."[95] The Supreme Court victory led to the perpetrator's incarceration. In 1989 Kwŏn received a reparation payment that provided the seed money for the Labor Human Rights Center (Nodong Inkwŏn Sentŏ).[96]

Transnational Contestations on Democracy in South Korea

In February 1986, the NKDP initiated a mass drive to collect nationwide ten million signatures in support of amending the constitution to allow for direct popular election in the upcoming 1988 presidential election. Opponents of the regime feared that without direct elections the ruling Democratic Justice Party and the authoritarian Chun regime would succeed in manipulating elections to their advantage. The Chun regime's response to this action was immediate. The signature drive was declared illegal; more than two hundred political dissidents, including Kim Dae-jung, Kim Young-sam, and NKDP president Yi Min-u, were placed under house arrest; scores of others were taken into custody for questioning, and police blockaded the entrances to opposition party offices.[97]

The crackdown was sharply criticized by the Reagan administration. The State Department dismissed the regime's claim that the nation's petition law did not allow collecting signatures for constitutional revision and called upon the regime to lift all restrictions.[98] However, many local and transnational activists did not believe that this statement went far enough, given that the same month the Reagan administration played a direct role in the overthrow of right-wing dictatorships in Haiti and in the Philippines. US actions in these countries prompted some to demand that the Reagan administration play a similar role in facilitating democratic transition in South Korea. For example, Eric P. Schwartz and Holly Burkhalter of Asia Watch wrote an op-ed for the *New York Times*, asking the Reagan administration to send a special envoy to Seoul to meet with pro-democratic actors and to declare openly that the United States would support neither "the regime's monopolization of power nor an undemocratic election that deprives South Koreans of an opportunity to choose their own leader."[99]

South Korean Christian church groups, both Protestant and Catholic, were also becoming more vocal in their opposition to the regime. On March 9, 1986, in a sermon that was unusual for its political content, Cardinal Kim Su-hwan told worshippers that the Chun regime must introduce the necessary constitutional revisions so that a successor could be chosen by direct election. Although Cardinal Kim did not directly reference the opposition's petition drive, his sermon made clear that the only way to achieve "national reconciliation" was through constitutional reform. Kim also repeated the opposition's comparison between the Chun regime and the recently deposed Marcos regime in the Philippines, warning that the South Korean government should not be so quick to dismiss the similarities: "Before they argue that Korea is different from the Philippines, political leaders must first show to the Korean people that Korea is free of corruption, torture, political oppression, rule by a handful of families, and violation of human rights, which were dominant in the Philippines." Both Kim Dae-Jung and Kim Young-sam attended the sermon; their presence in the front row, while outside more than 150 anti-government student activists marched, clearly demonstrated that the campaign for constitutional reform had gained the support of a broader spectrum of the population—the major opposition party, religious leaders, Christian human rights organizations, student activists, and college professors.[100] The US Congress also indicated its support for constitutional revision in South Korea through its endorsement of House Congressional Resolution 261 and Senate Congressional Resolution 100, "expressing the sense of the

Congress that the civil and political rights of Kim Dae-jung be restored" and that "the purpose of United States assistance to the Republic of Korea shall be to promote democracy in the Republic of Korea."[101]

In response to this pressure from human rights activists and the US Congress, the Reagan administration began reshaping its policy on promoting human rights and democracy abroad. In a policy statement delivered before Congress in mid-March 1986, Reagan claimed credit for ousting dictatorships in Haiti, the Philippines, and Chile and vowed in the name of human rights to "oppose tyranny in whatever form, whether of the left or right." This policy statement departed from his administration's earlier stance that authoritarian right-wing dictatorships should be treated differently than "totalitarian" Marxist regimes. However, US officials quickly clarified that this shift should not be interpreted as the abandonment of this distinction. As one White House official cautioned, Reagan's policy statement "should not be regarded as a hunting license to undermine friendly states, which often face external threats, and which can over time evolve nonviolently to evermore democratic forms of government." Thus, how this policy shift impacted South Korea remained unclear, especially given that Reagan's statement made no direct reference to South Korea.[102] Thus, human rights activists remained skeptical, with some viewing the shift as an attempt "to cloak the President's appeal for funding for the Nicaraguan contras, then under consideration in Congress, in the language of democracy and human rights."[103] This skepticism was exacerbated when in early April 1986, Ambassador Walker refused to meet with Kim Dae-jung. On April 17, before the Congressional Subcommittee on South Korea, Assistant Secretary of State for East Asian and Pacific Affairs Gaston J. Sigur stated that the Reagan administration did not support drawing "parallels between Korea and the Philippines," as was common practice in the media. Moreover, the administration had no plans to intervene directly in South Korea's democratic transition.[104]

The administration's insistence on nonintervention only intensified attacks on the Chun regime and on US policy on South Korea. In early April 1986 at Kim Dae-jung's request, the American Committee for Human Rights (ACHR) initiated a fact-finding mission on freedom of the press, electoral reform, and government-sponsored torture in South Korea. Like the NACHRK, CPAJ, and other advocacy groups, the ACHR focused on promoting the systemic and institutional reforms needed for democracy, rather than concentrating on amnesty for specific political dissidents.[105] On April 16, 1986, Edward Baker of Asia Watch testified before the US Congress on pending US aid to South Korea in the amount of $230 million for FMS credits. In his testimony, Baker insisted that US aid should be accompanied by "public statements indicating that democratization is integrally related to Korean stability and security and is thus of paramount importance to U.S. national security interests." The Reagan administration, he asserted, should "obtain an explicit guarantee that . . . the military will not intervene in the political process." Based on South Korean pro-democracy leaders' opinions, Baker emphasized that "a strong statement by President Reagan is essential" to prevent military interference in democratization. Baker's testimony thus incorporated indigenous perspectives to warn of the dangers of failing to learn from the lessons of the 1980 Kwangju Incident. A South Korean daily newspaper immediately translated Baker's testimony and published it in South Korea, thereby creating additional momentum for reform.[106]

Meanwhile in South Korea, tensions mounted. In early May 1986, approximately ten thousand protesters affiliated with the people's (*minjung*) movement gathered in Inch'ŏn to support a direct presidential election in 1988. The peaceful rally quickly deteriorated into violent clashes with the police. When protesters shouted slogans condemning the Chun regime, demanding US troop withdrawal from South Korea, and deriding what they saw as the accommodationist stance of the NKDP, the police fired tear gas into the crowds, and protesters retaliated by throwing rocks and homemade fire bombs. Although the NKDP claimed that the police provoked the riot by firing tear gas into the crowd, the party also denounced rising anti-Americanism and extremism. In a statement issued that same day, Kim Dae-jung cautioned protesters that violence risked discrediting the movement: "Moderation and nonviolence are the only way we can get the broad support of the people."[107]

Despite escalating violence in South Korea, the Reagan administration maintained its stance that no parallels existed between South Korea and the Philippines and emphatically affirmed its support of the Chun regime. During an in-flight news conference, Secretary of State Shultz described the situations in the two countries as "about as dissimilar as any two situations." He condemned those in the opposition who "incite violence" and declared that the United States "strongly supported" the Chun regime's "objective of moving more and more toward a democratic government." He also refused to meet with Kim Dae-jung and other opposition leaders during his visit.[108]

A few weeks after Shultz's departure, two human rights groups, the NACHRK and the Korea Institute for Human Rights (KIHR), both based in

Washington, DC, reported a sharp increase in the ROK government actions aimed at suppressing pro-democracy movements. The groups noted that since Shultz's departure over fifty dissidents had been arrested and dozens had been tortured while in police custody. In publicizing these incidents, both groups challenged Shultz's claim that the Chun regime was taking "impressive" steps toward instituting democracy. Shultz's failure to acknowledge the regime's human rights violations during his visit, according to Sim Ki-sŏp of the KIHR, communicated to the regime that "the United States doesn't care about the human rights situation" and therefore "Chun thinks he can do anything." When asked for comment about these two groups' findings, the State Department claimed that it was unaware of the crackdown, and the ROK Embassy in Washington, DC, denied the government's use of illegal interrogation and torture techniques.[109]

Despite White House efforts to downplay these allegations, some US congressional members demanded action. In June 1986, Congressman Michael A. Feighan introduced a resolution calling for "dialogue between the [ROK] government and the opposition in a spirit of reconciliation," the release of all political prisoners, and the guarantee for all citizens of freedom of speech, assembly, and due process, and "the peaceful and democratic transfer of the Presidency" through a fair election.[110] The resolution, which the KIHR helped draft, was approved unanimously by the US Congress. The following month, the US Senate passed a resolution in support of the South Korean campaign for direct presidential elections in 1988.[111]

At home and abroad, calls for the Chun regime to revise the constitution before the scheduled 1988 election grew. But rather than accommodating these calls, the regime continued its political crackdown. In early July 1986, the Kim Kŭn-t'ae case was back in the news, when the appeal court acknowledged that intelligence officers had tortured him but upheld his five-year prison sentence. The announcement immediately triggered protests by AI, Asia Watch, and the International Human Rights Law Group. In addition to his release, they also demanded the release of all POCs.[112] In September 1986, Congressman Stephen Solarz, chair of the Asian and Pacific Affairs Committee, along with fifty-one other congressmen sent President Chun a letter, in which they demanded that Kim Kŭn-t'ae's welfare be guaranteed and that all alleged torture and abuse cases be properly investigated.[113]

In late October, the White House received word of the most violent anti-American protest in South Korea since the 1980 Kwangju crisis. Students from twenty-seven universities occupied Konkook University in Seoul to protest

Chun's dictatorial rule and the presence of US troops and nuclear bases in South Korea. Approximately seven thousand riot police under orders from the government to crush the revolt, stormed five campus buildings occupied by students. The police fired thousands of canisters of tear gas, and firemen targeted students using twenty water cannons. Witnesses claimed that the police forced students to kneel and then clubbed them. News of the violence prompted thousands of students to launch protests at other universities in Seoul and in Pusan. As at Konkook, these demonstrations led to violent clashes with the police.

In response, the government accelerated its crackdown on dissidents. On December 31, 1986, the wife of the ecumenical activist Pang Pyŏng-gyu claimed that her husband was tortured and forced to confess to being an anti-state activist while in the custody of the Anti-Communist Bureau in Namyŏng-dong.[114] In early January 1987, a twenty-one-year-old college student, Pak Chong-ch'ŏl, died while detained at the same facility where Pang had been tortured. On January 14, 1987, the police attributed his death to "shock" and announced that an investigation into his death was underway. One day later, O Yŏn-sang, the doctor who conducted the autopsy, indicated that torture may have played a role in his death. On January 16, Asia Watch and the KIHR attributed Pak's death to "wounds sustained from torture" and called for an independent investigation. In response to these allegations, the US State Department condemned "torture as a violation of human rights" but did not explicitly denounce the ROK government, stating it would await the results of the regime's ongoing investigation.[115]

While the US government was willing to wait, South Korean and transnational activists were not. As in 1960 when a police tear-gas canister killed high school student Kim Chu-yŏl, Pak's death catalyzed a massive wave of pro-democracy protests. On January 22, 1987, Rev. Kim Sang-gŭn, chair of the NCCK's Anti-Torture Council, demanded full transparency from the government about the circumstances of Pak's death. He also called on all pro-democracy groups to launch anti-torture campaigns.[116] The ACTS organized an unprecedented national anti-torture coalition that included *chaeya* groups, student groups, and the opposition political parties.[117] The chair of the NK-DP's human rights committee claimed the government had illegally detained and tortured 238 people during the previous four months. Cardinal Kim Su-hwan concurred, stating that Pak's death was "not an anomaly."[118] AI substantiated their claims, noting they had identified seventy possible incidents of torture for the previous year.[119]

As anti-torture and pro-democracy protests gained momentum, pressure on the regime and on the Reagan administration substantially increased. After a massive rally on February 7, 1987, a second mass rally, "Grand March Against Torture and for Democratization," occurred on March 3, 1987. Despite the presence of thirty-five thousand armed police officers, ten thousand protesters, including students, religious groups, and opposition party members, gathered in Seoul and chanted "Down with Chun!" and "Restore Human Rights!"[120]

Against this backdrop, Assistant Secretary Sigur in an address before the U.S.-Korea Society in New York City proposed a "more open political system" in South Korea to resolve the nation's socioeconomic and political issues. However, his proposed "open system" did not appear to introduce any major shifts in US policy in South Korea. Rather than exhorting the Reagan administration to intervene as it had in Haiti and the Philippines, he emphasized the need for internal compromise and consensus among South Koreans.[121] A month later, while visiting Seoul, Secretary of State Shultz reaffirmed the United States' commitment to Chun's proposed plan, which he characterized as setting a "historical precedent for a peaceful transition of power."[122] In making this assertion, Shultz ignored the local and transnational voices that decried the regime's use of torture and other repressive measures. For example, just prior to his visit, Kim Dae-jung publicly appealed to Shultz to utilize his influence to exact from Chun a commitment to respect human rights, to enforce the military's political neutrality, and to allow a national referendum on the direct election of the South Korean president in 1988.[123] Asia Watch also publicly called on Shultz to address torture and other human rights abuses in South Korea.

Meanwhile, within the NKDP, there was growing turmoil over the constitutional issue. On December 24, 1986, Yi Min-u, the NKDP president, surprised NKDP leaders when he suggested that he would be willing to accept the ruling party's proposed cabinet system of government if the government agreed to implement his seven-point plan for democratization. Although Yi withdrew this controversial offer, there were growing signs that a party split was imminent. On April 13, 1987, Kim Dae-jung and Kim Young-sam left the NKDP to form the Party of Reunification and Democracy (RDP). Capitalizing on this schism, Chun canceled ongoing talks on constitutional revision and announced that in the name of protecting the constitution (*hohŏn*), the elections would take place under the existing system.

Chun's decision provoked harsh criticism in many circles. RDP chair Kim Young-sam denounced the decision, stating that the government's action reflected its lack of confidence. Cardinal Kim Su-hwan expressed "extreme disappointment" and noted that "Chun has no moral authority."[124] Students also protested the decision, and spring 1987 saw numerous clashes with the police. Still, Chun made only a token effort to liberalize his rule and restore confidence in his path to democracy. As he had done on multiple other occasions, on May 2, 1987, he announced the release of twenty-four political prisoners, in honor of Buddhist Day. Nearly two thousand POCs remained in custody and no systemic changes appeared on the immediate horizon.[125]

Just as the constitutional crisis reached critical mass, CPAJ disclosed important truths and details about Pak Chong-chŏl's death. On May 17, 1987, at the conclusion of Cardinal Kim's sermon at the Myŏngdong Cathedral in Seoul, Father Kim Sŭng-hun of the CPAJ produced evidence that contradicted the government's claim that two low-ranking officers bore sole responsibility for Pak's death. According to the CPAJ, three senior police officials induced the two junior officials to accept blame as part of a cover-up, designed to conceal the regime's endorsement of torture at the highest level. The very next day, the National Coalition for Democratic Constitution (NCDC, Kukbon), the largest coalition of anti-government groups to date, was established. The NCDC demanded the resignation of all cabinet members and announced its plans for a nationwide anti-government rally on June 10, 1987—the same day the ruling party would nominate its 1988 presidential candidate.[126]

In an effort to defuse tensions, the three senior police officials implicated in the cover-up were indicted, and Chun dismissed his entire cabinet. NSP director Chang Se-dong also resigned.[127] On May 30, 1987, the acting prime minister Yi Han-gi apologized for Pak's death and for the cover-up.[128] These concessions did little to assuage either anti-regime or anti-American sentiments. On June 10, hundreds of thousands of protesters took to the streets to protest the cover-up and demand that Chun revoke his April 13 decision. In addition to chanting anti-government slogans, protesters shouted, "Yankee go home" and burned an effigy of Reagan to protest the White House's support of the Chun regime.[129]

On Capitol Hill, Representatives Foglietta and Fortney H. Stark drafted a bill on June 18 that would deny favorable trade conditions to South Korea until that nation demonstrated "respect for internationally recognized human and labor rights" and introduced fair elections and freedom of the press.[130] The next day, a group of senators, including Senator Kennedy, introduced a tougher bill before the Senate's Committee on Foreign Relations. The bill, Democracy in South Korea Act (S. 1392), linked eligibility for multinational developmental bank loans and participation in US trade preference programs to a nation's human rights record. If enacted, it also would bar South Korea from receiving investment funds through the Overseas Private Investment Corporation. The bill drew harsh criticism from the White House, which on October 1987 sent a memo to the legislative liaison officer warning that "it is generally unwise to use economic sanctions for political purpose."[131]

As the situation in South Korea became more volatile, the Reagan administration became increasingly concerned that Chun would respond to mass anti-government demonstrations by reinstating martial law. This threat along with growing congressional dissatisfaction with the Reagan administration's foreign policy approach to South Korea compelled the Reagan administration to intervene in the South Korean democratic conflict. On June 20, 1987, James Lilley, who had replaced Richard Walker as US ambassador to South Korea in 1986, met with Chun to deliver a private letter from Reagan. The rationale for sending a "private" letter, rather than issuing a public statement, was that White House officials feared that open confrontation would provoke a backlash by Chun; this approach was also consistent with the administration's commitment to quiet diplomacy. The missive, composed by White House officials, was couched in "sympathetic, gentle and inoffensive language," and the content of the letter was deliberately kept vague. For example, the letter made no direct reference to the current crisis, but spoke broadly about how "dialogue, compromise and negotiation are effective ways to solve problems and maintain national unity."[132]

Meanwhile, Chun tried to placate the opposition by agreeing to meet with Kim Young-sam. At the meeting on June 24, 1987, Chun suggested that he would be willing to reopen parliamentary negotiations on constitutional revision. But Kim rejected Chun's offer, insisting that the government should agree to an immediate national referendum to choose between the current electoral system and direct presidential election—a concession that Chun was unwilling to make. Five days later, the ruling party's 1988 presidential nominee Roh Tae-woo surprised supporters and critics when he issued a statement outlining an eight-point proposal for democratization that largely acquiesced to opposition demands. The June 29 Declaration supported direct elections, the reinstatement of Kim Dae-jung's civil and political rights, the release of all political prisoners, and the promotion of human rights through, among other things, regular consultations with human rights organizations. The declaration also recognized freedom of speech, freedom of the press, and educational autonomy for universities.[133] The mood in South Korea in the immediate aftermath of the announcement was joyful; citizens celebrated "this delightful day" that they hoped would bring prosperity and real democratic rule.[134] But delight soon turned to disappointment for many activists, when, as political scientist Jang-Jip Choi illustrates, the democratization proved a "conservative democratization," owing to its failure to incorporate socioeconomic change.[135]

Conclusion

Although 1970s pro-democracy activism experienced a crushing blow in May 1980 at Kwangju, ecumenical and secular activists continued to develop the language and politics of human rights in order to create both transnational solidarity and local solidarity across religious and class boundaries. Through the language of human rights, the tentative bonds formed between workers, religious leaders, and student activists in the 1970s reached fruition in the 1980s. For example, in the 1980s, a significant number of students went undercover as "disguised workers" and risked their lives to help workers organize independent, democratic unions. Catholic and Protestant groups also at this time became more vocal in their advocacy for human rights and democracy, arguing that real economic growth required respecting workers' right to subsistence. From the pulpit, religious leaders spoke out against the regime's use of torture and called for constitutional reform.

Mass arrests and the use of torture to gain false confessions exposed the hypocrisy of Chun's "peaceful transition to democracy" and gave credence to local and transnational campaigns that saw democracy as the answer to South Korea's human rights crisis. The regime's repressive measures also unmasked the inefficacy of quiet diplomacy in advancing democratization. Although US officials secured the release of several prominent political prisoners, including Kim Dae-jung, through quiet diplomacy, its utilization never challenged the status quo. Nor was it intended to do so; consistent with the realpolitik orientation of earlier administrations, the Reagan administration believed that US security interests were contingent upon stabilizing the Chun regime. Thus, as anti-regime momentum grew in South Korea, US foreign policy became entangled in the Korean pro-democracy struggle at home and abroad. On the streets of South Korea, in the US Congress, and in the media, the challenge to US Cold War modernization policy grew as the struggle for democracy in South Korea became internationalized.

Human Rights in the Post-Democratization and Global Justice Age

This book examined the role of South Korean pro-democracy actors in (re) shaping the global history of human rights activism and politics in the 1970s and early 1980s. It showed how local pro-democracy activists pragmatically engaged with global advocacy groups, especially AI and the WCC, to maximize their socioeconomic and political struggles. It detailed how local pro-democracy protesters translated their sufferings into the language of international human rights that highlighted the role of US Cold War policies in impeding democratization in South Korea. In tracing the increasing coalitional ties between local pro-democracy protests and transnational human rights activism, the book also called attention to the parallel development of counteractive human rights policies by the South Korean regimes and US administrations. These counteractions were designed to safeguard the regime's legitimacy and to ensure the US Cold War security consensus. Thus, this book argued that local disputes over democratization in South Korea became transnational contestations on human rights through the development of transpacific human rights politics.

This epilogue extends its discussion of human rights in South Korea to the post-democratization era—a period in which predicting the demise of internationally endorsed human rights policies at the United Nations and elsewhere has increasingly gained sway among scholars. For example, in his recent monograph political scientist Stephen Hopgood foretells the imminent "endtimes" of human rights. Hopgood believes that we are entering a neo-Westphalian world, that is, a world of renewed national sovereignty and resurgent religious movements. In such a world, he argues, no hegemonic power will be able to globalize human rights effectively. Similarly, Eric

Posner contends that we are experiencing the "twilight of human rights law," which is misguided both in its endorsement of one set of legal norms for varying societies and its catalog of too many rights that most nations simply cannot afford to implement.[1] Yet, there has been some pushback on these views. For example, international relations scholar Monica Duffy Toft questions the negative effects of religion's resurgence on human rights, which Hopgood identifies as a prime characteristic of the emerging neo-Westphalian era that is so hostile to human rights. She points out that in four successive decades religious actors frequently played a positive role in democratization processes.[2] Political scientists, such as Todd Landman and Kathryn Sikkink, argue that Hopgood and Posner overstate their argument about the ineffectiveness of human rights policies in improving people's lives across the globe. They point to a series of empirical studies that demonstrate that the international human rights regime contributes positively to local struggles for human rights by providing important legal standards and public discourses that local groups leverage to realize their aims.[3] Finally, human rights scholar César Rodríguez-Garavito underscores that such negative assessments of human rights focus too much on uppercase Human Rights, that is, a global structure of laws, and not enough on lowercase human rights, that is, local and transnational networks that try to safeguard people's autonomy, integrity, and human dignity. This lopsided focus results in many connections and collaborations between uppercase and lowercase human rights being missed. Moreover, it misrepresents the human rights domain as two separate monocultures, when in fact human rights is better understood as a multipolar domain in which there is room for national and international diversity and multilateral connections between actors, topics, and strategies.[4]

Certainly, as this book has shown, local and transnational religious organizations played a critical role in the democratization process in South Korea in the 1970s and 1980s as well as in the vernacularization of universal human rights norms that allowed local activists to gain an international audience for their demands. Moreover, in keeping with Landman and Sikkink's assessment, international human rights standards not only provided South Korean activists and their allies a means of exerting pressure on the ROK government to institute change but also allowed activists to advance their cause in the US Congress. Finally, as this book has shown, a unilateral and static conception of human rights as radiating outward from the West simply does not capture the complex dynamics in play in South Korea. As we saw, South

Koreans advanced a definition of human rights that looked beyond the civil and political rights championed in the West. They did not merely adopt Western norms; they transformed the meaning of human rights and created unique strategies to fit local needs. This process of transformation continues today in South Korea and in other non-Western parts of the world, as increasingly lowercase human rights groups redefine the boundaries of the field, forming new connections and strategies in response to changing local and international affairs.

To illustrate this transformative process in contemporary South Korea, this epilogue focuses on three human rights issues in contemporary South Korea: "comfort women," forced labor, and human rights in North Korea. In so doing, it highlights vernacularization as a continued and critical mechanism for the transformation and globalization of human rights. It also spotlights the transformed and expanded spheres in which South Koreans contested human rights issues in the post-democratization era. In addition to campaigns targeting the US Congress, South Koreans developed campaigns aimed at United Nations offices and Korean institutions and also built bridges with other human rights organizations in Asia.

In the early 1990s, the issue of "comfort women" first appeared in the public discourse when Shoji Motooka, then a Socialist member of the House of Councillors of Japan, demanded that the Japanese government investigate the "'comfort women' question." The government responded by denying the involvement of the Japanese military in the "comfort station" operations and refused to launch an investigation. This denial prompted various Korean women's organizations, including the Korean Council for the Women Drafted for Military Sexual Slavery by Japan, to send the Japanese government multiple letters of protest demanding a resolution of this issue. In August 1991, Kim Hak-sun (1924–97), with the support of the Korean Council, came forward with her story, breaking over fifty years of silence on the topic. Kim and two other "comfort women" brought suit in a Japanese court in December 1991, demanding recognition and compensation for Japan's violation of their human rights. Kim's actions prompted other former "comfort women" and those who had been forced to labor in mines, airfields, and factories as part of the Japanese war effort to file lawsuits in Japanese courts.[5]

In addition to these eyewitness testimonies, in January 1992, Japanese historian Yoshiaki Yoshimi published documents contradicting the Japanese government's denial of responsibility. Since that time, numerous international organizations have researched and investigated the "comfort women" question. Most notably, in 1996, the special rapporteur on violence against women at the UN Human Rights Commission released a report describing the Japanese brothel system as "military sexual slavery," given "the status or condition of a person over whom any or all of the powers attaching to the right of ownership are exercised." Based on this report, the United Nations urged the Japanese government to take legal responsibility for the victims of "comfort women" operations. A written apology and compensation, the UN recommended, should be given to the victims.[6]

Still, the Japanese government refused to accept legal liability for violating the individual rights of the "comfort women" victims. As justification, the Japanese government argued that international criminal law cannot be applied retroactively. Since neither the crime of slavery nor acts of rape were prohibited by customary norms of international law at the time of the Second World War, the Japanese government cannot be held accountable. They also argued that under the terms of the 1965 Treaty on Basic Relations Between Japan and the Republic of Korea, "comfort women" and forced laborers cannot sue for compensation, because this treaty settled all outstanding claims between the two nations from the period of Japanese colonial rule. According to article 2 of the Agreement on the Settlement of Problems Concerning Property and Claims and on Economic Co-operation (signed in Tokyo on June 22, 1965), the issue of claims by individual victims during the colonial period "is settled completely and finally," and thus "no contention shall be made" with respect to "any claims" against the Japanese government and nationals. This agreement also required the Japanese government to provide the ROK government with a grant of $3 million and loans in the amount of $200 million for economic cooperation between the two countries. However, there was no prior consultation or follow-up consensus process on the issue of the right to claims for the colonial atrocities with the victims and anyone who was concerned with the treaty.[7]

In December 2015, it appeared that the stalemate on the long-running controversy would finally be broken, when the Japanese government led by Prime Minister Shinzo Abe and the ROK government led by President Park Geun-hye reached a resolution on the controversy. Per the agreement, Japan would apologize to the victims and accept "deep responsibility" for the issue. This act of contrition would be accompanied by a contribution of one billion yen (approximately $8.3 million at the time) to set up a foundation administered by the ROK government to support the living victims. In return, the ROK government agreed to remove "peace statues" symbolizing "comfort women," which activists erected outside the Japanese Embassy in Seoul in 2011 and in other locations. South Korea also agreed to recognize the matter, as resolved "finally and irreversibly" if Japan fulfilled its promises. Both governments extolled the treaty, predicting it would lead to enhanced diplomatic cooperation between the two nations in the fight against China's geo-economic military expansion as well as the nuclear threat from North Korea—both of which also challenged US global hegemony.

Yet, neither government took steps to ensure public support for the agreement. Thus, when the terms of the agreement, negotiated in secret, were made public, both leaders faced stiff opposition at home. Shinzo Abe came under attack from conservatives who condemned the agreement as unnecessary given previous Japanese expressions of remorse. More significantly, in South Korea, the Park government came under attack from some of the victims. Just as in 1965, the Park government had not consulted the victims prior to making the agreement. Many of the survivors and their supporters took issue with the wording of the agreement, which did not explicitly state that the "comfort women" would receive an apology and direct compensation from the Japanese government. Instead, the agreement stated that the fund would provide "support" and fund "projects for recovering the honor and dignity and healing the psychological wounds." This wording led to allegations that the ROK government in the name of improved security ties had sold out the victims and facilitated a process of historical forgetting. By late 2016, protests against the 2015 agreement with Japan had become a critical part of the massive "candlelight demonstrations," calling for President Park's impeachment on grounds of corruption and anti–human rights practices.[8]

Following President Park's removal from office and Moon Jae-in's election as president, the new ROK government immediately expressed its desire to Japan to revisit the 2015 agreement. In June 2017, Moon told Prime Minister Abe of Japan, "The reality is the majority of our people cannot emotionally accept the 'comfort women' agreement." In asking Abe to renegotiate the 2015 settlement, Moon was clear that the issue should not affect wider ROK-Japan relations, saying they should deal with the "comfort women" dispute and "work independently in order to respond to North Korean nuclear and missiles issues." Against the backdrop of continued popular disapproval of the 2015 agreement, the Moon Jae-in government in November 2018 announced the dissolution of the foundation for "comfort women." Despite Moon's plea for the contrary, the 2015 agreement's ultimate failure led to extraordinary diplomatic tensions between South Korea and Japan.[9] These tensions were further exacerbated by new developments on the issue of forced labor before and during the Second World War.

The state-dominated realpolitik approach to crimes against humanity during the colonial era experienced an unprecedented legal challenge when, in October 2018, the ROK Supreme Court ruled that Japan's Nippon Steel & Sumitomo Metal Corp. should compensate ninety-four-year-old Yi Ch'un-sik and three other Koreans for their wartime forced labor. The court rejected the company's claim that the 1965 treaty had permanently settled such cases and affirmed the right of individual victims to seek compensation for crimes against humanity. In responding to the verdict, Japanese foreign minister Taro Kono described the compensation order as "unthinkable" and as a clear violation of the 1965 treaty normalizing ties between the two countries. Kono warned that Tokyo might bring the case before the International Court of Justice. However, a group of Japanese lawyers and legal scholars insisted that "the issue of forced labor is a human rights issue," and thus "any settlement between countries that victims and society cannot accept is not a true settlement."[10] This pro–human rights perspective gained additional ground when one month later the ROK Supreme Court ruled that Mitsubishi Heavy Industries must compensate twenty-eight Koreans for their forced wartime labor. At the time of this decision, a dozen similar cases were pending in lower courts. In January 2019, a South Korean court approved a request by Yi, the plaintiff in the case against Japan's Nippon Steel & Sumitomo Metal Corp., to seize the company's local assets in South Korea as guarantee for payment of the settlement.[11]

Yi's victory was the culmination of a twenty-year effort. In the late 1990s and the early 2000s, Yi and other former forced laborers tried and failed in the Japanese court system to win compensation. But then in 2004, a South Korean court ordered the South Korean Foreign Ministry to declassify some of the documents related to the 1965 treaty. In 2005, a national commission reviewed the declassified documents and concluded that the treaty did not cover "illegal acts against humanity."[12] According to the documents, the secret proceeding for the 1965 treaty explored the issue of forced labor, but the final treaty did not properly and thoroughly cover it. In the interest of facilitating economic cooperation, the treaty focused on the transfer of money. These revelations, the Yonhap news agency in Seoul predicted, would lead to calls by ordinary Koreans for the treaty's renegotiation. When asked to comment on this development, the ROK government stated that although there

were obvious flaws in the original negotiations, it would not pursue renego-
tiations with Japan on the issue of individual claims, as the treaty had been
a comprehensive talk between the two nations.[13] Despite the ROK government's reaction, the court's decision opened the possibility of revisiting the
treaty and claims involving crimes against humanity in the framework of
human rights.

In tandem with this development, democratic and grassroots organizations in South Korea began building the institutional environment for
pursuing transitional justice on colonial and postcolonial atrocities as part
of the "justice cascade," which political scientists Kathryn Sikkink and Hun
Joon Kim describe as a "dramatic new trend in world politics toward holding individual state officials, including heads of state, criminally accountable
for human rights violations."[14] In South Korea, this pursuit culminated with
the establishment of the Truth and Reconciliation Commission of the Republic of Korea (TRCK) in 2005. The TRCK was tasked with investigating incidents of human rights abuses, violence, and massacres dating back to the
beginning of Japanese colonial rule. Its mandate covered approximately one
century, thus it also encompassed crimes committed against civilians during the Korean War and acts of political suppression during the democratic
transition. Although the commission did not have the authority to prosecute
violations, it did have the authority to investigate allegations and thus became
a forum in which charges of human rights violations were discussed, examined, and contested. Before its closure in December 2010, the commission received 11,174 cases based on petitions from individuals. Of these, the
commission confirmed 8,468, rejected 1,729, and another 967 were either referred to other bodies or closed due to insufficient information.[15] Legal
scholar Tae-Ung Baik notes that the TRCK proceedings elucidated the value
of "restorative justice," that is, justice that seeks to restore the dignity and
rights of survivors and victims.[16] Moreover, in 2012, the ROK Supreme Court
ruled that the 1965 treaty did not supersede the right of a victim of forced
labor to sue Japanese companies for compensation. It also ordered lower
courts to reconsider earlier verdicts.

However, the plaintiffs in these cases continued to face obstacles. The Foreign Ministry submitted an opinion to the Supreme Court seeking to block
the seizure of Japanese assets in South Korea, claiming that such a seizure
would be an "irreversible catastrophe," since other nations would brand
South Korea as untrustworthy for breaking international law. Because the
court took so long to rule on this matter, many accused then-president Park

Geun-hye of conspiring with the court to delay or overturn the decision. In early 2019, a truth commission, newly launched by the Moon Jae-in government, revealed that the rumors were in fact true. Former president Park Geun-hye had conspired with Chief Justice Yang Sŭng-t'ae in this counteraction against those seeking justice for forced laborers.[17] This revelation, for many South Koreans, raised the question of whether the 2015 "comfort women" agreement, also made under the Park government, might too have been part of a human rights counteraction in the name of security interests.

In July 2019, outraged by the court rulings, the Japanese government escalated the conflict when it announced that it would impose trade restrictions on South Korea. In the statement, Japan's Ministry of Economy, Trade, and Industry made thinly veiled allusions to the 1965 treaty and attacked South Korea's trustworthiness: "Through careful consideration among the relevant ministries in Japan, the Government of Japan cannot help but state that the Japan–[South Korea] relationship of trust, including in the field of export control and regulation, has been significantly undermined."[18] Specifically, Japan removed South Korea from its so-called "white list" of trusted trading partners. The trade-list demotion meant that exports to South Korea of a diverse range of materials, including some critical for South Korea's tech industry, were subjected to additional and stricter screenings than previously. Against the backdrop of mounting popular criticism of the Japanese government, including two self-immolations in front of the Japanese Embassy in Seoul, the ROK government took corresponding actions. It removed Japan from its list of preferred trading partners. Additionally, the ROK government announced that it would not renew the General Security of Military Information Agreement with Japan, citing a "grave change" in the environment for bilateral security cooperation owing to Japan's decision to lower South Korea's export status. This pact, signed by Japan and South Korea in December 2016, enabled the two nations to share information about North Korea's nuclear and missile development programs. As had been the case with the 1965 treaty, this pact had the strong backing of the United States. This decision not only escalated tensions with Japan, but also with the United States, as it affected US security interests in the region. But the ROK government insisted that it could not share security information with a nation that viewed it as untrustworthy.[19] Through this action, the ROK government hoped to pressure Japan and the United States to revisit the issue of individual compensation for victims of forced labor before and during the Second World War. As many human rights advocates noted, the United States had played a leading role in resolving German cases involving forced labor during the Second World War. Given the central role that the United States played in addressing how Japan's war conduct was dealt with after the war, legal experts, such as Timothy Webster, argue that the United States should also be actively involved in finding a solution to the impasse between Japan and South Korea over the forced labor cases.[20]

What had begun as a bilateral conflict between South Korea and Japan over human rights had morphed into a transnational dispute on economic and security agendas in East Asia. In challenging the legitimacy of the 1965 treaty, the contestation over crimes against humanity during the colonial era and the Pacific War reopened the 1970s and 1980s debate about the relationship between security and democracy. As at that time, the twenty-first-century debate recreated the oppositional binary that pitted the promotion of human rights and democracy against the realpolitik objective of advancing security interests in East Asia—interests that, despite the official end of the Cold War, still were informed by Cold War mentalities, ideologies, and agendas.

At roughly the same time that the human rights cases of "comfort women" and forced labor were unfolding, the issue of human rights in North Korea became part and parcel of post-democratization human rights talks and politics in South Korea. As with China, human rights violations in North Korea did not become part of the international "human rights" agendas until the late 1980s. In 1969, AI activist Ivan Morris had wanted to pursue impartial human rights campaigns in both South and North Korea. However, at the time, he admitted that AI's limited ability to conduct fact-finding mission on human rights violations in North Korea would seriously impair the organization's ability to internationalize human rights issues in North Korea. In 1985, the Minnesota Lawyers International Human Rights Committee attempted to overcome this issue by relying on alternative sources such as interviews with refugees and published accounts of life in North Korea.[21] In 1988, this Minnesota advocacy group together with Asia Watch released the first comprehensive report on human rights in North Korea. This report claimed specific violations of international human rights norms, such as an extensive surveillance system and no independent judiciary, based on North Korea's signing of the ICCPR and the ICESCR in 1981.[22] In 1991, one of the earliest direct challenges to North Korea's human rights record occurred in Pyongyang during an Inter-Parliamentary Union conference. Leni Fischer, a member of the German Christian Democratic Party, demanded to know if North Korea operated concentration camps for political prisoners and accused the North Korean government of denying its citizenry basic civil and political rights. An AI delegate, also at the conference, asserted that North Korea operated at least twelve political prisoners' camps (*kwanliso*), housing more than 100,000 inmates. North Korea's representatives to the conference denied all allegations.[23]

Since the 1990s, access to North Korea by international human rights monitors has not improved substantially, nor has North Korea developed any explicit form of civil society, yet, as I illustrate below, in the age of global justice, disputes on human rights in North Korea continued to grow against the backdrop of the worsening humanitarian crisis inside North Korea and deepening local and international confrontations over security interests on the Korean peninsula and in East Asia. The issues of political suppression and prisoners' camps were critical elements of these disputes. Still, the question of how to overcome the information monopoly of the North Korean government and ultimately how the protection and promotion of human rights in North Korea could be achieved without causing significant collateral damage, such as violent conflicts or war, remained contentious, opening up multilayered interactional contestations in local and international politics.

A critical stimulus for the expanding disputes on human rights in North Korea was the breakdown of North Korea's socioeconomic system in the aftermath of multiple natural disasters in the mid-1990s. Intermittent starvation, ongoing privation, and political repression led tens of thousands of North Koreans to cross the border into China, South Korea, and other nations. The testimonies of those who fled across the border into China led AI to issue a report in 2000 expressing concerns about the vulnerability of the refugees to human rights violations in China.[24] In the early 2000s, the US Congress also organized hearings on North Korea and in 2004 Congress issued the North Korea Human Rights Act, aimed at promoting human rights and freedom in that nation. The act is effective through 2022, after President Donald Trump reauthorized the bill in 2018. Specifically, the act provides US assistance to North Korean refugees, humanitarian aid to those living in North Korea, and grants to private nonprofit organizations that promote human rights, democracy, and a market economy in North Korea. It also seeks to increase the availability of information to North Koreans.[25] Also, in 2004, the UNCHR (now the UN Human Rights Council, UNHRC) appointed a special rapporteur to investigate and report on the human rights situation in North Korea. In December 2005, the UN General Assembly adopted for the first time a resolution on human rights violations in North Korea.[26]

These twenty-first-century approaches seem like an extension of 1970s and 1980s liberal internationalism, especially US foreign policy. In intervening in the domestic politics of authoritarian and totalitarian states, they established human rights mandates aimed at promoting democratic transitions. However, these efforts increasingly shifted in the direction of the emerging international doctrine known as the "Responsibility to Protect," or "R2P." This doctrine redefined sovereignty as a responsibility, rather than a privilege and was intended to legitimate interventions, including military ones, by the international community in cases where the regime perpetrated crimes against humanity. This doctrine crystallized, when the Rome Statute of the International Criminal Court (ICC) came into effect in 2002. The Rome Statute recognized victims as independent third parties, as opposed to their traditional role of witnesses for the prosecution or the defense. By 2013, against the backdrop of continuing privation in North Korea, the leadership's diversion of resources into pursuing nuclear weapons and ballistic missiles, international concerns about regional stability, and US worries about its security interests on the Korean peninsula, this new international doctrine had become a critical issue with reference to North Korea.

In March 2013, the UNHRC established a Commission of Inquiry (COI) to investigate human rights violations pertaining to, among other things, the rights to food and those associated with prison camps, torture, freedom of movement, arbitrary detention, and enforced disappearances. In February 2014, after hearing the testimony of more than three hundred witnesses in public hearings and private interviews, the COI released a four-hundred-page report that accused North Korean leaders of employing murder, torture, slavery, sexual violence, mass starvation, and other abuses as tools to maintain the state and terrorize "the population into submission."[27] In November 2014, the UN General Assembly voted 111 to 19, with 55 abstentions, in favor of a nonbinding resolution that recommended North Korea be referred to the ICC for crimes against humanity and other gross human rights violations. This resolution, however, was nonbinding, as only the UN Security Council can make such recommendations. In December 2014, the UN General Assembly adopted a resolution to submit the report to the UN Security Council for that purpose by a vote of 116 in favor, 20 against, and 53 abstentions. However, the North Korean leadership cadre has never been referred to the ICC, because repeatedly China and Russia have vetoed the referral.

As international calls to hold Kim Jong-un responsible for gross human rights violations escalated, so too did tensions over North Korea's nuclear missile tests.[28] In July 2016, the United States for the first time imposed economic sanctions on Kim Jong-un for what US officials called "notorious abuses of human rights." These human rights sanctions supplemented existing economic sanctions for nuclear testing. Similarly, since 2016, the United Nations has imposed economic sanctions against the North Korean regime for both its nuclear development program and for human rights violations. In this line, President Donald Trump's administration has pursued a "maximum pressure" campaign against North Korea designed to push Pyongyang toward denuclearization and addressing human rights violations.[29]

Ironically, the international community's intensifying human rights campaigns have exposed fundamental problems and tensions stemming from North Korea's highly suppressive polity as well as the division system established on the Korean peninsula under the 1953 armistice agreement. The verifiability and impartiality of the COI's 2014 report remain topics of contention, because no independent investigator, including the UN's special rapporteur, has been allowed access to North Korea. As foreign policy think-tank researcher Roberta Cohen notes, prior to 2012 the UN High Commissioner of Human Rights never actively pursued North Korea's human rights record, because of the lack of verifiable and impartial information obtained directly from North Korea. However, in 2013, the COI heard testimony from survivors, including former gulag inmate Shin Dong-hyuk. The testimony of Shin and other eyewitnesses became a critical source for the allegations made in the 2014 COI report.[30] Shin's testimony, in particular, received international attention, because he claimed that he was born and raised in North Korea's most notorious gulag, Camp 14. His story received further attention thanks to journalist Blaine Harden's 2012 best-selling book *Escape from Camp 14* about Shin's life experience.[31] However, in 2015, Shin recanted parts of his testimony, after the North Korea government released a video message from his father denying Shin's account. The revisions Shin made to his story immediately sparked a debate about the admissibility of such testimony in criminal proceedings. As during the Cold War, the ideological agenda of the defector and the political biases of the listener, many argued, made such eyewitness testimony suspect.[32]

Political scientist Hazel Smith also points out that the 2014 report's conclusions about the violation of food rights in North Korea were not consistent with the statistical indicators provided by various UN humanitarian and development agencies since the 1990s. This incongruence, which led to charges of gross human rights violation, she argues, "is not primarily due to conscious bias but much more because of the unconscious adoption of a securitized perspective through which knowledge about Korea is filtered." This securitized narrative is based on a Cold War ideological bifurcation of the world into anti-Communist and Communist camps, in which the latter as the enemy must be destroyed. The danger with unreflexively accepting this perspective is that it can potentially lead to war based on false assumptions.[33] Similarly, peace specialist Suh Bo-hyuk argues that the approach to human rights on the Korean peninsula has focused too narrowly on alleged North Korean abuses, failing to take into consideration the way in which the US-sanctioned system of division created hostile mutual interdependencies between the two Koreas. He suggests that the ROK's co-optation as part of the United States' neo–Cold War agenda in the Asia-Pacific region, including South Korea's disproportionately high expenditure on military modernization, threatens "the Korean people's right to peace," as it reinforces the volatile militarized foundation of inter-Korean relations first established in 1953. Instead, what is needed is "a comprehensive human rights approach" on the Korean peninsula that "aims at once to abolish militarism and to improve human rights through peaceful, cooperative, and constructive means."[34]

Balancing North Korean human rights and peace-building efforts on the Korean peninsula has been a highly debated topic in South Korea, even since President Kim Dae-jung (1998–2002) introduced the Sunshine Policy aimed at normalizing relations between the two Koreas and promoting economic cooperation. Presidents Roh Moo-hyun (2003–7) and Moon Jae-in (2017–present) respectively continued and revitalized this approach, which initiated a marked departure from the traditional zero-sum confrontational approach. Like Willy Brandt's *Ostpolitik* begun in the late 1960s, the Sunshine Policy envisioned a de facto unification through reconciliation, cooperation, trust-building, and peaceful coexistence. As political scientists Jong-Yun Bae and Chung-in Moon clearly capture, this vision entails balancing the basic needs of the North Korean people with creating the conditions under which North Korea becomes open to market and political reform and the development of a genuine civil society. Proponents of this policy "constrained their open pursuit of a human rights campaign against North Korea" in the belief that democracy and human rights were best promoted through domestic developments and movements, rather than being imposed by external forces. Kim Dae-jung, winner of the Nobel Peace Prize in 2000 "for his work for democracy and human rights in South Korea and in East Asia in general, and for peace and reconciliation with North Korea in particular," explained the rationale: "Yes, we are aware of severe human rights problems in the North, but it is not wise to raise the issue openly. Given its contextual uniqueness, openly raising the issue will neither help ameliorate human rights conditions nor improve inter-Korean relations."[35]

This statement immediately brings to mind the contentious debates over the US use of quiet diplomacy in South Korea in the 1970s and 1980s. At that time, Kim Dae-jung was an outspoken critic of how the United States employed quiet diplomacy to legitimize South Korea's authoritarian regimes. Yet now, Kim Dae-jung, as head of state, was championing the approach Kim Dae-jung, the dissident, had lambasted. This seeming about-face exposed Kim to charges of hypocrisy, but such criticism failed to take into consideration important differences between the two situations—differences of which Kim, as a former dissident, was painfully aware. For example, unlike the South Korean case, no strong pro-democracy organizations existed in North Korea for the ROK government to support. Moreover, the ROK government did not have the means of pressuring North Korea that were available to the United States. Not to mention, the United States actively utilized quiet diplomacy to stabilize three successive authoritarian regimes in South Korea. In addition, Kim was fully aware of the danger of pursuing hard-line and provocative policies in the "unique" context of an unending war and the almost permanent division of the Korean peninsula, which had separated families and entangled Korea in Cold War superpower geopolitics. Furthermore, although the ROK constitution specified South Korea's territory as consisting of the Korean peninsula and adjacent islands, in reality, South Korea has no de facto sovereignty over North Korea. Thus, Kim Dae-jung and proponents of the Sunshine Policy saw it as a long-term project intended to build the type of leverage needed to bring sociopolitical and cultural changes to North Korea through peaceful means, that is, the introduction of a market economy, the expansion of civil society, and the advent of a middle class.

This engagement policy's pragmatic and strategic "silence" on North Korea's human rights record, however, exposed it to severe criticism from anti-Communist/anti–North Korean political parties and advocacy groups, especially under Presidents Lee Myung-bak (2008–12) and Park Geun-hye (2013–17), as Bae and Moon note. These conservative critics believed that the best way to achieve human rights in North Korea was through regime change. Thus, they argued that the best prescription for improving human rights was isolation, containment, and strangulation so as to hasten the regime's fall and emancipate North Koreans.[36] Labeling supporters of the engagement policy as *chongbuk chwap'a* (pro–North Korea followers/leftists), in 2016, opponents in the ROK National Assembly pushed back, passing the North Korea Human Rights Act. The act tasked the ROK government with investigating the human rights situation in North Korea and ensuring that humanitarian aid delivered to North Korea was distributed with the goal of promoting the human rights of North Korean citizens. To ensure implementation, the act provided for the establishment of four bodies: (1) North Korean Human Rights Advisory Committee, (2) Center for North Korean Human Rights Records at the Ministry of Unification, (3) North Korean Human Rights Documentation Office, and (4) North Korean Human Rights Foundation.[37] Without any measures aimed at overcoming the fundamental dilemma of the division system, this act has achieved little. In fact, its passage may have had more to do with domestic politics than with improving human rights in North Korea. Just five days before parliamentary elections, the Park Geun-hye administration announced that twelve female workers and the manager of a state-run North Korean restaurant in China had defected to South Korea. Because disclosures of defections are rare, the announcement immediately led to speculation that South Korea's intelligence agency may have been behind the defection in an attempt to influence the upcoming elections. This speculation, in turn, resulted in a team of international lawyers investigating the allegations. In 2019, the international team concluded that the women had been kidnapped by the ROK intelligence office for partisan and propaganda motives.[38]

Concomitant with South Korean debates on the engagement policy, an international debate developed on the Trump administration's approach to North Korea. In 2017, following a series of North Korean nuclear tests, Trump took a hard-line approach on the issue of ballistic missiles and human rights. His comment that any North Korean threat against the United States would be met with "fire and fury like the world has never seen" was followed by others that linked the administration's hard line on nuclear weapons to a similar hard line on human rights.[39] For example, on June 30, 2017, during a press conference at the White House with South Korea's President Moon-Jae in, Trump stated: "The nuclear and ballistic missile programs of that regime require a determined response. The North Korean dictatorship has no regard for the safety and security of its people or its neighbors and has no respect for human life. And that's been proven over and over again."[40] This outspoken approach on nuclear weapons and human rights conditions in North Korea continued into early 2018. During Trump's State of the Union Address in January 2018, he recounted the story of Ji Seong-ho, a North Korean refugee: "Seong-ho traveled thousands of miles on crutches all across China and Southeast Asia to freedom." Ji Seong-ho, who had been invited by Trump to attend, was then given a standing ovation by congressional members.[41] In February 2018, to protest North Korea's human rights abuses, Vice President Mike Pence attended the Pyeongchang Winter Olympics in South Korea with the parents of deceased US college student Otto Warmbier, who had been imprisoned on charges of sedition for removing a propaganda poster from the wall of the hotel where he was staying.[42]

However, as Trump and Kim Jong-un prepared for the June 2018 Singapore Summit, where they would meet with Kim Jong-un to discuss North Korea's denuclearization, the Trump administration abruptly turned to the quiet diplomacy that earlier administrations had used with the ROK government during the democratic transition to gain concessions, such as amnesty for political prisoners. For example, the Trump administration suspended military exercises targeting North Korea and stopped openly criticizing human rights abuses in North Korea. This silence was contingent upon the Kim Jong-un regime releasing US nationals detained in North Korea and returning the remains of US soldiers from the Korean War.

The Trump administration's sudden and continuing embrace of quiet diplomacy sparked criticism from some leading human rights advocates. In October 2019, the UN Special Rapporteur urged the Trump administration not to sideline human rights in its negotiations on denuclearization and sanction relief: "Integrating fundamental human rights into the current negotiations is crucial for the sustainability of any agreement for denuclearization and peace for the Korean Peninsula and beyond."[43] Jeff Sifton, the Asia advocacy director at Human Rights Watch, also expressed frustration with the administration's shift in policy: "Everyone says they care about human rights in North Korea—but when it comes to action, people get soft."[44] Thus, the efficacy of quiet diplomacy in bringing about systemic human rights reform and democracy remains at the heart of the transnational debate about human rights on the Korean peninsula today. And like human rights politics in South Korea in the 1970s and 1980s, the issue of human rights remains deeply entangled with geopolitical issues of security and economic development.

In addition to the continuing transpacific politics of human rights, the post-democratization vernacularization of human rights in South Korea introduced a new trans-Asian regional human rights network as well as a

trans-Asia-Africa connection. For example, the May 18 Memorial Foundation, established in 1994 in Kwangju to commemorate the 1980 Kwangju
Uprising and to stand in solidarity with democratic and human rights struggles in Asia and beyond, has played a leading role in building a regional
human rights network in Asia. On March 17, 1998, in collaboration with the
Hong Kong–based Asian Human Rights Commission (AHRC), the May 18
Memorial Foundation promulgated the Asian Human Rights Charter, "a
people's charter." The charter denounced authoritarian regimes that "have
enacted legislation to suppress people's rights and freedoms and colluded
with foreign firms and groups in the plunder of national resources." These
regimes, it continued, when confronted by individuals demanding their
rights, hide behind "spurious theories of 'Asian Values,'" claiming that such
rights are foreign to the religious and cultural traditions of the region.[45]
Each year, the foundation also hosts the annual Gwangju [Kwangju]–Asia
Forum that brings together human rights organizations from across Asia
to discuss pertinent issues of human rights and democracy. In 2018, the forum marked the twentieth anniversary of the Asian Human Rights Charter
and as part of the celebration announced the Asian declarations on the
rights to justice, culture, and peace.[46]

Similarly, other South Korean groups have sought to build human rights
connections between Asia and Africa. On March 8, 2012, International
Women's Day, two former "comfort women" and the Korean Council for the
Women Drafted for Military Sexual Slavery by Japan established the Nabi
(Butterfly) Fund, promising to use any future compensation they received
from the Japanese government to help female victims of war across the globe.
Since its establishment, the fund has provided aid to women in countries that
have been ravaged by conflict, such as Vietnam, Congo, and Uganda.[47]

The three campaigns discussed in this epilogue—"comfort women,"
forced labor, and human rights in North Korea—are by no means the only
human rights campaigns during the post-democratization era in South Korea.
Other human rights campaigns have centered on, among other things, issues
such as students' rights, environmental rights, the rights of migrant workers, housing rights, and gender equality. In each case, as in the 1970s and
1980s, these campaigns have had to contend with anti–human rights coun-
terreactions. Under the Lee Myung-bak and Park Geun-hye administrations,
for example, the independence of the National Human Rights Commission
of Korea (NHRCK), established in 2001, was curbed; the TRCK was terminated; and anti-Communist nationalism was utilized to shut down earlier

administrations' engagement policy with North Korea as well as to crack-down on dissident protests. These reversals prompted AI in 2015 to issue its first report, since democracy was established in South Korea, expressing concern about human rights conditions in that nation.[48] Within South Korea, the worsening human rights situation under President Park Geun-hye, daughter of Park Chung-hee, was euphemistically referred to as the "Yushin Redux."[49]

The tide, however, turned after hundreds of thousands of South Koreans took part in a series of protests, known as the Candlelight Demonstration, calling for Park's impeachment for corruption and for anti–human rights policies. Since then, the Moon Jae-in administration has revitalized the NHRCK as a site for discussions on human rights. But, as we have seen, the revitalization of human rights campaigns has also strained diplomatic relations with Japan and the United States, as South Korea's unresolved co-lonial past and Cold War tensions and interests continue to define the con-tours of human rights on the Korean peninsula. At the same time, newly emerging regional and transregional networks in Asia and Africa point to the vibrancy of human rights movements across the globe and the evolution of strategies for securing a livable world.

NOTES

Introduction

1. Kukche Aemnest'i Han'guk Wiwŏnhoe, *Han'guk Aemnesŭt'i 5-yŏn yaksa* [AI Korea's five-year chronology] (Seoul, 1977), 1.

2. Hammarberg to IEC, memorandum, March 28, 1972, SGO–NS Korea 1971–72, microfilm (hereafter, MF) 16, Collection of AIIS, International Institute of Social History (hereafter, IISH).

3. On concepts of imagination and vernacularization in the globalization of human rights, see Mark Philip Bradley, *The World Reimagined: Americans and Human Rights in the Twentieth Century* (New York: Cambridge University Press, 2016).

4. Samuel Huntington, *The Third Wave: Democratization in the Late Twentieth Century* (Norman: University of Oklahoma Press, 1991).

5. See, for example, Kirsten Sellars, *The Rise and Rise of Human Rights* (Stroud, UK: Sutton, 2002); and Micheline Ishay, *The History of Human Rights: From Ancient Times to the Globalization Era* (Berkeley: University of California Press, 2004).

6. Samuel Moyn, *The Last Utopia: Human Rights in History* (Cambridge, MA: Belknap Press of Harvard University Press, 2010).

7. Kenneth Cmiel, "Emergence of Human Rights Politics in the United States," *Journal of American History* 86, no. 3 (1999): 1232–33, 1250.

8. Bradley, *The World Reimagined*.

9. Kathryn Sikkink, *Evidence for Hope: Making Human Rights Work in the 21st Century* (Princeton, NJ: Princeton University Press, 2017), 81.

10. Patrick William Kelly, *Sovereign Emergencies: Latin America and the Making of Global Human Rights Politics* (New York: Cambridge University Press, 2018), 17.

11. See, for example, Samuel Moyn, *Christian Human Rights* (Philadelphia: University of Pennsylvania Press, 2016).

12. An Pyŏng-uk et al., eds., *Yushin kwa panyushin* [The Yushin system versus the anti-Yushin opponents] (Seoul: Minjuhwa Undong Kinyŏm Saŏphoe, 2005).

13. Namhee Lee, *The Making of Minjung: Democracy and the Politics of Representation in South Korea* (Ithaca, NY: Cornell University Press, 2007).

14. Hak-kyu Sohn, *Authoritarianism and Opposition in South Korea* (New York: Routledge, 1989).

15. Paul Y. Chang, *Protest Dialectics: State Suppression and South Korea's Democracy Movement, 1970–1979* (Stanford, CA: Stanford University Press, 2015).

16. Son Sŭng-ho, *Yusin ch'eje wa Han'guk Kidokkyo in'gwŏn undong* [The Yushin system and South Korean Christian community's human rights movements] (Seoul: Han'guk Kidokkyo Yŏksa Yŏn'guso, 2017).

17. Minjuhwa Undong Kinyŏm Saŏphoe, *Han'guk minjuhwa undongsa* [The history of the Korean democratization movements], vol. 3 (Seoul: Tolbegae, 2010), 675–77.

18. Sang-young Rhyu, ed., *Democratic Movements and Korean Society* (Seoul: Yonsei University Press, 2007).

19. Hyug Baeg Im, "Christian Churches and Democratization in South Korea," in *Religious Organizations and Democratization: Case Studies from Contemporary Asia*, ed. Tun-jen Cheng and Deborah A. Brown (Armonk, NY: Sharpe, 2006), 136–56; Misook Lee, "South Korea's Democratization Movements of the 1970s and 80s Communicative Interaction in Transnational Ecumenical Networks," *International Journal of Korean History* 19, no. 2 (2014): 241–70; Patrick Chung, "The 'Pictures in Our Heads': Journalists, Human Rights, and U.S.–South Korean Relations, 1970–1976," *Diplomatic History* 38, no. 5 (2014): 1136–55.

20. Jerome Cohen and Edward Baker, "U.S. Foreign Policy and Human Rights in South Korea," in *Human Rights in Korea: Historical and Policy Perspectives*, ed. William Shaw (Cambridge, MA: East Asian Legal Studies Program of the Harvard Law School and the Council on East Asian Studies, Harvard University, 1991), 170–219.

21. Yong-Jick Kim, "The Security, Political, and Human Rights Conundrum, 1974–1979," in *The Park Chung Hee Era: The Transformation of South Korea*, ed. Byung-Kook Kim and Ezra Vogel (Cambridge, MA: Harvard University Press, 2011), 457–82; Yi Sam-sŏng, *Migukŭi yaehan chŏngch'aek kwa han'guk minjokjuŭi* [American foreign policy toward Korea and Korean nationalism] (Seoul: Han'gilsa, 1993).

22. Sarah Snyder, *From Selma to Moscow: How Human Rights Activists Transformed U.S. Foreign Policy* (New York: Columbia University Press, 2018), 87–115.

23. This book adopts the term "transnational" to indicate "various types of interactions across national boundaries," while indicating the "worldwide" or global scope and scale of the interactions. Although "transnational" still contains the sense of "national," it is distinctive from a similar term, "international," which underlines a "state-bound" orientation. See Akira Iriye, "Internationalizing International History," in *Rethinking American History in a Global Age*, ed. Thomas Bender (Berkeley: University of California Press), 51–52. For more perspectives on "transnational" history," see C. A. Bayly et al., "AHR Conversation: On Transnational History," *American Historical Review* 111, no. 5 (2006): 1441–64.

24. Iriye, "Internationalizing International History," 47–62.

25. Charles Bright and Michael Geyer, "Where in the World Is America? The History of the United States in the Global Age," in Bender, *Rethinking American History*, 63–99.

26. Mark Philip Bradley and Patrice Petro, "Introduction," in *Truth Claims: Representation and Human Rights*, ed. Bradley and Petro (New Brunswick, NJ: Rutgers University Press, 2002), 1.

27. Brad Simpson, "'Human Rights Are Like Coca-Cola': Contested Human Rights Discourses in Suharto's Indonesia, 1968–1980," in *The Breakthrough: Human Rights in the 1970s*, ed. Jan Eckel and Samuel Moyn (Philadelphia: University of Pennsylvania Press, 2014), 186–203.

28. On the emergence of the national security state, see Michael Hogan, *A Cross of Iron: Harry S. Truman and the Origins of the National Security State, 1945–1954* (New York: Cambridge University Press, 1998); Bruce Cumings, *Dominion from Sea to Sea: Pacific Ascendancy and American Power* (New Haven, CT: Yale University Press, 2009), 388–423.

29. For more on the 1970s rise of liberal internationalism in US foreign policy in relation to global human rights activism and politics, see Barbara Keys, *Reclaiming American Virtue: The Human Rights Revolution of the 1970s* (Cambridge, MA: Harvard University Press, 2014),

153–77; see also John Inkberry, *Liberal Leviathan: The Origins, Crisis, and Transformation of the American World Order* (Princeton, NJ: Princeton University Press, 2011).

30. For more on the relationship between the concepts of quiet diplomacy and human rights advocacy, see David P. Forsythe, *Human Rights in International Relations*, 3rd ed. (New York: Cambridge University Press, 2012), 199; Sandy Vogelgesang, "Diplomacy of Human Rights," *International Studies Quarterly* 23, no. 2 (1979): 219–20.

31. For exemplary works, see Mark Philip Bradley, *Imagining Vietnam and America: The Making of Postcolonial Vietnam, 1919–1950* (Chapel Hill: University of North Carolina Press, 2000); Mary Dudziak, *Cold War Civil Rights: Race and the Image of American Democracy* (Princeton, NJ: Princeton University Press, 2000); and Matthew Connelly, *A Diplomatic Revolution: Algeria's Fight for Independence and the Origins of the Post–Cold War Era* (New York: Oxford University Press, 2002).

32. Bruce Cumings, *Korea's Place in the Sun*, rev. ed. (New York: W. W. Norton, 2005); Bruce Cumings, *The Origins of the Korean War* (Princeton, NJ: Princeton University Press, 1981–90), vol. 1.

33. Jang-Jip Choi, *Democracy After Democratization: The Korean Experience* (Stanford, CA: Walter H. Shorenstein Asia-Pacific Research Center, 2012), 24–51.

34. Gregg Brazinsky, "Koreanizing Modernization: Modernization Theory and South Korean Intellectuals," in *Staging Growth: Modernization, Development, and the Global Cold War*, ed. David C. Engerman et al. (Amherst: University of Massachusetts Press, 2003), 253–54.

35. Odd Arne Westad, *The Global Cold War: Third World Interventions and the Making of Our Time* (Cambridge: Cambridge University Press, 2006).

36. Victor Korchmann, "Modernization and Democratic Values: The 'Japanese Model' in the 1960s," in Engerman et al., *Staging Growth*, 225–49.

37. Gregg Brazinsky, *Nation Building in South Korea: Koreans, Americans, and the Making of a Democracy* (Durham: University of North Carolina Press, 2007); Brazinsky, "Koreanizing Modernization," 251–73; Pak T'ae-gyun, *Wŏnhyŏng kwa pyŏnyong: Han'guk kyŏngje kaebal kyehoek ŭi kiwŏn* [Archetype and metamorphosis: The origins of Korea's economic development plans] (Seoul: Seoul National University Press, 2007).

38. Alice Amsden, *Asia's Next Giant: South Korea and Late Industrialization* (New York: Oxford University Press, 1989), 200–201.

39. Rosemary Foot, "The Cold War and Human Rights," in *The Cambridge History of the Cold War*, vol. 3, ed. Melvyn Leffler and Odd Westad (New York: Cambridge University Press, 2010), 445–65.

40. Eric Posner, *The Twilight of Human Rights Law* (New York: Oxford University Press, 2014), 15–19.

41. Roland Burke, *Decolonization and the Evolution of International Human Rights* (Philadelphia: University of Pennsylvania Press, 2010), 1

42. Vanessa Ogle, "State Rights Against Private Capital," *Humanity* 5, no. 2 (Summer 2014): 211–34.

43. Akira Iriye, Petra Goedde, and William I. Hitchcock, eds., *The Human Rights Revolution: An International History* (Oxford: Oxford University Press, 2012); Eckel and Moyn, *The Breakthrough.*

44. Cumings, *Origins of the Korean War*, 2:205; Robert Cottrell, *Roger Nash Baldwin and the American Civil Liberties Union* (New York: Columbia University Press, 2000), 315–19;

"Chosŏn Inkwŏn Ongho Yŏnmaeng kyŏlsŏng" [The foundation of the Korea Civil Liberties Union], *Kyŏnghyang sinmun*, May 25, 1947, 3.

45. Su-kyoung Hwang, *Korea's Grievous War* (Philadelphia: University of Pennsylvania Press, 2016), 59–117.

46. "Segye kigu e chŏngsik kaip taehan 'Inkwŏn Ongho Yŏnmaeng'" [The Korean League for the Rights of Man, registered for the international organization], *Tonga ilbo*, April 24, 1955, 3.

47. On human rights discourse before 1970 in Korea, see Yi Chŏng-ŭn, "Haebang hu inkwŏn tamnon ŭi hyŏngsŏng kwa chedohwa e kwanhan yŏn'gu, 1945-yŏn–1970-yŏn ch'o" [Human rights discourse and the institutionalization of human rights in Korea from 1945 to the early 1970s] (Ph.D. diss., Seoul National University, 2008).

Chapter 1. Protest Language

1. Petitioners to Kim Sŏng-sŏp, "Chinjŏngsŏ" [Petition], January 1973, serial no. 01130855-001, National Institute of Korean History (hereafter, NIKH); Yim Kyŏng-ja, "Kangje yebae to yebae imnikka" [Is a forced prayer even a prayer?], April 11, 1973, serial no. 01130855-004, NIKH.

2. In *Korean Workers*, Hagen Koo makes no reference to women workers' invocation of human rights; in fact, "human rights" does not appear in the index; see Koo, *Korean Workers: The Culture and Politics of Class Formation* (Ithaca, NY: Cornell University Press, 2001).

3. "Inkwŏn sŏnŏn 13-junyŏn, Pak Chŏng-hŭi Ŭijang kimyŏnsa" [The 13th anniversary of the UDHR—Chairman Park Chung-hee's speech], *Chosŏn ilbo*, December 10, 1961.

4. "Inkwŏn Onghogwa sinsŏl" [Establishment of the section for the protection of human rights], *Chosŏn ilbo*, May 19, 1962.

5. "'Kŏri ŭi hwaje'—sŏng'ŏp inkwŏn sangdamsil" [News on the street—Consulting office for human rights' large practice], *Chosŏn ilbo*, March 10, 1962.

6. "Kukche Inkwŏn Ongho Han'guk Yŏnmaeng Yi Hwal hoejang" [Yi Hwal of the International Human Rights League of Korea], *Chosŏn ilbo*, December 12, 1971.

7. For selected newspaper coverage, see "Han'guk ch'uk yogu chiji, Chuhan Migun Sinbun Hyŏpchŏng ch'egyŏl ŭl ch'okku, Kukche Inkwŏn Ongho Hyŏphoe ponbu sŏ hoehan" [International League for the Rights of Man reply: Supporting the Korean side's demands and urging the conclusion of the SOFA], *Chosŏn ilbo*, April 10, 1962; "Mi Chŏngbu t'aedo rŭl Inkwŏn Yŏnmaeng sŏ t'onggo, Haenghyŏp ch'egyŏl e noryŏk" [The International Human Rights League of Korea, reporting on the US government's efforts to conclude the SOFA], *Chosŏn ilbo*, June 30, 1962.

8. Yi Chŏng-ŭn, "Haebang hu inkwŏn tamnon," 186; for more, see 185–210.

9. See "Yusinjŏk ch'eje kaehyŏk tanhaeng" [Decisive actions for Yushin-style reform], *Kyŏnghyang sinmun*, October 18, 1972; "Pak Chŏnghŭi Ŭijang ŭi minjujuŭigwan" [Chairman Park Chung Hee's perspective on democracy], *Chosŏn ilbo*, March 3, 1962.

10. On changes in Third World nations' human rights policy, see Burke, *Decolonization*, 13–58; 112–44.

11. Jan Eckel, "The International League for the Rights of Man, Amnesty International, and the Changing Fate of Human Rights Activism from the 1940s Through the 1970s," *Humanity* 4, no. 2 (2013): 205.

12. Cmiel, "Emergence of Human Rights Politics," 1242.

13. *Amnesty International, 1961-1976: A Chronology* (London: Amnesty International, 1976), 1–3.

14. "Embassies," ca. April 1962, Correspondence with Embassies, 1961–1964, MF 450, IISH; AI, *Annual Report, 1961–1962* (London: Amnesty International, 1962).

15. "Choe In-gyu, Kwak Yŏng-ju, Cho Yong-su, Yim Hwa-su, Choe Paek-kun sahyŏng hwakin" [Confirming the death sentences of Ch'oe In-gyu, Kwak Yŏng-ju, Cho Yong-su, Yim Hwa-su], *Kyŏnghyang sinmun*, December 21, 1961; "Ŏje hao kyosuhyŏng chiphaeng" [The execution enforced yesterday afternoon], *Tonga ilbo*, December 22, 1961.

16. AI, *Annual Report, 1961–1962*, 14. It is unclear whether AI's 1961 intervention saved Song's life, as Song often claimed in the early 1970s. In his prison diary, published in the mid-1980s, he never mentioned AI's 1961 campaign. In fact, it was the PEN Club campaigns that garnered the Korean media's attention. See Song Chi-yŏng, *Usu ŭi sewŏl 1963–1969* [Prison diary, 1963–1969] (Seoul: Yungsŏng Ch'ulp'an, 1986), 13–14, 595, and 1027.

17. "Some Lawyers in the Prisoners of Conscience Library," no date, Appeal for Amnesty 1962, MF 481, IISH.

18. For a comparable case, see Peter Slezkine, "From Helsinki to Human Rights Watch: How an American Cold War Monitoring Group Became an International Human Rights Institution," *Humanity* 5, no. 3 (2014): 345–70.

19. AI, *Annual Report, 1980* (London: AI, 1980), 14; *Annual Report, 1968–1969* (London: AI, 1969), 0; *Annual Report, 1970–1971* (London: AI, 1971), 13; *AI Annual Report, 1972–1973* (London: AI, 1973), 12.

20. AI, *Annual Report, 1969–1970* (London: AI, 1970), 1–2.

21. For statistical data on AI's rapid growth in the 1970s, see AI, *Annual Report, 1980*, 6–7.

22. AI, *Annual Report, 1969–1970*, 4 and 6; AI, *Annual Report, 1970–1971*, 50–51.

23. Morris to Ennals, December 6, 1969, Ivan Morris Correspondence, MF 464, IISH.

24. Morris, memo, "Mission to South Korea by Ivan Morris for Amnesty International December 1969: Report," December 12, 1969, Mission—General, Box 6, Ivan 4, Ivan Morris Papers, Rare Book and Manuscript Library, Columbia University (hereafter, Morris Papers).

25. Ibid.

26. On the Truth Commission report, see Kukchŏngwŏn Kwagŏ Sagŏn Chinsil Kyumyŏng ŭl T'onghan Palchŏn Wiwŏnhoe, *Kwagŏ wa taehwa, mirae ŭi sŏngch'al* [Dialogue with the past, introspection for the future], vol. 2 (Seoul: National Intelligence Service, 2007), 429.

27. Morris, memo, "Mission to South Korea."

28. Ibid.

29. Morris to Hinze, January 4, 1970, Mission—General, Box 6, Ivan 4, Morris Papers.

30. Breidenstein to Hinze, March 7, 1970, SGO–NS Korea 1971–72, MF 16, IISH.

31. "South Korea—Formation of Amnesty Section," ca. March 1970, IEC Meeting March 1970, MF 243, IISH.

32. Breidenstein to Ennals, October 6, 1970, SGO–NS Korea 1971–72, MF 16, IISH.

33. Minjuhwa Undong Kinyŏm Saŏphoe Yŏn'gusŏ, ed., *Han'guk minjuhwa undongsa yŏnp'yo* [A chronological history of the Korean democratization movements] (Seoul: Sŏnin, 2006), 191–92.

34. Kukche Aemnest'i Han'guk Chibu 30-chunyŏn Kinyŏm Saŏp Wiwŏnhoe, *Han'guk Aemnest'i 30-yŏn! Inkwŏn 30-yŏn!* [Thirty years of AI Korea! The thirty-year human rights movement!] (Taegu: Kukche Aemnest'i Han'guk Chibu, 2002), 138–39.

35. Kwŏn Ŭn-jŏng, "Inkwŏn kwa chayu ka hŭrŭnŭn t'ongil ŭi kkum" [The dream of unification running with human rights and freedom], *Inkwŏn* 66 (2011): 5.

36. Pak Ŭn-gyŏng, "Yŏksa ŭi surye pak'wi nŭn kkŭdŏpsi tonda kŭrŏna nugun'ga kullyŏya tonda" [History goes on endlessly, what will move it], *Shindong'a* 578 (2007): 528.

37. Kukche Aemnest'i Han'guk Chibu, *Han'guk Aemnest'i 30-yŏn!*, 137–38; Yun Hyŏn, interview with author, Seoul, October 7, 2011.

38. Breidenstein to Ennals, October 6, 1970, SGO–NS Korea 1971–72, MF 16, IISH.

39. Ibid.

40. Ibid.

41. Kukche Aemnest'i Han'guk Chibu, *Han'guk Aemnest'i 30-yŏn!*, 139.

42. Ennals to Breidenstein, January 19, 1971, SGO–NS Korea 1971–72, MF 16, IISH.

43. Yoon to Ennals, July 6, 1971, SGO–NS Korea 1971–72, MF 16, IISH.

44. Breidenstein to Hinze, July 10, 1971, SGO–NS Korea 1971–72, MF 16, IISH.

45. Ennals to Yoon, July 26, 1971, SGO–NS Korea 1971–72, MF 16, IISH; Ennals to Breidenstein, July 30, 1971, SGO–NS Korea 1971–72, MF 16, IISH; Yoon to Ennals, November 19, 1971, SGO–NS Korea 1971–72, MF 16, IISH.

46. Ennals to Yoon, October 15, 1971, SGO–NS Korea 1971–72, MF 16, IISH.

47. Yoon to Ennals, November 19, 1971, SGO–NS Korea 1971–72, MF 16, IISH; Yoon to Ennals, December 2, 1971, SGO–NS Korea 1971–72, MF 16, IISH.

48. *Amnesty Newsletter Korea*, no. 1, December 1971, SGO–NS Korea 1971–72, MF 16, IISH; Yoon to Ennals, December 2, 1971, SGO–NS Korea 1971–72, MF 16, IISH; Yoon to Ennals, January 22, 1972, SGO–NS Korea 1971–72, MF 16, IISH; *Amnesty Newsletter Korea*, no. 3, February 1972, SGO–NS Korea 1971–72, MF 16, IISH.

49. Ennals to Yoon, March 2, 1972, SGO–NS Korea 1971–72, MF 16, IISH.

50. For a history of the *chaeya* movements, see Myung-Lim Park, "The *Chaeya*," in Kim and Vogel, eds. *Park Chung Hee Era*, 373–400.

51. "Son'ŏnmun" [Inaugural statement], ca. March 1972, SGO–NS Korea 1971–72, MF 16, IISH.

52. Moyn, *Christian Human Rights*, 22.

53. Ibid., 9–34.

54. Ibid., 33.

55. David Johnson, ed., *Uppsala to Nairobi, 1968–1975* (New York: WCC, 1975), 33, 48–50.

56. CCIA (Commission of the Churches on International Affairs of the WCC), *The Churches in International Affairs: Reports, 1970–1973* (Geneva: WCC, 1974), 112.

57. AI, *Annual Report, 1980*, 4.

58. CCIA, *Churches in International Affairs*, 112; Johnson, *Uppsala to Nairobi*, 134.

59. CCIA, *Churches in International Affairs*, 113–14.

60. Ibid., 115–17.

61. Ibid., 83–84.

62. Ibid., 111.

63. Korean Association of Urban Industrial Mission Groups (KAUIMG), memo, "Chŏn'guk Tosi San'ŏp Sŏn'gyo Yŏn'guhoe pogosŏ" [Report on Urban Industrial Mission Groups' research], ca. September 1973, Folder 24, Box 2, George Ogle Papers, Pitts Theology Library, Emory University (hereafter, Ogle Papers); "Inkwŏn suho panghyang mosaek" [Exploring the ways to protect human rights], *Han'guk kidok kongbo* [Korean Christian Press], November 17, 1973.

64. Pak Hyŏng-gyu, *Pak Hyŏng-gyu hoegorok* [Pak Hyŏng-gyu's memoir] (P'aju: Ch'angbi, 2010), 172–73; Kim Kwan-sŏk Moksa Kohui Kinyŏm Mujip Ch'ulp'an Wiwŏnhoe, ed., *I ttang*

e p'yŏnghwa rŭl: 70-yŏndae ŭi inkwŏn undong [Bringing peace to this land: Human rights movements in the 1970s] (Seoul: Kim Kwan-sŏk Moksa Kohui Kinyŏm Mujip Ch'ulp'an Wiwŏnhoe, 1991), 330.

65. O Chae-sik, interview with author, Seoul, November 18, 2010; Pak Hyŏng-gyu, *Pak Hyŏng-gyu hoegorok*, 141–43.

66. Kim Kwan-sŏk Moksa, *I ttang e*, 328–29; O Chae-sik interview.

67. Margaret White and Herbert White, eds., *The Power of People: Community Action in Korea* (Tokyo: UIM, East Asia Christian Conference, 1973).

68. Saul Alinsky, *Rules for Radicals: A Pragmatic Primer for Realistic Radicals* (1971; repr., New York: Vintage Books, 1989).

69. Bruce Cumings, *Parallax Visions: Making Sense of American–East Asian Relations* (Durham, NC: Duke University Press, 2000), 112. See also Charles Armstrong, *North Korean Revolution, 1945–1950* (Ithaca, NY: Cornell University Press, 2003); and Suzy Kim, *Everyday Life in the North Korean Revolution, 1945–1950* (Ithaca, NY: Cornell University Press, 2013).

70. White and White, *The Power of People*, 91–92.

71. Alinsky, *Rules for Radicals*, xxv.

72. Pak Hyŏng-gyu, review of *Haksaeng kwa sahoe chŏngŭi* [Students and social justice], by Pu Kwang-sŏk, *Kidokkyo sasang* 15, no. 8 (1971): 116.

73. For an outline of these theologies along with selected works, see Carl E. Braaten and Robert W. Jenson, eds., *A Map of Twentieth-Century Theology: Readings from Karl Barth to Radical Pluralism* (Minneapolis: Fortress, 1995).

74. *Haksadan News*, vol. 1, no. 3, October 1, 1969, serial no. 58530, Korea Democracy Foundation (hereafter, KDF).

75. Pu Kwang-sŏk, *Haksaeng kwa sahoe chŏngŭi* [Students and social justice] (Seoul: Taehan Kidokkyo Sŏhoe and KSCF, 1971); Gerhard Breidenstein, *Christians and Social Justice: A Study Handbook on Modern Theology, Socio-Political Problems in Korea, and Community Organization* (Privately published, 1971); Han'guk Kidokkyo Kyohoe Hyŏbŭihoe, *1970-yŏndae minjuhwa undong* [The 1970s democratization movements] (Seoul: Han'guk Kidokkyo Kyohoe Hyŏbŭihoe, 1987), 1:99.

76. O Chae-sik interview.

77. O Chae-sik, "1970-yŏndae wa kidokkyo undong ŭi taeŭng" [Christian movements in the 1970s], in Kim Kwan-sŏk Moksa, *I ttang e*, 73.

78. J. Bryan Hehir, "The Modern Catholic Church and Human Rights: The Impact of the Second Vatican Council," in *Christianity and Human Rights: An Introduction*, ed. John Witte Jr. and Frank S. Alexander (New York: Cambridge University Press, 2010), 119–24.

79. Don Baker, "The Transformation of the Catholic Church in Korea: From a Missionary Church to an Indigenous Church," *Journal of Korean Religion* 4, no. 1 (2013): 11–42.

80. Kim Chi-ha, "Kim Chi-ha hoegorok" [Kim Chi-ha's memoir], series no. 160, *Pressian*, October 17, 2002, available from https://www.pressian.com, last visited on October 26, 2020.

81. Kim Kwan-sŏk Moksa, *I ttang e*, 328–29.

82. Kim Kwan-sŏk Moksa, *I ttang e*, 328–29; Han'guk Kidokkyo Kyohoe Hyŏbŭihoe, *1970-yŏndae minjuhwa undong*, 1:256–60.

83. KSCF, "Striving for the Righteousness of Christ," October 5, 1973, serial no. 01130996–004, NIKH; Linda Jones, "Rŭppo chesam segye wa inkwŏn" [Reportage on the Third World and human rights], *Wŏlgan Taehwa* [Monthly dialogue], February 1977, 238–99.

84. "Special Labor Union Training—Activities of Labour Union & Human Rights," ca. 1970, serial no. 359590, KDF; Yoon to Ennals, January 23, 1972, SGO–NS Korea 1971–72, MF 16, IISH.

85. Yu Pyŏng-gwan to Kim Chong-dae, "Kŭlloja inkwŏn pojang ŭl wihan ch'onghoejŏkin hyŏpcho ŭi il" [Letter to the Presbyterian Church of Korea on safeguards for workers' human rights], April 2, 1973, serial no. 357139, KDF.

86. Ibid.

87. Petitioners to Taehan Mobang Company Chair, "Taehan mobang esŏ haego doen 4-myŏng ŭn pokjik toeŏya hamnida" [We demand the four fired workers' reinstatement], April 1973, serial no. 01130855–006, NIKH.

88. Ko Sŏng-sin to Seoul District Prosecutor Office Director, "Kosojang" [Accusation], May 9, 1973, serial no. 357111, KDF.

89. KAUIMG, memos, "Ch'ŏngju ch'ŏngsobu (170-myŏng) e taehan munje" [Issues of cleaners in Ch'ŏngju], September 12, 1973, and "Chŏn'guk Tosi San'ŏp Sŏn'gyo Yŏn'guhoe pogosŏ" [no date], both in Folder 24, Box 2, Ogle Papers.

90. Pak Hyŏng-gyu, Pak Hyŏng-gyu hoegorok, 145–47, 166–68, 174–75; Kim Kwan-sŏk Moksa, I ttang e, 334.

91. "Report of National Council of Churches, Japan and National Council of Churches, USA, East Asia Working Group Team, Visit to Korea, Aug 1–3, 1973," August 10, 1973, Folder 26, Box 2, Ogle Papers.

92. Han'guk Kidokkyo Kyohoe Hyŏbŭihoe, 1970-yŏndae minjuhwa undong, 1:296.

93. Kim Kwan-sŏk Moksa, I ttang e, 342–43.

94. "'Inkwŏn munje hyŏbŭihoe' rŭl wihan charyo (ch'oan)" [Consultation on human rights (draft) material], ca. October 1973, serial no. 452379, KDF; "Kyohoe, sŏn'gyo, inkwŏn kŭ killo" [The future of church, mission, and human rights], Han'guk kidok kongbo, November 17 and 24, 1973; CCIA, Churches in International Affairs, 111–17.

95. Han'guk Kidokkyo Kyohoe Hyŏbŭihoe, 1970-yŏndae minjuhwa undong, 1:296–300.

96. "Kyohoe wa inkwŏn kido chugan" [Church and human rights prayer week], December 1, 1973, serial no. 445821, KDF.

97. Kukche Aemnest'i Han'guk Wiwŏnhoe, Han'guk Aemnest'i 5-yŏn yaksa, 2–6.

98. Han'guk Kidokkyo Kyohoe Hyŏbŭihoe, 1970-yŏndae minjuhwa undong, 1:292–94.

99. Kukche Aemnest'i Han'guk Wiwŏnhoe, Han'guk Aemnest'i 5-yŏn yaksa, 5.

100. Han'guk Kidokkyo Kyohoe Hyŏbŭihoe, 1970-yŏndae minjuhwa undong, 1:300.

101. "Kach'ing Han'guk Kyohoe Tosi San'ŏp Munje Hyŏbŭihoe—ch'onghoe charyo" [Tentative title—The Korean Christian Action Organization for Urban Industrial Mission—General meeting material], ca. September 1971, serial no. 105555, KDF; Pak Hyŏng-gyu, Pak Hyŏng-gyu hoegorok, 166–68, 195–98.

102. Hyung Kyu Pak and Seung Hyuk Cho [This report was written in English], "Activity Report (1973)," December 31, 1973, serial no. 05-012444, Kim Dae-Jung Presidential Library; "Kyohoe wa inkwŏn yŏnhap yebae" [United worship service: Church and Human Rights Week], December 16, 1973, serial no. 97860, KDF.

103. Han'guk Kidokkyo Kyohoe Hyŏbŭihoe, 1970-yŏndae minjuhwa undong, 1:299–300; "Silhaeng Wilwŏnhoe hoeŭirok sabon" [NCCK Executive Committee minutes], December 10, 1973, serial no. 103341, KDF; "Inkwŏn Wiwŏnhoe hoeŭi: Han'guk Kidokkyo Kyohoe Hyŏbŭihoe Inkwŏnwi hoech'ik" [Meeting on bylaws for the NCCK's Human Rights Committee], serial no. 102832, KDF; "1974-yŏndo Han'guk Kidokkyo Kyohoe Hyŏbŭihoe Inkwŏn Wiwŏnhoe saŏp

kyehoek an" [Discussion of NCKK Human Rights Committee plans, 1974], ca. May 1974, serial no. 360506, KDF.

104. See Yoon to Ennals, April 4, 1972, SGO–NS Korea 1971–72, MF 16, IISH; "April 1, 9, 1972, Weekly Chosun," SGO–NS Korea 1971–72, MF 16, IISH.

105. Yi Pyŏng-rin Pyŏhosa Munjip Kanhaeng Wiwŏnhoe, *Simdang Yi Pyŏng-rin pyŏhosa munjip* [Lawyer Yi Pyŏng-rin's collective works] (Seoul: Ture, 1991), 53–54; Han Sŭng-hŏn, *Wijang sidae ŭi jŭngŏn* [Testimonies in the era of camouflage] (Seoul: Pŏmusa, 1974), 346–69; Kukche Aemnest'i Han'guk Wiwŏnhoe, *Han'guk Aemnesŭt'i 5-yŏn yaksa.*

106. Kim Chae-jung, "Chi Hak-sun Chukyo ŭi yangsim sŏnŏn" [Bishop Chi Hak-sun's declaration of conscience], *Kyŏnghyang sinmun*, June 15, 2003, available at http://news.khan.co .kr, last accessed April 9, 2017; Chi Hak-sun, "Yangsim sŏnŏn" [Declaration of conscience], July 23, 1974, serial no. 59833, KDF.

107. Bruce Cumings, "The Kim Chi Ha Case," *New York Review of Books* 22, no. 16 (1975).

108. Minjuhwa Undong Kinyŏm Saŏphoe Yŏn'guso, *Han'guk minjuhwa undongsa yŏnp'yo*, 265–69, 296, and 310.

109. Yi Pyŏng-rin Pyŏhosa Munjip Kanhaeng Wiwŏnhoe, *Simdang Yi Pyŏng-rin pyŏhosa munjip*, 53–54; Kukche Aemnest'i Han'guk Wiwŏnhoe, *Han'guk Aemnest'i 5-yŏn yaksa*, 7–9.

110. See AI Korea, "Hanŭl ŭl pogo ttang ŭl pogo, yŏnsujaryo 1" [Look up at the sky, look down at the earth: Research material no. 1] (February 1978), back cover, Folder 13, Box 1, Series 1.1, Research Group IV, AIUSA Collection, Rare Book and Manuscript Library, Columbia University, New York (hereafter, AIUSA Collection).

111. Han Sŭng-hŏn, interview with author, Seoul, September 22, 2011; Yun Hyŏn interview.

112. Kukche Aemnest'i Han'guk Chibu, *Han'guk Aemnest'i 30-yŏn!*, 37 and 53–56.

113. "Guidelines on the Relevance for AI's Work of Economic, Social and Cultural Rights in Relation to Civil and Political Rights," ca. January 1976, IEC POL, January 1976, MF 245, IISH.

114. Coordination Unit to all national sections, memorandum, "Working Rules for AI (Draft)," March 31, 1976, IEC for comment, April 1976, MF 246, IISH; Richard to Ennals et al., memo, "NS Work in Their Own Countries," November 17, 1977, Sections Work on Own Countries 1977–1979, MF 265, IISH.

115. AI, *AI Handbook*, 7th ed. (London: AI, 1991).

116. See Kukche Aemnest'i Han'guk Chibu, *Han'guk Aemnest'i 30-yŏn!*

117. George Todd, "Mission and Justice: The Experience of Urban and Industrial Mission," *International Review of Mission* 65, no. 259 (1976): 251–61.

118. For *Abstract Service* issues, see Boxes 83–87, ICUIS Records, Richard Daley Library Special Collections, University of Illinois at Chicago.

Chapter 2. Transpacific Politics

1. Kukchŏngwŏn Kwagŏ Sagŏn Chinsil Kyumyŏng ŭl T'onghan Palchŏn Wiwŏnhoe, "Inmin hyŏngmyŏngdang mit minch'ŏng hangnyŏn sagŏn chinsil kyumyŏng" [Telling the truth about the PRP and the NDYSF cases], in *Kwagŏ wa taehwa, mirae ŭi sŏngch'al*, 99–291.

2. "74-yŏn ŭi inkwŏn, Aemnesŭt'i Han'gukwi segye inkwŏn sŏnŏn" [Human Rights in 1974: AI Korea's public lecture for the UDHR celebration], *Chosŏn ilbo*, December 12, 1974.

3. Ibid. An English translation of the article was delivered to AI IS. See "The *Chosun ilbo*, December 12, 1974," SGO–NS Korea 1973–75, MF 16, IISH.

4. Harris to Morris, February 4, 1974, National Sections—General Corres 1973–74, MF 562, IISH. On the concept of *chaeya*, see Myung-Lim Park, "The *Chaeya*," 373–400.

5. Kurata to Harris, February 8, 1974, SGO–NS Japan 1974–75, MF 17, IISH.

6. "South Korean Mission Proposal," memo, February 15, 1974, HORO—Kor Corr 1970–75, MF 557, IISH.

7. Grant to Morris, March 20, 1974, Asia National Section 1973–74, MF 562, IISH.

8. Shimizu to Ennals, April 12, 1974, HORO—Kor Corr 1970–75, MF 557, IISH.

9. Morris to Ennals, April 17, 1974, IEC ASA 1974, MF 245, IISH.

10. Ibid.

11. Harris to Ennals, April 19, 1974, SGO–NS Japan 1974–75, MF 17, IISH.

12. Harris to Cheng, May 31, 1974, HORO—Kor Corr 1970–75, MF 557, IISH.

13. Shimizu to Ennals, June 14, 1974, IEC ASA July 1974, MF 82, IISH.

14. Ennals to Harris, May 8, 1974, SGO–NS Japan 1974–75, MF 17, IISH; and Shimizu to Ennals, June 14, 1974.

15. Ennals to Butler, June 21, 1974, SGO Korea 1974, AI MF 8, IISH.

16. Kurata to Cheng, June 30, 1974, SGO–NS Japan 1974–75, MF 17, IISH.

17. See Moyn, *The Last Utopia*, 132 and 150–51.

18. Cheng to Ennals and Grant, July 5, 1974; Rodley to Cheng, June 27, 1974; Nigel Rodley to Cheng, June 14, 1974, SGO Korea 1974, MF 8, IISH.

19. For a concise discussion on the intersection between human rights and humanitarianism, see Michael Barnett, *Empire of Humanity: A History of Humanitarianism* (Ithaca, NY: Cornell University Press, 2011), 19.

20. "AI Urges South Korea to Commute Death Sentences," AI news release, July 12, 1974, SGO Korea 1974, MF 8, IISH; Cheng, memo, "Trial of 54 South Koreans Charged Under Emergency Regulation 4," July 15, 1974, HORO—Kor Corr 1970–75, MF 557, IISH; Minjuhwa Undong Kinyŏm Saŏphoe Yŏn'guso, *Han'guk minjuhwa undongsa yŏnp'yo*, 265.

21. US Congress, House Committee on Foreign Affairs, *International Protection of Human Rights: The Work of International Organizations and the Role of U.S. Foreign Policy . . .* (Washington, DC: US Government Printing Office, 1974), 554.

22. US Congress, House Committee on Foreign Affairs, *Human Rights in the World Community: A Call for U.S. Leadership . . .* (Washington, DC: US Government Printing Office, 1974), 1, 3, 9.

23. From Section 502B, currently codified as 22 U.S.C. § 2304, available at https://codes.findlaw.com, last accessed September 23, 2019.

24. Butler to Ennals, July 11, 1974, SGO Korea 1974, MF 8, IISH.

25. Grant, memo, "Telephone Conversation with William Butler," July 16, 1974, SGO Korea 1974, MF 8, IISH.

26. "Conversation with Arthur Michaelson," memo, July 16, 1974, SGO Korea 1974, MF 8, IISH.

27. Grant to Michaelson, July 19, 1974, HORO—Kor Corr 1970–75, MF 557, IISH.

28. Butler to Ennals, July 25, 1974, SGO Korea 1974, MF 8, IISH.

29. Ibid.

30. Butler, "Political Repression in South Korea," report (updated), October 1974, Mission Report South Korea—July 1974, MF 564, IISH.

31. Ibid.; see also Bruce Cumings, "Is America an Imperial Power?," *Current History*, November 2003, 355–60.

32. Butler, "Political Repression in South Korea."

33. Following the Korean War, Averell Harriman, the undersecretary of state for East Asian affairs during the Kennedy administration was the first to broach the idea of withdrawing US troops from South Korea. See Cumings, "The Structural Basis of 'Anti-Americanism,'" in *Korean Attitudes Toward the United States: Changing Dynamics*, ed. David Steinberg (Armonk, NY: Sharpe, 2005), 104.

34. Cheng to Grant, memo, "Amnesty's Role in South Korea," September 23, 1974, HORO—Kor Corr 1970–75, MF 557, IISH.

35. Ann Marie Clark, *Diplomacy of Conscience: Amnesty International and Changing Human Rights Norms* (Princeton, NJ: Princeton University Press, 2001), 14.

36. Memo, Yutaka Ogita's letter, October 30, 1974, SGO Korea 1974, MF 8, IISH [no further information on who created and sent or who received]; Kim Sŏl-i and Yi Kyŏng-ŭn, *Chaetpit sidae pora pit koun kkum* [A beautiful purple-color dream in the gray-color era] (Seoul: KDF, 2006), 49–50.

37. The shunning of those accused of espionage or of having Communist ties continued in the 1980s. See Minjuhwa Undong Kinyŏm Saŏphoe, *Han'guk minjuhwa undongsa*, 2:507.

38. Memo, Ogita's letter, October 30, 1974.

39. "Situation of Members of the Korean Committee of Amnesty," memo, January 1975, SGO Korea 1974, MF 8, IISH.

40. Yun Hyŏn, interview with author, October 7, 2011.

41. Kim and Yi, *Chaetpit sidae*, 61–65.

42. George Ogle, *Liberty to the Captives: The Struggle Against Oppression in South Korea* (Atlanta: John Knox Press, 1977), 136–37.

43. AI Asia Research Department, memo, "Brief Outline of Events in the '54' Case, South Korea," February 5, 1975, NS Circulars 1974 ASIA, MF 113, IISH.

44. George Ogle, *Liberty to the Captives*, 136–37.

45. James Sinnott, *Hyŏnjang chŭngŏn 1975-yŏn 4-wŏl 9-il* [On-the-spot testimony on the 9 April 1975 incident], trans. Kim Kŏn-ok and Yi U-kyŏng (Seoul: Pitture, 2004), 121–25.

46. Friends of Rev. George Ogle, memo, "Special to Mainichi Shimbun Publications," January 30, 1975, SGO–NS Japan 1974–75, MF 17, IISH.

47. Fox Butterfield, "7 Dissidents Doomed by Seoul Are Said to Be Spies for North," *New York Times* (hereafter, *NYT*), November 26, 1974.

48. George Ogle, *Liberty to the Captives*, 135–42.

49. Rustand to Davis, memo, November 4, 1974, TR 11–2 Seoul, Korea, 10–22 to 23–74, 1–30–4 to 10–29–74, General, Box 40, WHCF Subject File, Gerald Ford Presidential Library (hereafter, GFPL).

50. Sinnott, *Hyŏnjang chŭngŏn*, 145–47. Quote translated by author.

51. George Ogle, *Liberty to the Captives*, 150–54; for a scholarly account on the declining threats from North Korea post-1968, see Pak T'ae-gyun, *Ubang kwa cheguk, Han-Mi kwan'gye ŭi tu sinhwa: 8.15 esŏ 5.18 kkaji* [Ally and empire, two myths in US-Korean relations: From national liberation in 1945 to the Kwangju Uprising in 1980] (P'aju: Ch'angbi, 2006).

52. "U.S. Bishop Leads Catholics in a Protest March in Seoul," *NYT*, October 21, 1974; Fox Butterfield, "2,000 Catholics Protest in Seoul," *NYT*, November 7, 1974; Fox Butterfield, "Coming Ford Visit Debated in Seoul," *NYT*, November 11, 1974.

53. "Kim oemu panjŏng temo e palk'yŏ" [Foreign Minister Kim speaks against the anti-government protests], *Tonga ilbo*, November 9, 1974; "Kim Oemu sŏn'gyosa ch'ubang palŏn ŭl

puin" [Foreign Minister Kim's denial of his remark on the missionaries' expulsion], *Kyŏnghyang sinmun*, November 12, 1974.

54. "Yŏlolin ch'ongmu sŏngt'o" [NCCK general secretary condemns Premier Kim's religious denunciation], *Tonga ilbo*, November 11, 1974. For the original biblical verse, see *New International Version*, Romans 13:1–2, accessed January 15, 2017, http://www.biblegateway.com.

55. Sinnott, *Hyŏnjang chŭngŏn*, 185–92; Sinnott, memo, "The Protest by Wives of Political Prisoners at the U.S. Embassy in Seoul, Korea: The Testimony of James Sinnott, M.M.," November 21, 1974, Folder 34, Box 4, Ogle Papers.

56. George Ogle, *Liberty to the Captives*, 133, 162–65.

57. AI Asia Research Department, "Brief Outline of Events in the '54' Case."

58. Rosemary Foot, "The Cold War and Human Rights," in *The Cambridge History of the Cold War*, vol. 3, *Endings*, ed. Melvin P. Leffler and Odd Arne Westad (New York: Cambridge University Press, 2010), 445–65.

59. See Moyn, *The Last Utopia*; Sarah Snyder, *Human Rights Activism and the End of the Cold War: A Transnational History of the Helsinki Network* (New York: Cambridge University Press, 2011); and Keys, *Reclaiming American Virtue*.

60. US Congress, House Committee on Foreign Affairs, *Human Rights in the World Community*, 10–11.

61. US Congress, House Committee on Foreign Affairs, *Human Rights in South Korea: Implications for U.S. Policy . . .* (Washington: US Government Printing Office, 1974), 1–4.

62. US Department of State, Bureau of Public Affairs, "Special Report: Human Rights in the Republic of Korea," East Asia and Pacific Series 212 (September 1974), TR 11–2, 12–1–74 to 1–26–75, External, Box 40, WHCF Subject File, GFPL.

63. See "Pat M. Holt, Chief of Staff, Foreign Relations Committee," Oral History Interviews, Senate Historical Office, Washington, DC, accessed June 20, 2016, www.senate.gov.

64. Bureau of Public Affairs, "Special Report."

65. East Asia Researcher to All National Sections, memo, "Trial of 54: Commutation of Five Death Sentences," July 28, 1974, HORO—Kor Corr 1970–75, MF 557, IISH.

66. House Committee on Foreign Affairs, *Human Rights in South Korea*, 6–9.

67. Butler, "Political Repression in South Korea."

68. "'Han'guk inkwŏn munje' Mi Kukmusŏng t'ŭkpyŏl pogosŏ" [State Department's special report on 'Human rights in Korea'], *Tonga ilbo*, October 3, 1974.

69. Keys, "Congress, Kissinger, and the Origins of Human Rights Diplomacy," *Diplomatic History* 34, no. 5 (September 2010): 839; Department of State, Secret, Secretary's Principles and Regionals Staff Meeting, December 23, 1974, National Security Archive Electronic Briefing Book No. 110, "The Pinochet File," accessed June 29, 2016, http://nsarchive.gwu.edu.

70. "P'odŭ, 11-wŏl 22-il naehan Ch'ŏngwadae-Paegakkwan palp'yo" [White House and Blue House announce President Ford's visit to Korea], *Kyŏnghyang sinmun*, September 21, 1974.

71. Richard A. Ericson to Kissinger, telegram, "Korean Interest in Presidential Visit," September 6, 1974, Korea–State Department Telegrams to SECSTATE-EXDIS (I), Box 11, NSA Presidential Country Files for East Asia and the Pacific (hereafter, PCFEAP), GFPL.

72. Hodgson to Kissinger, telegrams, "Japanese-Korean Difficulties," September 9, 1974, and "Current Japan-ROK Dispute," September 10, 1974, Japan-State Department Telegrams to SECSTATE-EXDIS (I), Box 8, NSA PCFEAP, GFPL.

73. Kissinger to Sneider, telegram, "Presidential Visit," September 17, 1974, Korea–State Department Telegrams from SECSTATE—NODIS (I), Box 11, NSA PCFEAP, GFPL; Sneider

to Kissiner, telegram, "Presidential Visit," September 17, 1974, Korea–State Department Telegrams to SECSTATE—NODIS (I), Box 11, NSA PCFEAP, GFPL.

74. "Panghan e uryŏ p'yomyŏng K'enedi Sang-wŏn Ŭiwŏn" [Senator Kennedy expresses his concern about Ford's visit to Korea], *Tonga ilbo*, September 21, 1974.

75. Edwin O. Reischauer, "The Korean Connection: Is It Time to Disengage?," *New York Times Magazine*, September 22, 1974, 64.

76. Richard Halloran, "Park Seems Ready to Ease Seoul Curbs," *NYT*, September 23, 1974; "Seoul Students Ask Prisoners' Release," *NYT*, September 24, 1974; "2,000 Catholics in Seoul Renew Protests," *NYT*, September 27, 1974.

77. "Mi Hawŏn Oegyowi sujŏngan ch'aet'aek Taehan kunwŏn 6-ch'ŏnman talla sakkam" [The International Relations Committee of the House of Representatives passed a revised bill to cut 60 million in aid to Korea], *Tonga ilbo*, September 25, 1974.

78. Bernard Gwertzman, "Ford's Visit Is Tied to Belief Repression Will Ease," *NYT*, September 28, 1974; "'Pisang sat'ae wanhwa,' Mi kowi kwalli chŏnmang" [High-ranking US officials predict Seoul's political amelioration], *Tonga ilbo*, September 28, 1974.

79. "P'odŭ panghan ch'ŏn mojong choch'ŏ" [A sort of measure made in Seoul before Ford's visit], *Tonga ilbo*, September 30, 1974; "Po'odŭ panghan apsŏ mojong choch'ŏ [A sort of measure made in Seoul prior to Ford's visit], *Chosŏn ilbo*, October 1, 1974.

80. "Mi Kukmusŏng kunwŏn sakkam, inkwŏn munje kwallyŏn" [US State Department is reducing military aid based on human rights], *Tonga ilbo*, October 2, 1974.

81. "NYT podo, 'chŏngch'aek wanhwa' wa chikkyŏl" [*NYT*'s report: A direct connection exists between Ford's visit and political moderation in Seoul], *Tonga ilbo*, September 30, 1974; "P'odŭ chŏngch'ibŏm sŏkpang tŭng kidae panghan tongŭi NYT podo" [*NYT*'s report: Ford agreed to visit Korea owing to anticipated release of political prisoners], *Chosŏn ilbo*, October 1, 1974.

82. "P'odŭ inp'a, Sŏul ŭi yŏlgwang" [Excited crowds greet Ford in Seoul], *Chosŏn ilbo*, November 23, 1974.

83. Richard Smyser to Kissinger, "Draft Memorandum of Conversation Between President Ford and South Korean President Park," November 27, 1974, November 22, 1974—Ford, Kissinger, South Korean President Park Chung-Hee, Box 7, NSA Memoranda of Conversations, 1973–1977, GFPL.

84. Kissinger to Sneider, telegram, "ROK Emergency Measure," June 21, 1975, Korea–State Department Telegrams From SECSTATE–NODIS (3), Box 11, NSA PCFEAP, GFPL.

85. Memorandum of Conversation (Ford, Kissinger, Scowcroft), November 12, 1974 (9:20–10:10 A.M.), Ford, Kissinger, Box 7, NSA Memoranda of Conversations, 1973–1977, GFPL.

86. Kissinger to Sneider, telegram, "ROK Emergency Measure," June 21, 1975.

87. "Habibŭ paegyŏng sŏlmyŏng So Chunggong i Han'guk sŭngin apsŏ Misŏ mŏnjŏ Pukhan sŭnginanhae" [Habib's explanation: US did not endorse North Korea before the Soviets and China endorsed South Korea], *Tonga ilbo*, November 23, 1974.

88. Halloran, "Ford Hints Seoul Repression Perils Aid," *NYT*, November 23, 1974.

89. On the role of Halloran and other American journalists in transnational human rights campaigns for human rights and democracy, see Chung, "The 'Pictures in Our Heads.'"

90. "P'odŭ pojwagwan onŭl saebyŏk e Mi sŏn'gyosa 5-myŏng myŏndam" [Early morning meeting between Ford's aide and 5 American missionaries], *Chosŏn ilbo*, November 23, 1974; "Habibŭ Mi Ch'agwanbo ka palkhin naeyong kungnae eso kija hoegyŏn" [Assistant Secretary

Habib's remarks at the press conference for domestic and international media], *Tonga ilbo*, November 25, 1974; "Sŭmaijŏ Anbo Wiwŏn chuhan Mi sŏngjikcha 9-myŏng kwa kandam" [Smyser, the NSC staff, meeting with nine American missionaries living in Korea], *Tonga ilbo*, November 23, 1974; Smyser to Kissinger, memo, "My Meeting with American Missionaries in Korea," November 29, 1974, Korea (2), Box 9, NSA PCFEAP, GFPL.

91. George Ogle, *Liberty to the Captives*, 159–60.

92. "Kim Che-wŏn Ŭiwŏn ch'okku, pŏboein oeguk chonggyoin ch'ubang myŏngnyŏng naerirago" [Assemblyman Kim Che-wŏn urges government to expel foreign missionaries for violating the law], *Tonga ilbo*, November 28, 1974.

Chapter 3. Washington

1. Peter Hazelhurst, "Freed Opponents of the S. Korean Regime Tell of Torture to Extract False Confessions," *The Times* (London), February 18, 1975, Mission Report ROK March–April 1975, MF 564, IISH; Robert Whymant, "Students Tell of Korean Tortures," *The Guardian*, February 18, 1975, Mission Report ROK March–April 1975, MF 564, IISH; "Kadŭn komun ta tang'haetta" [All forms of torture enforced], *Tonga ilbo*, February 17, 1975.

2. "Bishop Chi Hak-sun" and "The Declaration of Conscience of Bishop Chi Hak-soon," Folder 25, Box 4, Ogle Papers.

3. Kippŭm kwa Hŭimang Samok Yŏn'guso, ed., *Amhŭk sok ŭi hwaetpul* [A torchlight in the dark age], vol. 1 (Kippŭm kwa Hŭimang Samok Yŏn'guso, 1996), 284–85 and 426–28.

4. Han'guk Kidokkyo Kyohoe Hyŏbŭihoe, *1970-yŏndae minjuhwa undong*, 2:583–84.

5. Kim Chŏng-nam, *Chinsil, kwangjang e sŏda* [The truth stands upon the square] (P'aju: Ch'angbi, 2005), 92–93.

6. "Tortured by KCIA: Poet Kim," August 5, 1975, *Japan Times*, Folder 12, Box 4, Ogle Papers; Kim Chŏng-nam, *Chinsil*, 124–33; Kim Chi-ha, "From a Seoul Prison," *NYT*, December 17, 1975.

7. Yuasa et al., "The Poet, for Kim Chi Ha—Seeking a Wider International Support," June 12, 1975, SGO Japan 1970–79, MF 8, IISH.

8. Kim to Embassy in Sweden and Norway, memo, August 16, 1975; Embassy in Norway to Kim, memo, August 20, 1975, "Kim Chi-ha siin e taehan 1976-yŏndo Nobel Pyŏnghwasang hubo tŭngnok munje," Folder 6, MF B–06–0026, Korean Diplomatic Archives (hereafter, DA).

9. Geoffrey Wilkinson to John Humphreys, memo, "Kim Chi Ha/ South Korea/ Dutch Section," 18, 1977, Correspondence with NS 1977, MF 560, IISH.

10. Ennals to the Chief Judge, "Second Trial of Soh Sung and Soh Joon-shik Between January 13 and January 22, 1972," January 14, 1972, SGO Korea 1972–73, MF 8, IISH; Ennals to Sanguinetti, January 18, 1973, SGO Korea 1972–73, MF 8, IISH.

11. "Hyŏng hwakchŏngja onŭl p'ullyŏ" [Prisoners having imprisonment decision released today], *Tonga ilbo*, February 15, 1975.

12. "'Minju hoebok kusokcha hyŏbuihoe' kyŏlsŏng" [The establishment of the Council of Prisoners for the Restoration of Democracy], *Tonga ilbo*, March 28, 1975.

13. "'Minju suho ch'urok t'usa hwanyŏngoe kaech'oe" [A welcoming assembly for released prisoners], *Tonga ilbo*, February 21, 1975.

14. Minjuhwa Undong Kinyŏm Saŏphoe Yŏn'guso, *Han'guk minjuhwa undongsa yŏnp'yo*, 286–87; "Minju Hoebok Kungmin Hoeŭi, minch'ŏng hangnyŏn sagŏn chojong kongso sasil edo ŏmnŭn kŏt konggae chaep'an haeya" [NCRD demands public trial in the PRP case], *Tonga ilbo*, February 22, 1975; Ch'ŏnjugyo Chŏngŭi Kuhyŏn Sajedan and Kusokcha Kajok Hyŏbŭihoe,

"Inhyŏktang chinsang ŭl chosa palp'yo hamyŏnsŏ" [Investigation announced into the truth of the so-called PRP case], February 24, 1975, Folder 19, Box 4, Ogle Papers.

15. Minjuhwa Undong Kinyŏm Saŏphoe, *Han'guk minjuhwa undongsa*, 2:167.

16. Peter Hazelhurst, "S. Korean Plea to Amnesty over Torture," *The Times*, February 20, 1975, Mission Report ROK March–April 1975, MF 564, IISH.

17. "8-dae yadang ŭiwŏn 12myŏng i chasulhan komun tanghan naeyong" [Twelve former opposition party members reveal that they were tortured], *Tonga ilbo*, February 28, 1975; "South Korea, 13 Former Parliamentarians Denounce Torture They Have Undergone," *Le Monde*, March 1, 1975, Mission Report ROK March–April 1975, MF 564, IISH.

18. Kim Chi-ha, "Kohaeng—1974" [Asceticism—1974], *Tonga ilbo*, February 26, 1975; Kim Chŏng-nam, *Chinsil*, 123.

19. For more, see Chang, *Protest Dialectics*, 111–38.

20. "Amnesty International Reflected in Korean Journalism, March 1972–March 1975," SGO-NS Korea 1973–75, MF, IISH.

21. Hazelhurst to AIIS, telegram, "Today's London Times," February 21, 1975, Folder 13, Box 7, S5, RG II, AIUSA Collection.

22. Amnesty Korean Section Newsletter, March 1, 1975," SGO–NS Korea 1973–75, MF 16, IISH.

23. Huang and Sherman Carroll, memo, "Request for Special Project Funds for Mission to South Korea," March 5, 1975, SGO Korea 1975, MF 8, IISH.

24. Huang to Salzburg, March 6, 1975, Mission Report ROK March–April 1975, MF 564, IISH.

25. Salzburg to Huang, March 17, 1975, Mission Report ROK March–April 1975, MF 564, IISH; Stephanie to Huang and Sherman, memo, "Donald Fraser," March 17, 1975, Mission Report ROK March–April 1975, MF 564, IISH.

26. Arlette Laduguie and—Marguerite Garling to Stephanie, memo, "PRP Cases in South Korea, Mission Proposal from Lynn Miles," January 10, 1975, SGO Korea 1975, MF 8, IISH; Ennals to Miles, January 13, 1975, SGO Korea 1975, MF 8, IISH.

27. Kurata et al. to Garling et al., March 14, 1975, SGO–NS Japan 1974–75, MF 17, IISH.

28. Huang to Pedersen and Wrobel, memo, "Korean Mission," March 17, 1975, Mission Report ROK March–April 1975, MF 564, IISH.

29. Ibid.; Schmitz to Ennals, memo, "Korea Committee," February 20, 1975, SGO–NS Korea 1973–75, MF 16, IISH.

30. Ennals to Yoon, January 8, 1975, SGO–NS Korea 1973–75, MF 16, IISH.

31. AIIS to AIUSA, cable, "South Korea News Release," March 19, 1975, Mission Report ROK March–April 1975, MF 564, IISH.

32. "Yŏ-ya kyŏktol pulgap'i" [Inevitable confrontation between the ruling and opposition parties], *Maeil kyŏngje*, March 19, 1975.

33. Sinnott, *Hyŏnjang chŭngŏn*, 325–29.

34. Grant to Hammarberg, cable, March 20, 1975, Mission Report ROK March–April 1975, MF 564, IISH.

35. Huang to Hans et al., memo, "Korean Mission, "Final Phase," March 21, 1975, Mission Report ROK March–April 1975, MF 564, IISH.

36. Kissinger to Sneider, telegram, "FonMin Kim Visit: Call on Deputy Secretary Ingersoll," March 28, 1975, Korea–State Department Telegrams from SECSTATE–EXDIS, Box 11, NSA, PCFEAP, GFPL.

37. Huang to Stephanie et al., memo, "Telephone Conversation with Brian Wrobel," April 9, 1975, SGO Korea 1975, MF 8, IISH.

38. Ennals to Kim, April 9, 1975, SGO Korea 1975, MF 8, IISH.

39. Sinnott, *Hyŏnjang chŭngŏn*, 356.

40. Youngju Ryu, *Writers of the Winter Republic* (Honolulu: University of Hawaii Press, 2016).

41. Chang, *Protest Dialectics*, 159–72.

42. Hagen Koo, "Strong State and Contentious Society," in *State and Society in Contemporary Korea*, ed. Hagen Koo (Ithaca, NY: Cornell University Press, 1993), 232.

43. No Yun-jŏng and Cho Sŏng-jin, "'Inhyŏktang mujoe' hwakchŏng ŭimi" [Final ruling of innocence in the PRP case], *Munhwa ilbo*, January 23, 2007.

44. Yi Sŏng-hŭi, "8-il saebyŏk 3-si inhyŏktang chaegŏnwi sahyŏng chiphaeng t'ongji, ojŏn 10-si taebŏp sahyŏng sŏn'go" [Notification of PRP prisoners' executions at 3 A.M. on April 8, Supreme Court ruling, however, at 10 A.M.], *Kyŏnghyang sinmun*, September 14, 2012.

45. See Kim Tong-hyŏn, "Pakjŏnghŭi pisŏg'wan 'Pakjŏnghŭi, inhyŏktang sahyŏng chisi anhae'" [Park Chung-hee's secretary: "Park Chung-hee did not order PRP prisoners' execution"], *Pyujŭ aen nyujŭ*, October 26, 2012.

46. Sneider to Kissinger, telegram, "Meeting with Prime Minister," April 10, 1975, Korea–State Department Telegrams to SECSTATE–NODIS (5), Box 11, NSA, PCFEAP, GFPL.

47. Kissinger to Sneider, telegram, "Review of US Policies Toward Korea," April 22, 1975, Korea–State Department Telegrams to SECSTATE–NODIS (5), Box 11, NSA, PCFEAP, GFPL.

48. Sneider to Kissinger, telegram, "Meeting with President Park: Missile Strategy," May 1, 1975, Korea–State Department Telegrams to SECSTATE–EXDIS (2), Box 11, NSA, PCFEAP, GFPL.

49. Sneider to Kissinger, telegram, "New Korean Emergency Measures," May 12, 1975, Korea–State Department Telegrams to SECSTATE–EXDIS (2), Box 11, NSA, PCFEAP, GFPL.

50. Sneider to Kissinger, telegram, "Reassessment of Assumptions Regarding ROKG Internal Situation," June 20, 1975, Korea–State Department Telegrams to SECSTATE–EXDIS (2), Box 11, NSA, PCFEAP, GFPL.

51. Ibid.

52. See John Lewis Gaddis, *Strategies of Containment*, rev. and expanded ed. (New York: Oxford University Press, 2005); on dual containment, see Cumings, *Parallax Vision*, 130.

53. Kissinger to Sneider, telegram, "ROKG Emergency Measure," June 21, 1975, Korea–State Department Telegrams from SECSTATE–NODIS (3), Box 11, NSA, PCFEAP, GFPL. For more on the hearing, see US Congress, House Committee on International Relations, *Human Rights in South Korea and the Philippines: Implications for US Policy; Hearings Before the Subcommittee on International Organizations of the Committee on International Relations . . .* (Washington, DC: US Government Printing Office, 1975).

54. Kissinger to Sneider, telegram, "ROKG Emergency Measure," June 21, 1975.

55. Sneider to Kissinger, telegram, "ROKG Emergency Measure," June 23, 1975, Korea–State Department Telegrams to SECSTATE–NODIS (6), Box 11, NSA, PCFEAP, GFPL.

56. Bernard Gwertzman, "Top U.S. Aide Indicts Seoul and Manila, but He Says Security Requires Support," *NYT*, June 25, 1975.

57. Sneider to Kissinger, telegram, "US Policy Towards Korea," June 24, 1975, Korea–State Department Telegrams to SECSTATE–NODIS (6), Box 11, NSA, PCFEAP, GFPL.

58. Richard Halloran, "U.S. Press Is Part of Seoul Politics," *NYT*, September 8, 1975.

59. Chin Hwan Row, "Korea: A Time for a New Understanding," Letters to the Editor, *NYT*, August 18, 1975.

60. Richard Halloran, "Park Sees Seoul Needing U.S. Force Only till 1980," *NYT*, August 21, 1975.

61. Sneider to Kissinger, telegram, June 20, 1975, Korea–State Department Telegrams to SECSTATE–EXDIS (2), Box 11, NSA, PCFEAP, GFPL.

62. "Seoul Asks 5 Years for Rival Leader," *NYT*, September 13, 1975.

63. Richard Halloran, "Curbs Are Tighter on South Koreans," *NYT*, September 22, 1975.

64. David Binder, "A Critic in Seoul Warns on Curbs," *NYT*, September 25, 1975.

65. Richard Halloran, "Seoul Court Delays Case of Park's Foe," *NYT*, September 27, 1975.

66. "House Votes to Ban Foreign Aid for Human-Rights Violations," *NYT*, September 11, 1975.

67. Leslie H. Gelb, "Phasing Out of Direct U.S. Arms Aid Is Expected over Two Years," *NYT*, October 15, 1975; "United States: Mutual Defense Assistance Act of 1949," *American Journal of International Law* 44, no. 1, Supplement: Official Documents (January 1950): 29–38.

68. Bernard Gwertzman, "President Asking $4.7-Billion in Aid, Most for Mideast," *NYT*, October 31, 1975.

69. Bernard Gwertzman, "U.S. Blocks Rights Data on Nations Getting Arms," *NYT*, November 19, 1975.

70. Ibid.

71. "Bill Calls on U.S. to Remove Forces from South Korea," *NYT*, December 18, 1975.

72. For a few exemplary works, see Daniel Thomas, *The Helsinki Effect: International Norms, Human Rights and the Demise of Communism* (Princeton, NJ: Princeton University Press, 2001); Moyn, *The Last Utopia*; and Snyder, *Human Rights Activism*.

73. Memorandum of Conversation, "President's First Meeting with Prime Minister Miki," August 5, 1975, Ford, Japanese Prime Minister Takeo Miki, Box 14, NSA Memoranda of Conversations, 1973–1977, GFPL; Christopher S. Wren, "Moscow's Renewed Interest in Asia," *NYT*, September 14, 1975.

74. Memorandum of Conversation, "President's First Meeting with Prime Minister Miki."

75. Ibid.

76. Ibid.

77. *Foreign Relations of the United States* (hereafter, *FRUS*), 1969–1976, vol. 17, China, 1969–1972, ed. Steven Phillips (Washington, DC: US Government Printing Office, 2006), 67–68; Henry Kissinger, *White House Years* (Boston: Little, Brown, 1979), 182.

78. *FRUS*, 1969–1976, 17:973; *FRUS*, 1969–1976, vol. 18, China 1973–1976, ed. David P. Nickles (Washington, DC: US Government Printing Office, 2007), 603–4.

79. *FRUS*, 1969–1976, 17:814; and 18:723–24.

80. Memorandum of Conversation, "President's Second Meeting with Prime Minister Miki," August 6, 1975, Ford, Japanese Prime Minister Takeo Miki, Box 14, NSA Memoranda of Conversations, 1973–1977, GFPL.

81. Memorandum of Conversation, "Inkwŏn munje wa kwallyŏnhan kwan'gye puch'ŏkan hoeŭi" [Meeting of offices concerned with human rights issues], November 8, 1976, "Han'guk inkwŏn munje pogosŏ chech'ul" [On the submission of the Report on Human Rights Issues in Korea], Folder 7, MF 0737, DA.

82. Ministry of Foreign Affairs to KCIA Director, memo, "Chŏngbu ŭigyŏnsŏ (an) e tae-han ŭigyŏn" [Opinions on the Korean government's draft statement], December 2, 1976, "Han'guk inkwŏn munje pogosŏ chech'ul," Folder 7, MF 0737, DA.

83. Ambassador in Washington to Foreign Minister, memo, February 3, 1977, "Kakkuk chach'i kyosŏp mit hoeŭi kyŏlgwa" [The results of autonomous negotiations and meetings from each country's delegates], Folder 8, MF 0737, DA.

84. Ambassador in Geneva to Foreign Minister, memo, February 25, 1977, "Kakkuk chach'i kyosŏp mit hoeŭi kyŏlgwa," Folder 8, MF 0737, DA.

85. Margo Picken to IEC et al., memo, "54th Session of the UN Commission on Human Rights (February 6–March 10, 1978, Geneva)," March 13, 1978, IEC–For Information, Folder 131, IISH.

86. KCIA Director to Ministry of Foreign Affairs, memo, "Inkwŏn munje e taehan chŏngbu ŭigyŏnsŏ t'ongbo" [On the Korean government's response on human rights issues in Korea], July 29, 1979, "UN Inkwŏn Wiwŏnhoe hoeŭi, che 35-ch'a, Geneva, 1979.2.12–3.16" [The 35th meeting of the UN Human Rights Commission, February 12–March 16, 1979], Folder 9, MF 951, DA.

87. "A Proposal for Special Pilot Project on Korea" [undated, ca. June 1975], Folder 11, Box 5, Collection on Democracy and Unification in Korea (Collection 358), Department of Special Collections, Charles E. Young Research Library, UCLA (hereafter, UCLA Collection).

88. Luidens to East Asia Working Group Administration Committee, memo, "Proposal for Korean Human Rights Project," July 3, 1975, Folder 11, Box 5, UCLA Collection.

89. "Working Paper: Proposal for Washington, D.C.–Based American Working on Korean Issue," memo, August 18, 1975, Folder 11, Box 5, UCLA Collection.

90. L. Newton Thurber, memo, "Proposal for Coalition on Human Rights in Korea," August 29, 1975, Folder 11, Box 5, UCLA Collection; Luidens to Korea Joint Action Group, memo, "Dealing with Korean Human Rights Concerns in North America," September 3, 1975, Folder 11, Box 5, UCLA Collection.

91. Ann Marie Clark, Diplomacy of Conscience, 132; Keys, Reclaiming American Virtue, 205–11.

92. Grant to Blane, memo, "Guidelines for Approaches to Washington," ca. March 1976, AI Correspondence, Box 4, Ivan 4, Morris Papers.

93. David Hawk to Chairman of the Board and Executive Committee, memo, "Agenda Item 5: Discussion of Washington Office," July 5, 1977, Washington, DC, Office, 1976–1979, B11, S2, RG II; Jones to members of Ad Hoc Committee on Governmental Relations, memo, "Preliminary Discussion of Issues," September 7, 1976, Washington, DC, Office, 2 of 3, 1975–1980, B5, S1, RG II; Weissbrodt, memo, "Report of the Amnesty International Washington Office," September 20, 1976, Washington, DC, Office, 2 of 3 1975–1980, Box 5, S1, RG II; Memorandum of Conversations, Weissbrodt, "Report of the Amnesty International (U.S.A.) Washington Committee," October 22, 1976, Washington, DC, Office, 2 of 3, 1975–1980, Box 5, S1, RG II, AIUSA Collection.

94. McRae to the Executive Committee, memo, August 22, 1977, Washington, DC, Office, 1 of 3, 1975–1980, Box 5, S1, RG II, AIUSA Collection.

95. Keys, Reclaiming American Virtue, 208.

Chapter 4. The 1976 March 1 Incident

1. On Charter 77, see, for example, Jonathan Bolton, *Worlds of Dissent: Charter 77, the Plastic People of the Universe, and Czech Culture Under Communism* (Cambridge, MA: Harvard University Press, 2012).

2. See Kang Man-gil, "3·1 minju kuguk sŏnŏn ŭi yŏksajŏk sŏnggyŏk" [Historical features of the March First Declaration of Democratic National Salvation], in 3·1 Minju Kuguk Sŏnŏn Kwallyŏnja, *Saeropke t'aorŭnŭn 3·1 minju kuguk sŏnŏn* [The reignited March First Declaration of Democratic National Salvation] (Seoul: Sagyejŏl, 1998), 23–30. For other studies with the same approach, see Sohn, *Authoritarianism and Opposition*, 89–111; Cohen and Baker, "U.S. Foreign Policy and Human Rights," 170–219; Chang, *Protest Dialectics*, 145–74.

3. See Moyn, *The Last Utopia*; Keys, *Reclaiming American Virtue*.

4. See Gaddis Smith, *Morality, Reason, and Power: American Diplomacy in the Carter Years* (New York: Hill and Wang, 1986); Tony Smith, *America's Mission: The United States and the Worldwide Struggle for Democracy* (Princeton, NJ: Princeton University Press, 2012).

5. Tony Smith, *America's Mission*, 243; William Stending, *Presidential Faith and Foreign Policy: Jimmy Carter the Disciple and Ronald Reagan the Alchemist* (New York: Palgrave Macmillan, 2014), 1 and 39–56.

6. For the exception, see, for example, Tony Smith, *America's Vision*; note, in making this argument, Smith does not examine the South Korean case.

7. Chae-Jin Lee, *A Troubled Peace: U.S. Policy and the Two Koreas* (Baltimore: Johns Hopkins University Press, 2006), 64–111; Brazinsky, *Nation Building in South Korea*, 223–50; Yong-Jik Kim, "Security, Political, and Human Rights Conundrum," 457–82.

8. Margaret E. Keck and Kathryn Sikkink, *Activists Beyond Borders: Advocacy Networks in International Politics* (Ithaca, NY: Cornell University Press, 1998), 13–78 and 148–219.

9. On ties between democratization movements and Christianity, see Donald Clark, "Protestant Christianity and the State: Religious Organizations as Civil Society," in *Korean Society: Civil Society, Democracy and the State*, ed. Charles Armstrong (New York: Routledge, 2006), 171–90; and Hyug Baeg Im, "Christian Churches and Democratization," 136–56.

10. Kim Chŏng-nam, *Chinsil*, 144–49; Richard Halloran, "South Korea Calm as Curbs Continue," *NYT*, February 6, 1976.

11. Kim Hyŏng-su, *Mun Ik-hwan p'yŏngjŏn* [A critical biography of Mun Ik-hwan] (Seoul: Silch'ŏn Munhaksa, 2004), 434–48; Kim Chŏng-nam, *Chinsil*, 144–49; Kim Kwan-sŏk Moksa, *I ttang e*, 347–75.

12. 3·1 Minju Kuguk Sŏnŏn, *Saeropke t'aorŭnŭn*, 17–21.

13. Ibid., 321–22; Kim Kwan-sŏk Moksa, *I ttang e*, 375–80.

14. "Leading Seoul Dissidents Ask Resignation of President Park," *NYT*, March 3, 1976; "Prayers to Be Offered in U.S.," *NYT*, March 5, 1976.

15. Marjorie Hyer, "Korean Arrests Protested," *Washington Post* (hereafter, *WP*), March 12, 1976; "Dissidents' Release Asked by Quakers," *WP*, March 25, 1976.

16. 3·1 Minju Kuguk Sŏnŏn, *Saeropke t'aorŭnŭn*, 332–34.

17. "Ilbu chaeya insa chŏngbu chŏnbok sŏndong kwallyŏnja 11-myŏng kusok" [11 opposition leaders imprisoned for subversive agitation], *Chosŏn ilbo*, March 11, 1976.

18. No record of Kim's confession has ever been found. In 1997, when Yi Chong-ch'an, a former KCIA officer in the 1970s, became head of the National Intelligence Service (KCIA's successor), he conducted an exhaustive search of KCIA records on Kim Dae-jung and found

no record. See 3·1 Minju Kuguk Sŏnŏn, *Saeropke t'aorŭnŭn*, 31–107; Kim Sŏng-jae, interview, November 22, 2015; Yi, interview, November 23, 2015.

19. 3·1 Minju Kuguk Sŏnŏn, *Saeropke t'aorŭnŭn*, 7.

20. Sneider to Kissinger, telegram, "Korean Policy," June 20, 1975, Korea–State Department Telegrams (hereafter, KSTEL) to SECSTATE–EXDIS (2), Box 11, NSA, PCFEAP, GFPL.

21. Sneider to Kissinger, telegram, "Myongdong Cathedral Incident and Kim Tae Jung Confession," March 13, 1976, KSTEL to SECSTATE–NODIS (10), Box 12, NSA, PCFEAP, GFPL.

22. Kissinger to Sneider, telegram, "Arrest of Korean Political and Religious Figures," March 16, 1976, KSTEL from SECSTATE–NODIS (4), Box 11, NSA, PCFEAP, GFPL.

23. Sneider to Kissinger, telegram, "Arrest of Korean Political and Religious Figures," March 18, 1976, KSTEL to SECSTATE–NODIS (10), Box 12, NSA, PCFEAP, GFPL.

24. "South Korea's Most Dangerous Man," *WP*, March 19, 1976; Sneider to Kissinger, telegram, "ROK Domestic Policy," March 25, 1976, KSTEL to SECSTATE–NODIS (10), Box 12, NSA, PCFEAP, GFPL.

25. Sneider to Kissinger, telegram, "Aftermath of Myongdong Incident," March 27, 1976, KSTEL to SECSTATE–NODIS (10), Box 12, NSA, PCFEAP, GFPL.

26. Kissinger to Sneider, telegram, "ROK Domestic Political Actions," April 1, 1976, KSTEL from SECSTATE–NODIS (4), Box 11, NSA, PCFEAP, GFPL.

27. Fraser and 119 Congress Members to Ford, April 2, 1976, CO 78–2, 1–1–76 to 1–20–77—Executive, Box 33, WHCF Subject File, GFPL.

28. Philip Habib, "U.S. Security Relationship with the Republic of Korea," Department of State News Release, April 8, 1976, CO 78–2, 9–1–76 to 1–31–77—General, Box 34, WHCF Subject File, GFPL.

29. Sneider to Kissinger, telegram, "Foreign Minister Park's Meeting with the Secretary," April 8, 1976, KSTEL to SECSTATE–NODIS (11), Box 12, NSA, PCFEAP, GFPL.

30. Sneider to Kissinger, telegram, "ROKG Domestic Affairs," April 16, 1976, KSTEL to SECSTATE–NODIS (11), Box 12, NSA, PCFEAP, GFPL.

31. Ford to Morgan, May 19, 1976; Ford to Derwinski, June 4, 1976, FO 3–2 CO 78–2–CO 81—Executive, Box 23, WHCF Subject File, GFPL.

32. For more on this incident, see Don Oberdorfer and Robert Carlin, *The Two Koreas: A Contemporary History* (New York: Basic Books, 2014), 59–66.

33. Keys, *Reclaiming American Virtue*, 236.

34. Fox Butterfield, "U.S. Facing a Dilemma in Its Korea Policy," *NYT*, August 31, 1976.

35. Memo, "Korea" (*WP*, March 21, 1976) and "South Korea" (*Newsweek*, May 10, 1976), Carter Quotes—Korea, South, Box H28, President Ford Committee Records 1975–1976, GFPL.

36. For the overall legislative illustration around this period, see Mark L. Schneider, "A New Administration's New Policy: The Rise to Power of Human Rights," in *Human Rights and U.S. Foreign Policy*, ed. Peter Brown and Douglas MacLean (Lexington, MA: Lexington Books, 1979), 3–13.

37. Memo, "South Korea/Human Rights" (*Chicago Tribune*, July 30, 1976) and "South Korea/ Defense Policy/ NATO" (*WP*, September 2, 1976), Carter Quotes—Korea, South, Box H28, President Ford Committee Records 1975–1976, GFPL.

38. Don Oberdorfer, "Carter Speaks on Human Rights," *WP*, September 9, 1976.

39. Keys, *Reclaiming American Virtue*, 236–37.

40. Charles Mohr, "Carter Suggests That U.S. Foster Rights Overseas," *NYT*, September 9, 1976.

41. Leslie Gelb, "Human-Rights and Morality Issue Runs Through Ford-Carter Debate," *NYT*, October 8, 1976; Bernard Gwertzman, "Some Major Differences," *NYT*, October 8, 1976.

42. Memorandum of Conversation (Ford, Kissinger, Scowcroft), October 19, 1976—Ford, Kissinger, Scowcroft, Box 21, NSA Memoranda of Conversation, 1973–1977, GFPL.

43. Lincoln Bloomfield, "The Carter Human Rights Policy: A Provisional Appraisal," January 11, 1981, Subject File, NSA Accomplishment—Human Rights: 1–81, Box 34, Brzezinski Collection (donated), Jimmy Carter Presidential Library (hereafter, JCPL).

44. "154 in Congress Condemn Jailings in South Korea," *NYT*, October 28, 1976.

45. Armacost, "US Forces in Korea," November 5, 1976, Korea [2 of 2], Box H–311, NSC Subject, Miscellaneous Institutional Files of the Nixon Administration, NSC H–Files, Richard Nixon Presidential Library.

46. Cyrus Vance, *Hard Choices: Critical Years in America's Foreign Policy* (New York: Simon and Schuster, 1983), 32.

47. Scowcroft, memo, "National Security Council Meeting on the NSSM 246 Report on U.S. Defense Policy and Military Posture and the NSC Study on Naval Force Requirements," no date, NSC Meeting December 15, 1976, Box 2, NSA NSC Meeting File, GFPL.

48. Davis to Scowcroft, memo, "Minutes of NSC Meeting Held December 15, 1976," January 3, 1997, NSC Meeting December 15, 1976, Box 2, NSA NSC Meeting File, GFPL.

49. Maxine Cheshire and Scott Armstrong, "Seoul Gave Millions to U.S. Officials," *WP*, October 24, 1976.

50. Cumings, *Korea's Place in the Sun*, 459–61.

51. Sneider to Kissinger, telegram, "Kim Case and Its Aftermath in Korea," December 3, 1976, KSTEL to SECSTATE–NODIS (13), Box 12; Sneider to Kissinger, telegram, "Growing Korean Concern About Future of US-ROK Relations," November 22, 1976, KSTEL to SECSTATE–NODIS (12), Box 12, NSA, PCFEAP, GFPL.

52. William H. Gleysteen Jr., *Massive Entanglement, Marginal Influence: Carter and Korea in Crisis* (Washington, DC: Brookings Institute Press, 1999), 31.

53. Bernard Gwertzman, "U.S. Says 6 Nations Curb Human Rights," *NYT*, January 2, 1977.

54. Oberdorfer and Carlin, *The Two Koreas*, 69.

55. Michael Armacost, interview with author, Stanford, CA, April 30, 2010.

56. Tuchman and Kimmitt to Brzezinski, memo, February 7, 1977, Human Rights, 2–4/77, Box 28, NSA (7), JCPL.

57. Zbigniew Brzezinski, *Power and Principle: Memoirs of the National Security Adviser, 1977–1981* (New York: Farrar, Straus, Giroux, 1983), 126–27.

58. Brzezinski to Carter, memo, "Information Items," February 7, 1977, Declassified: 2005/02/02 NCL–1–1–8–32–6, JCPL.

59. Vance to Sneider, telegram, "Letter to President Park," February 14, 1977, Presidential Correspondence with Foreign Leaders File, Korea, Republic of, 2/77–12/78, Box 12, NSA Brzezinski Material, JCPL.

60. Vance to Sneider, telegram, "Presidential Letter to President Park" [no date], Country File, Korea, Republic of, 5–6/77, Box 43, NSA Brzezinski Material, JCPL.

61. Sneider to Brzezinski, cable, "Reply to President Carter's Letter," February 26, 1977, Armacost Chron File (hereafter, ACF), 3/1–9/77, Box 2, NSA Staff Material Far East (hereafter, SMFE), JCPL.

62. Brzezinski to Carter, memo, "President Park's Reply to Your Letter of February 15" [no date], ACF, 3/1–9/77, Box 2, NSA SMFE, JCPL.

63. Vance to Sneider, telegram, "President Park's Comments on Human Rights," March 4, 1977, Country File, Korea, Republic of, 1–4/77, Box 43, NSA Brzezinski Material, JCPL.

64. Carter to Brzezinski and Vance, memo [no title], March 5, 1977, Country File, Korea, Republic of, 1–4/77, Box 43, NSA Brzezinski Material, JCPL.

65. Oberdorfer and Carlin, *The Two Koreas*, 71.

66. Sellars, *The Rise and Rise of Human Rights*, 122–26.

67. Keys, *Reclaiming American Virtue*, 236–37 and 259–64.

68. Gleysteen, *Massive Entanglement*, 31–33.

69. Memo of Conversation (March 9, 1977), ACF, 3/10–15/77, Box 2, NSA SMFE, JCPL.

70. Armacost to Brzezinski, memo, "President's Meeting with South Korean Foreign Minister Pak Tong-chin," and attachment, "Meeting with South Korean Foreign Minister Pak Tong-chin," March 8, 1977; Armacost to Brzezinski, memo, "Your Appointment with Korean Foreign Minister Park Tong-chin," March 9, 1977, ACF, 3/1–9/77 Box 2, NSA SMFE, JCPL.

71. Donald M. Fraser, "Freedom and Foreign Policy," *Foreign Policy* 26 (1977): 147 and 156.

72. Fraser to Carter, March 3, 1977, Subject File, Countries, Co 82–2, 1/20/77–3/31/77, Box Co–41, WHCF, JCPL.

73. Cyrus Vance, "Human Rights and Foreign Policy," *Georgia Journal of International and Comparative Law* 7, no. 223 (1977): 226.

74. Patricia M. Derian, "Human Rights in American Foreign Policy," *Notre Dame Law* 55, no. 2 (1979): 271.

75. Jack Donnelly, "Human Rights and Foreign Policy," *World Politics* 34, no. 4 (1982): 594–95.

76. Yun Po-sŏn et al. to Carter, March 1977; Fraser to Moe, April 1, 1977, ACF, 4/1–12/77, Box 2, NSA SMFE, JCPL.

77. Gleysteen, *Massive Entanglement*.

78. Armacost to Aaron, memo, "Letter to President from South Koreans," April 6, 1997; Brzezinski to Carter, memo, "Letter on Human Rights from South Koreans" [no date], ACF, 4/1–12/77, Box 2, NSA SMFE, JCPL.

79. Vance to Brzezinski, cable, "Korea Troop Withdrawal and Human Rights," April 5, 1977, ACF, 4/1–12/77, Box 2, NSA SMFE, JCPL.

80. Vance to Brzezinski, cable, "Meeting with President Park on Current Korean Problems," April 9, 1977, ACF, 4/1–12/77, Box 2, NSA SMFE, JCPL. The suggested connection between Park's about-face and possible US support for regime change was not without merit. In October 1976 during a public talk at the University of Texas in Austin, Donald Gregg, former CIA station chief in Korea (1973–75) noted that if President Park sought reelection, "he will probably not live to serve out his term," and he also revealed that he intervened in saving Kim Dae-jung in the KCIA's attempt to kidnap Kim for murder in Tokyo in August 1973. Although far from explicit, this remark by a former CIA station chief in Korea and current CIA official pointed to possible tensions between the Park regime and the US intelligence office, which very well may have fueled Park's belief that the United States intended to replace him with Kim Dae-jung. See Steve McGuire, "Revelations from CIA's Former Korea Chief," *Counterspy* 3, no. 2 (1976), 34; Donald Gregg, interview with author, New York, Jun 24, 2015.

81. Poitras to Fraser, February 20, 1977; Fraser to Brzezinski, April 11, 1977, Country File, Korea, Republic of, 1–4/77, Box 43, NSA Brzezinski Material, JCPL.

82. Armacost to Brzezinski, memo, "Don Fraser's Letter About Human Rights in Korea," April 20, 1977, Country File, Korea, Republic of, 1–4/77, Box 43, NSA Brzezinski Material, JCPL.

83. Vance to Brzezinski, cable, "President Park and Human Rights," April 25, 1977, Country File, Korea, Republic of, 1–4/77, Box 43, NSA Brzezinski Material, JCPL; Brzezinski to Vance, memo, "Release of Kim Dae Jung," April 26, 1977, ACF, 4/13–26/77, Box 2, NSA SMFE, JCPL.

84. Charles A. Beard, *The Idea of National Interest: An Analytical Study in American Foreign Policy* (New York: Macmillan, 1934), 388.

85. Brzezinski to Carter, memo, "NSC Meeting on Korea," April 26, 1977, and attachment, "U.S. Ground Force Withdrawals from Korea: Advantages and Disadvantages" [no date], ACF, 4/13–26/77, Box 2, NSA SMFE, JCPL.

86. Brzezinski to Carter, memo, "Korean Policy," May 3, 1977, and attachment, "National Security Council Meeting," April 27, 1977, ACF, 4/27–30/77, Box 3, NSA, SMFE, JCPL.

87. Fraser to Brzezinski, April 25, 1977; Armacost to Brzezinski, memo, "Don Fraser's Most Recent Letter," April 29, 1977, ACF, 4/27–30/77, Box 3, NSA SMFE, JCPL.

88. John Saar, "Singlaub's Colleagues Also Oppose GI Pullout," *WP*, May 21, 1977; Warren Brown, "Carter Had 'No Choice' on Singlaub, Byrd Says," *WP*, May 23, 1977.

89. Sneider to Vance, telegram, "Human Rights: Meeting with President Park," May 27, 1977, Country File, Korea, Republic of, 5–6/77, Box 43, NSA Brzezinski Material, JCPL.

90. Sneider to Vance, telegram, "Possible Progress on Human Rights Issue," May 20, 1977, Country File, Korea, Republic of, 5–6/77, Box 43, NSA Brzezinski Material, JCPL.

91. Henry Kamm, "Park Said to Yield Reluctantly to U.S. Korea Plan," *NYT*, May 26, 1977; Kamm, "Americans End Seoul Talks," *NYT*, May 27, 1977.

92. Keck and Sikkink, *Activists Beyond Borders*.

93. Memorandum of Conversation (Carter, Brown, Brzezinski, and Armacost), "Security Consultative Meeting in Korea," July 14, 1977, ACF, 7/15–31/77, Box 4, NSA SMFE, JCPL.

94. Armacost to Brzezinski, memo, "Your Meeting with Ambassador Kim Yong Shik," July 15, 1977, ACF, 7/15–31/77, Box 4, NSA SMFE, JCPL.

95. "Kinggŭp choch'i wiban 14-myŏng sŏkpang" [Release of 14 prisoners charged under Decree No. 9], *Chosŏn ilbo*, July 19, 1977.

96. "Kinkŭp choch'i wiban 11-myŏng sŏkpang" [Release of 11 prisoners charged under Decree No. 9], *Chosŏn ilbo*, December 27, 1977; "Myŏngdong sagŏn kwallyŏn 5-myŏng sŏkpang" [Release of 5 prisoners from the Myŏngdong Incident], *Chosŏn ilbo*, January 1, 1978.

97. "Myŏngdong sagŏn sŏkpang inkwŏn ŭi chin'ilbo" [Release of prisoners from Myŏngdong Incident, signaling the one-step advance of human rights], *Chosŏn ilbo*, January 5, 1978.

98. Vance to Carter, memo, "Letter to Korean President Park," January 13, 1978, Presidential Correspondence with Foreign Leaders File, Korea, Republic of, 2/77–12/78, Box 12, NSA Brzezinski Material, JCPL.

99. Brzezinski, *Power and Principle*, 126.

100. Bloomfield, "The Carter Human Rights Policy," 8–9, and 41.

101. Billings and Kim to Carter, March 1, 1978, NACHRK, 3/76–5/78, Box 29, Public Liaison Contanza, JCPL.

102. Wives to Mrs. Carter [no date], Subject File, Countries, Co 82–2 1/20/77–1/20/81, Box Co–42, WHCF, JCPL.

103. Lee to Brzezinski, May 14, 1978, and Brzezinski to Lee, June 15, 1978, Subject File, Countries, Co 82–2, 1/20/77–1/20/81, Box Co–41, WHCF, JCPL; Carter to Park, May 17, 1978, Presidential Correspondence with Foreign Leaders File, Korea, Republic of, 2/77–12/78, Box

12, NSA Brzezinski Material, JCPL; "Kinkŭp choch'i wiban 8-myŏng sŏkpang" [Release of 8 prisoners charged under Decree No. 9], *Chosŏn ilbo*, May 16, 1978.

104. Brzezinski to Carter, memo, "Summary of April 11, 1978, Meeting on Korea and China," April 18, 1978; Memo of Conversation, "Summary Minutes of the April 11, 1978 Meeting on Korea and China," April 11, 1978, ACF, 4/11–18/78, Box 7, NSA SMFE, JCPL.

105. Terence Smith, "Carter Cuts Totals of U.S. Troops to Leave South Korea This Year," *NYT*, April 22, 1978.

Chapter 5. People's Protests

1. An Chae-sŏng, "YH sagŏn—Yŏgongdŭl, minjujuŭi pomŭl purŭda" [The YH Incident: Female factory workers, calling out the democratic spring], in the Korea Democracy Foundation (KDF) Open Archives, accessed January 4, 2014, http://archives.kdemo.or.kr.

2. Simpson, "'Human Rights Are Like Coca-Cola,'" 186–203.

3. "Pak Taet'ongnyŏng kimnyŏmsa yoji" [Summary of President Park's address], *Kyŏnghyang sinmun*, March 1, 1974.

4. "Pan'gong kyoyuk ŭn kot saengjonkwŏn suho" [The education on anti-Communism is to protect the rights to subsistence], *Kyŏnghyang sinmun*, October 26, 1974.

5. Marina Svensson, *Debating Human Rights in China: A Conceptual and Political History* (New York: Rowman & Littlefield, 2002), 274–75.

6. "Human Rights and Reconciliation," message of the 1974 Synod of Bishops, October 23, 1974, in *The Pope Speaks* 19 (1974–75): 216–19.

7. "Minju hoebok chujang, yŏksa ŭi hŭrŭm" [Calling for the restoration of democracy as a historical current], *Kyŏnghyang sinmun*, January 6, 1975.

8. "Chayukwŏn kwa saengjonkwŏn" [Civil liberty and rights to subsistence], *Tonga ilbo*, January 9, 1975.

9. Pak Sŭng-ok, "Ppaeakkin nodongjŏl ŭi 33-yŏn yŏksa" [The 33-year lost history of Labor Day], *Wŏlgan Mal* 47 (May 1990): 98–103.

10. Cho Sŭng-hyŏk, "Sanŏp sŏn'gyo wa nodongja ŭi inkwŏn" [The UIM and laborers' human rights], *Ssial ŭi sori*, November 1978, 27–37.

11. Laborers' Day Joint Protestant-Catholic Mass, "1977 Declaration on the Human Rights of Laborers," March 10, 1977, serial no. 01130913–022, NIKH.

12. Pyŏnghwa Sijang Kŭlloja Inkwŏn Munje Hyŏbŭihoe, "Sŏngmyŏngsŏ" [Statement], November 1, 1977, Serial No. 105258, KDF; Pyŏnghwa Sijang Kŭlloja Inkwŏn Munje Hyŏbŭihoe, "Sŏngmyŏngsŏ" [Statement], November 18, 1977, Serial No. 419607, KDF.

13. Pyŏnghwa Sijang Kŭlloja Inkwŏn Munje Hyŏbŭihoe, "Han'guk nodong inkwŏn hŏnjang" [Korean Laborers' Charter for Human Rights], December 23, 1977, serial no. 443694, KDF.

14. "The Catholic Farmers Association and the Sweet Potato Scandal," May 8, 1978, serial no. 01130905–003, NIKH.

15. "Nongminhoe kidohoe annae" [Information on the Catholic Farmers Association prayer meeting], serial no. 01130837–070, NIKH.

16. An anonymous visitor, "Korean Farmers Continue Two-Year Struggle, 500 Demonstrate," May 5, 1978, serial no. 01130905–013, NIKH.

17. Memo of Conversation, Chŏn'guk Nongmin Inkwŏn Wiwŏnhoe [The National Committee for Farmers' Human Rights], April 28, 1978; Chŏn'guk Nongmin Inkwŏn Wiwŏnhoe,

"Nongmin ŭi t'ujaeng e tongch'am ŭl sŏnŏn hamyŏ" [On declaring our participation in the farmers' struggle], May 1, 1978, serial no. 213461, KDF.

18. Chŏn'guk Nongmin Inkwŏn Wiwŏnhoe, "Nongmin ŭi t'ujaeng e tongch'am ŭl sŏnŏn hamyŏ," May 1, 1978; Minjuhwa Undong Kinyŏm Saŏphoe Yŏn'guso, *Han'guk minjuhwa undongsa yŏnp'yo*, 330.

19. Ch'ŏngju Tosi Sanŏp Sŏgyohoe, "Ŏgruhan nongmindŭr ŭi inkwŏn hoebok ŭl wihan paegil kido sunsŏ" [A one-hundred-day prayer for the restoration of the human rights of farmers, who have been unfairly treated], June 21, 1978, serial no. 429444, KDF.

20. Nodongja nongmin ŭi inkwŏn ŭl wihan kidohoe chuch'oeja, "Kyŏrŭimun" [Resolution], May 29, 1978, serial no. 01130905–017–0, NIKH.

21. Minju ch'ŏngnyŏn inkwŏn hyŏbŭihoe, "Sŏngmyŏngsŏ" [Statement on the repression of the Democratic Youth Council for Human Rights], May 26, 1978, serial no. 85383, KDF.

22. Minju ch'ŏngnyŏn inkwŏn hyŏbŭihoe, "Kyŏrŭimun" [Resolution], June 2, 1978, serial no. 01130906–003, NIKH; Minjuhwa Undong Kinyŏm Saŏphoe Yŏn'guso, *Han'guk minjuhwa undongsa yŏnp'yo*, 337.

23. Han'guk Kidokkyo Kyohoe Hyŏbŭihoe Inkwŏn Wiwŏnhoe, "Inkwŏn chugan annae" [On the Human Rights Week], in *Human Rights Newsletter*, November 22, 1977, serial no. 569594, KDF; memo, "Ŏmmu pogo, 77. 11.17.–12.16" [Report on the NCCK's Human Rights Committee's activities from November to December 1977], serial no. 102838, KDF.

24. Han'guk Inkwŏn Undong Hyŏbŭihoe, "Han'guk Inkwŏn Undong Hyŏbŭihoe ch'ŏngsik paljok" [Inauguration of the Coalition of Human Rights Movements in Korea], January 1978, serial no. 40940, KDF.

25. Han'guk Inkwŏn Undong Hyŏbŭihoe, "Uri ŭi inkwŏn hyŏnsil," February 27, 1978, serial no. 445950, KDF; Han'guk Inkwŏn Undong Hyŏbŭihoe, "Han'guk kungmin ŭi inkwŏn sŏnŏn," February 27, 1978, serial no. 40942, KDF.

26. Coalition for Human Rights Movements in Korea, "Our Human Rights Situation," February 27, 1978; Han'guk Kidokkyo Kyohoe Hyŏbŭihoe, *1970-yŏndae minjuhwa undong*, vol. 5, 1903–1907.

27. Han'guk Inkwŏn Undong Hyŏbŭihoe, "Och'ŏnman ŭi inkwŏn," June 9, 1978, serial no. 59809, KDF.

28. Kim Tae-yŏng, "Pan Yusin chaeya undong" [The *chaeya* movements against the Yushin regime], in *Yushin kwa panyushin*, 425; Minjuhwa Undong Kinyŏm Saŏphoe, *Han'guk minjuhwa undongsa*, 2:272–73.

29. NACHRK, "S.O.S.!!," February 1978, Folder 30, Box 3, Ogle Papers.

30. Koo, *Korean Workers*, 84

31. Quoted in ibid., 88.

32. NACHRK, "S.O.S.!!"

33. Koo, *Korean Workers*, 69–99; Sohn, *Authoritarianism and Opposition*, 112–46.

34. Memorandum of Conversations, NACHRK Executive Committee Meeting, January 30, 1978, NACHRK 1978–1979, Box 10, Linda Jones Papers, Archives of the Korea Democracy Foundation (hereafter, Jones Papers); NACHRK, "Overview of the Program (8/76–8/78)," NACHRK 1978–1979, Box 10, Jones Papers.

35. Grant to Humphreys, memo, "Meeting with John Salzberg," January 9, 1978, AIUSA Correspondence 1978, MF 560, IISH; Huang to Grant, January 27, 1979, AIUSA Correspondence 1978, MF 560, IISH.

36. NACHRK, "S.O.S.!!"

37. Soonok Chun, *They Are Not Machines: Korean Women Workers and Their Fight for Democratic Trade Unionism in the 1970s* (Burlington, VT: Ashgate, 2003), 126–34.

38. Kim to Potter, March 16, 1978, Folder 5, Box 6, UCLA Collection.

39. Harvey to McIntyre, April 22, 1978, Folder 19, Box 29, UCLA Collection.

40. Ogle to Meany, June 23, 1978, Folder 30, Box 3, Ogle Papers.

41. Ernest Lee to Ogle, July 5, 1978, Folder 30, Box 3, Ogle Papers.

42. Ogle to Lee, August 30, 1978, Folder 30, Box 3, Ogle Papers; McIntyre et al. to Mikva, memo, "Summary of Dong-il Textile Workers' Problems as a Part of Larger Korean Labor Struggle," November 8, 1978, Folder 30, Box 3, Ogle Papers; McIntyre to Howard et al., memo, "Report on Korean Concerns/ Washington," March 20, 1979, Folder 8, Box 21, UCLA Collection.

43. Jang Jip Choi, *Labor and the Authoritarian State: Labor Unions in South Korean Manufacturing Industries, 1961–1981* (Seoul: Korea University Press, 1989), 144–45.

44. Im Song-ja, "1970-yŏndae Tosisanŏp Sŏn'gyohoe wa Han'guk Noch'ong ŭi kaltŭngtaerip" [Conflicts and confrontations between UIM Groups and the FKTU in the 1970s], *Sarim* 35 (2010): 311–44.

45. Shorrock, "Labor's Cold War," *The Nation*, May 19, 2003, 15–22.

46. See, for example, Kim Scipes, *AFL-CIO's Secret War Against Developing Country Workers: Solidarity or Sabotage?* (Lanham, MD: Lexington Books, 2010); and Ronald Cox, ed., *Corporate Power and Globalization in US Foreign Policy* (New York: Routledge, 2012).

47. McIntyre et al. to Mikva, memo, "Summary of Dong-il Textile Workers' Problems."

48. For exemplary works, see Meredith Woo-Cumings, ed., *The Developmental State* (Ithaca, NY: Cornell University Press, 1999); Amsden, *Asia's Next Giant*; Jang Jip Choi, *Labor and the Authoritarian State*.

49. See Clair Apodaca and Michael Stohl, "United States Human Rights Policy and Foreign Assistance," *International Studies Quarterly* 43, no. 1 (March 1999): 185–98; Steven Poe et al., "Human Rights and US Foreign Aid Revisited: The Latin American Region," *Human Rights Quarterly* 16, no. 3 (1994): 539–58.

50. "U.S.-Korea Cotton Politics," June 1978, cir, Folder 30, Box 3, Ogle Papers.

51. "H.R. 6714 (95th): International Development and Food Assistance Act" (text of bill as of August 3, 1977), accessed July 31, 2019, https://www.govtrack.us/congress/bills/95/hr6714/text.

52. Kukche kyŏngjeguk, memo, "PL 480 kwa inkwŏn munje" [PL 480 and human rights], March 13, 1978, *FY79 Miguk ŭi kukche kaebal singyang wŏnjobŏp (PL–480) 1977–78* [International development and US food aid in FY 1979], vol. 1, July 1977–June 1978, Folder 16, MF 2009-74, DA; Dan Morgan, *Merchants of Grain: The Power and Profits of the Five Giant Companies at the Center of the World's Food Supply* (Harmondsworth: Penguin Books, 1980), 376.

53. On Sneider's discussion with ROK officials, see Kukche kyŏngjeguk, memo, "PL 480 ch'agwan chongnyo wa aguk nongsanmul toip chŏngch'aek kaesŏn" [Termination of PL 480 loan and policy reform on the Korean import of agricultural products], June 27, 1978, *FY79 Miguk ŭi kukche kaebal singyang wŏnjobŏp (PL–480) 1977–78*, vol. 1, July 1977–June 1978, Folder 16, MF 2009-74, DA.

54. For more on the Senate vote, see Library of Congress Foreign Affairs Division, *Chronologies of Major Developments in Selected Areas of International Relations* (Washington, DC: US Government Printing Office, 1978), 198; see also Acting Foreign Minister to

President and Prime Minister, memo, "Chuhan Mi Taesa Taeri wa ŭi myŏndam pogo" [Report on a conversation with the charge d'affairs of the United States], February 24, 1978, *FY79 Miguk ŭi kukche kaebal singyang wŏnjobŏp (PL-480) 1977-78*, vol. 1, July 1977–June 1978, F16, MF 2009-74, DA.

55. Ambassador to Foreign Minister, memo, April 13, 1978, *FY79 Miguk ŭi kukche kaebal singyang wŏnjobŏp (PL-480) 1977-78*, vol. 1, July 1977–June 1978, F16, MF 2009-74, DA; Kukche kyŏngjeguk, memo, "PL 480 ch'agwan chongnyo wa aguk nongsanmul toip chŏngch'aek kaesŏn," June 27, 1978.

56. "Seoul President Pledges All Possible Cooperation," *NYT*, August 6, 1978; Acting Foreign Minister to President and Prime Minister, memo, "Nongŏp kwangye chich'ul pŏban Mi Sangwŏn pohoeŭi t'onggwa" [The US Senate passes agricultural funds bill, rejecting Korea aid cut-off], August 12, 1978, *FY79 Miguk ŭi kukche kaebal singyang wŏnjobŏp (PL-480) 1977-78*, vol. 1, July–September 1978, Folder 17, MF 2009-74, DA.

57. Tom Harkin, "A Speech in International Development Conference," February 8, 1978, Folder 3, Box 19, UCLA Collection.

58. "U.S.-Korea Cotton Politics."

59. "Chadong wan'gu chipchung kaebal" [The intensive development of mass-produced toys], *Maeil kyŏngje*, July 8, 1975.

60. Taehyup Workers, "The Taehyup Factory Workers Appeal," June 10, 1977, Folder 30, Box 3, Ogle Papers.

61. Lavender to Ogle, June 21, 1977, Folder 29, Box 3, Ogle Papers.

62. CWU, memo, "Worker Profile—Taehyup," June 1977, cir, Folder 30, Box 3, Ogle Papers.

63. Amsden, *Asia's Next Giant*, 195–204.

64. On South Korean state corporatism, see Jang Jip Choi, *Labor and the Authoritarian State*; Ch'oi Chang-jip, *Minjuhwa ihu ŭi minjujuŭi* [Democracy in the post-democratization era] (Seoul: Humanit'asŭ, 2002). For a comparable study on North Korea, see Cumings, *Korea's Place in the Sun*, 408–24.

65. Hwasook Nam, *Building Ships, Building a Nation* (Seattle: University of Washington Press, 2009), 198–99.

66. CWU, memo, "Worker Profile—Taehyup."

67. Andrew H. Malcolm, "South Korean Labor Force Shows Increasing Unrest," *NYT*, August 8, 1977.

68. Ed Kinchley, "Signetics Korea, Seoul," *New Asia News Notes*, October 28, 1977, Folder 32, Box 2, Ogle Papers.

69. Maud Easter, "Mattel in Korea," *Christianity and Crisis*, June 1978, cir, Folder 30, Box 3, Ogle Papers.

70. Ibid.; Chŏng Un-yŏng, "Nondan—Kongjang saemaŭl undong kwa nosa hyŏpcho punwigi chosŏng" [Forum: Factory–New Village Movements and the creation of labor-management cooperation], *Sallim Munhwa* (1979), accessed December 1, 2016, http://www.sanrimji.com; "YH chŏngguk anp'ak ch'wijae pangdam" [Reporters' at-random commentaries on the YH Incident], *Tonga ilbo*, August 31, 1979.

71. Easter, "Mattel in Korea."

72. Kim to Friends, June 26, 1978, Folder 30, Box 3, Ogle Papers.

73. Easter, "Mattel in Korea"; "Taehyŏp such'ulsŏn kkŭnkyŏ kyŏngyŏngnan" [Taehyŏp's financial problems due to export route loss], *Maeil kyŏngje*, August 7, 1980.

74. *Korea Communique*, no. 19 (March 1, 1978), NACHRK, 3/76–5/78, Box 29, Public Liaison, Seymour Wishman's Subject Files, JCPL.

75. Sinnott to Ogle, February 26, 1978, Folder 18, Box 3, Ogle Papers.

76. Kim to Friends, March 30, 1978, NACHRK 1978–1979, Box 10, Jones Papers; "Washington Notes—NACHRK—#8," March 1978, Folder 18, Box 3, Ogle Papers.

77. McIntyre, "Annual Report—Michael McIntyre," May 22, 1978, Folder 5, Box 6, UCLA Collection.

78. Shoji to Friends, March 13, 1979, Folder 24, Box 66, UCLA Collection.

79. Platt to Brzezinski, memo, October 2, 1978, Platt Chron File, 10/78, Box 65, NSA (26); Platt to Brzezinski, memo, September 28, 1978, Country File, Korea, Republic of, 10/77–12/78, Box 43, NSA Brzezinski Material, JCPL.

80. Fifteen Concerned Foreigners in Korea to Carter, September 1, 1978; Thompson to Carter, October 20, 1978, Subject File, Countries, Co 82–2 1/1/78–1/20/81, Box Co–42, WHCF, JCPL.

81. Maud Easter to Friends, 3 January 1979, with enclosure, An anonymous foreigner living in Seoul, "A Criticism of Jimmy and a Message to the American People from South Korea," December 3, 1978, Folder 3, Box 8, UCLA Collection.

82. Ibid.

83. In 2003, T.K.'s identity as Professor Chi Myŏng-gwan was revealed. See T.K., "Carter's Korea Visit," December 3, 1978, *Sekai*, February 1979, Folder 6, Box 91, UCLA Collection.

84. Ham et al. to Carter, [undated], Subject File, Countries, Co 82–2 1/20/77–1/20/81, Box Co–41, WHCF, JCPL.

85. Richard Halloran, "Aide on Rights Mission to Seoul Before Carter Trip," *NYT*, May 27, 1979.

86. Platt to Brzezinski, memo, April 27, 1979, Platt Chron File, 4/26–30/79, Box 66, NSA (26), JCPL.

87. Gleysteen, *Massive Entanglement*, 31–40.

88. Pŏngyŏk Munje Taech'aek Chŏn'guk Haptong Wiwŏnhoe, "Sŏnŏnmun" [Statement], June 1, 1979, serial no. 85382, KDF.

89. NACHRK, [Untitled: Chronology: June to December 1979], Folder 6, Box 42, UCLA Collection.

90. Halloran, "Aide on Rights Mission to Seoul"; "Why We Koreans Oppose President Carter's Visit to Korea," *NYT*, June 15, 1979.

91. Harkin et al. to Carter, June 19, 1979, Subject File, Countries, Co 82–2 9/1/78–12/31/79, Box Co–41, WHCF, JCPL.

92. "Edŭwŏdŭ K'enedi sangwŏn ŭiwŏn chipmusil paep'o" [Senator Kennedy circulates list of political prisoners], June 21, 1979, serial no. 486572, KDF.

93. Minjuhwa Undong Kinyŏm Saŏphoe Yŏn'guso, *Han'guk minjuhwa undongsa yŏnp'yo*, 359; NACHRK, [Untitled: Chronology: June to December 1979]; Han Sŭng-hŏn, interview with author, Seoul, Korea, September 22, 2011.

94. Cumings to Oksenberg, November 2, 1979, Platt Chron File, 11/79, Box 68, NSA (26), JCPL.

95. Oberdorfer and Carlin, *The Two Koreas*, 84.

96. Platt to Brzezinski, memo, July 11, 1979, Platt Chron File, 6/15–30/79, Box 67, NSA (26), JCPL.

97. Platt to Brzezinski, memo, May 31, 1979; Gleysteen to H. Brown, telegram, May 18, 1979, Country File, Korea, Republic of, 1–6/79, Box 44, NSA Brzezinski Material, JCPL; Platt to Brzezinski, memo, October 1, 1979, Platt Chron File, 10/79, Box 68, NSA (26), JCPL.

98. Sterba, "U.S. Presses Seoul to Free Dissidents as Carter Departs," *NYT*, July 2, 1979; White House Press Secretary, "The White House Press Briefing by Cyrus R. Vance," July 1, 1979, *Carter, Jimmy Miguk taet'ongnyŏng panghan, 1979.6.29–7.1.*, vol. 3, Folder 9, MF 2009–24, DA.

99. Gleysteen, *Massive Entanglement*, 50.

100. "Kinkŭp choch'i wiban 86-myŏng sŏkpang" [Release of 86 prisoners charged with violating Emergency Decree No. 9], *Chosŏn ilbo*, July 18, 1979.

101. Brzezinski to Brown, memo, July 21, 1979, Platt Chron File, 7/13–31/79, Box 67, NSA (26), JCPL.

102. Atwood to Pease, July 25, 1979, Subject File, Countries, Co 82–2 9/1/78–12/31/79, Box Co–41, WHCF, JCPL.

103. NACHRK, "Chronology: June to December 1979."

104. Bernard Gwertzman, "U.S. Rift with Seoul over Rights Widens," *NYT*, October 6, 1979.

105. Minjuhwa Undong Kinyŏm Saŏphoe, *Han'guk minjuhwa undongsa*, 2:281–82.

106. "Kinkŭpchoch'iwiban 53-myŏng sŏkpang" [Release of 53 prisoners charged under Emergency Decree No. 9], *Chosŏn ilbo*, August 15, 1979.

107. Kukche Aemnest'i Han'guk Chibu, *Han'guk Aemnest'i 30-yŏn!*, 61–66 and 146–47.

108. Minjuhwa Undong Kinyŏm Saŏphoe, *Han'guk minjuhwa undongsa*, 2:260–65 and 280–81.

109. Henry Scott Stokes, "Foe of Seoul Regime Asks Decision by U.S.," *NYT*, September 16, 1979.

110. "Ŏch' ŏguni ŏpnŭn sadaejuŭi ŏndong" [Tendency toward senseless subservience in speech and action], *Sŏul sinmun*, September 18, 1979.

111. Oberdorfer and Carlin, *The Two Koreas*, 89.

112. Vance to Carter, memo, October 12, 1979, Presidential Correspondence, Korea, Republic of: President Park, 1–10/79, Box 12, NSA Brzezinski Material, JCPL.

113. Tarnoff to Brzezinski, memo; Dodson to Clift, memo, October 12, 1979, Platt Chron File, 10/79, Box 68, NSA (26), JCPL.

114. Brzezinski to Carter, memo, October 13, 1979; Carter to Park, October 13, 1979, Presidential Correspondence, Korea, Republic of: President Park, 1–10/79, Box 12, NSA Brzezinski Material, JCPL.

115. "Pusan Masan sat'ae" [Pusan-Masan Incident], November 28, 1979, cir, Folder 6, Box 66, UCLA Collection.

116. "Pusan Masan sat'ae"; "1980-yŏn kongp'an kirok" [Trial records for 1980], Folder 5, Box 66, UCLA Collection.

117. PuMa Minju Hangjaeng Kinyŏm Saŏphoe, *PuMa Minju Hangjaeng 10-chunyŏn Kinyŏm Charyojip* [Sourcebook on the Tenth Anniversary of Pusan-Masan Incident] (Puma Minju Hangjaeng Kinyŏm Saŏphoe, 1989), 31–33 and 107–12.

118. "1980-yŏn kongp'an kirok"; PuMa Minju Hangjaeng Kinyŏm Saŏphoe, *PuMa Minju Hangjaeng 10-chunyŏn*, 142–44 and 151–55; Kukche Aemnest'i Han'guk Chibu, *Han'guk Aemnest'i 30-yŏn!*, 162–67.

119. Sŏ Chung-sŏk, "PuMa hangjaeng ŭi yŏksajŏk chaejomyŏng" [Rethinking the Pusan-Masan Uprising], in the 2009 conference packet "Pak Chŏng-hŭi ch'eje wa PuMa hangjaeng

ui yŏksajŏk chaejomyŏng" [Rethinking the Park Chung-hee regime and the Pusan-Masan Uprising], 3–37.

120. Kim Chae-gyu, "Hangso iyu poch'ungsŏ" [Statement of reason for appeal], in Kim Tae-gon, *Kim Chae-gyu X-p'ail* [Kim Chae-gyu's X-file] (Seoul: Sanha, 2005), 247–50.

121. Ibid.

122. Richard Halloran, "Brown Pledges U.S. Will Not Force South Korea to Ease Repression," *NYT*, October 19, 1979.

123. Platt to Brzezinski, memo, October 24, 1979, Platt Chron File, 10/79, Box 68, NSA (26), JCPL.

Chapter 6. Kwangju

1. Gi-Wook Shin, "Introduction," in *Contentious Kwangju: The May 18 Uprising in Korea's Past and Present*, ed. Gi-Wook Shin and Kyung Moon Hwang (Lanham, MD: Rowman & Littlefield, 2003), xxv.

2. See, for example, Shin and Hwang, *Contentious Kwangju*; Donald Clark, ed., *The Kwangju Uprising: Shadows over the Regime in South Korea* (Boulder, CO: Westview Press, 1988); and Steinberg, *Korean Attitudes Toward the United States*.

3. Drennan, "The Tipping Point: Kwangju, May 1980," in Steinberg, *Korean Attitudes*, 280–306.

4. Lee Jai-eui, *Kwangju Diary: Beyond Death, Beyond the Darkness of the Age*, trans. Kap Su Seol and Nick Mamatas (Los Angeles: UCLA Asian Pacific Monograph Series, 1999); Cumings, "Structural Basis of 'Anti-Americanism,'" 91–115; Yi Sam-sŏng, *Miguk ŭi Taehan chŏngch'ak kwa Han'guk minjokjuŭi*; Namhee Lee, *The Making of Minjung*, 109–44.

5. Kim Dae-jung, *Conscience in Action: The Autobiography of Kim Dae-jung*, trans. Jeon Seung-hee (New York: Palgrave Macmillan, 2019), 242.

6. Minjuhwa Undong Kinyŏm Saŏphoe Yŏn'guso, *Han'guk minjuhwa undongsa yŏnp'yo*, 368–71.

7. "South Korea's Second Spring," *NYT*, March 8, 1980; "South Korea Amnesty Set Today," *NYT*, February 29, 1980.

8. Minjuhwa Undong Kinyŏm Saŏphoe Yŏn'guso, *Han'guk minjuhwa undongsa yŏnp'yo*, 375–81.

9. Henry Scott Stokes, "South Korea Leader Voices Worry on Student Unrest," *NYT*, April 10, 1980.

10. "79 on Trial in Secret Korean Case," *NYT*, April 17, 1980.

11. "More Unrest in S. Korea," Other World Events, *NYT*, April 27, 1980.

12. Pak also claimed that since March 1980, the US intelligence office had been kept informed by the South Korean government about tactical developments and their implementation. However, his reference is not sufficient to cross-check. See Pak Man-gyu, "Singunbu ŭi Kwangju hangjaeng chinap kwa Miguk munje" [The new military regime's crackdown on the Kwangju Uprising and the role of the United States], *Minjujuŭi wa Inkwŏn* 3, no. 1 (2003), 211–42.

13. Gleysteen to SecState (Seoul 05907), telegram, "Korea Focus: Meeting with General Chun and Blue House SYG Choi," May 9, 1980; Gleysteen to SecState (Seoul 05921), telegram, "Korea Focus: May 9 Conversation with Blue House SYG Kwang Soo Choi," May 10, 1980, in Tim Shorrock's collection, accessed August 1, 2014, http://timshorrock.com (hereafter, Shorrock's Collection).

14. "Korea General Gets Intelligence Post," *NYT*, April 15, 1980; Henry Scott Stokes, "New Intelligence Chief Is Now South Korea's Strongman," *NYT*, April 16, 1980.

15. "Seoul's Intelligence Chief Pledges an End of Political Surveillance," *NYT*, April 30, 1980.

16. "Students' Protests Worry South Korea," *NYT*, May 11, 1980.

17. Tim Shorrock, "Kwangju Diary: The View from Washington," in Lee Jae-eui, *Kwangju Diary*, 151–72.

18. Gleysteen to SecState (Seoul, 05781), telegram, "ROKG Shifts Special Forces Units," May 7, 1980, Korea, Republic of, 1–5/80, Box 44, NSA Brzezinski Country File, JCPL.

19. Christopher to AmEm Seoul (State 122052), telegram, "Korea Focus: Tensions in the ROK," May 8, 1980, Shorrock's Collection.

20. Gleysteen to SecState (Seoul 05907), telegram, "Korea Focus: Meeting with General Chun and Blue House SYG Choi," May 9, 1980; Gleysteen to SecState (Seoul 05921), telegram, "Korea Focus: May 9 Conversation with Blue House SYG Kwang Soo Choi," May 10, 1980.

21. Brzezinski to Carter, memo, "Daily Report," May 9, 1980, 5/1/80–5/10/80, Box 15, NSA Brzezinski President's Daily Report File, JCPL; Gregg to Brzezinski, memo, "The Situation in Korea," May 8, 1980, Korea, Republic of, 1–5/80, Box 44, NSA Brzezinski Country File, JCPL.

22. "50,000 Battle Police in Seoul Protests," *NYT*, May 15, 1980.

23. Gleysteen to SecState (Seoul 8282), telegram, "Crackdown in Seoul," May 17, 1980, Korea, Republic of, 1–5/80, Box 44, NSA Brzezinski Country File, JCPL.

24. James P. Sterba, "Tough Steps Taken by Seoul to Quell Students' Protests," *NYT*, May 18, 1980.

25. For more on the peasant uprising, see Albert L. Park, *Building a Heaven on Earth: Religion, Activism, and Protest in Japanese-Occupied Korea* (Honolulu: University of Hawaii Press, 2015); on the student movement, see Charles Kim, *Youth for Nation: Culture and Protest in Cold War South Korea* (Honolulu: University of Hawaii Press, 2018).

26. Ahn Jean, "The Socio-economic Background of the Gwangju Uprising," in *South Korean Democracy: The Legacy of the Gwangju Uprising*, ed. Georgy N. Katsiaficas and Na Kanch'ae, (New York: Routledge, 2006), 24–46, here 42.

27. Minjuhwa Undong Kinyŏm Saŏphoe Yŏn'guso, *Han'guk minjuhwa undongsa yŏnp'yo*, 386–88.

28. James P. Sterba, "Seoul Vows New Restrictions Won't Delay Democracy," *NYT*, May 19, 1980.

29. "U.S. 'Disturbed' Over Crackdown," *NYT*, May 20, 1980.

30. Jungwoon Choi, *The Gwangju Uprising: The Pivotal Democratic Movement That Changed the History of Modern Korea*, trans. Yu Young-nan (Paramus, NJ: Homa & Sekey Books, 2006), 139.

31. Henry Scott Stokes, "Cabinet Resigns in South Korea as Riots Grow," *NYT*, May 21, 1980; and Shim Jae Hoon, "Protesters Control South Korean City," *NYT*, May 22, 1980.

32. Gleysteen to SecState (Seoul 06463), telegram, "The Kwangju Crisis," May 21, 1980, Korea, Republic of, 1–5/80, Box 44, NSA Brzezinski Country File, JCPL; Gregg to Brzezinski, memo, "Up-Date on Korea," May 21, 1980, serial no. CK3100466141, Declassified Documents Reference System (hereafter, DDRS).

33. Gregg to Brzezinski, memo, "Up-Date on Korea," May 21, 1980.

34. Dodson to Mondale et al., memo, "Summary of Conclusions," May 30, 1980, with an enclosure, Memorandum of Conversations, Policy Review Committee, "Korea," May 22, 1980, Shorrock's Collection.

35. Gleysteen to SecState (Seoul 06525), telegram, "Possible Further U.S. Statement on Kwangju Crisis," May 22, 1980, Korea, Republic of, 1–5/80, Box 44, NSA Brzezinski Country File, JCPL.

36. Gleysteen to SecState (Seoul 06610), telegram, "Initial Call on Acting Prime Minister," May 23, 1980, Korea, Republic of, 1–5/80, Box 44, NSA Brzezinski Country File, JCPL.

37. NACHRK, "Chronology of Recent Events in Korea" (October 1979–May 1980), Folder 6, Box 42, UCLA Collection.

38. Shim Jae Hoon, "Unsuccessful Truce Talks Held in South Korean City," *NYT*, May 23, 1980.

39. Committee for Democratic Struggle of Chosun University, "An Urgent Cry for Help," May 22, 1980, Folder 8, Box 55, UCLA Collection; Oh Jaeshik to British Council et al., cable, "Statement: Chun Du Hwan's Genocidal Operation in Kwangju," May 28, 1980, Folder 2, Box 21, UCLA Collection.

40. Jones and Overton, letter to the editor, *Chicago Tribune*, May 21, 1980; Jones and Overton, "U.S. Policy Neglected Korean Aspirations," *Chicago Tribune*, June 5, 1980, CCHRA–1980, Box 6, Jones Papers.

41. Jones and Overton, letter to the editor, *Chicago Sun-Times*, May 23, 1980; Jones and Overton, "Long U.S. Support to Blame for Korean Woe," *Chicago Sun-Times*, June 2, 1980, CCHRA–1980, Box 6, Jones Papers.

42. Anonymous citizen to Mr. Foreign Correspondent, May 23, 1980, Folder 1, Box 7, UCLA Collection.

43. Henry Kamm, "Seoul Seems to Plan a Move on Kwangju," *NYT*, May 26, 1980.

44. Gleysteen to SecState (Seoul 06663), telegram, "May 26 Meeting with Blue House SYG Choi," May 26, 1980, Korea, Republic of, 1–5/80, Box 44, NSA Brzezinski Country File, JCPL.

45. Henry Scott Stokes, "Rebels Seek U.S. Help," *NYT*, May 27, 1980.

46. NACHRK, "Chronology of Recent Events in Korea" (October 1979–May 1980).

47. Henry Kamm, "South Korea Troops Recapture Kwangju in Predawn Strike," *NYT*, May 27, 1980; Henry Scott Stokes, "When the Troops Finally Came, Kwangju Revolt Became a Rout," *NYT*, May 28, 1980. The official casualty numbers, released by the ROK government in 1995, are similar to those cited. However, not a few scholars, activists, and journalists place the numbers much higher (Pharis Harvey, interview, April 29, 2010).

48. "United States Government Statement on the Events in Kwangju, Republic of Korea, in May 1980," June 19, 1989, accessed November 1, 2019, http://kr.usembassy.gov.

49. Bernard Gwertzman, "Military Rule in South Korea Gives White House a Major Challenge," *NYT*, May 29, 1980.

50. Billings et al. to Carter, May 27, 1980, Folder 1, Box 7, UCLA Collection.

51. "Korean Exile Assails U.S. Stand on Revolt," *NYT*, May 30, 1980.

52. Wilson to McCloud, memo, June 9, 1980, with enclosure, Underwood to Thurber, May 30, 1980, Folder 2, Box 22, UCLA Collection.

53. For more, see Charles Kim, *Youth for Nation*, 137–75.

54. McConaughy to SecState (962), telegram, April 25, 1960 [795B.00/4–2560 HBS], Folder 3–2960, Box 2180, Department of State Central Decimal File 1960–1963, RG 59, National Archives and Records Administration, College Park, MD (hereafter, NARA).

55. McConaughy to SecState (962), telegram, April 25, 1960 [795B.00/4–2560 HBS].

56. Wilson to McCloud, memo, June 9, 1980, with enclosure, Underwood to Thurber, May 30, 1980.

57. "Ch'oe Taet'ongnyŏng Ŭijang Kukka Powi Pisang Taechaekwi sinsŏl" [President Ch'oe launches Special Committee for National Security Measures], *Tonga ilbo*, May 31, 1980.

58. Memo [no title], June 6, 1980, Folder 5, Box 49, UCLA Collection.

59. Office of News and Information of National Council of Churches, "U.S. Repeating Iran Mistakes in South Korea, Church Leaders Warn," June 11, 1980, Folder 2, Box 21, UCLA Collection.

60. Gleysteen to SecState (Seoul 08159), telegram, "Korea Focus: June 25 Talk with Blue House SYG," June 25, 1980, Shorrock's Collection.

61. Pharis Harvey, "In Korea, Savage Repression Brings a Timid US Response," *Christianity and Crisis* 40, no. 12 (July 21, 1980): 212–15, July 21, 1980, 212–15, NACHRK 1980–1981, Box 10, Jones Papers.

62. Billings to Luidens et al., memo, "August 9–August 16, 1980 Trip to Korea" [no date], Folder 17, Box 22, UCLA Collection. AI also tried to conduct a fact-finding mission, but its delegates were barred from entering South Korea. See "AI Says South Korea Bars Factfinding Mission," AI news news release, August 5, 1980, South Korean Mission 1980, MF 473, IISH.

63. On increased arsons targeting US installations, see Keun-sik Jung, "Has Kwangju Been Realized" in Shin and Hwang, *Contentious Kwangju*, 47.

64. Chief of SRS/DDI to Director of Central Intelligence, memo, "Proposal for U.S. Action in South Korea," April 21, 1960 [CIA–RDP80–01446R000100060004–7], CIA Records Search Tool (CREST), NARA (hereafter, CREST–NARA).

65. Peer de Silva, *Sub Rosa: The CIA and the Uses of Intelligence* (New York: Times Books, 1978).

66. Poitras et al. to Carter, June 6, 1980, Subject File, Countries, Co 82–2 1/1/78–1/20/81, Box Co–42, WHCF, JCPL.

67. Gleysteen to SecState (Seoul 06463), telegram, "The Kwangju Crisis," May 21, 1980, Korea, Republic of, 1–5/80, Box 44, NSA Brzezinski Country File, JCPL; Brzezinski to Gregg, memo, "Possible Policy Options: South Korea," July 3, 1980, Korea, Republic of, 6–8/80, Box 44, NSA Brzezinski Country File, JCPL.

68. Gregg to Brzezinski, memo, "United States Government Reactions to Events in Korea," August 14, 1980, Korea, Republic of, 6–8/80, Box 44, NSA Brzezinski Country File, JCPL; Gregg to Brzezinski, memo, "Presidential Interest in the Trial of Kim Dae Jung," August 15, 1980, Korea, Republic of, 6–8/80, Box 44, NSA Brzezinski Country File, JCPL; Sullivan to Brzezinski and Aaron, memo, "US Policy Options in Connection with the Kim Dae Jung Trial," August 20, 1980, Korea, Republic of, 6–8/80, Box 44, NSA Brzezinski Country File, JCPL; Sam Jameson, "U.S. Support Claimed for S. Korea's Chon," *LAT*, August 8, 1980.

69. Henry Scott Stokes, "General Says South Korea Needs 'New Leaders' and He Is Willing," *NYT*, August 9, 1980.

70. Carter to Chun, August 27, 1980 [#2], with one draft letter [#2H], serial no. CK3100117778, DDRS.

71. Muskie to AmEm Seoul (State 240037), telegram, "President Chun's Response to President Carter," September 10, 1980, Korea, Republic of, 9/80–1/81, Box 44, NSA Brzezinski Country File, JCPL.

72. Brzezinski to Carter, memo, "Kim Dae Jung," September 16, 1980, Korea, Republic of, 9/80–1/81, Box 44, NSA Brzezinski Country File, JCPL; Gregg to Brzezinki, memo, "Kim Dae Jung," September 16, 1980, Korea, Republic of, 9/80–1/81, Box 44, NSA Brzezinski Country File, JCPL; Turner to Brzezinski, memo, "Korea: Policy Options," September 15, 1980, serial no. CK3100670528, DDRS; Gregg to Brzezinki (5148 Add on), memo, "Kim Dae Jung," September 16, 1980, Korea, Republic of, 9/80–1/81, Box 44, NSA Brzezinski Country File, JCPL.

73. Tarnoff to Brzezinski, memo, "Release of Part of a Letter from President Chun of Korea," September 19, 1980, Korea, Republic of, 9/80–1/81, Box 44, NSA Brzezinski Country File, JCPL.

74. Hutcheson to Brzezinski, memo, October 21, 1980, Korea, Republic of, 9/80–1/81, Box 44, NSA Brzezinski Country File, JCPL; Brzezinski to Carter (5613 Add on), memo, "Letter to the President from Mrs. Kim Dae Jung," October 20, 1980, with enclosures, "Letter, Kinney to Whom It May Concern," October 6, 1980, and "Letter, Mrs. Kim Dae Jung to President and Mrs. Carter," October 1, 1980, Korea, Republic of, 9/80–1/81, Box 44, NSA Brzezinski Country File, JCPL; Gregg to Brzezinski (5613), memo, "Letter to the President from Mrs. Kim Dae Jung," October 16, 1980, Korea, Republic of, 9/80–1/81, Box 44, NSA Brzezinski Country File, JCPL.

75. Hutcheson to Brzezinski, memo, October 21, 1980; Brzezinski to Carter (5613 Add on), memo; Gregg to Brzezinski (5613), memo.

76. Aaron to Carter, memo, "Kim Dae Jung," November 4, 1980, Korea, Republic of, 9/80–1/81, Box 44, NSA Brzezinski Country File, JCPL; Gregg to Aaron, memo, "Kim Dae Jung," November 14, 1980, Korea, Republic of, 9/80–1/81, Box 44, NSA Brzezinski Country File, JCPL.

77. Carter to Brzezinski et al., memo [no title], [no date; 20 November 1980, cir], [Declassified, June 11, 2009: NLC–127–1–41–1–4], CK3100595051, DDRS.

78. Mansfield to SecState (Tokyo 20249), telegram, "Ambassador's November 19 Meeting with Chief Cabinet Secretary: Kim Dae Jung Case," November 19, 1980, CK3100510117, DDRS; Muskie to AmEm Tokyo (State 308256/01), telegram, "Consultations with Japan on the Kim Dae Jung Issue," November 20, 1980, CK3100521467, DDRS.

79. Gleysteen to SecState (Seoul 15600), telegram, "Korea Focus: Discussion on Kim Dae Jung with [redacted]," November 21, 1980, Korea, Republic of, 9/80–1/81, Box 44, NSA Brzezinski Country File, JCPL; Gleysteen to SecState (Seoul 15601), telegram, "Korea Focus: November 21 Conversation with President Chun Re Kim Dae Jung," November 21, 1980, Korea, Republic of, 9/80–1/81, Box 44, NSA Brzezinski Country File, JCPL.

80. Muskie to AmEm Tokyo (State 317140), telegram, "Gleysteen/Okawara Discussion Re Kim Dae Jung," November 28, 1980, CK3100521465, DDRS; Muskie to Carter, memo, "Meeting Korean Rice Import Needs," [no date; November 25, 1980, cir.], Korea, Republic of, 9/80–1/81, Box 44, NSA Brzezinski Country File, JCPL; Gregg to Brzezinski, memo, "Korean Rice," November 25, 1980, Korea, Republic of, 9/80–1/81, Box 44, NSA Brzezinski Country File, JCPL; Brzezinski to Carter, memo, "Korean Rice Imports," November 26, 1978, Korea, Republic of, 9/80–1/81, Box 44, NSA Brzezinski Country File, JCPL; Aaron to Brzezinski, memo, November 26, 1980, Korea, Republic of, 9/80–1/81, Box 44, NSA Brzezinski Country File, JCPL.

81. Muskie to Carter, memo [no title], November 25, 1980 [#16], with an enclosure, (draft) letter, Carter to Chun, CK3100109089, DDRS.

82. Gleysteen to SecState (Seoul 16166), telegram, "Brown Visit to Korea," December 4, 1980, Korea, Republic of, 9/80–1/81, Box 44, NSA Brzezinski Country File, JCPL; Christopher to AmEm Seoul (State 322462), telegram, "Secretary Brown Visit to Korea," December 5,

1980, Korea, Republic of, 9/80–1/81, Box 44, NSA Brzezinski Country File, JCPL; Gleysteen to SecState (Seoul 16264), telegram, "Delivery of Presidential Letter," December 6, 1980, Korea, Republic of, 9/80–1/81, Box 44, NSA Brzezinski Country File, JCPL; Situation Room to Brzezinski, memo, "Noon Notes," December 5, 1980, CK3100638725, and December 10, 1980, CK3100634631, DDRS; Gleysteen to SecState (Seoul 16596), telegram, "Korea Focus: Secretary Brown's Korea Visit—Kim Dae Jung," December 13, 1980, Korea, Republic of, 9/80–1/81, Box 44, NSA Brzezinski Country File, JCPL.

83. Gleysteen to SecState (Seoul 17308), telegram, "Korea Focus: Prospects on Kim Dae Jung," December 31, 1980, Korea, Republic of, 9/80–1/81, Box 44, NSA Brzezinski Country File, JCPL.

84. Gleysteen to SecState (Seoul 17309), telegram, "Kim Dae Jung," December 31, 1980, Korea, Republic of, 9/80–1/81, Box 44, NSA Brzezinski Country File, JCPL.

85. Gleysteen to SecState (Seoul 16261), telegram, "Report of Chun Emissary to the US," December 6, 1980, Korea, Republic of, 9/80–1/81, Box 44, NSA Brzezinski Country File, JCPL.

Chapter 7. Aftermath

1. See Chun to Reagan, January 22, 1981, CO082–02 Korea S–1, WHORM Subject File, Ronald Reagan Presidential Library (hereafter, RRPL).

2. Gleysteen to Haig (00845), cable, "Kim Dae Jung Verdict," January 22, 1981, KOR S (1/22/1981–2/27/1981), Box 9, NSC ES CO, RRPL.

3. Gleysteen to Haig (00773), cable, "Announcement of Supreme Court Decision on Kim Dae Jung January 23," January 22, 1981, KOR S (1/22/1981–2/27/1981), Box 9, NSC ES CO, RRPL.

4. Gleysteen to Haig (00844), cable, "Agenda Suggestion for Reagan-Chun Meeting," January 22, 1981, Korea President Chun Visit February 10, 1981 (5–5), Box 91434, NSC ES VIP Visits, RRPL.

5. Gleysteen to Haig, cable, "Supreme Court Upholds Kim Dae Jung's Death Sentence," January 23, 1981, Korea South (1/22/1981–2/27/1981), Box 9, NSC ES CO, RRPL; Yu Sŏn-hŭi, "Ojŏn 'sahyŏng' ohu e 'mugi' ro" [Death sentence in the morning made life sentence in the afternoon], *Hankyŏrye*, February 14, 2016, accessed November 3, 2019, http://www.hani.co.kr.

6. Bernard Gweertzman, "U.S. Put Off Report on Human Rights to Avoid Embarrassing Chun," *NYT*, February 3, 1981.

7. "Talking Paper for Conduct of the Summit Meeting" [no date], Department of State Briefing Book re the Official Visit of Chun, February 1–3, 1981 (1/2), Box 91434, NSC ES VIP Visits, RRPL.

8. "South Korea, Prospects for the Fifth Republic" [no date], Korea President Chun Visit, February 1–3, 1981 (3/5), Box 91434, NSC ES VIP Visits, RRPL.

9. Allen to Reagan, memo, "President Chun of Korea," January 29, 1981, Chun Visit—February 1981 (1of 2), RAC Box 10, Donald Gregg Files, RRPL.

10. Adair to Reagan, January 22, 1981, CO082–02 Korea S–1, WHORM Subject File, RRPL.

11. Harkin et al. to Reagan, January 28, 1981, CO082–02 Korea S–2, WHORM Subject File, RRPL.

12. Randall et al. to Reagan, January 29, 1981, CO082–02 Korea S–1, WHORM Subject File, RRPL.

13. "Department of State Briefing Paper, Human Rights" [no date], Department of State Briefing Book re the Official Visit of Chun, February 1–3, 1981 (2/2), Box 91434, NSC ES VIP Visits, RRPL.

14. Allen to Reagan, memo, "Secretary Haig's Memo on Korea," February 2, 1981, Chun Visit—February 1981 (1of 2), RAC Box 10, Donald Gregg Files, RRPL.

15. Allen to Reagan, memo, "Your Meeting with President Chun of Korea," February 6, 1981, Memoranda of Conversation (3), Box 48, NSC ES Subject File, RRPL.

16. Joint communiqué, February 2, 1981, Department of State Briefing Book re the Official Visit of Chun, February 1–3, 1981 (1/2), Box 91434, NSC ES VIP Visits, RRPL.

17. Allen to Reagan, memo, "Your Meeting with President Chun of Korea," February 6, 1981, Memoranda of Conversation (3), Box 48, NSC ES Subject File, RRPL.

18. Ernest Lefever, *Human Rights and Foreign Policy* (Washington, DC: Ethics and Public Policy Center, 1980).

19. Judith Miller, "Heat over Lefever's Nomination Brings Some Senators to a Boil," *NYT*, May 24, 1981; Miller, "Percy and Majority of Senate Panel Are Expected to Reject Rights Choice," *NYT*, June 5, 1981; Miller, "Rebuffed in Senate, Lefever Pulls Out as Rights Nominee," *NYT*, June 6, 1981.

20. Quoted in Kathryn Sikkink, *Mixed Signals: U.S. Human Rights Policy and Latin America* (Ithaca, NY: Cornell University Press, 2004), 155.

21. Bernard Gwertzman, "Haig Favors Stand Against Violations of Rights Abroad," *NYT*, April 21, 1981.

22. Gleysteen to Haig, cable, "Korea in the Perspective of the Last Three Years," June 9, 1981, ROK (4–4), RAC Box 10, Donald Gregg Files, RRPL.

23. Gleysteen to Haig, cable, "ROKG Non-Proliferation Assurances," June 9, 1981, Korea South (4/22/1981–6/30/1981), Box 9, NSC ES CO, RRPL.

24. Harvey to Reagan, July 7, 1981, CO082–02 Korea S–4, WHORM Subject File, RRPL.

25. Henry Scott Stokes, "Seoul Dissidents Bitter About U.S.," *NYT*, August 25, 1981.

26. Gleysteen to Haig, cable, "Conversation with Yoo Hak Seong," June 1, 1982, Korea South (4/24/1981–6/30/1981), Box 9, NSC ES CO, RRPL.

27. The details of this meeting between Kalicki and Kim were reported by the US ambassador to South Korea, Richard Walker, to Haig. See Walker to Haig, cable, "Kalicki Conversation with Kim Kyung Won," August 23, 1981, Korea South (7/1/1981–9/15/1981), Box 9, NSC ES CO, RRPL.

28. Henry Scott Stokes, "Prisoner Beatings Reported in Seoul," *NYT*, September 6, 1981.

29. Henry Scott Stokes, "Seoul Said to Hold 15,000 in Camps Without Trial," *NYT*, September 20, 1981.

30. Henry Scott Stokes, "South Korea Says It Is Holding 3,228 Criminals Without Charges," *NYT*, September 26, 1981.

31. Walker to Haig, cable, "South Korea," October 29, 1981, ROK (3–4), RAC Box 10, Donald Gregg Files, RRPL.

32. Haig to Holdridge et al., memo, "Human Rights Policy," January 21, 1982, Folder 8, Box 91, UCLA Collection; Tamar Jacoby, "The Reagan Turnaround on Human Rights," *Foreign Affairs* 64, no. 5 (Summer 1986): 1066–86.

33. Barbara Crossette, "Central America Found to Regress on Human Rights," *NYT*, February 8, 1982.

34. Henry Scott Stokes, "Seoul Reduces Life Sentence of Top Dissident to 20 Years," *NYT*, March 3, 1982. On this announcement, see also Stokes, "Seoul Urged to Ease Up on Prisoners," *NYT*, March 15, 1982.

35. Richard Halloran, "Weinberger Vows Support for Seoul," *NYT*, March 30, 1982.

36. Henry Scott Stokes, "Bush Visiting Seoul Amid Worry over Anti-U.S. Acts," *NYT*, April 25, 1982.

37. Walker to Haig, cable, "Bush's Breakfast Meeting with Korean Opinion Leaders," April 29, 1982, Korea South (4/14/1982–4/30/1982), Box 9, NSC ES CO, RRPL.

38. Bruce Cumings, "Devil to Pay in Seoul," *NYT*, July 6, 1982.

39. "Notes on Hearing Before Joint Sub-Committees on Human Rights and Asia Pacific," August 10, 1982, Edward J. Baker (EJB) Collection, Chestnut Hill, MA (hereafter, EJB Collection).

40. "Testimony of the Honorable Richard Holbrooke Before Subcommittee on Asian and Pacific Affairs and the Subcommittee on Human Rights and International Organizations of the Committee on Foreign Affairs," August 10, 1982, EJB Collection.

41. Bob to Sigur, memo, September 14, 1982, Korea 1982 (9/14/1982–10/31/1982), RAC Box 10, Gaston Sigur Files (hereafter, GSF), RRPL; "South Korea Won't Get High Voltage Batons," *NYT*, September 17, 1982.

42. Don Bonker, "Opening Statement," September 21, 1982, EJB Collection; Edward Baker, "Prepared Statement on Reconciling Human Rights and Strategic Interests in South Korea," September 21, 1982, EJB Collection.

43. Harvey to Reagan, November 12, 1982, CO082-02 Korea S–7, Box 116, WHORM Subject File, RRPL.

44. Walker to Shultz, cable, "Conversation with Mrs. Kim Dae-jung," December 20, 1982, Korea South (9/11/1982–2/28/1983), Box 9, NSC ES CO, RRPL.

45. "U.S. Welcomes Seoul's Move to Release 1,200 Prisoners," *NYT*, December 25, 1982.

46. Seth S. King, "Kim Says Many in Korea Speak of U.S. Betrayal," *NYT*, December 27, 1982.

47. "Freeman Reports," CNN, January 5, 1983, Folder 6, Box 74, UCLA Collection.

48. *Korea Scope* 3, no. 1 (March 1983), Korea 1982 (1/1/1983–3/2/1983), RAC Box 10, GSF, RRPL.

49. "Exiled South Korean Plans to Return Soon to Press Fight for Rights," *NYT*, November 12, 1984.

50. Matthew C. Quinn, "South Korea Opposition Leader Kim Dae-Jung Left for Home," February 6, 1985, UPI Archives, accessed June 5, 2019, https://www.upi.com.

51. "Kim Dae Jung Is Beaten by Police on Arrival in Seoul, Escort Says," *NYT*, February 6, 1985.

52. Bernard Gwertzman, "U.S. Says Seoul Failed to Use an Agreed Plan," *NYT*, February 9, 1985; Clyde Haberman, "Melee at Airport in Seoul Prompts New Accusations," *NYT*, February 11, 1985.

53. Ben A. Franklin, "Reagan Faults Both Sides in Seoul Melee," *NYT*, February 12, 1985.

54. EAP to Seoul Embassy, cable, "Washington Post Interview Concerning Kim Dae Jung," February 19, 1985, Talking Points—Korean Issues (2 of 2), Box 15, Linda Kojelis Files, RRPL.

55. Harvey to Reagan, January 26, 1983, PR 013 Petitions, Box 6, WHORM Subject File, RRPL.

56. Shultz to Walker, cable, "Appeal for Clemency for Pusan Arson Defendants," February 19, 1983, Korea South (9/11/1982–2/28/1983), Box 9, NSC ES CO, RRPL.

57. Walker to Shultz, cable, "Supreme Court Upholds Death Sentence for Pusan Arsonists," March 8, 1983, Korea South (3/1/1983–4/15/1983), Box 9, NSC ES CO, RRPL.

58. Walker to Shultz, cable, "Pusan Arson Case Demarche," March 14, 1983, Korea South (3/1/1983–4/15/1983), Box 9, NSC ES CO, RRPL.

59. Ibid.

60. Hill to Gregg, memo, "Briefing Memo for the Vice President's Meeting with the Korean Foreign Minister," April 19, 1983, Korea—Visit of Min. of Foreign Affairs, RAC Box 10, GSF, RRPL.

61. Shultz to Walker, cable, "Foreign Minister Lee's Meeting with the President," May 5, 1983, Korea—Visit of Min. of Foreign Affairs, RAC Box 10, GSF, RRPL.

62. Clyde Haberman, "Security Tightened in Seoul in Advance of Reagan Visit," *NYT*, November 12, 1983.

63. "Excerpts from President's Address in Seoul," *NYT*, November 12, 1983; on Chun's secret plan, see "Preparatory Research for the Peaceful Regime Change in 1988" [ca. June 1984], Folder 5, Box 46, UCLA Collection.

64. "Uri ŭi siljŏng" [Our realities], memo [ca. October 1981], Folder 8, Box 42, UCLA Collection.

65. On the rise of mass demonstrations in June 1987, see Hagen Koo, *Korean Workers*.

66. Chŏng Sŏn-sun to Kyohoe Yŏsŏng Yŏnhaphoe, memo, "Yŏsŏng kŭlloja ka tanghin inkwŏn ch'imhae haegyŏl ŭl wihan hyŏpcho yoch'ŏng" [Request for cooperation on settlement of human rights violations against female workers], June 23, 1982, serial no. 14790, KDF; Harvey to Hiatt, October 18, 1982, serial no. 528063, KDF.

67. Minjuhwa Undong Kinyŏm Saŏphoe Yŏn'gusŏ, *Han'guk minjuhwa undongsa yŏnp'yo*, 256, 401–05; "[1981–yŏn] K'ont'ŭrol Teit'a Nodong Chohap, tagukchŏk kiŏp kwa kwŏllyŏk e massŏn t'ujaeng" [Control Data union's struggle against multinational company and the regime], accessed June 13, 2019, http://demos-archives.or.kr.

68. Han'guk K'ont'ŭrol Teit'a Nodong Chohap, memo, "Tagukchŏk kiŏb esŏ yŏsŏng kŭlloja ka tanghago innŭn inkwŏnch'imhae" [Human rights violations against female workers at multinational companies], serial no. 443701, KDF.

69. Walker to Shultz, cable, "'Young Priests' Letter to President Reagan on Control Data Korea," July 30, 1982, Korea South (5/1/1982–9/10/1982), Box 9, NSC ES CO, RRPL.

70. Hyung Kyu Park to the Secretary of State, August 8, 1982, serial no. 843251, KDF.

71. "Human Rights Declaration," October 6, 1982, Folder 24, Box 66, UCLA Collection.

72. "Human Rights Declaration," October 1983, Folder 14, Box 67, UCLA Collection.

73. "Inkwŏn sosik" [Human rights news], NCCK's Human Rights Committee, no. 81, December 15, 1983, serial no. 521463, KDF.

74. Chŏngŭi P'yŏnghwa Wiwŏnhoe, "Che2hoe inkwŏnjuil e chŭŭmhayŏ" [On the occasion of the second Human Rights Day], December 4, 1983, serial no. 835731, KDF.

75. Chŏngŭi P'yŏnghwa Wiwŏnhoe, "Saengjonkwŏn ŭi pojang ŭl wihayŏ" [Assuring the right to subsistence], December 9, 1984, serial no. 78935, KDF.

76. Directorate of Intelligence, "South Korea: Seoul's Campus Strategy," April 4, 1984, Korea South 1984 (4 of 7), RAC Box 10, GSF, RRPL.

77. Clyde Haberman, "Student Protests May Test Seoul's Recent Easing of Political Curbs," *NYT*, March 12, 1984.

78. Directorate of Intelligence, "South Korea: Seoul's Campus Strategy," April 4, 1984..

79. On the student-labor alliance, see Namhee Lee, *The Making of Minjung*, 213–40; Minjuhwa Undong Kinyŏm Saŏphoe Yŏn'gusŏ, *Han'guk minjuhwa undongsa yŏnp'yo*, 413–27.

80. On student vanguardism, see Charles Kim, *Youth for the Nation*; Minjuhwa Undong Kinyŏm Saŏphoe Yŏn'gusŏ, *Han'guk minjuhwa undongsa yŏnp'yo*, 411–23.

81. "Han'guk chŏngbu, 'pŭllaengnisŭt'ŭ' ro nodongja t'anap" [The ROK government's use of "blacklist" to suppress workers], *Korean Street Journal*, January 1, 1984, 6, MF 0054, KSJ series, Korean Heritage Library, University of Southern California.

82. Kim Yong-ja and Sŏ Ki-hwa, "Haego nodongja inkwŏn sŏnŏn" [The fired workers' declaration of human rights], December 10, 1983, serial no. 835033, KDF.

83. Chŏnnam Inkwŏn Sŏn'gyo Wiwŏnhoe, "Inkwŏn sŏnŏn" [Declaration of human rights], October 1, 1984, serial no. 879266, KDF.

84. SNU Students' Association et al., "Naemubu Changgwan e ponae nŭn konggae hangŭisŏ" [Open complaint to Minister of Home Affairs], April 13, 1985, serial no. 89764, KDF.

85. Han'guk Kidokkyo Kyohoe Hyŏbŭihoe Inkwŏn Wiwŏnhoe et al., "Sŏngmyŏngsŏ" [Statement], June 5, 1985, serial no. 521493, KDF; "85-yŏndo inkwŏn munje chŏn'guk hyŏbŭihoe tŭngnokcha myŏngdan" [Enrollment for the 1985 national consultation on human rights], September 6, 1985, serial no. 841750, KDF.

86. Cho Yong-sul to Haet'ai Chegwa sajang, memo, "Nodongja pudang t'anap e taehan hangŭi ŭi kŏn" [Complaint on unjust oppression of workers], July 5, 1985, serial no. 334039, KDF.

87. Namhee Lee, *The Making of Minjung*, 264.

88. Organization for Demilitarization and Neutralization of Korea to the Members of the United Nations, October 9, 1982, Korea South 1982 (11/1/1982–12/31/1982), RAC Box 10, GSF, RRPL; Stoessel to Walker, cable, "Torture in Pusan Arson Case," July 23, 1982, Korea South (5/1/1982–9/10/1982), Box 9, NSC ES CO, RRPL; Walker to Shultz, cable, "Torture in Pusan Arson Case," July 27, 1982, Korea South (5/1/1982–9/10/1982), Box 9, NSC ES CO, RRPL.

89. Minjuhwa Undong Kinyŏm Saŏphoe, *Han'guk minjuhwa undongsa*, 3: 683.

90. Ibid., 683–84.

91. "South Koreans Protest over Purported Torture," *NYT*, November 12, 1985; "South Korean Sit-In," *NYT*, November 13, 1985.

92. "South Korea: The Detention of Prisoner of Conscience Kim Keun-tae," AI IS, March 1986, EJB Collection.

93. Waller, "AFKN and Host Country Sensitivities," August 6, 1987, Korea—Military [11/6/1987], RAC Box 4, James Kelly Files, RRPL.

94. Quoted in James West and Edward Baker, "The 1987 Constitutional Reforms in South Korea: Electoral Processes and Judicial Independence" in Shaw, *Human Rights in South Korea*, 221–52, here 247.

95. Asia Watch Committee, *Freedom of Expression in the Republic of Korea* (Washington, DC: Asia Watch, 1988), 51.

96. Minjuhwa Undong Kinyŏm Saŏphoe, *Han'guk minjuhwa undongsa*, 3:684–85, 897–99.

97. "U.S. Sees a Crackdown on the Seoul Opposition," *NYT*, February 15, 1986. See also Ronald E. Yates, "S. Korean, Foes Meet on Petitions," *Chicago Tribune*, February 25, 1986.

98. "U.S. Sees a Crackdown on the Seoul Opposition," *NYT*, February 15, 1986.

99. Eric Schwartz and Holly Burkhalter, "Press Seoul for Democracy, Too," *NYT*, February 24, 1986.

100. Clyde Haberman, "Korean Cardinal Backs Opposition," *NYT*, March 10, 1986.

101. McDaniel to Peterson, memo, "State Draft Reports on H.Con.Res. 261 and S.Con.Res. 100 Regarding the Civil Rights of Kim Dae Jung in Korea," March 18, 1986, CO082-02 Korea S–15, Box 117, WHORM Subject File, RRPL.

102. Leslie H. Gelb, "U.S. Vows to Resist Despots of Rights as Well as of Left," *NYT*, March 14, 1986; Bernard Weinraub, "The U.S. and Dictators," *NYT*, March 15, 1986.

103. Jacoby, "Reagan Turnaround," 1067.

104. Shultz to Walker, cable, "Assistant Secretary Sigur's Testimony on Korea," April 17, 1986, Korea (4/16/1986–5/15/1986), RAC Box 3, James Kelly Files, RRPL.

105. Fine to Teitel, April 9, 1986, EJB Collection.

106. "Testimony of Edward J. Baker on Behalf of the Asia Watch, Wednesday, April 16, 1986, Subcommittees on Asian and Pacific Affairs and Human Rights and International Organizations"; "Mi, Han'guk minjuhwa kyesok kwŏnjang" [US recommendation for Korea's continued democratization], *Tonga ilbo*, April 19, 1986, EJB Collection.

107. Quoted in Stephen B. Butler, "Student Riot Deals Major Blow to S. Korea Opposition," *Christian Science Monitor*, May 5, 1986. On the riot, see also "Protesters Battle Police in South Korea," *NYT*, May 4, 1986.

108. Bernard Gwertzman, "Shultz, in Seoul, Says U.S. Backs Korea's Efforts," *NYT*, May 8, 1986.

109. Kendall Wills, "Rights Abuses Said to Rise Sharply in South Korea," *NYT*, June 1, 1986.

110. Martin Tolchin, "High Profile for South Korean 'Embassy in Exile,'" *NYT*, October 10, 1986.

111. Peterson to NSC and Department of Justice, memo, "State's Draft Report on S.Res. 392," July 29, 1986, Korea (7/1/1986–8/11/1986), RAC Box 3, James Kelly Files, RRPL.

112. "South Korea Is Urged to Release 2 Prisoners," *NYT*, July 15, 1986.

113. Solarz et al. to Chun Doo-hwan, September 26, 1986, EJB Collection.

114. Chŏng Yŏng-nan, "Pang Pyŏng-gyu Chŏndosa nim ŭi komun chinsang ŭl palkimnida" [Full and true account of the torture of evangelist Pang Pyŏng-gyu], December 31, 1986, serial no. 521405, KDF.

115. Kendall J. Wills, "Seoul to Investigate Man's Death in Police Custody," *NYT*, January 18, 1987; Pak Ki-yong, "Pak Chong-ch'ŏl komun ch'ŏt p'ongno ŭisa" [Doctor exposed Pak Chong-ch'ŏl's torture for the first time], *Hankyŏrye*, January 9, 2018, accessed November 3, 2019, http://www.hani.co.kr.

116. Kim Sang-gŭn, "Sŏngmyŏngsŏ" [Statement], January 22, 1987, serial no. 59587, KDF.

117. Minjuhwa Undong Kinyŏm Saŏphoe, *Han'guk minjuhwa undongsa*, 3: 281–82.

118. Clyde Haberman, "Seoul Student's Torture Death Changes Political Landscape," *NYT*, January 31, 1987.

119. Wills, "Seoul to Investigate Man's Death in Police Custody."

120. David Pitt, "Protesters in Seoul Routed by Tear Gas," *NYT*, March 4, 1987.

121. Bureau of Public Affairs, "Korean Politics in Transition," Current Policy No. 917 [no date], Korea (3/16/1987–4/30/1987), RAC Box 3, James Kelly Files, RRPL.

122. David Shipler, "Seoul Gives Shultz a Democracy Vow," *NYT*, March 7, 1987.

123. "New U.S. Ambassador to Korea, Possible Policy Changes Viewed," *Seoul Wolgan Kyonghyang*, May 1987, Korea (10/26/1987–11/30/1987), RAC Box 3, James Kelly Files, RRPL.

124. Rockefeller to Carlucci, May 7, 1987, CO082–02 Korea S–17, Box 117, WHORM Subject File, RRPL.

125. "24 Political Prisoners to Be Freed by Seoul," *NYT*, May 3, 1987.

126. Minjuhwa Undong Kinyŏm Saŏphoe, *Han'guk minjuhwa undongsa*, 3: 300–303.

127. "1,000 Arrested in Seoul During Street Protests," *NYT*, May 24, 1987.

128. "Seoul Apologizes for Student's Killing but Warns Protesters," *NYT*, May 31, 1987.

129. Susan Chira, "South Koreans' Anger at Rulers Is Also Turned Against U.S.," *NYT*, June 20, 1987.

130. "On Trade with Korea," *NYT*, June 17, 1987.

131. Peterson to Legislative Liaison Officer, memo, "State Draft Report on S. 1392," October 9, 1987, CO082–02 Korea S–20, Box 117, WHORM Subject File, RRPL.

132. Quoted in Oberdorfer and Carlin, *The Two Koreas*, 168. For more on the very real threat of martial law, see "Former Defense Minister Interviewed on Politics," JPRS–KAR–88–010, April 26, 1988, Korea (4/26/1988–5/3/1988), RAC Box 4, James Kelly Files, RRPL; "Profile of Kim Pok-tong, Man Behind 29 June Affair" [no date], Korea (10/26/1987–11/30/1987), RAC Box 3, James Kelly Files, RRPL.

133. Shultz to Lilley, cable, "Roh Tae Woo Calls for Direct Presidential Election," June 29, 1987, Korea (6/20/1987–7/1/1987), RAC Box 3, James Kelly Files, RRPL.

134. Susan Chira, "For Koreans, Sighs of Relief as Air Clears," *NYT*, June 30, 1987.

135. Jang-Jip Choi, *Democracy After Democratization: The Korean Experience* (Stanford, CA: Walter H. Shorenstein Asia-Pacific Research Center, 2012), 187–89.

Epilogue

1. Stephen Hopgood, *The Endtimes of Human Rights* (Ithaca, NY: Cornell University Press, 2013) and Posner, *The Twilight of Human Rights Law*.

2. Monica Duffy Toft, "False Prophecies in the Service of Good Works," in *Debating "The Endtimes of Human Rights": Activism and Institutions in a Neo-Westphalian World*, ed. Doutje Lettinga and Lars van Troost (Amsterdam: Amnesty International Netherlands, 2014), 47–51.

3. Todd Landman, "Social Magic and the Temple of Human Rights: Critical Reflections on Stephen Hopgood's *Endtimes of Human Rights*," in Lettinga and van Troost, *Debating "The Endtimes of Human Rights*," 25–32; Sikkink, *Evidence for Hope*, 7–13.

4. César Rodríguez-Garavito, "Towards a Human Rights Ecosystem," in Lettinga and van Troost, *Debating "The Endtimes of Human Rights*," 39–46.

5. Etsuro Totsuka, "Commentary on a Victory for 'Comfort Women': Japan's Judicial Recognition of Military Sexual Slavery," *Pacific Rim Law & Policy Journal* 8, no. 1 (1999): 47–61.

6. For the 1996 report, see *Report of the Special Rapporteur on Violence Against Women, Its Causes and Consequences*, UN Commission on Human Rights, 52nd Sess., Provisional Agenda Item 9(a), UN Doc. E/CN.4/1996/53/Add.1. For more on the history of comfort women, see Sarah Soh, *The Comfort Women: Sexual Violence and Postcolonial Memory in Korea and Japan* (Chicago: University of Chicago Press, 2008).

7. For more on the treaty, see United Nations Treaty Collection, accessed November 1, 2019, https://treaties.un.org/doc/Publication/UNTS/Volume%20583/volume-583-I-8473-English.pdf. For more on Japanese arguments, see Totsuka, "Commentary on a Victory," 52–54.

8. Ankit Panda, "The 'Final and Irreversible' 2015 Japan–South Korea Comfort Women Deal Unravels," *The Diplomat*, January 9, 2017, https://thediplomat.com.

9. See James Griffiths, "South Korea's New President Questions Japan's 'Comfort Women' Deal," *CNN World*, June 5, 2017, cnn.com. See also Benjamin Haas, "Anger in

Japan as South Korea Dissolves 'Comfort Women' Foundation," *The Guardian*, November 21, 2018.

10. Wooyoung Lee, "Japan to Bring South Korean Court Ruling on Forced Labor to International Court," United Press International (UPI), November 6, 2018, https://www.upi.com.

11. Choe Sang-Hun and Motoko Rich, "The $89,000 Verdict Tearing Japan and South Korea Apart," *NYT*, February 14, 2019.

12. Ibid.

13. "Han Il hyŏpchŏng munsŏ konggae ŭimi wa p'ajang" [The declassification of the ROK-Japan treaty documents and its impact], *Han'gyŏre*, January 17, 2005, http://www.hani.co.kr.

14. Kathryn Sikkink and Hun Joon Kim, "The Justice Cascade: The Origins and Effectiveness of Prosecutions of Human Rights Violations," *Annual Review of Law and Social Science* 9 (2013): 269–85.

15. Kim Dong-Choon, "The Long Road Toward Truth and Reconciliation," *Critical Asian Studies* 42, no. 4 (2010): 525–52. For the statistics on TRCK cases, see the United States Institute of Peace, "Truth Commission: South Korea 2005," accessed November 11, 2019, usip.org.

16. Tae-Ung Baik, "Fairness in Transitional Justice Initiatives: The Case of South Korea," *Buffalo Human Rights Law Review* 19 (2012): 169–91.

17. Choe and Motoko, "The $89,000 Verdict."

18. Grace Shao, "Tension Between Japan and South Korea Is Rising," *CNBC*, accessed November 13, 2019, at cnbc.com.

19. Justin McCurry and Agencies, "South Korea Cuts Intelligence Ties with Japan, Raising Fears over North Korea," *The Guardian*, August 22, 2019.

20. Victoria Kim, "Japan, Korea and the Messy Question of How to Pay for Historic Wrongs," *LAT*, August 17, 2019.

21. Weissbrodt et al. to Henderson, October 18, 1985; and Fraser to Colleague, November 1, 1985; both in Human Rights—1970s Ideas + Talks (1), Box 9, Gregory Henderson Papers on Korea, Harvard-Yenching Library.

22. Susan Chira, "For North Korea, a Harsh Portrait," *NYT*, December 23, 1988; Asia Watch and Minnesota Lawyers International Human Rights Committee, *Human Rights in the Democratic People's Republic of Korea* (Washington, DC: Asia Watch and Minnesota Lawyers International Human Rights Committee, 1988).

23. "Visitors to North Korea Denounce Rights Abuses," *NYT*, May 5, 1991.

24. AI, "Democratic People's Republic of Korea: Persecuting the Starving; The Plight of North Koreans Fleeing to China," December 15, 2000, amnesty.org.

25. H.R. 4011 (108th): North Korean Human Rights Act of 2004; H.R. 2061(115th): North Korean Human Rights Reauthorization Act of 2017, accessed November 17, 2019, govtrack.us.

26. See "UN General Assembly Adopts Resolution on Human Rights Abuse in DPR Korea," *UN News*, December 16, 2005, news.un.org.

27. "DPRK/Human Rights: Key Report Must Be Sent to UN Security Council, Says UN Special Rapporteur," October 28, 2014, https://www.ohchr.org.

28. "Yuen 'Puk in'gwŏn ch'imhae ch'aegimja, Kukche Hyŏngsa Chaep'anso e kisohaeya'" [UN should indict the North Korean human rights violators to the ICC], March 9, 2019, http://news.chosun.com.

29. Josh Rogin, "Opinion: Trump's North Korea Policy Is 'Maximum Pressure' but Not 'Regime Change,'" *WP*, April 14, 2017.

30. Roberta Cohen, "The High Commissioner for Human Rights and North Korea," in *The United Nations High Commissioner for Human Rights: Conscience for the World*, ed. Felice D. Gaer and Christen L. Broecker (Leiden: Nijhoff, 2014), 293–310.

31. Blaine Harden, *Escape from Camp 14: One Man's Remarkable Odyssey from North Korea to Freedom in the West* (New York: Viking/Penguin, 2012).

32. "T'albukcha Sin Tong-hyŏk 'Pukhan inkwŏn undong chungdanhal sudo itta" [North Korean defector Sin Tong-hyŏk, "I may stop human rights campaigns for North Korea"], *Yŏnhap nyusŭ*, January 18, 2015, https://www.yna.co.kr; Oliver Stone and Peter Kuznick, *The Untold History of the United States* (New York: Gallery Books, 2012), 476.

33. Hazel Smith, "Crimes Against Humanity?," *Critical Asian Studies* 46, no. 1 (2014): 127–43.

34. Suh Bo-hyuk, "The Militarization of Korean Human Rights," *Critical Asian Studies* 46, no. 1 (2014): 3–14.

35. For this quote and more on the awarding of the prize, see "The Nobel Prize: Kim Dae-jung," accessed November 16, 2019, nobelprize.org. See also Jong-Yun Bae and Chung-in Moon, "South Korea's Engagement Policy," *Critical Asian Studies* 46, no. 1 (2014): 15–38.

36. Bae and Moon, "South Korea's Engagement Policy."

37. For more on the act, see http://www.law.go.kr, accessed November 2, 2019.

38. "Kukche chosadan, 'Pak Kŭn-hye chŏngbu ttae chiptan t'albuk yŏjongŏbwŏndŭl . . . napch'idoen kŏt' kyŏllon" [International investigation team concludes, "Waitresses kidnapped under the Park Geun-hye administration"], *Kungmin ilbo*, September 6, 2019, http://news.kmib.co.kr.

39. Peter Baker and Choe Sang-Hun, "Trump Threatens 'Fire and Fury' Against North Korea if It Endangers U.S.," *NYT*, August 8, 2017.

40. Quoted in Meghan Keneally, "From 'Fire and Fury' to 'Rocket Man,' the Various Barbs Traded Between Trump and Kim Jong Un," *ABC News*, June 12, 2018, abcnews.go.com.

41. "President Donald J. Trump's State of the Union Address," issued on January 30, 2018, accessed November 17, 2019, whitehouse.gov.

42. "Otto Warmbier's Father to Attend Olympics in South Korea," BBC, February 5, 2018, bbc.com.

43. Office of the High Commissioner for Human Rights, "North Korea: UN Expert Calls for Engagement amid Continuing Rights Violations," October 24, 2019, https://www.ohchr.org.

44. Dan Spinelli, "Trump Has Abandoned Human Rights in North Korea," *Mother Jones*, February 14, 2019, motherjones.com.

45. Pak Ho-jae, "2018 Kwangju Asia P'orŏm" [2018 Kwangju Asia Forum], *Chungang ilbo*, April 22, 2018.

46. *Asian Human Rights Charter: A People's Charter* (Hong Kong: Asian Human Rights Commission, Asian Legal Resource Centre, 1998), 5.

47. For more, see http://womenandwar.net/kr/tag/butterfly-fund/, accessed November 1, 2019.

48. "Pak kŭn-hye chŏngbu 2-yŏn, Han'guk inkwŏn sangwang hut'oe" [South Korea's human rights in regression during the two-year rule of the Park Geun-hye government], *Yŏnhap nyusŭ*, February 25, 2015, accessed May 21, 2019, https://www.yna.co.kr.

49. Youngju Ryu, "Conclusion: From Yusin Redux to *Yuch'e it'al*," in *Cultures of Yusin: South Korea in the 1970s*, ed. Youngju Ryu (Ann Arbor: University of Michigan Press, 2018), 279–92.

BIBLIOGRAPHY

Archives

AIIS Secretariat Collection. International Institute of Social History, Amsterdam, the Netherlands.

AIUSA Collection. Rare Book and Manuscript Library, Columbia University, New York.

CIA Records Search Tool. NARA, College Park, MD.

Collection on Democracy and Unification in Korea. Department of Special Collections, Charles E. Young Research Library, UCLA.

Declassified Documents Reference System.

EJB Collection. Papers of Edward J. Baker. Chestnut Hill, MA.

Gerald Ford Presidential Library, Ann Arbor, MI.

Henderson, George. Papers on Korea. Harvard–Yenching Library.

ICUIS Records. Richard Daley Library Special Collections, University of Illinois at Chicago.

Jimmy Carter Presidential Library.

Kim Dae-jung Presidential Library, Seoul, South Korea.

Korea Democracy Foundation Open Archives, Gyeonggi-do, South Korea. https://archives.kdemo.or.kr.

Korean Diplomatic Archives, Ministry of Foreign Affairs, Republic of Korea, Seoul, South Korea.

Korean Heritage Library, University of Southern California.

Morris, Ivan. Papers. Rare Book and Manuscript Library, Columbia University, New York.

National Archives and Records Administration (NARA), College Park, MD.

National Institute of Korean History, Gyeonggi-do, South Korea.

National Security Archive. http://nsarchive.gwu.edu.

Ogle, George. Papers. Pitts Theology Library, Emory University, Atlanta, GA.

Oral History Interviews. Senate Historical Office, Washington, DC. www.senate.gov.

Richard Nixon Presidential Library, Yorba Linda, CA.

Ronald Reagan Presidential Library, Simi Valley, CA.

Shorrock's Collection. Washington-based investigative journalist Tim Shorrock's online collection, http://timshorrock.com.

Interviews

Armacost, Michael. Interview by author, Stanford, CA, April 30, 2010.

Gregg, Donald. Interview by author, Armonk, NY, June 24, 2015.

Han Sŭng-hŏn. Interview by author, Seoul, South Korea, September 22, 2011.

Harvey, Pharis. Interview by author, San Jose, CA, April 29, 2010.

Kim Sŏng-jae. Interview by author, Seoul, South Korea, November 22, 2015.
O Chae-sik. Interview by author, Seoul, South Korea, November 18, 2010.
Yi Chong-ch'an. Interview by author, Seoul, South Korea, November 23, 2015.
Yun Hyŏn. Interview by author, Seoul, South Korea, October 7, 2011.

Newspapers, News Media, and Periodicals

ABC News, New York, NY
BBC, London, United Kingdom
Chicago Tribune,
Chosŏn ilbo, Seoul, South Korea
Chungang ilbo, Seoul, South Korea
CNBC, Englewood Cliffs, New Jersey
CNN, Atlanta, GA
The Diplomat, Washington D.C.
The Guardian, London, United Kingdom
Han'guk kidok kongbo, Seoul, South Korea
Hankyŏrye, Seoul, South Korea
Korean Street Journal, Los Angeles, CA
Kungmin ilbo, Seoul, South Korea
Kyŏnghyang sinmun, Seoul, South Korea
Los Angeles Times, Los Angeles, CA
Maeil kyŏngje, Seoul, South Korea
Munhwa ilbo, Seoul, South Korea
New York Times
Pressian, Seoul, South Korea
Pyujŭ aen nyujŭ, Seoul, South Korea
Sŏul sinmun, Seoul, South Korea
Tonga ilbo, Seoul, South Korea
UN News, New York, NY
UPI, Washington D.C.
Washington Post
Yŏnhap nyusŭ, Seoul, South Korea

Published Primary Sources

AI (Amnesty International). *Amnesty International Handbook.* 7th ed. London: Amnesty International, 1991.
——. *Amnesty International, 1961–1976: A Chronology.* London: Amnesty International, 1976.
——. *Annual Report.* London: Amnesty International, 1962–.
Alinsky, Saul. *Rules for Radicals: A Pragmatic Primer for Realistic Radicals.* 1971. Reprint, New York: Vintage Books, 1989.
Asian Human Rights Commission. *Asian Human Rights Charter: A People's Charter.* Hong Kong: Asian Human Rights Commission, Asian Legal Resource Centre, 1998.
Asia Watch and Minnesota Lawyers International Human Rights Committee. *Human Rights in the Democratic People's Republic of Korea.* Washington, DC: Asia Watch and Minnesota Lawyers International Human Rights Committee, 1988.

Asia Watch Committee. *Freedom of Expression in the Republic of Korea.* Washington, DC: Asia Watch, 1988.

Bible. *New International Version.* http://www.biblegateway.com.

Breidenstein, Gerhard. *Christians and Social Justice: A Study Handbook on Modern Theology, Socio-Political Problems in Korea, and Community Organization.* Privately published, 1971.

Brzezinski, Zbigniew. *Power and Principle: Memoirs of the National Security Adviser, 1977–1981.* New York: Farrar, Straus, Giroux, 1983.

CCIA (Commission of the Churches on International Affairs of the World Council of Churches). *The Churches in International Affairs: Reports, 1970–1973.* Geneva: WCC, 1974.

Cho Sŭng-hyŏk. "Sanŏp sŏn'gyo wa nodongja ŭi inkwŏn" [The UIM and laborers' human rights]. *Ssial ŭi sori,* November 1978, 27–37.

Derian, Patricia M. "Human Rights in American Foreign Policy." *Notre Dame Law* 55, no. 2 (1979): 264–78.

de Silva, Peer. *Sub Rosa: The CIA and the Uses of Intelligence.* New York: Times Books, 1978.

Foreign Relations of the United States [FRUS]. 1969–1976. Vol. 17, China, 1969–1972. Edited by Steven E. Phillips. Washington, DC: US Government Printing Office, 2006.

———. 1969–1976. Vol. 18, China, 1973–1976. Edited by David P. Nickles. Washington, DC: US Government Printing Office, 2007.

Fraser, Donald M. "Freedom and Foreign Policy." *Foreign Policy* 26 (1977): 140–56.

Gleysteen, William H., Jr. *Massive Entanglement, Marginal Influence: Carter and Korea in Crisis.* Washington, DC: Brookings Institute Press, 1999.

Han Sŭng-hŏn. *Wijang sidae ŭi jŭngŏn* [Testimonies in the era of camouflage]. Seoul: Pŏmusa, 1974.

Han'guk Kidokkyo Kyohoe Hyŏbŭihoe. *1970-yŏndae minjuhwa undong* [The 1970s democratization movements]. 3 vols. Seoul: Han'guk Kidokkyo Kyohoe Hyŏbŭihoe, 1987.

"Human Rights and Reconciliation." Message of the 1974 Synod of Bishops, October 23, 1974. *The Pope Speaks* 19 (1974–75): 216–19.

Johnson, David, ed. *Uppsala to Nairobi, 1968–1975.* New York: WCC, 1975.

Jones, Linda. "Rŭppo chesam segye wa inkwŏn" [Reportage on the Third World and human rights]. *Wŏlgan Taehwa* [Monthly dialogue], February 1977, 238–99.

Kim Chŏng-nam. *Chinsil, kwangjang e sŏda* [The truth stands upon the square]. P'aju: Ch'angbi, 2005.

Kim Dae-jung. *Conscience in Action: The Autobiography of Kim Dae-jung.* Translated by Jeon Seung-hee. New York: Palgrave Macmillan, 2019.

Kim Hyŏng-su. *Mun Ik-hwan p'yŏngjŏn* [A critical biography of Mun Ik-hwan]. Seoul: Silch'ŏn Munhaksa, 2004.

Kim Kwan-sŏk Moksa Kohui Kinyŏm Mujip Ch'ulp'an Wiwŏnhoe, ed. *I ttang e p'yŏnghwa rŭl: 70-yŏndae ŭi inkwŏn undong* [Bringing peace to this land: Human rights movements in the 1970s]. Seoul: Kim Kwan-sŏk Moksa Kohui Kinyŏm Mujip Ch'ulp'an Wiwŏnhoe, 1991.

Kim Sŏl-i and Yi Kyŏng-ŭn. *Chaetpit sidae pora pit koun kkum* [A beautiful purple-color dream in the gray-color era]. Seoul: KDF, 2006.

Kippŭm kwa Hŭimang Samok Yŏn'guso, ed. *Amhŭk sok ŭi hwaetpul* [A torchlight in the dark age]. Vol. 1. Seoul: Kippŭm kwa Hŭimang Samok Yŏn'guso, 1996.

Kissinger, Henry. *White House Years.* Boston: Little, Brown, 1979.

Kukche Aemnest'i Han'guk Chibu 30-chunyŏn Kinyŏm Saŏp Wiwŏnhoe. *Han'guk Aemnest'i 30-yŏn! Inkwŏn 30-yŏn!* [Thirty years of AI Korea! The thirty–year human rights movement!]. Taegu: Kukche Aemnest'i Han'guk Chibu, 2002.

Kukchŏngwŏn Kwagŏ Sagŏn Chinsil Kyumyŏng ŭl T'onghan Palchŏn Wiwŏnhoe. *Kwagŏ wa taehwa, mirae ŭi sŏngch'al* [Dialogue with the past, introspection for the future]. Vol. 2. Seoul: National Intelligence Service, 2007.

Kwŏn, Ŭn-jŏng. "Inkwŏn kwa chayu ka hŭrŭnŭn t'ongil ŭi kkum" [The dream of unification running with human rights and freedom]. *Inkwŏn* 66 (2011): 4–8.

Lee Jai-eui. *Kwangju Diary: Beyond Death, Beyond the Darkness of the Age.* Translated by Kap Su Seol and Nick Mamatas. Los Angeles: UCLA Asian Pacific Monograph Series, 1999.

Library of Congress Foreign Affairs Division. *Chronologies of Major Developments in Selected Areas of International Relations.* Washington, DC: US Government Printing Office, 1978.

McGuire, Steve. "Revelations from CIA's Former Korea Chief." *Counterspy* 3, no. 2 (1976): 34–35.

Morgan, Dan. *Merchants of Grain: The Power and Profits of the Five Giant Companies at the Center of the World's Food Supply.* Harmondsworth: Penguin Books, 1980.

Ogle, George. *Liberty to the Captives: The Struggle Against Oppression in South Korea.* Atlanta: John Knox Press, 1977.

Pak Hyŏng-gyu. *Pak Hyŏng-gyu hoegorok* [Pak Hyŏng-gyu's memoir]. P'aju: Ch'angbi, 2010.

———. Review of "Haksaeng kwa sahoe chŏngŭi" [Students and social justice], by Pu Kwang-sŏk. *Kidokkyo sasang* 15, no. 8 (1971): 116.

Pak Ŭn-gyŏng. "Yŏksa ŭi surye pak'wi nŭn kkŭdŏpsi tonda kŭrŏna nugun'ga kullyŏya tonda" [History goes on endlessly, what will move it]. *Shindong'a* 578 (2007): 526–33.

Pu Kwang-sŏk. *Haksaeng kwa sahoe chŏngŭi* [Students and social justice]. Seoul: Taehan Kidokkyo Sŏhoe and KSCF, 1971.

Sinnott, James. *Hyŏnjang chŭngŏn 1975-yŏn 4-wŏl 9-il* [On-the-spot testimony on the 9 April 1975 incident]. Translated by Kim Kŏn-ok and Yi U-kyŏng. Seoul: Pitture, 2004.

US Congress. House. Committee on Foreign Affairs. *Human Rights in South Korea: Implications for U.S. Policy; Hearings Before the Subcommittees on Asian and Pacific Affairs and on International Organizations and Movements of the Committee on Foreign Affairs, House of Representatives, Ninety-Third Congress, Second Session, July 30, August 5, and December 20, 1974.* Washington, DC: US Government Printing Office, 1974.

———. *Human Rights in the World Community: A Call for U.S. Leadership; Report of the Subcommittee on International Organizations and Movements of the Committee on Foreign Affairs, House of Representatives, March 27, 1974.* Washington, DC: US Government Printing Office, 1974.

———. *International Protection of Human Rights: The Work of International Organizations and the Role of U.S. Foreign Policy; Hearings Before the Subcommittee on International Organizations and Movements of the Committee on Foreign Affairs, House of Representatives, Ninety-Third Congress, First Session.* Washington, DC: US Government Printing Office, 1974.

US Congress. House. Committee on International Relations. *Human Rights in South Korea and the Philippines: Implications for US Policy; Hearings Before the Subcommittee on International Organizations of the Committee on International Relations, House of Representatives, Ninety-Fourth Congress.* Washington, DC: US Government Printing Office, 1975.

Todd, George. "Mission and Justice: The Experience of Urban and Industrial Mission." *International Review of Mission* 65, no. 259 (1976): 251–61.

"United States: Mutual Defense Assistance Act of 1949." *American Journal of International Law* 44, no. 1, Supplement: Official Documents (January 1950): 29–38.

Vance, Cyrus. *Hard Choices: Critical Years in America's Foreign Policy.* New York: Simon and Schuster, 1983.

———. "Human Rights and Foreign Policy." *Georgia Journal of International and Comparative Law* 7, no. 223 (1977): 223–29.

White, Margaret, and Herbert White, eds. *The Power of People: Community Action in Korea.* Tokyo: UIM, East Asia Christian Conference, 1973.

Yi Pyŏng-rin Pyŏhosa Munjip Kanhaeng Wiwŏnhoe. *Simdang Yi Pyŏng-rin pyŏhosa munjip* [Lawyer Yi Pyŏng-rin's collective works]. Seoul: Ture, 1991.

Unpublished Primary Sources

Kukche Aemnest'i Han'guk Wiwŏnhoe. *Han'guk Aemnesŭt'i 5-yŏn yaksa* [AI Korea's five-year chronology]. Seoul, 1977.

Chŏng Un-yŏng. "Nondan—Kongjang saemaŭl undong kwa nosa hyŏpcho punwigi chosŏng" [Forum: Factory–New Village Movements and the creation of labor-management cooperation]. *Sallim Munhwa* (1979). Accessed December 1, 2016. http://www.sanrimji.com,

Kim Tae-gon. *Kim Chae-gyu X-p'ail* [Kim Chae-gyu's X-file]. Seoul: Sanha, 2005.

"United States Government Statement on the Events in Kwangju, Republic of Korea, in May 1980." June 19, 1989. http://kr.usembassy.gov.

Unpublished Secondary Sources

An Chae-sŏng. "YH sagŏn—Yŏgongdŭl, minjujuŭi pomŭl purŭda" [The YH Incident: Female factory workers, calling out the democratic spring]. In the Korean Democracy Foundation (KDF) Open Archives. Accessed January 5, 2014. http://archives.kdemo.or.kr.

PuMa Minju Hangjaeng Kinyŏm Saŏphoe. *PuMa Minju Hangjaeng 10-chunyŏn Kinyŏm Charyojip* [Sourcebook on the tenth anniversary of Pusan-Masan Incident]. Puma Minju Hangjaeng Kinyŏm Saŏphoe, 1989.

Sŏ Chung-sŏk. "PuMa hangjaeng ŭi yŏksajŏk chaejomyŏng" [Rethinking the Pusan-Masan Uprising]. In the 2009 conference packet "Pak Chŏng-hŭi ch'eje wa PuMa hangjaeng ui yŏksajŏk chaejomyŏng" [Rethinking the Park Chung-hee regime and the Pusan–Masan Uprising], 3–37.

Yi Chŏng-ŭn. "Haebang hu inkwŏn tamnon ŭi hyŏngsŏng kwa chedohwa e kwanhan yŏn'gu, 1945-yŏn–1970-yŏn ch'o" [Human rights discourse and the institutionalization of human rights in Korea from 1945 to the early 1970s]. Ph.D. diss., Seoul National University, 2008.

Published Secondary Sources

3·1 Minju Kuguk Sŏnŏn Kwallyŏnja. *Saeropke t'aorŭnŭn 3·1 minju kuguk sŏnŏn* [The reignited March First Declaration of Democratic National Salvation]. Seoul: Sagyejŏl, 1998.

Amsden, Alice. *Asia's Next Giant: South Korea and Late Industrialization.* New York: Oxford University Press, 1989.

An Pyŏng-uk et al., eds. *Yushin kwa panyushin* [The Yushin system versus the anti–Yushin opponents]. Seoul: Minjuhwa Undong Kinyŏm Saŏphoe, 2005.

Apodaca, Clair, and Michael Stohl. "United States Human Rights Policy and Foreign Assistance." *International Studies Quarterly* 43, no. 1 (1999): 185–98.

Armstrong, Charles. *North Korean Revolution, 1945–1950*. Ithaca, NY: Cornell University Press, 2003.

Bae, Jong-Yun, and Chung-in Moon. "South Korea's Engagement Policy." *Critical Asian Studies* 46, no. 1 (2014): 15–38.

Baik, Tae-Ung. "Fairness in Transitional Justice Initiatives: The Case of South Korea." *Buffalo Human Rights Law Review* 19 (2012): 169–91.

Baker, Don. "The Transformation of the Catholic Church in Korea: From a Missionary Church to an Indigenous Church." *Journal of Korean Religion* 4, no. 1 (2013): 11–42.

Barnett, Michael. *Empire of Humanity: A History of Humanitarianism*. Ithaca, NY: Cornell University Press, 2011.

Bayly, C. A., Sven Beckert, Matthew Connelly, Isabel Hofmeyr, Wendy Kozol, and Patricia Seed. "AHR Conversation: On Transnational History." *American Historical Review* 111, no. 5 (2006): 1441–64.

Beard, Charles. *The Idea of National Interest: An Analytical Study in American Foreign Policy*. New York: Macmillan, 1934.

Bender, Thomas, ed. *Rethinking American History in a Global Age*. Berkeley: University of California Press, 2002.

Bolton, Jonathan. *Worlds of Dissent: Charter 77, the Plastic People of the Universe, and Czech Culture Under Communism*. Cambridge, MA: Harvard University Press, 2012.

Braaten, Carl, and Robert Jenson, eds. *A Map of Twentieth-Century Theology: Readings from Karl Barth to Radical Pluralism*. Minneapolis: Fortress, 1995.

Bradley, Mark Philip. *Imagining Vietnam and America: The Making of Postcolonial Vietnam, 1919–1950*. Chapel Hill: University of North Carolina Press, 2000.

———. *The World Reimagined: Americans and Human Rights in the Twentieth Century*. New York: Cambridge University Press, 2016.

Bradley, Mark Philip, and Patrice Petro, eds. *Truth Claims: Representation and Human Rights*. New Brunswick, NJ: Rutgers University Press, 2002.

Brazinsky, Gregg. "Koreanizing Modernization: Modernization Theory and South Korean Intellectuals." In *Staging Growth: Modernization, Development, and the Global Cold War*, edited by David C. Engerman, Nils Gilman, Mark H. Haefele, and Michael E. Latham, 251–73. Amherst: University of Massachusetts Press, 2003.

———. *Nation Building in South Korea: Koreans, Americans, and the Making of a Democracy*. Durham: University of North Carolina Press, 2007.

Bright, Charles, and Michael Geyer. "Where in the World Is America? The History of the United States in the Global Age." In *Rethinking American History in a Global Age*, edited by Thomas Bender, 63–99. Berkeley: University of California Press, 2002.

Burke, Roland. *Decolonization and the Evolution of International Human Rights*. Philadelphia: University of Pennsylvania Press, 2010.

Ch'a Sŏng-hwan. *1970-yŏndae minjung undong yŏn'gu* [A study of people's movements in the 1970s]. Seoul: Sŏnin, 2005.

Chang, Paul Y. *Protest Dialectics: State Suppression and South Korea's Democracy Movement, 1970–1979*. Stanford, CA: Stanford University Press, 2015.

Ch'oi Chang-jip. *Minjuhwa ihu ŭi minjujuŭi* [Democracy in the post–democratization era]. Seoul: Humanit'asŭ, 2002.

Choi, Jang-Jip. *Democracy After Democratization: The Korean Experience.* Stanford, CA: Walter H. Shorenstein Asia-Pacific Research Center, 2012.

Choi, Jang Jip. *Labor and the Authoritarian State: Labor Unions in South Korean Manufacturing Industries, 1961–1980.* Seoul: Korea University Press, 1989.

Choi, Jungwoon. *The Gwangju Uprising: The Pivotal Democratic Movement That Changed the History of Modern Korea.* Translated by Yu Young-nan. Paramus, NJ: Homa & Sekey Books, 2006.

Chun, Soonok. *They Are Not Machines: Korean Women Workers and Their Fight for Democratic Trade Unionism in the 1970s.* Burlington, VT: Ashgate, 2003.

Chung, Patrick. "The 'Pictures in Our Heads': Journalists, Human Rights, and U.S.–South Korean Relations, 1970–1976." *Diplomatic History* 38, no. 5 (2014): 1136–55.

Clark, Ann Marie. *Diplomacy of Conscience: Amnesty International and Changing Human Rights Norms.* Princeton, NJ: Princeton University Press, 2001.

Clark, Donald, ed. *The Kwangju Uprising: Shadows over the Regime in South Korea.* Boulder, CO: Westview Press, 1988.

———. "Protestant Christianity and the State: Religious Organizations as Civil Society." In *Korean Society: Civil Society, Democracy and the State,* edited by Charles Armstrong, 171–90. New York: Routledge, 2006.

Cmiel, Kenneth. "Emergence of Human Rights Politics in the United States." *Journal of American History* 86, no. 3 (December 1999): 1231–50.

Cohen, Jerome, and Edward Baker. "U.S. Foreign Policy and Human Rights in South Korea." In *Human Rights in Korea: Historical and Policy Perspectives,* edited by William Shaw, 170–219. Cambridge, MA: East Asian Legal Studies Program of the Harvard Law School and the Council on East Asian Studies, Harvard University, 1991.

Cohen, Roberta. "The High Commissioner for Human Rights and North Korea." In *The United Nations High Commissioner for Human Rights: Conscience for the World,* edited by Felice Gaer and Christen Broecker, 293–310. Leiden: Nijhoff, 2014.

Connelly, Matthew. *A Diplomatic Revolution: Algeria's Fight for Independence and the Origins of the Post–Cold War Era.* New York: Oxford University Press, 2002.

Cottrell, Robert. *Roger Nash Baldwin and the American Civil Liberties Union.* New York: Columbia University Press. 2000.

Cox, Ronald, ed. *Corporate Power and Globalization in US Foreign Policy.* New York: Routledge, 2012.

Cumings, Bruce. *Dominion from Sea to Sea: Pacific Ascendancy and American Power.* New Haven, CT: Yale University Press, 2009.

———. "Is America an Imperial Power?" *Current History,* November 2003, 355–60.

———. "The Kim Chi Ha Case." *New York Review of Books* 22, no. 16 (1975).

———. *Korea's Place in the Sun.* Rev. ed. New York: W. W. Norton, 2005.

———. *The Origins of the Korean War.* 2 vols. Princeton, NJ: Princeton University Press, 1981–90.

———. *Parallax Visions: Making Sense of American–East Asian Relations.* Durham, NC: Duke University Press, 2000.

———. "The Structural Basis of 'Anti-Americanism' in the Republic of Korea." In *Korean Attitudes Toward the United States: Changing Dynamics,* edited by David Steinberg, 91–115. Armonk, NY: Sharpe, 2005.

Donnelly, Jack. "Human Rights and Foreign Policy." *World Politics* 34, no. 4 (1982): 574–95.

Drennan, William. "The Tipping Point: Kwangju, May 1980." In *Korean Attitudes Toward the United States: Changing Dynamics*, edited by David Steinberg, 280–306. Armonk, NY: Sharpe, 2005.

Dudziak, Mary. *Cold War Civil Rights: Race and the Image of American Democracy*. Princeton, NJ: Princeton University Press, 2000.

Eckel, Jan. "The International League for the Rights of Man, Amnesty International, and the Changing Fate of Human Rights Activism from the 1940s Through the 1970s." *Humanity* 4, no. 2 (2013): 183–214.

Eckel, Jan, and Samuel Moyn, eds. *The Breakthrough: Human Rights in the 1970s*. Philadelphia: University of Pennsylvania Press, 2014.

Engerman, David C., Nils Gilman, Mark H. Haefele, and Michael E. Latham, eds. *Staging Growth: Modernization, Development, and the Global Cold War*. Amherst: University of Massachusetts Press, 2003.

Foot, Rosemary. "The Cold War and Human Rights." In *The Cambridge History of the Cold War*, vol. 3, *Endings*, edited by Melvyn P. Leffler and Odd Arne Westad, 445–65. New York: Cambridge University Press, 2010.

Forsythe, David P. *Human Rights in International Relations*. 3rd ed. New York: Cambridge University Press, 2012.

Gaddis, John Lewis. *Strategies of Containment: A Critical Appraisal*. Rev. and expanded ed. New York: Oxford University Press, 2005.

Harden, Blaine. *Escape from Camp 14: One Man's Remarkable Odyssey from North Korea to Freedom in the West*. New York: Viking/Penguin, 2012.

Hehir, J. Bryan. "The Modern Catholic Church and Human Rights: The Impact of the Second Vatican Council." In *Christianity and Human Rights: An Introduction*, edited by John Witte Jr. and Frank S. Alexander, 113–34. New York: Cambridge University Press, 2010.

Hogan, Michael. *A Cross of Iron: Harry S. Truman and the Origins of the National Security State, 1945–1954*. New York: Cambridge University Press, 1998.

Hopgood, Stephen. *The Endtimes of Human Rights*. Ithaca, NY: Cornell University Press, 2013.

Huntington, Samuel. *The Third Wave: Democratization in the Late Twentieth Century*. Norman: University of Oklahoma Press, 1991.

Hwang, Su-kyoung. *Korea's Grievous War*. Philadelphia: University of Pennsylvania Press, 2016.

Im, Hyug Baeg. "Christian Churches and Democratization in South Korea." In *Religious Organizations and Democratization: Case Studies from Contemporary Asia*, edited by Tun-jen Cheng and Deborah A. Brown, 136–56. Armonk, NY: Sharpe, 2006.

Im Song-ja. "1970-yŏndae Tosisanŏp Sŏn'gyohoe wa Han'guk Noch'ong ŭi kaltŭng-taerip" [Conflicts and confrontations between UIM Groups and the FKTU in the 1970s]. *Sarim* 35 (2010): 311–44.

Inkberry, John. *Liberal Leviathan: The Origins, Crisis, and Transformation of the American World Order*. Princeton, NJ: Princeton University Press, 2011.

Iriye, Akira. "Internationalizing International History." In *Rethinking American History in a Global Age*, edited by Thomas Bender, 47–62. Berkeley: University of California Press, 2002.

Iriye, Akira, Petra Goedde, and William I. Hitchcock, eds. *The Human Rights Revolution: An International History*. Oxford: Oxford University Press, 2012.

Ishay, Micheline. *The History of Human Rights: From Ancient Times to the Globalization Era*. Berkeley: University of California Press, 2004.

Jacoby, Tamar. "The Reagan Turnaround on Human Rights." *Foreign Affairs* 64, no. 5 (Summer 1986): 1066–86.

Jean Ahn. "The Socio-economic Background of the Gwangju Uprising." In *South Korean Democracy: The Legacy of the Gwangju Uprising*, edited by Georgy Katsiaficas and Na Kanchae, 24–46. New York: Routledge, 2006.

Jung, Keun-sik. "Has Kwangju Been Realized?" In *Contentious Kwangju: The May 18 Uprising in Korea's Past and Present*, edited by Gi-Wook Shin and Kyung Moon Hwang, 43–50. Lanham, MD: Rowman & Littlefield, 2003.

Keck, Margaret E., and Kathryn Sikkink. *Activists Beyond Borders: Advocacy Networks in International Politics*. Ithaca, NY: Cornell University Press, 1998.

Kelly, Patrick William. *Sovereign Emergencies: Latin America and the Making of Global Human Rights Politics*. New York: Cambridge University Press, 2018.

Keys, Barbara. "Congress, Kissinger, and the Origins of Human Rights Diplomacy." *Diplomatic History* 34, no. 5 (September 2010): 823–51.

———. *Reclaiming American Virtue: The Human Rights Revolution of the 1970s*. Cambridge, MA: Harvard University Press, 2014.

Kim, Byung-Kook, and Ezra Vogel, eds. *The Park Chung Hee Era: The Transformation of South Korea*. Cambridge, MA: Harvard University Press, 2011.

Kim, Charles. *Youth for Nation: Culture and Protest in Cold War South Korea*. Honolulu: University of Hawaii Press, 2018.

Kim Dong-Choon. "The Long Road Toward Truth and Reconciliation." *Critical Asian Studies* 42, no. 4 (2010): 525–52.

Kim, Suzy. *Everyday Life in the North Korean Revolution, 1945–1950*. Ithaca, NY: Cornell University Press, 2013.

Kim, Yong-Jick. "The Security, Political, and Human Rights Conundrum, 1974–1979." In *The Park Chung Hee Era: The Transformation of South Korea*, edited by Byung-Kook Kim and Ezra Vogel, 457–82. Cambridge, MA: Harvard University Press, 2011.

Koo, Hagen. *Korean Workers: The Culture and Politics of Class Formation*. Ithaca, NY: Cornell University Press, 2001.

———. "Strong State and Contentious Society." In *State and Society in Contemporary Korea*, edited by Hagen Koo, 231–49. Ithaca, NY: Cornell University Press, 1993.

Korchmann, Victor. "Modernization and Democratic Values: The 'Japanese Model' in the 1960s." In *Staging Growth: Modernization, Development, and the Global Cold War*, edited by David C. Engerman, Nils Gilman, Mark H. Haefele, and Michael E. Latham, 225–49. Amherst: University of Massachusetts Press, 2003.

Landman, Todd. "Social Magic and the Temple of Human Rights: Critical Reflections on Stephen Hopgood's *Endtimes of Human Rights*." In *Debating "The Endtimes of Human Rights": Activism and Institutions in a Neo-Westphalian World*, edited by Doutje Lettinga and Lars van Troost, 25–32. Amsterdam: Amnesty International Netherlands, 2014.

Lee, Chae-Jin. *A Troubled Peace: U.S. Policy and the Two Koreas*. Baltimore: Johns Hopkins University Press, 2006.

Lee, Misook. "South Korea's Democratization Movements of the 1970s and 80s Communicative Interaction in Transnational Ecumenical Networks." *International Journal of Korean History* 19, no. 2 (2014): 241–70.

Lee, Namhee. *The Making of Minjung: Democracy and the Politics of Representation in South Korea*. Ithaca, NY: Cornell University Press, 2007.

Lefever, Ernest W. *Human Rights and Foreign Policy*. Washington, DC: Ethics and Policy Center, 1980.

Lettinga, Doutje, and Lars van Troost, eds. *Debating "The Endtimes of Human Rights": Activism in a Neo-Westphalian World*. Amsterdam: Amnesty International Netherlands, 2014.

Minjuhwa Undong Kinyŏm Saŏphoe. *Han'guk minjuhwa undongsa* [The history of the Korean democratization movements]. Vols. 2 and 3. Seoul: Tolbegae, 2009–10.

Minjuhwa Undong Kinyŏm Saŏphoe Yŏn'gusŏ, *Han'guk minjuhwa undongsa yŏnp'yo* [A chronological history of the Korean democratization movements]. Seoul: Sŏnin, 2006.

Moyn, Samuel. *Christian Human Rights*. Philadelphia: University of Pennsylvania Press, 2016.

———. *The Last Utopia: Human Rights in History*. Cambridge, MA: Belknap Press of Harvard University Press, 2010.

Nam, Hwasook. *Building Ships, Building a Nation*. Seattle: University of Washington Press, 2009.

Oberdorfer, Don, and Robert Carlin. *The Two Koreas: A Contemporary History*. New York: Basic Books, 2014.

Ogle, Vanessa. "State Rights Against Private Capital." *Humanity* 5, no. 2 (Summer 2014): 211–34.

Pak Man-gyu. "Singunbu ŭi Kwangju hangjaeng chinap kwa Miguk munje" [The new military regime's crackdown on the Kwangju Uprising and the role of the United States]. *Minjujuŭi wa Inkwŏn* 3, no. 1 (2003): 211–42.

Pak Sŭng-ok. "Ppaeakkin nodongjŏl ŭi 33-yŏn yŏksa" [The 33-year lost history of Labor Day]. *Wŏlgan Mal* 47 (May 1990): 98–103.

Pak T'ae-gyun. *Ubang kwa cheguk, Han-Mi kwan'gye ŭi tu sinhwa: 8.15 esŏ 5.18 kkaji* [Ally and empire, two myths in US-Korean relations: From national liberation in 1945 to the Kwangju Uprising in 1980]. P'aju: Ch'angbi, 2006.

———. *Wŏnhyŏng kwa pyŏnyong: Han'guk kyŏngje kaebal kyehoek ŭi kiwŏn* [Archetype and metamorphosis: The origins of Korea's economic development plans]. Seoul: Seoul National University Press, 2007.

Park, Albert L. *Building a Heaven on Earth: Religion, Activism, and Protest in Japanese-Occupied Korea*. Honolulu: University of Hawaii Press, 2015.

Park, Myung-Lim. "The *Chaeya*." In *The Park Chung Hee Era: The Transformation of South Korea*, edited by Byung-Kook Kim and Ezra Vogel, 373–400. Cambridge, MA: Harvard University Press, 2011.

Poe, Steven, et al. "Human Rights and US Foreign Aid Revisited: The Latin American Region." *Human Rights Quarterly* 16, no. 3 (1994): 539–58.

Posner, Eric. *The Twilight of Human Rights Law*. New York: Oxford University Press, 2014.

Rhyu, Sang-young, ed. *Democratic Movements and Korean Society*. Seoul: Yonsei University Press, 2007.

Rodríguez-Garavito, César. "Towards a Human Rights Ecosystem." In *Debating "The Endtimes of Human Rights": Activism and Institutions in a Neo-Westphalian World*, edited by Doutje Lettinga and Lars van Troost. 39–46. Amsterdam: Amnesty International Netherlands, 2014.

Ryu, Youngju. "Conclusion: From Yusin Redux to *Yuch'e it'al*." In *Cultures of Yusin: South Korea in the 1970s*, edited by Youngju Ryu, 279–92. Ann Arbor: University of Michigan Press, 2018.

———. *Writers of the Winter Republic*. Honolulu: University of Hawaii Press, 2016.

Schneider, Mark. "A New Administration's New Policy: The Rise to Power of Human Rights." In *Human Rights and U.S. Foreign Policy*, edited by Peter Brown and Douglas MacLean, 3–13. Lexington, MA: Lexington Books, 1979.

Scipes, Kim. *AFL-CIO's Secret War Against Developing Country Workers: Solidarity or Sabotage?* Lanham, MD: Lexington Books, 2010.

Sellars, Kirsten. *The Rise and Rise of Human Rights*. Stroud, UK: Sutton, 2002.

Shaw, William, ed. *Human Rights in South Korea: Historical and Policy Perspectives*. Cambridge, MA: East Asian Legal Studies Program of the Harvard Law School and the Council on East Asian Studies, Harvard University, 1991.

Shin, Gi-Wook, and Kyung Moon Hwang, eds. *Contentious Kwangju: The May 18 Uprising in Korea's Past and Present*. Lanham, MD: Rowman & Littlefield, 2003.

Shorrock, Tim. "Kwangju Diary: The View from Washington." In Lee Jai-eui, *Kwangju Diary: Beyond Death, Beyond the Darkness of the Age*, translated by Kap Su Seol and Nick Mamatas, 151–72. Los Angeles: UCLA Asian Pacific Monograph Series, 1999.

———. "Labor's Cold War." *The Nation*, May 19, 2003, 15–22.

Sikkink, Kathryn. *Evidence for Hope: Making Human Rights Work in the 21st Century*. Princeton, NJ: Princeton University Press, 2017.

———. *Mixed Signals: U.S. Human Rights Policy and Latin America*. Ithaca, NY: Cornell University Press, 2004.

Sikkink, Kathryn, and Hun Joon Kim. "The Justice Cascade: The Origins and Effectiveness of Prosecutions of Human Rights Violations." *Annual Review of Law and Social Science* 9 (2013): 269–85.

Simpson, Brad. "'Human Rights Are Like Coca-Cola': Contested Human Rights Discourses in Suharto's Indonesia, 1968–1980." In *The Breakthrough: Human Rights in the 1970s*, edited by Jan Eckel and Samuel Moyn, 186–203. Philadelphia: University of Pennsylvania Press, 2014.

Slezkine, Peter. "From Helsinki to Human Rights Watch: How an American Cold War Monitoring Group Became an International Human Rights Institution." *Humanity* 5, no. 3 (2014): 345–70.

Smith, Gaddis. *Morality, Reason, and Power: American Diplomacy in the Carter Years*. New York: Hill and Wang, 1986.

Smith, Hazel. "Crimes Against Humanity?" *Critical Asian Studies* 46, no. 1 (2014): 127–43.

Smith, Tony. *America's Mission: The United States and the Worldwide Struggle for Democracy*. Princeton, NJ: Princeton University Press, 2012.

Snyder, Sarah. *From Selma to Moscow: How Human Rights Activists Transformed U.S. Foreign Policy*. New York: Columbia University Press, 2018.

———. *Human Rights Activism and the End of the Cold War: A Transnational History of the Helsinki Network*. New York: Cambridge University Press, 2011.

Soh, Sarah. *The Comfort Women: Sexual Violence and Postcolonial Memory in Korea and Japan*. Chicago: University of Chicago Press, 2008.

Sohn, Hak-kyu. *Authoritarianism and Opposition in South Korea*. New York: Routledge, 1989.

Son Sŭng-ho. *Yusin ch'eje wa Han'guk Kidokkyo in'gwŏn undong* [The Yushin system and South Korean Christian community's human rights movements]. Seoul: Han'guk Kidokkyo Yŏksa Yŏn'guso, 2017.

Song Chi-yŏng. *Usu ŭi sewŏl 1963–1969* [Prison diary, 1963–1969]. Seoul: Yungsŏng Ch'ulp'an, 1986.

Steinberg, David, ed. *Korean Attitudes Toward the United States: Changing Dynamics*. Armonk, NY: Sharpe, 2005.

Stending, William. *Presidential Faith and Foreign Policy: Jimmy Carter the Disciple and Ronald Reagan the Alchemist*. New York: Palgrave Macmillan, 2014.

Stone, Oliver, and Peter Kuznick. *The Untold History of the United States*. New York: Gallery Books, 2012.

Suh Bo-hyuk. "The Militarization of Korean Human Rights." *Critical Asian Studies* 46, no. 1 (2014): 3–14.

Suri, Jeremi. *Power and Protest: Global Revolution and the Rise of Detente*. Cambridge, MA: Harvard University Press, 2003.

Svensson, Marina. *Debating Human Rights in China: A Conceptual and Political History*. New York: Rowman & Littlefield, 2002.

Thomas, Daniel. *The Helsinki Effect: International Norms, Human Rights, and the Demise of Communism*. Princeton, NJ: Princeton University Press, 2001.

Toft, Monica Duffy. "False Prophecies in the Service of Good Works." In *Debating "The Endtimes of Human Rights": Activism and Institutions in a Neo-Westphalian World*, ed. Doutje Lettinga and Lars van Troost, 47–51. Amsterdam: Amnesty International Netherlands, 2014.

Totsuka, Etsuro. "Commentary on a Victory for 'Comfort Women': Japan's Judicial Recognition of Military Sexual Slavery." *Pacific Rim Law & Policy Journal* 8, no. 1 (1999): 47–61.

Vogelgesang, Sandy. "Diplomacy of Human Rights." *International Studies Quarterly* 23, no. 2 (1979): 216–45.

West, James, and Edward Baker. "The 1987 Constitutional Reforms in South Korea: Electoral Processes and Judicial Independence." In *Human Rights in South Korea: Historical and Policy Perspectives*, edited by William Shaw, 221–52. Cambridge, MA: East Asian Legal Studies Program of the Harvard Law School and the Council on East Asian Studies, Harvard University, 1991.

Westad, Odd Arne. *The Global Cold War: Third World Interventions and the Making of Our Time*. Cambridge: Cambridge University Press, 2006.

Woo-Cumings, Meredith, ed. *The Developmental State*. Ithaca, NY: Cornell University Press, 1999.

Yi Sam-sŏng. *Migukŭi yaehan chŏngch'aek kwa han'guk minjokjuŭi* [American foreign policy toward Korea and Korean nationalism]. Seoul: Han'gilsa, 1993.

INDEX

ACKNOWLEDGMENTS

This book would not have been possible without the input and assistance of many persons and organizations. First, I would like to thank the members of my dissertation committee—Bruce Cumings, Mark Bradley, and Michael Geyer. To Bruce Cumings, I owe an immense debt for his unwavering support and wise counsel throughout my time at the University of Chicago. Without his encouragement, what began as a first-year seminar paper would never have become a dissertation or book. I would like to thank Mark Bradley whose groundbreaking work on the transnational and diasporic forces shaping human rights claims first inspired me to rethink the implications of global-local relations for Korean history. To Michael Geyer, I express my gratitude for pushing me to delve deeper into the intersectional relationship between global human rights history, international relations, and Korea's struggle for democratization. As a fellow immigrant scholar, he also provided me with invaluable assistance in navigating American academic culture.

I would also like to thank Park Myung-lim, Rhyu Sang-young, and Kim Dong-no whose mentorship during and after my time at Yonsei University gave me the academic foundation to complete my studies. In particular, I would like to thank Professor Park for hiring me as his research assistance and allowing me to accompany him on research trips to the United States. The research and interviews I conducted during my employment generated the idea of this book.

The research behind this book could not have been completed without the generous funding of the University of Chicago, the Lyndon B. Johnson Library Foundation, Korea Foundation, the Harvard Yenching Library, the USC Korean Heritage Library, and Boston College. Its publication was gratefully supported by the 2020 Korean Studies Grant Program of the Academy of Korean Studies (AKS–2020–P04). I would also like to thank the countless librarians and archivists who generously gave their time. Although I cannot possibly mention all by name, I would like to extend my special thanks to Yi Ch'ung-ŭn at the Kim Dae-jung Presidential Library; Hyŏn Chong-ch'ŏl, Yang Kyŏng-hŭi, Pae Sŏn-hwa, and Wŏn Chong-gwan at the Korea Democracy Foundation, Hwang Pyŏng-ju, Yi Sang-rok, Yun Tŏk-yŏng, and Kim So-nam at the National Institute of Korean History; Kim Dong-choon and Sŏ Hŭi-kyŏng at the ROK Truth and Reconciliation Commission; Yi Ko-un at the Korean Section of Amnesty International; Yi Ch'ang-hun at the April 9 Unification and Peace Foundation; Norma-Rae Mandera at Emory University Pitts Theology Library; Marja Musson at the International Institute of Social History; William McNitt and Donna Lehman at the Ford Presidential Library; James Yancey Jr. at the Carter Presidential Library; Jeeyoung Park and Jeongsoo Kim at the University of Chicago Regenstein Library; Joy Kim at the USC East Asian Library; Mikyung Kang at the Harvard Yenching Library; and Julia Hughes at Boston College. I would also like to express my gratitude to Han Sŭng-hŏn, Yun Hyŏn, O Chae-sik, Pharis Harvey, Michael Armacost, Yi Chong-ch'an, and Kim Sung-jae who in interviews shared their knowledge and experience of the events described in this book. To Albert Park, Philip Dorsey Iglauer, Kevin Kim, and Cho Hyŏk-jin, I extend a heartfelt thanks for the hospitality, conversation, and research assistance each of you provided while I was doing fieldwork.

This book also benefited from the constructive feedback that the following individuals gave: Sam Lebovic, James Sparrow, Emily Osborne, Patrick W. Kelly, Lael Weinberger, Kyeong-hee Choi, Shinyoung Kwon, James Matray, Mitchell Lerner, Brandon Gauthier, David Fields, Robert Brier, Benjamin Nathans, Sarah Snyder, Bradley Simpson, Ray Wang, Hung-ling Yeh, Chang-ho Kim, Jun Hyung Chae, Jeongha Lee, Vanessa Walker, Sungwoo Park, Henry Em, Youngju Ryu, Myunsham Suh, Kun-woo Kim, You Jae Lee, Jong Chol An, Taejin Hwang, Jiehyun Lim, Selçuk Esenbel, Arzu Öztürkmen, Hakan Yılmaz, Hyun Woong Hong, Song Hwan Kwon, Lee Sang-cheol, and Kim Jinho. I specially thank Kimba Allie Tichenor, whose Socratic approach to editing this manuscript helped me solidify arguments and improve my writing.

I would also like to thank my colleagues and friends at Boston College. First, I would like to thank Greg Kalscheur and Billy Soo whose decision to promote Korean studies opened the door for me to find an academic home at Boston College. For their encouragement, support, and advice during the revision stage, I am deeply indebted to Erik Owens, Robert Murphy, Hiroshi Nakazato, and Franziska Seraphim. I would also like to thank Jessica Lipton,

Young Hoon Oh, Jisoo Park, and Daniel Pu for their hard work on my project as undergraduate research fellows.

My book project has been greatly encouraged and assisted by former University of Pennsylvania Press editor-in-chief Peter Agree, present editor-in-chief Water Beggins, and series editor Professor Bert Lockwood. I am grateful to Lily Palladino for walking me through the production process and Kristen Bettcher and Jennifer Shenk for handling the copyediting of this work. I also would like to thank the anonymous readers, whose comments helped me clarify and improve my thoughts and writing.

For their unwavering moral support, I thank the following individuals: Kim Mun-sik, Hŏ Ch'ŏn-t'aek, Kim Sung-jae, Nammok Zo, Jeeyoung Park, Cathryn Bearov, Hiroyoshi Noto, Jaehong Yi, Colin Astron Rennison, Robert Garnett Jr., Pak Tong-hyŏn, and Monk Hyekwang. Without their compassionate intercession, I could not have completed this arduous academic journey. I would like to extend a special thanks to Ed and Diane Baker whose warm embrace upon our arrival in Boston allowed Kang Hye-seung and I, as newlyweds, to adjust quickly to life in a new city.

To my parents, siblings, nephews, and cousins whose love and support has served as a beacon throughout my life, I humbly thank you. To my in-laws, Kang Mun-su and Um Un-ja, I express my deep gratitude for welcoming me into your family. To my wife Kang Hye-seung, I want to acknowledge not only the encouragement that you provided me but also your tremendous courage in embracing a new life in a foreign country.

Lastly, I extend my deepest admiration to all those who devoted their lives to promoting democracy and human rights in South Korea.

www.ingramcontent.com/pod-product-compliance
Lightning Source LLC
Chambersburg PA
CBHW020454270326
41926CB00008B/596